JN320136

Edited by **Masae Tsutsumi**

A Turning Point of Women, Families and Agriculture in Rural Japan

GAKUBUNSHA

Copyright © 2010 by Gakubunsha, Inc.
  All rights reserved. No part of this book may be reproduced
  in any form, by photostat, microfilm, retrieval system, or any
  other means, without the prior written permission of the publisher.

Gakubunsha, Inc., Publishers
  3-6-1 Shimomeguro, Meguro-Ward, Tokyo

Library of Congress Catalog in Publication Data
Edited by Tsutsumi Masae
A Turning Point of Women, Families and Agriculture in Rural Japan

Includes bibliographical references and index.
  ISBN 978-4-7620-2015-5

Printed in Japan

Contents

Foreword vii

Chapter 1 Changes of Women, Families and Agriculture in Rural Japan 1

1. Trends of Japanese Farming Families and Farm Management 3
    1. Introduction 3
    2. Rural Communities, Families, and Lifestyle in Japan at a Turning Point 4
    3. Changes in Japanese Families 8
    4. Changes in Farm Management and Labor 14
    5. Conclusion 18
2. Change and Problems Regarding Women Farmers in Japan 22
    1. Image versus Reality 22
    2. The Changing Lifestyle of the Rural Family 23
    3. Individualism within the Stem Family 24
    4. The Empowerment of Women Farmers 24
    5. A Case of One of the Leaders of Women Farmers 28
    6. Problems for Women Farmers 31
3. The Characteristics and the Challenges of Rural Women's Entrepreneurial Activities in Japan 35
    1. Introduction 35
    2. Characteristics of Rural Women's Entrepreneurial Activities 35
    3. Present Status of RWEAs and Policy Support 42
    4. Challenges for RWEAs 42

Chapter 2 Network and Socioeconomic Activity of Women 45

1. Network of Female New Farmers in Japan Who Come from the Non-agricultural Sector 47
    1. Introduction 47
    2. Method and Respondents 48
    3. Process of Taking up Farming 49
    4. Personal Network in the Community 51
    5. Problems in Daily Life and Degree of Satisfaction 56
    6. Discussion 58
2. How Rural Women's Entrepreneurship drawn from Life Improvement Practice Group Developed: A Case Study on Tochigi and Nagano, Japan 61
    1. Introduction 61
    2. Purpose and Research Issues 61
    3. Case Study 64

    4. Summary and Comments   69
3. Issues and Characteristics of the Economic Activities by Women in Japanese Farming Villages: From the Examination of a Business Establishment Process 73
    1. Introduction   73
    2. General Characteristics of Economic Activities   73
    3. Business Establishment Process Models   76
    4. Conclusion   78
4. Background and Factors Promoting the Empowerment of Women in the Rural Society of Japan 80
    1. The Purpose and Method   80
    2. Framework   81
    3. Experience of Tense Relationships by Women Farmers and Their Responses   86
    4. Background of Promoting Empowerment   89
    5. Promoting Factors of Women's Empowerment   91
    6. Conclusion   95

Chapter 3 Women Balancing Family and Farming 97
1. Maternity Leave for Farmers and the Potentiality of the Family Management Agreement in Japan 99
    1. Introduction   99
    2. Support Frameworks for Farmers in Birth and Child-rearing Periods from an International Point of View   100
    3. The Status of Farming Women during the Period when They Give Birth in Japan   102
    4. The Possibilities of Gaining Maternity Leave Utilizing a Family Management Agreement   105
    5. Conclusion   107
2. Mother and Daughter-in-law Dyads in Farming Families Executing the Family Management Agreement 109
    1. Introduction   109
    2. Methods   110
    3. Cases of Mother and Daughter-in-law Dyad   111
    4. Comparison and Conclusion   121
3. Experimental Study on Work Life Balance of Women Farmers in Japan 124
    1. Introduction   124
    2. Dynamic Trends in Population, Agrarian Labor and Way of Working in Japan   127
    3. Result of Research Analysis   130
    4. Conclusion   141

Contents   iii

Chapter 4 The Roles of Female Farmers 145
1. Can Farm Women's Activities Reconstruct the Community? 147
    1. Introduction   147
    2. Objectives   148
    3. Results—The effect of the activities to the community—   149
    4. Discussion—The role of farm women for reconstruction of community—   153
2. The Social Norm and the Awareness of the Constraints of Rural Women in Japan 157
    1. Introduction   157
    2. Method   157
    3. Findings and Implications   158
    4. Conclusion   161
3. Career Formation of Farming Women and Agricultural Policy in Postwar Japan: A case of Katsunuma Town 163
    1. Introduction   163
    2. Generational Change in Career Formation of Farming Women   165
    3. Working Status of Farming Women   166
    4. Social Activities and Career Formation of Farming Women   171
    5. Conclusion and Discussion   179
4. Effects of the Family Management Agreement on Gender Equality 183
    1. Introduction   183
    2. Gender Issues in Rural Japan   184
    3. Promotion of the Family Management Agreement   189
    4. Data Collecting   191
    5. Cases of Farming Families Executing the Family Management Agreement   192
    6. Conclusion   198

Chapter 5 Family Strategy on Succession and Family Farm Management ... 209
1. New Trends in Stem-families Succession in Rural Japan: A case of Katsunuma Town 211
    1. Introduction   211
    2. Findings   212
    3. Conclusion   220
2. Property Inheritance of Farming Families 224
    1. Introduction   224
    2. Characteristics of Challenges and Subjects, and Contents of Inheritance   226
    3. Characteristics of Inheritance by Investigation Year   230
    4. Case Study on Generations of Succession and Inheritance upon the Father's Death   231
    5. Succession and Inheritance Due to Unexpected Family Events   235

6. Conclusion—Inheritance of property the tendencies that persist   238
3. Family Strategy in Farm Succession: A Case of Farming Families Executing the Family Agreement in Takasaki City 244
    1. Introduction   244
    2. The Post-war Agricultural Policy in Japan and Family Farming   244
    3. Family Agreement in Takasaki City   246
    4. Family Agreement and Rural Communities in Takasaki City   248
    5. Farming Holdings and Family-Farm Successions   251
    6. Conclusion and Discussion   256

Chapter 6 Today's Subsistence Production and Agro-food Initiatives in Japan 259

1. The Present Situation of Local Supply and Consumption of Agricultural Products from the Aspect of Acquisition and Utilization by Local People............................. 261
    1. Introduction   261
    2. Research Area and Method   263
    3. Results and Discussions   266
    4. Conclusion   278
2. Alternative Agro-food Movement in Contemporary Japan....................................... 281
    1. Introduction   281
    2. The Transition of the Relationship between Farmers (Agriculture) and Consumers (Food)   281
    3. Emergence of the Localization Movement in the U.S.   285
    4. The Alternative Agriculture Movement in Contemporary Japan   288
    5. Criticism   294
    6. Conclusion   295
Afterword   298
index   300

About the Authors

Masae Tsutsumi, Ph.D. (Human Sciences) ················· Ch.1-1, Ch.5-2
Faculty of International Policy Management and Communications, Yamanashi
Prefectural University, Professor, Family Sociology/Area Studies

Tokuya Kawate, Ph.D. (Agriculture) ················· Ch.1-2
College of Bioresources Sciences, Nihon University, Associate Professor,
Rural Development/Agricultural Economics

Kyoko Morofuji, Ph.D. (Agriculture) ················· Ch.1-3, Ch.6-1
NPO Research Institute for Rural Community and Life, Director, Agriculture Economics

Juri Hara-Fukuyo, Ph.D. (Agriculture) ················· Ch.2-1
National Agricultural Research Center, National Agriculture and Food Research
Organization, Senior Researcher, Rural Sociology

Tomoko Ichida, Ph.D. (Agriculture) ················· Ch.2-2
School of Agriculture, Meiji University, Associate Professor, Agriculture policy/
Rural Sociology

Kumi Sawano, Ph.D. (Agriculture) ················· Ch.2-2
Meiji University, Organization for the Strategic Coordination of Research and
Intellectual Property, Guest Researcher, Agricultural Economics

Miki Shibuya, Ph.D. (Academic Sciences) ················· Ch.2-3
National Agricultural Research Center for Tohoku Region, National Agriculture and Food
Research Organization, Senior Researcher, Rural Sociology

Rieko Tsuru, Ph.D. (Sociology) ················· Ch.2-4
School of Sociology, Kibi International University, Associate Professor, Rural Sociology

Chie Katayama, M.A. (Health Sciences) ················· Ch.3-1, Ch.6-1
Department of Rural Planning, National Institute for Rural Engineering, National
Agriculture and Food Research Organization, Contracted Researcher, Health
Sociology/Public Nutrition

Yukiko Otomo, M.A. (Literature) ·························· Ch.3-2, Ch.4-3, 4-4, Ch.5-1, 5-3
    Faculty of Social and Information Sciences, Jumonji University, Associate Professor,
    Family Sociology

Michi Tsutsumi, Ph.D. Student (Agriculture) ··· Ch.3-3
    United Graduate School of Agricultural Science, Tokyo University of Agriculture and
    Technology, Agricultural Economics

Mima Nishiyama, Ph.D. (Agriculture) ······································ Ch.4-1, Ch.6-2
    Graduate school of horticulture, Chiba University, Associate Professor,
    Agricultural Economics

Masashi Yamashita, Ph.D. (Engineering) ·· Ch.4-2
    Department of Rural Planning, National Institute for Rural Engineering, National
    Agriculture and Food Research Organization, Contracted Researcher, Rural
    Planning/Regional Planning/Architecture

Keiko Yoshino, Ph.D. (Agriculture) ·· Ch.6-1
    Department of Global Agricultural Sciences, Graduate school of Agricultural and
    Life Sciences, University of Tokyo, Research Assistant, Regional Studies/
    Subsistence/Gender

Edited by Masae Tsutsumi

Foreword

This book was based on the report for the International Rural Sociological Association (IRSA), and it was presented at a group session that dealt with issues regarding women, family, network, group activities, and Japanese agriculture. The subjects of research are women in rural Japan, family as a life base, network, and communities. Here, rural communities in Japan are explained in detail for international comparison. The new trends of Japanese society are looked at closely from various viewpoints in hopes of introducing the actual conditions of rural villages, families, women, and agriculture in Japan to the international community.

When we reported on the current conditions of rural villages, families, and agriculture in Japan at international conferences, many people from different countries took interest. Our reports brought up questions that were common to all and led to discussions. We also became aware of the fact that many things that are accepted as common sense by the Japanese were not widely known outside Japan. One of the main reasons for publishing this book was to provide people who are interested in Japan with an opportunity to learn about the rural side of our country, how we live in our families, our culture, our lifestyle, and how we do what we do.

Japan experienced high economic growth and rapid urbanization, leaving agriculture and farming areas to follow a course of decline. This is still a critical problem. Recently, however, more people have taken interest in the area of farming and agriculture from such standpoints as ecology, food issues, nonprofit activities, and community business. A farming community is the producer and the provider of our food, and it is where our life and culture are nurtured. It is also a base for understanding our traditional culture, the very hub of our living. One of the characteristics of this book is that it focuses on this cultural foundation as well as on the new trends.

Each chapter has a summary in the beginning. The main topics of each chapter are as follows.
Chapter 1: Historical changes of Japanese society. How Japanese families and rural communities have been changing will be explained. An overview on Japanese women, families, and agriculture will be given.
Chapter 2: How women's networking, social participation, entrepreneurship, and life study groups have helped women to improve their status and to participate in farm management, transforming the traditional way of thinking will be examined. The

importance and meaning of women's personal, group, and social activities will be discussed.

Chapter 3: What support do women farmer need to have children and continue to work while raising them without worries? What kind of work environment do they want? The significance of family management agreement will also be presented.

Chapter 4: Farming women's local activities and their hindrances. Gender equality, family management agreement, and food issues will be discussed.

Chapter 5: Generational succession from parents to children, and inheritance of farmland and assets. Generational changes will be analyzed, shedding light on today's heir problem.

Chapter 6: New trends, new roles, and the future of rural Japan. Suggestions such as communication between urban and rural regions through food, and local production for local consumption as an alternative movement against globalization will be given.

These topics will be discussed in the fields of sociology, economy, and agriculture.

The authors are mostly young researchers who have been and will continue to be addressing various issues of Japanese rural communities to the world. Masae Tsutsumi is the chief editor, Tokuya Kawate the associate editor. The author of the first clause of each chapter oversaw the whole chapter. This book was truly a product of the cooperation of each and every author.

It is our hope that through this book the readers will gain understanding of the current conditions of Japanese society, farming regions, and families. We also hope that, while entrusting the readers with any judgment, problems common to all countries will be recognized and discussed, creating rich soil for international comparison. Time is needed for such intentions to be fully realized. But if this book opens up more studies on the international level, global policymaking and solution, it will be a great pleasure for all the authors.

Masae Tsustumi, Chief Editor/Author

Chapter 1

Changes of Women, Families and Agriculture in Rural Japan

Abstract

Chapter 1 presents the overview of historical changes that the Japanese society went through. Characteristics of the changes in Japanese families and agriculture will be examined based on statistical data from the national census and the agriculture and forestry census. In rural areas which had seen little transformation, family forms have started to change, with nuclear families and single-person households on the rapid rise. It will be pointed out how the farming population is aging and the percentage of women is increasing as farm size and labor forms change. The once-solid family forms are now changing, and personalization within the stem family is spreading. Active and important roles women play in farming and in the community will be discussed. The emergence of female entrepreneurs in rural areas with the governmental support helps improve women's economic activities, social positions, and quality of life. Today's trend of changing families, the significance and effects of agriculture and women's regional activities will be laid out.

1
Trends of Japanese Farming Families and Farm Management
Masae Tsutsumi

1. Introduction
1-1. Purpose
In this article, it is hoped to suggest themes for an international comparison study through analyzing current conditions of women in rural Japan, their families as the center of their lives, networks, groups, rural villages[1], and agriculture, while keeping the universal challenges in perspective. Here, the present condition of the Japanese society will be examined in terms of its structure and system, and the new trends will be scrutinized from multiple angles. The turning point that the Japanese society is facing will be presented.

In this chapter, the history of socio-economic changes in the Japanese society will be traced, and changes in families and people's lives will be explained. How life in Japan has changed after World War II will thus be revealed, which will help clarify the turning point that present Japan faces. Specific data will be referred to in order to describe the changes in families and households as well as farm management and farm labor. Household structures and sizes are important indexes of familial change analysis. Management scale, work arrangement, and labor input are indicative of the conditions of family farming. Such data will be gained from censuses and repeated research.[2]

1-2. Viewpoint of Continuance and Change
A general look at our lives indicates that cities change more rapidly than rural villages. The rural regions we study seem to have more persistent factors than cities. Today, however, what used to rarely change are changing dramatically. This is what the

---

1) The rural villages mentioned here refer to regions with general characteristics of a farming village and includes non-urban regions.
2) The author explained in my book *Nihon Nouson Kazoku no Jizoku to Hendou* (Continuance and Changes of the Stem Family Households in Rural Japan) 2009, Gakubunsha, how Japanese families had changed, what aspects of life had remained unchanged, and how the unchanged aspects had been passed down. Based on the knowledge gained through examining the persistence and change in Japanese families, the trends of Japanese rural families and agriculture will be investigated in this article.

turning point in the Japanese society signifies.

Life never changes uniformly; some elements change rapidly while others seem to remain the same. One may focus either on what changes, or on what does not change and persists. All social phenomena change during the course of time. It takes a long time to understand what does not change. On the other hand changes are more easily perceived. Which social phenomenon change, and which do not is difficult to grasp. How much modification is needed to bring about a real change, or when such a turning point is passed, are hard to know and often recognized later in time.

Various viewpoints need to be examined when trying to study the ever changing lifestyle of people. Some aspects of life are more likely to change, as there are also different speeds of change. When one is too focused on changes, things that do not change may be overlooked. Changes take many forms; they never occur uniformly or in a linear manner.

As for the concept of family [Morioka & Mochizuki, 1983], its forms and functions tend to change, but ties and relationships hardly do. Parents delight in the healthy growth of their children, and children worry about their aging parents in any age or type of society. Ties among family members are universal and rarely change. Forms and functions of family are often influenced by social changes and therefore prone to change.

This article aims to understand trends and characteristics of persistence and change in various fields and levels of study for international comparison.

2. Rural Communities, Families, and Lifestyle in Japan at a Turning Point

Since the end of World War II until today, the Japanese society has experienced four turning points, including the current one, prompted by socio-economic changes. At each turning point, rural regions, families, and lifestyles underwent changes. The first turning point was the institutional change that took place soon after the war. The second one occurred during the high economic growth. The third came during the period of economic stability, which heralded the age of localism or the age of women. During this period, a shift from mass production to low-volume production of various kinds took place. Today, as the new century dawns, confusion reigns both inside and outside Japan, new systems are being put forth, and government organizations are being restructured and reformed. This is the beginning of the fourth great transition. This transition is related to changes in rural regions, families, and lifestyles [Tsutsumi, Tokuno, & Yamamoto, 2008, 29-39]. The following is an overview of the historical turning points in the Japanese society.

2-1. Institutional Changes Regarding Families and Lifestyles: From Confusion to Stability

Soon after the war around 1946-1948, various regulations that concern our everyday and family lives were set up, such as the Constitution, Civil Code, Labor Union Act, School Education Act, and land reform. The latter especially transformed the social structure. The dissolution of the financial clique also had a great impact on both urban and rural areas.

The abolition of the traditional "Ie" or family system and the emergence of the conjugal family system was a big change. It is widely known how this change prompted a shift of focus in human relations from the parent-child to the husband-wife relationship. The emphasis of social relations in general also shifted from hierarchical (vertical) to equal (horizontal) relationships. Also showing signs of disappearing were the main and branch family relationships which are an important part of the "Ie" system. The subordinates were liberated, especially women, the social subordinates, experienced great changes in various fields.

Democracy was introduced to every aspect of life. Institutional changes, however, did not bring about immediate changes in people's lives. They gradually occurred as the people's consciousness slowly changed. The first baby boom had a long-lasting influence on various fields. High rates of birth and infant mortality were replaced with high birthrates and low infant mortality. In the early 1950s, less than ten years after the war, the birthrate also dropped. The Japanese society started to age rapidly with the birthrate decline being greater than the increase in life expectancy.

"Sazae-san," a story comic, first published around this time, depicts parents living with their daughter and her husband, an ideal form of family for both parents and children of the time. But their family standards and consciousness are those of the traditional family system. Their relationship appears to be equal and democratic, but their code of conduct gives men the priority and demands women to stay one step back. The ways a mother and daughter give support to their respective husbands are different. The child generation prefers a modern behavioral pattern to a traditional one. Sazae-san, the main character, is a homemaker, a model of a woman supporting working men during the next big change of the high economic growth. Sazae-san's lifestyle has been adjusted as the Japanese society developed, but when it was first published, it showed a new way of life for women, a new way of family. It was rather the high economic growth than the institutional changes that quickly transformed people's lives. The next rapid economic growth was the second wave of change in post-war Japan.

2-2. High Economic Growth that Changed Life: From Rural to Urban

For three years around 1960, the primary sector declined and the secondary and tertiary sectors expanded[3]. The population moved from rural to urban areas searching for jobs. While this happened, their consumption behavior changed to an urban style. Due to the limited size of the urban residence, the number of people per household was small. The high education orientation also helped limit the number of children, altering the family forms and functions.

Urban lifestyles were introduced to rural regions after they lost population. As the population concentrated in urban areas, the urban lifestyle became considered the average Japanese lifestyle. It was around this time that Japanese families rapidly became nuclear and small. The stem family system, indigenous in rural regions, did not change drastically as long as the family continued farming. But it started to change greatly when the urban lifestyle permeated into rural regions, creating a time lag. The modification of family forms affected the family functions, which led to a transformation of life.

The issuance of 10,000-yen bills and the emergence of instant ramen were remarkable signs of the transformation of life. Refrigerators, TVs, and washing machines, "the three sacred treasures," became common, which helped reduce housework. Farming families during this time also purchased consumer durable goods and their life was revolutionized. Such changes on a day-to-day life level created a vector for changing the way of families.

Few women in rural regions went to work in factories because farming was the main industry. But on the national level, married women started to go to work. Depending on the farm management method, women in farming families also started to get a job. Since more women were working outside their homes, finding one's own partner became easier, and traditional, conventional arranged marriages decreased. This transformed the family system and perception about marriage and family slowly started to change.

Ever since the high economic growth, forms of rural families gradually changed along with family structures and human relationships. As people migrated from rural regions to cities, many villages became depopulated, which led to the aging and decreasing farming workforce.

---

3) *Chihou Kara no Shakaigaku*, 2007, Gakubunsha, Figure1-1:p.31. The Change of Industrial Structures, Zenkoku Shakaifukushi Kyogikai Shakaifukushigaku-Shu Sousho Henshuiinkai ed., *Shakaigaku* 10, 104.

2-3. Changes in Day-to-Day Life: To the Age of Localism

The flexible rate system was introduced in the 1970's. There were also the dollar and oil shocks, and the economy was far from being stabilized. Stabilization did not happen until around 1980 when the Japanese economy started to grow again. The way people lived changed, and the Age of Localism and the Age of Women began.

Various economic and social indicators and data reveal that Japan started to give international aid that was appropriate for a developed country on an international level. The yen grew stronger, and the effects of development were evident in local regions as seen by the new Tohoku and Joetsu Shinkansen lines. Everything used to concentrated in the metropolitan area, but decentralization was starting to happen. The population concentration in cities created traffic congestion, housing problems and environmental problems. Multipolar decentralization instead of overconcentration was called for, and a movement to boost rural development started.

The Equal Employment Act was implemented to secure equal opportunity and treatment between men and women. The system for women to be in the social workforce was gradually established. Advancement of computerization changed the employment structure, and internationalization brought about deregulation. Social restructuring also started in order to improve the international competitive power. Division and privatization of Japan National Railways, privatization of telephone services, introduction of shorter working hours and a five-day work-week system, and implementation of a consumption tax all indicated the new social structure.

Once Japan joined the ranks of developed countries, people's living standards improved, higher education became more popular, the number of nuclear families increased, and more women went into the workforce. In addition to the increase of nuclear and smaller families, many were now living alone, strengthening the tendency toward individualism. People's values were changing from material and economy-oriented to comfortable living-oriented. Both death and birth rates dropped, heightening the concerns about the aging society, caring for the elderly, and the lack of successors. For farming families, lack of successors had always been a cause of concern, but it became increasingly serious during this time. After the 1.57 birth rate shock, the problem of the declining birthrate gained social recognition. The quality of life became an issue in various fields and people's values became more diverse.

2-4. Structural Adjustment: Widening Disparity

In 1995, the Great Hanshin-Awaji Earthquake occurred. Witnessing the calamity, many people realized how precious it was to have a safe and stable life. Learning the enormous damage that natural disasters could cause led them to appreciate living harmoniously within a natural environment. In order to live a safe and stable life, the environment must be protected. A shift from mass production and mass consumption to low-volume production of multiple kinds took place, and people started to seek for more quality in their lives. The increase of gourmet and brand-conscious people is evidence of the shift from quantity to quality. More people now wanted a beautiful environment as well as convenience and comfort, the best of both rural and urban living. Quality of life was becoming more important for many.

There are many problems springing up everywhere from usual daily life to the worldwide, global level. There has been much talk about the need for all, regardless of their generation, to work together in order to face the challenges of further computerization and globalization, the garbage and industrial waste problem, and protection and preservation of the environment. The advancement of automation drastically changed both workplaces and homes. Everyone was hard-pressed to comply with technological innovation and the IT revolution. The fear of terrorism also helped turn people toward safety and stability.

Observation of tendencies in everyday life reveals the increase in women's social participation and married women entering the workforce. On the other hand, the unemployment rate has gone up, and attention has been attracted to the job problems of the young. The declining birthrate has been recognized as a social problem, and the government has started taking measures to reverse this trend. About one out of three Japanese live alone, confirmation of spreading individualism. The increase of the midlife divorce rate indicates the change in family relationships and how families operate. The tax and consumption units had been per household but may be changing to per individual.

Recessions in other countries affect Japan greatly. New viruses spread worldwide. Globalization, computerization, and aging are keenly felt in daily lives. It has been more than half a century since many systems of the post-war Japan were established, and there are some discrepancies between the systems and reality. It is time to amend them according to the present conditions. Life sometimes needs to adjust to the system, but sometimes the system must be adjusted according to reality. The industrial structural switch and disparity problem do not only concern the gap between urban and rural regions, but it is a matter of transforming the entire social structure. People's lifestyles have been changing since before the dawn of the 21st century, and waves of change have been reaching the rural regions.

3. Changes in Japanese Families

In this section the characteristics of Japanese rural families will be investigated in terms of their transformation from the stem family system to the conjugal family system. Families have been shrinking in size during the rural society's modernization.

3-1. Characteristics of Japanese Rural and Urban Families

In modern Japan, the conjugal family system is most prevalent. Families are established by marriage and each being the last generation because the family becomes dissolved by the death of one or both spouses. By general rule, parents do not live with their children's reproductive families. This way of family life has gone mainstream and has increased as the economic structure has changed. The ideology of the conjugal family system encourages independence of younger generations and values individual will over the logic of the mass, which appears favorable to the younger generations. Recently, because of the housing problem and the increase of dual-income households, the child generation often wishes to live with their parents for convenience, which is not always favored by the parent generation. As the recent increase of the Kangaroos[4] shows, diversity is on the rise. In the past, parents' wish to live with their child's family was often not granted because of the child's work situation, but now both parents and children have a say in this matter.

In terms of the system, modern Japanese families are conjugal families, but some traditions of the stem family system still remain. Some actively seek to live with their parents for practical reasons. The way families operate has been changing little by little. In the modern stem family system, under the influence of the conjugal family system, the successor's family living separately is sometimes even accepted. Because of this, the actual conditions and the family's ideal do not necessarily match. Efforts are made to turn the ideal into reality, but the historical typological changes are based on the system change and are advanced with economic changes in the background. In reality families live together or separately for convenience, but the proportion accounted for by the conjugal family system has certainly been increasing. Some parents live in a separate house on the same site with their children in rural areas where more space is available.

The ratio of the stem family system is higher and the family size larger in rural regions. It was generally acknowledged that the opposite was true in rural regions. Japanese families shifted from the stem family system to the conjugal system, therefore these two systems can be considered to characterize the modern and present ages, pre-war and post-war. The recent transformation of Japanese families is one from "Ie" to present families, from the stem family to the conjugal family. In this sense, they are perfect

---

4) Lifestyle in which the struggling child generation live with and is supported by the parent generation. They do not share a household with the ideal of the stem family system, but mainly for financial reasons.

examples of urban and rural families.

Historically, however, these two have coexisted. During the age of the stem family system, the pre-war age of the "Ie" system, there were conjugal families. In the present age, the conjugal system is considered the norm, but stem families still exist. Even though conjugal families are the majority today, there is still some inclination toward the stem family system. Both are weaved together in various ways. Even in a single household, they sometimes both exist in different spears of control.

The "historical typological changes" in Japanese families mentioned above means the majority shift from the stem family system to the conjugal family system as well as the increase in ratio of the conjugal family elements in situations where both exist. Changes in the society as a whole can often be measured by studying the ratio. Today, as urban lifestyles have spread in rural regions, changes in families are becoming more individual and diverse [Tsutsumi, 1980].

3-2. Changes in Family Forms

Family forms refer to the number of family members, or "size", and the relationships of the members, or "composition". Changes in family forms are also discussed in terms of both size and composition. When the number of family members decreases, it is a change in size. The trend toward the nuclear family is the trend toward a simpler household composition. Therefore, these changes are of different aspects, even though in Japan both emerged simultaneously during the high economic growth as is widely known.

Japan's industrialization started later than that of the United States and Britain, and because of this, the Japanese family size shrank rapidly compared to that of the West. The average number of household members between 1920 and 1955 was around five, and no drastic change occurred during this period. Despite modest increases and decreases, the family size was stable throughout the pre- and post-war period. During a short period of time between 1955 and 1980, when Japan's industrialization finally kicked in, the number dropped to around 3.5, the same level as that of in the West. Such a rapid change in size should be considered an evidence of changes in various fields.

The trend toward the nuclear family refers to the actual shift from the expanded family form to the nuclear family, and the increase of the nuclear family ratio. Families in post-war Japan have simpler compositions than those of the pre-war period. This tendency is apparent in the increase of the nuclear and single-person households. Especially, the increase of people living alone shows a notable tendency of individualization.

Industrialization, demographic shift, urbanization, and the emergence of wage earners all have an effect on the transformation of family forms. Some argue that

Chapter 1: Changes of Women, Families and Agriculture in Rural Japan   11

industrialization helps turn stem families into nuclear families, while others oppose this view. This depends on each country, and under different circumstances, both are possible. But the reduction in family size and the increase in nuclear families are now a worldwide phenomena. Even in countries where the nuclear family has been a tradition, more young people marry later, stay single, become Kangaroos or parasite singles, contributing to the increase in three-generation families. Let us examine the tendencies of smaller, nuclear, and, single-person households in Japan and their regional characteristics.

3-3. Tendency of Smaller Families

Table 1-1-1: Looking at the tendency of smaller families from the number of households by size, households have been increasing every single year. The period between 1960 and 1970 saw the greatest increase, but each period shows an upward trend. In 2000, one out of four Japanese lived alone, this being the highest percentage. In 2005, it almost reached the level of one out of three.

Table 1-1-1 Number of Households by Size and Index Transition (National)

Year	1	2	3	4	5	6	7 and up	Total
1960	3,722,110	2,519,576	3,154,512	3,704,488	3,391,318	2,605,060	3,441,581	22,538,645
1970	6,137,443	4,183,902	5,321,911	6,884,785	3,907,031	2,285,353	1,576,589	30,297,014
1975	6,561,316	5,256,774	6,258,725	8,301,309	3,904,137	2,036,681	1,276,786	33,595,728
1980	7,105,246	6,001,075	6,475,220	9,070,100	3,981,763	2,032,848	1,157,357	35,823,609
1985	7,894,636	6,985,292	6,813,402	8,988,042	4,201,242	1,984,619	1,112,751	37,979,984
1990	9,389,660	8,370,087	7,350,639	8,787,908	3,805,147	1,903,065	1,063,969	40,670,475
1995	11,239,389	10,079,958	8,131,151	8,277,047	3,511,770	1,712,927	947,681	43,899,923
2000	12,911,318	11,743,432	8,810,437	7,924,827	3,167,227	1,448,960	776,182	46,782,383
2005	14,457,083	13,023,662	9,196,084	7,707,216	2,847,699	1,207,777	623,009	49,062,530

Year	1	2	3	4	5	6	7 and up	Total
1960	100.0	100.0	100.0	100.0	100.0	100.0	100.0	100.0
1970	164.9	166.1	168.7	185.8	115.2	87.7	45.8	134.4
1975	176.3	208.6	198.4	224.1	115.1	78.2	37.1	149.1
1980	190.9	238.2	205.3	244.8	117.4	78.0	33.6	158.9
1985	212.1	277.2	216.0	242.6	123.9	76.2	32.3	168.5
1990	252.3	332.2	233.0	237.2	112.2	73.1	30.9	180.4
1995	302.0	400.1	257.8	223.4	103.6	65.8	27.5	194.8
2000	346.9	466.1	279.3	213.9	93.4	55.6	22.6	207.6
2005	388.4	516.9	291.5	208.1	84.0	46.4	18.1	217.7

Source: Created from National Census results 1960-2005

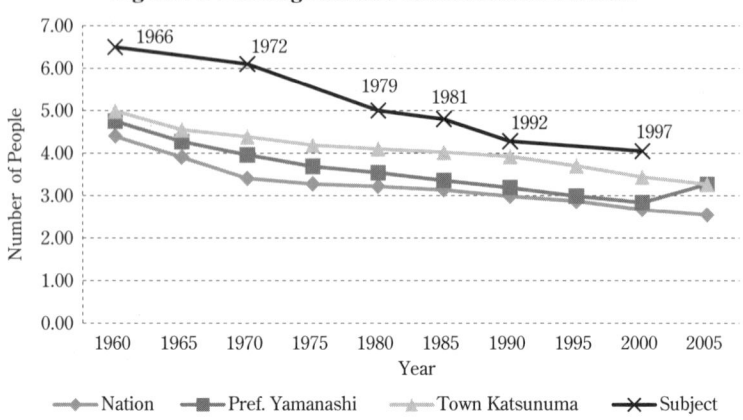

Figure1-1-1 Average Number of Household Members

(Chart showing number of people from 1960 to 2005 for Nation, Pref. Yamanashi, Town Katsunuma, and Subject. Subject line data points: 1966, 1972, 1979, 1981, 1992, 1997.)

On the national level, the total number of households more than doubled in forty years between 1960 to 2000. As shown in the table, the single-person households increased 3.5 fold, two-person 4.7 fold, three-person 2.8 fold, and four-person 2.1 fold. The number of five-person households was rather stagnant between 1960 and 1995, but in 2000 it dropped below the 1960 level. The number of six-person households decreased almost by half, and that of the households with seven or more people are now less than one-fifth of what it was in the 1960s.

On the prefectural level, the number of households shows the same upward trend. On a smaller municipal level, the data become more diverse, but the reduction in family size is quite apparent in many regions. This trend is worth noting.

Figure 1-1-1 indicates the changes in the average number of household members. Until the 1950s, the average number was five, but it started to decline from the 1960s. It decreased by one between 1960 and 1970. Later, until the mid 1980s, it stayed above three, and then it dropped to two in the 1990s. The decline has been gradual but definite. The prefectural data shows the same downward trend, but it is about five years behind the national trend. The number has steadily been declining, most greatly between 1960 and 1965. The average number of household members in Katsunuma Town has always been greater than the national or prefectural numbers.

3-4. From Nuclear Family to Single-person

The number of stem families in our country has been gradually decreasing in the

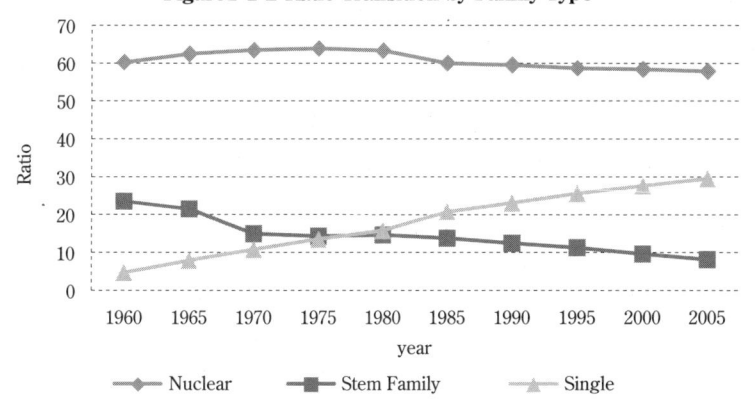

Figure 1-1-2 Ratio Transition by Family Type

[Line graph showing ratio (0-70) on y-axis, years 1960-2005 on x-axis, with three lines: Nuclear, Stem Family, and Single]

recent years. Stem families as an ideal type have also lost its appeal and today "Ie" is said to have disappeared. But what should be noted is that while the ratio of stem family households has definitely decreased, the actual number has not changed much. Even with the tendency toward the nuclear family, many couples still live with their aging parents. As the population as a whole ages further, more elderly living by themselves present many problems in terms of care and support.

Let us examine the national ratio transition by type for the changes in family forms (Figure 1-1-2). The nuclear family ratio is down, the single-person household ratio is up, and the stem family ratio is down. Although not shown, the regional and prefectural nuclear family ratios are a little lower than the national ratio. It was even lower on the town level, but has jumped up in recent years.

The data of the stem family households indicates the opposite trend: its municipal ratio is higher than the prefectural ratio, which is higher than the national. The municipal ratio was much higher until it dropped sharply in the 1990s. The national and prefectural single-person household ratios have drastically increased, a trend that started on the municipal level in 1990.

In regard to the family changes and regional characteristics of rural Japan, Yukiko Otomo pointed out that the changes in families are diversified depending on the level of urbanization and family norm. She quoted Tadashi Fukutake[1949], "For farming families that need successors, the stem family has been the ideal. But while the families from the north-east strongly feel that the stem family system is the norm, the families from south-west consider the conjugal family system as the norm." [Otomo, 2007: 83]

Factors for the nuclear family are related to those for the small family. What is common is the highly-developed industrial structure, demographic changes, and the spread of the concept of the conjugal family system [Morioka & Mochizuki, 1997: 161-162]. The trend of the nuclear family is considered to be especially influenced by the highly-developed industrial structure. On the other hand, demographic changes such as lower birthrates and the decline in the number of newborns have a great impact on the small family trend.

The national family trend and regional characteristics show that regional families experience changes more than ten years later than the national average. There is a wide gap among the regional families, national average, and urban families. The changing regional families need wisdom and ingenuity for preserving the merits of tradition.

3-5. Families in Pre-War Japan were not Large?

Many people may imagine that Japanese families before the war were mostly stem families and large in size. The national census was first conducted in 1920 in Japan and at that time, the "Ie" system was prevalent. 55.3% of the households were nuclear families so more than half were already nuclear.

Since 1920, the total number of households increased as the population increased, and the number of nuclear households has almost quadrupled and the number of stem families has doubled. While the nuclear family increased in ratio, the stem family decreased. This makes it appear as though the stem family sharply decreased in number, but despite the lower ratio, the actual number has not changed much. Recently, the single-person household increased and the stem family started to decrease, but not by much. The average family size used to be five before the war, but it started to go down rapidly and is now less than three.

There have been tendencies toward smaller, nuclear, or single-person households, but even before the war there were many nuclear families in Japan. Although many people hold an image of pre-war families being all large, what the statistics tell us is different.

4. Changes in Farm Management and Labor

Let us now discuss the operation scale, work forms, and changes in labor of farming families. These are indexes of farming transitions. As the lifestyles become urbanized and values become diversified, farm management seeks to secure appropriate income for their living level. Japan has mostly small family farming, and the reduction of farming families often leads to the increase of nuclear families[5].

4-1. Transition of Management Scale—Polarization in Farm Management—

After World War II, economic growth widened the gap between agriculture and industry. In terms of industrial structure, agriculture, being the primary industry, declined. The number of industrial workers, secondary industrial workers, people in the service business, and tertiary industrial workers have increased. The gap between large scale farming families that can support themselves with only farming and small scale farmers that cannot live by farming alone is widening. Farmers with small scale operations turned to part-time work, and the farming population divided into large and small scale farming and farms started to disintegrate.

The actual numbers in farming in total greatly decreased, dropping to one third, between 1960 and 2005. But the scale of farming families of 2.0ha and larger increased. In particular, 1501 households had 5.0ha or larger in 1965, and the number increased to 54,176 households in 1995, (decreased to) 43,438 in 2000, and 83,411 in 2005, an increase most notable after 2000. Recently, there has been a tendency toward group farming, which most likely contributes to this phenomenon.

The index changes by scale compared to 1960 (100) go parallel to the changes of actual numbers. But as a whole, the period between 1960 and 2005 saw a decline of about 40%. The scale of 2.0ha and over kept its upward trend until 1970. Other classes all decreased. 0.5ha or less was down to 20%, 0.5-1.0ha to one third, 1.5ha or over about 40%.

Large-scale farmers increased, while small-scale farmers decreased. The former started its upward trend in the 1970s and it continued in 1980 and 1990. There seems to be some entrepreneurship emerging among farmers, and how it is related to higher productivity, more development, technology, diversified management, and a wide variety of production will be a very important subject. (Figure 1-1-3[6])

---

5) In *Nihon Nouson Kazoku no Jizoku to Hendou* (Cuntinuance and Changes of the Stem Family Households in Rural Japan) 2009, Gakubunsha, Masae Tsutsumi analyzed the tendencies on the national, prefectural (Yamanashi), and municipal (Katsunuma) levels, based on the socio-economic data from "Agriculture Census Annual Statistics (1904-2000)," "Agriculture Census Yamanashi Statistics (1960-2005)," "Katsunuma Town Census," "Town Residents Poll," "Katsunuma Town Agricultural Vision," "Fruit Farming in Katsunuma," recent data from the Internet, and data from repetition research on subject households. Their results will be explained here.

6) In the Agriculture Census Annual Statistics, the operation area sections were different every year. Since 1985, commercial farmers were separated from private farmers, changing the counting method. From 1985 to 2005, the numbers are for commercial farmers. Since around 1985, how members of farming households are operating has greatly changed.

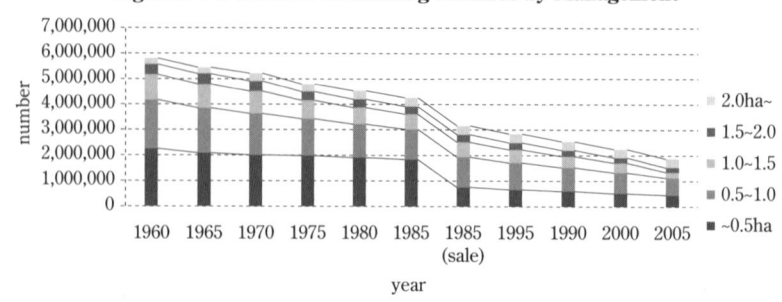

Figure 1-1-3 Number of Farming Families by Management

[Bar chart showing number of farming families from 1960 to 2005, with categories: 2.0ha~, 1.5~2.0, 1.0~1.5, 0.5~1.0, ~0.5ha. X-axis years: 1960, 1965, 1970, 1975, 1980, 1985, 1985 (sale), 1995, 1990, 2000, 2005.]

Note: The numbers from 1985 to 2005 are for sale farmers.

4-2. Shifting away from Agriculture—Full-time/Part-time Farming Family Composition (See Figure 1-1-4)

The number of full-time farming families has been decreasing and that of part-time farming families, especially Type II, has been on the rise. The decline of full-time farmers was most notable between 1965 and 1985. The decline had been parallel to economic growth, but recently that started to increase. The majority of the farmers are part-time.

The number of full-time farming families sharply dropped between 1960 (2,078,124) to 1965 (1,218,723) and between 1965 and 1975 (844,828). There was another major decline between 1980 (623,133) and 1985 (498,299). The drop that occurred between 1995 (427,584) and 2000 (426,355) was relatively small and the number went slightly up in 2005 (443,158).

The increase of part-time farmers was most notable between 1960 (3,978,506) and 1965 (4,446,040). The upward trend continued through 1975 and 1980. It then decreased starting in 1985 (2,816,632) to 2000 (1,910,554). In 2005 (1,520,266), the total number of farming families dropped, and part-time farmers decreased even further. During the period from 1955-1960, Type I part-time farmers were the majority, but that changed in 1965 when Type II came to the top.

In 1955, 34.8% of the farming families were full-time, then dropped drastically in 1965. In 1970, it came down to 15.6%, in 1975 2.4%, and in 1980 back up to 13.4%. It was 15.0% in 1985 and continued to increase to 16.1% in 1990 and 18.2% in 2000. Type I part-time farmers were 37.7% of the total in 1955, and Type II were 27.5%. In 1960, Type I was 33.6% and Type II was 32.1%. After 1970, Type II exceeded 50%, reaching 66.8% in 2000. In 2005, however, it went back down to the 1975 level.

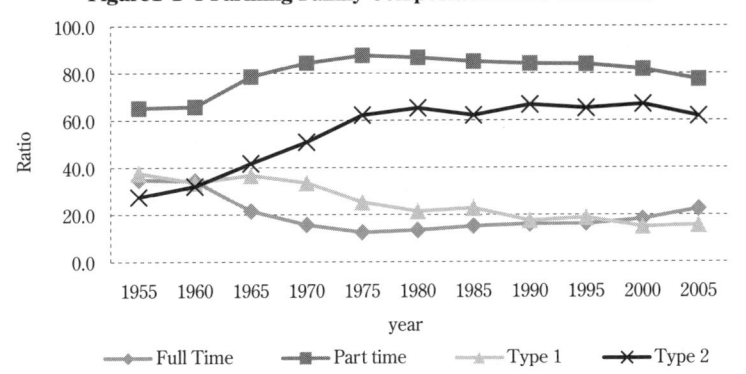

Figure 1-1-4 Farming Family Composition Ratio Transition

Ratio vs. year (1955–2005). Series: Full Time, Part time, Type 1, Type 2.

4-3. Changes in Farm Labor

The number of household members that joined their family farm is shown below by gender. The transition is described in Figure 1-1-5 in comparison to 1960.

As a national tendency, the workforce, considered from the viewpoint of the number of family members working on their farm, decreased by half between 1985 and 2000. As for the number of workdays, 29, the lowest, accounted for one third, and 150 or more, the highest, also took up one third.

Women tended to work fewer days than men. Women accounted for most of those who worked 29 days a year. Those who worked 150 days or more were mostly men. Polarization in the number of workdays can be seen in both genders. Female farmers have been increasing, and their workforce is becoming more important. The elderly work more than the rest of the age groups. Women in the child-rearing years worked less, and therefore, women usually joined the workforce after that period.

In both genders, young people did not participate in farming much. Those who were 60 or older worked more, actually supporting agriculture. This may mean working after retirement.

Let us examine the characteristics of the recent farming workforce based on a Census in 2000 in rural regions, the author's research subject. About half of the full-time farmers' households are living with a successor. The average age of the men was 33.7 years old, and the women's average age was 29.6 years old. The average age of farming successors living outside of the household was 36.1 (male) and 30.3 (female), higher than live-in successors'.

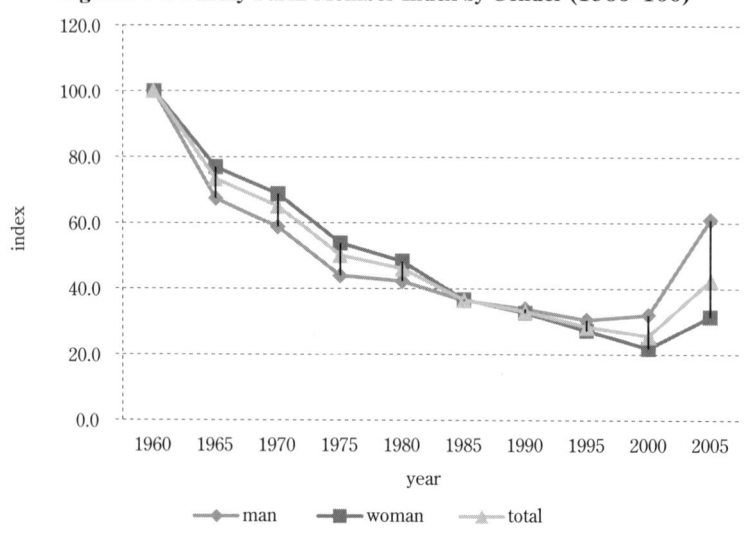

Figure 1-1-5 Family Farm Member Index by Gender (1960=100)

(Line graph showing index values from 1960 to 2005 for man, woman, and total. Values start at 100 in 1960 and decline to roughly 20–30 by 2000, with an uptick by 2005.)

The average age of farmers was 55.5, that of the principle farmer was 61.3, and that of those who work on the family farm 150 days or more was 61.3. Men's labor participation ratio was about 80%, women's 60%. In 1980, agriculture dropped to around 60%, then to 40% in 2000, and at this point, the number of female farmers was 10% larger than the male's. More men work in the secondary industry than women.

As we have seen, the farming population's aging and the increase of women in the workforce is very significant in rural regions.

5. Conclusion

Changes in Japanese families and farming have been investigated from analysis data from the Census, Agriculture and Forestry Census, and repetitive research of subject households. As a result, it has become clear that Japanese families and farming are at a great turning point. Families, our intimate life group, have been turning into nuclear, small, or single-person households, and shrinking. Agriculture that supports our environment has been getting smaller, and small farm management, part-time farming, discontinuation of farming, and a decline in farm laborers were recognized. Clearly, a great change is now taking place.

The following is a summary of the above.

(1) It is generally considered that the traditional "Ie" has disappeared from Japanese

Chapter 1: Changes of Women, Families and Agriculture in Rural Japan   19

families. They rapidly became small and nuclear during the high economic growth, but today, the increase of single-person households is even more dramatic. The nuclear family has been changing in quality. It is apparent from the changes in lifestyles, such as new values, diversity, and activities. In particular, the aging problem in rural regions presents problems in various fields of life. It is presumed that the families are becoming more nuclear internally while maintaining the form of the stem family system.

(2) Relation between family forms and operation size seems different depending on the social environment. In order to maintain the stem family system, the operation scale needs to be large. Since 1980, the number of stem families has been decreasing, but farms with large scale operations are also increasing. Transition since 1980 seemed to show that family form and farming scale were not related, but technology, methods, and farm management seem to be related.

(3) Part-time farmers often increased while stem families decreased. The number of full-time farmers has not decreased much, but stem families seem to be declining since 1990. Situations are different depending on the type of farming and regions. In general, the stem family and the work method are related. There is no obvious sign that the stem family and the number of farm workdays are related.

(4) When families changed, employment forms changed, and so did the significance of owning a piece of land. Who is going to succeed and how a daughter or son should be raised are major challenges for the future. Agriculture plays a significant role in creating traditional industries and for environmental preservation. Agriculture supports our livelihood. How can we integrate its management with traditional industry to be succeeded and to develop? How can we create a comfortable environment and communicate? These are the important challenges for the future.

References
Arahi, Yutaka, 2004, *Nouson Hendou to Chiikikasseika* (Changes and Vitalization of Rural Communities), Tokyo: Souzoushobou. (in Japanese)
Hasegawa, Akihiko, 1981, "Chiikishakai to Kazoku no Kinou (Functions of Local Community and Family)," Takeo Shinohara and Hideo Tsuchiya eds., *Chiikishakai to Kazoku* (Local Community and Family), Tokyo: Baifukan, 47-61. (in Japanese)
Hasumi, Otohiko, 1980, "Nouka no Kazoku to Nouka-Seikatsu (Farming Family and Farming Life)," Kazuo Aoi and Koukichi Shouji eds., *Kazoku to Chiiki no Shakaigaku* (Sociology of Family and Community), Tokyo: University of Tokyo Press, 121-141. (in Japanese)
Hiroshima, Kiyoshi, 1998, "Nihon no Kazoku Jinkougaku 20 nen (20 Years of Family Demography in Japan)," *Jinkougaku Kenkyu* (Demographic Research), 22: 31-37. (in Japanese)
Hosoya, Takashi, 1998, *Gendai to Nihon-Nouson-Shakaigaku* (Sociology of Today's Rural Japan),

Sendai: Tohoku University Press. (in Japanese)

Ishihara, Toyomi, 1996, *Nouka no Kazoku-Hendou* (Changes in Farming Family), Tokyo: Nippon-Hyoron-sha. (in Japanese)

Kawaguchi, Akira, 1995, *Ie to Mura: Kyousei to Kyouzon no Kouzou* (Ie and Mura: Structure of Coexistence and Codependence), Tokyo: Rural Culture Association. (in Japanese)

Morioka, Kiyomi and Takashi Mochizuki, [1983] 1987, 1993, 1997, 2000, *Atarashii Kazoku Shakaigaku* (New Family Sociology), Tokyo: Baifukan. (in Japanese)

Otomo, Yukiko, 1993, "Chokkei-Sei Kazoku ni okeru Kazoku-Kousei no Henka to Sedai no Koushin (Change in Family Composition and Generational Renewal of Stem-Family Households)," Kiyomi Morioka, Kunio Ishihara, Hiroto Satake, Masae Tsutsumi and Takashi Mochizuki eds., *Kazoku Shakaigaku no Tenkai* (The Development of Family Sociology), Tokyo: Baifukan, 99-121. (in Japanese)

———, 1998, "Chokkei-Sei Kazoku no Hendou ni tsuite no Jisshou-teki Kenkyu: Yamanashi-Ken Katsunuma-Cho ni okeru Paneru Deta wo mochiite (Empirical Study on Change in Stem-family Households Based on the Panel in Katsunuma Town, Yamanashi Prefecture)," *Research Journals on Household Economics*, 37: 70-73. (in Japanese)

The Japanese Association for Rural Studies and Hiroyuki Torigoe eds., 2007, *Mura no Shakai wo Kenkyu suru* (Study on Village Society), Tokyo: Rural Culture Association. (in Japanese)

———and Kouichi Ikegami eds., 2007, *Mura no Shigen wo Kenkyu suru* (Study on Village Resources), Tokyo: Rural Culture Association. (in Japanese)

Tsutsumi, Masae, 1980, "Kazokuhendou to Sono-Nihonteki-Tokucho (Changes in Family and Their Japanese Characteristics)," Gendaishakai-Kenkyukai (Society of Modern Social Studies) ed., *Gendaishakai no Shakaigaku* (Sociology of Today's Society), Tokyo: Kawashima-Shoten: 24-46. (in Japanese)

———ed., 2000, *Women and Families in Rural Japan,* Tokyo: Tsukuba Shobo.

———, 2003, "Tenkanki ni aru Nihon-Nouson-Kazoku to Nougyo (Japanese Farming Families and Agriculture at a Turning Point): Analysis of National Census, Agriculture and Forestry Census, and Longitudinal Research," *Yamanashi-Kenritsu Joshi-Tankidaigaku Chiiki Kenkyu* (Yamanashi Prefectural Women's Junior College Area Studies), 3: 41-82. (in Japanese)

Tsutsumi, Masae, Sadao Tokuno and Tsutomu Yamamoto eds., 2008, *Chihoukara no Shakaigaku* (Sociology from Local Region), Tokyo: Gakubunsha. (in Japanese)

Tsutsumi, Masae, 2009, *Nihon Nouson Kazoku no Jizoku to Hendou* (Continuance and Changes of the Stem Family Households in Rural Japan), Tokyo: Gakubunsha. (in Japanese)

Tsutsumi, Masae and Michi Tsutsumi, 2004, "A Turning Point of Household and Agriculture in Rural Japan: Analysis of National Census, Agriculture and Forestry Census, and Longitudinal Research," (http://www.irsa-world.org/prior/XI/papers/18-12.pdf, January 13, 2010).

Chapter 1: Changes of Women, Families and Agriculture in Rural Japan   21

Analysis Data
National Census
1960: Japan's Population; Population Compendium No.1 Japan; National Census Report Vol.2; National Census No.19 Yamanashi
1965: National Census Vol.4 Administrative Divisions No.19 Yamanashi; Approximate Numbers of Households and Population; Japan's Population
1970: Households and Families
1975-2005: National Census, Japan's Population: National Census, Vol.5, No.19 Yamanashi

World Agriculture & Forestry Census, Ministry of Agriculture & Forestry, Statistics Research Dada.
1960: World Agriculture & Forestry Census, Statistics by Municipals No.19
1965: Agricultural Census, Yamanashi Statistics, No.19
1970: World Agriculture & Forestry Census, Yamanashi Statistics, No.19
1975: Agricultural Census, Yamanashi Statistics, No.19
1980: World Agriculture & Forestry Census, Yamanashi Statistics
1985: Agricultural Census, Vol.1 Statistics on Administrative Divisions, No.19 Yamanashi
1990-2005: World Agriculture & Forestry Census, Vol.1 Yamanashi Statistics, (Agriculture).
2000: World Agriculture & Forestry Census Result Report, March 2001,Yamanashi
2000: Agricultural Census Annual Figures: Statistics (1899-2000), March 2003 Ministry of Agriculture, Forestry, and Fishery, Statistics Information Data.

Katsunuma Town References
March 1992: 3rd Long-term Total Plan
October 1992: Katsunuma Municipal Census Outline
October 1993: Katsunuma Town Organization 40th Anniversary Commemorative Booklet
May 1994: Industry and Life Revitalization Research
March 1991: Approach to the 21st Century–Katsunuma Agriculture Vision
March 1997: Fruit Farming of Katsunuma–Town of Grapes, Wine, and Flowers
March 2001: 4th Katsunuma Town Total Plan
October 2001: Municipal Census, Town Opinion Poll Report
March 2002: Katsunuma Human Plan Town Opinion Poll Report
October 2002: Municipal Census, Town Opinion Poll Report

2
Change and Problems Regarding Women Farmers in Japan
Tokuya Kawate

1. Image versus Reality

What is the common perception of families and women in rural farming villages in Japan?

The prototype for the rural family image can be found before Japan's period of rapid economic growth from middle 1950's to early 1970's. The rural (agricultural) family was essentially a patriarchal stem family which is called "Ie". Because families included unmarried collateral relatives, they tended to be quite large. Live-in workers lived on a large farm with the farm owners. Inheritance of the family business and property was based on an established system. The basic rural community in Japan, a rural village which is called "Mura" was conceived and governed as Japanese traditional household "Ie" coalitions. Self-government had been managed by "Omodachi", representatives of influential "Ie" who were almost all old and middle aged men in the "Mura". A Homogeneous rural community was enumerated as the major feature. This network of geographical and sanguinary relations often interfered with the running of individual households. Women were seen solely as unpaid laborers bearing and rearing children, or "hornless cows."

However, the rural family has changed greatly in recent years. The family structure in Japan has changed to include more singles, single-generation, and nuclear families, but in the case of rural families, the stem family remains a distinguishing characteristic. Still, the characters of rural families have been greatly altered from the "Ie" (household) system. In other words, diverse management styles and lifestyles have emerged within the stem family. As farming families increasingly supplement their income with side businesses, family members are more and more engaged in different jobs. Even those working in agriculture are subject to greater division of labor. Lifestyle changes have affected life outside of work as well: farming families increasingly separate their family budgets, meals, and living quarters into smaller family units. Living areas are often divided using the married couple as the base unit of ownership, and there are also more cases of commuting to the farm to work. These phenomena do not signal the end of the stem family. If anything, they are the reflection of the rural family's attempts to adapt to changing social conditions while respecting each family member's individuality.

Regarding rural communities, growing heterogeneity of the rural community can be enumerated since the period rapid economic growth. Recently about 90% of residences of rural villages are non-farm households. The way of management of rural communities is changing, but women farmers are still excluded from the decision making [Kawate, 2000].

2. The Changing Lifestyle of the Rural Family

It goes without saying that Japan's period of rapid economic growth was a major factor in altering the landscape for agriculture and rural farming villages. During this period, agriculture and farmers' lifestyles "modernized" in a clearly visible way. A significant shift to urban lifestyles was made. Washing machines, refrigerators, televisions, interior toilets and baths became fixtures of life, and the farm kitchen was also rapidly improved. As a result, the amount of heavy labor families performed decreased markedly. Houses also changed: from multi-generational families living in neighboring rooms separated only by thin walls or sliding doors to homes ensuring a greater measure of privacy for couples. The movement of younger sons, women, and finally eldest sons to other industries spurred the addition of supplementary businesses and the move to "urbanization." Values also changed. Examples include (1) the emergence of individualism (equality under the law and respect for self-determination of career, living arrangement, and marriage), (2) changing attitudes about nature (from feared to conquerable or developable), (3) a partial shift to economic rationalism. All of these developments led to the spread of economic orientation.

Consequently, the rural family underwent major change. One might call this, "the coupling of the stem family," meaning the move to a married couple level family structure. Patriarchal family relations weakened, and the emotional bonds between couples and their children in particular came to be emphasized. Parent-child agreements provided impetus for the further differentiation of lifestyles for each married couple family unit. Factors in this include, (1) the assignment of management responsibilities to farm heirs and encouragement of participation in farming, (2) the shift away from treating farm heirs as "unpaid labor" and the accompanying provision of wages and allowances to each family member, and (3) housing improvements.

While the stem family remained the rule, the changing demographics of 1950s Japan meant a precipitous drop in children per couple and loss of collateral family to other enterprises. Overall (with regional variation), the family shrank. Live-in employees and other labor disappeared. And most of family business (farming) ceased to be the subject of inheritance, and only family assets continued to be passed down.

Multi-generational cohabitation, which had been the rule for farming families, gave way to an ideal family based on married couple family units. Farm heirs had less disposable income than their white collar peers, and men were at a disadvantage in finding wives because of the heavy labor awaiting women on farms. Some heirs made the effort to carve out their own management divisions to overcome this adversity. This was simultaneous to efforts by many farmers to avoid relying on supplementary (non-agricultural) income by moving away from rice-only farming.

Women, however, were still unpaid labor, with little chance of self-realization. Traditional views of gender roles and "women's work" remained strong. As agricultural productivity rose, the division between productive labor and housework was drawn with increasing clarity. Because of fixed gender role prejudices, women were increasingly shunted into housework—more and more their labor was "shadow work." Farming women thus came to be defined as "wife's help in the background" for their husbands, the "entrepreneurs" of modern farming in Japan [Kawate, 2000].

3. Individualism within the Stem Family

Rural families today, particularly those engaged solely in agriculture (but excluding those in depopulated areas and in regions like Kagoshima where the youngest son is traditionally the heir) have evolved from a period of unaltered stem family morphology with the married couple forefronted to one of unaltered stem family morphology with the *individual* forefronted.

In other words, the family structure remains within the parameters of the stem family. Despite increased intergenerational lifestyle differentiation and separate or two-generation living quarters, what is actually occurring is that the three-generation family arrangement is barely holding on or that the families themselves are falling apart; this is not a paradigm shift to a new household model. It is worth noting that individual lifestyle differentiation as mentioned above is predicated on intragenerational and intergenerational lifestyle balance, but because of the general trend to individualization, this balance is not easily attained and maintained. Individualization and heterogenization are affecting even farming families, and that today's farm families tend not to be coherent in this sense. Families are also shrinking. Traditional inheritance systems have mostly faltered. Of these, family asset inheritance has been particularly weakened by rising urban land prices and population loss in rural villages[1].

4. The Empowerment of Women Farmers

Contemporary women farmers in Japan are far from "miserable".

---

1) These changes can be summarized as: (1) unaltered stem family morphology, (2) increasing emphasis on the emotional bonds between couples and their children, (3) a shift to farm management by

Chapter 1: Changes of Women, Families and Agriculture in Rural Japan

In Japanese farming villages, the number of women accounts for approximately 55% of total farming population, making the role of women very important in agricultural production as they handle their work of housekeeping, child rearing and care taking of the elderly and so on at the same time. Recently the number of women farmers, mainly their leaders, who play an active role in the society of farming villages has been increasing (Table 1-2-1).

Leaders of women farmers now in their 50s and 60s play key roles in changing the rural family. These women were born in the post-War period, and were among the first generation to receive democratization education throughout their school careers. Many of these women began farming only after marriage, regardless of whether they were born on a farm or not. The majority began to seriously take on leadership roles in their 30s—after the busiest childrearing period had ended. Many were born in cities to white collar families and had no premarital knowledge of or experience with agriculture. Paradoxically, it was this previous ignorance that allowed them to posit themselves as active subjects at the same time agriculture and rural farming villages slipped deeper into trouble. They take on new important roles or businesses in agriculture, (1) as the

Table 1-2-1 Percentage of Women in Farm Population in Japan

Item	Farm Household Population	Farm Population
	(Unit : 1,000 people)	(Unit : 1,000 people)
Total	9647	3684
Female	4926	2039
Ratio(%)	51.1	55.4

Source : The Ministry of Agriculture, Forestry and Fisheries, "Agricultural Cesus" 2005

---

individuals, and (4) increasing an increasing level of lifestyle differentiation. (2) has been problematic since Japan's period of rapid economic growth. It proved an important factor in the progression of (3) and (4) and continues to grow stronger.

(3) and (4) are relatively new changes. They share the following characteristics: (a) increasing responsibility and participation in farm management by women, (b) decreased treatment of women as "unpaid labor" sources and the corresponding personal budgets, and (c) increasing individual human networking outside the family structure. It must be added that (c) represents a shift away from traditional autochthonic and consanguinary bonds to relationships based on choice. This means the creation of new human pipelines in the family and community. In this context, the bases for individual expression are being established at the same time that communities are evolving into new forms. It is worth noting that individual lifestyle and farm management differentiation as mentioned above are predicated on intragenerational and intergenerational lifestyle balance, but because of the general trend to individualization, this balance is not easily attained and maintained. These changes in family relations are of vast importance in considering the changes in rural farming society.

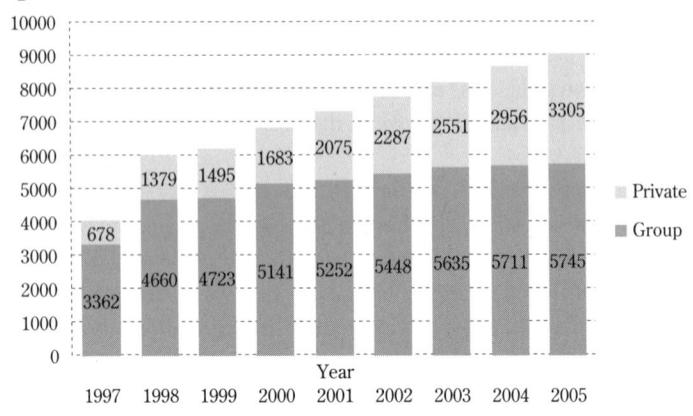

Figure 1-2-1 Trends of Rural Women Entrepreneurial Activities in Japan

Year	Group	Private	Total
1997	3362	678	
1998	4660	1379	
1999	4723	1495	
2000	5141	1683	
2001	5252	2075	
2002	5448	2287	
2003	5635	2551	
2004	5711	2956	
2005	5745	3305	

Source : The Division of Agricultural Extension and Women, MAFF, 2007

manager or the management partner, (2) the processing and selling of farm products, agriculture for tourism and so on, giving women responsibility for initiating a new business as well.

Their sphere of activity has expanded from their own farms and lifestyles to include the community and even the urban side of the equation. Their activities are not limited to empowering rural farming women. They are involved with farmers' markets, direct sales, processing agricultural products, passing down received traditions and creating new ones, community building, managing local resources, responding to environmental issues, welfare for the elderly, liaising with urbanites and consumers, and more.

Background of new roles or businesses of women farmers, the Japanese consumers are begging to demand fresh, delicious, safe and real farm products. On the other hand, farmers are begging to process and sell their farm products directly to consumers at higher prices in order to increase their income. After rapid economic development in Japan, for the promotion of agriculture and farm villages, a kind of harmonization with urbanization and industrialization has become very important, including intercourse between urbanites and ruralites or consumers and producers [kawate, 2000; Tsuru, 2007].

Recently, many women in farm households have been initiating new businesses in rural areas. These economic activities include processing of farm products, direct selling to consumers, delivery of meals to the elderly, running a special restaurant featuring famous foods of the area and green tourism activities. The amount of annual

Table1-2-2 Type of Rural Women Entrepreneurial Activities in Japan, 2005 (multi answer)

Type	Number	%
Total	9050	100
Agricultural Production	1421	15.2
Food Processing	6816	75.3
Other Processing	343	3.8
Direct Sales, Distribution	3999	44.2
Interchange with City	995	11
Service	55	0.6
Other	42	0.5
Unkown	7	0.1

Source : The Division of Agricultural Extension and Women, MAFF, 2007

sales and profits from these businesses are generally not so great, but they are stimulating local economies.

Such new businesses are called "Rural Women Entrepreneurial Activities" or "New Work by Rural Women Entrepreneurs", Which are promoted, and getting support from the Ministry of Agriculture, Forestry and Fishery, local governments, Agricultural Cooperatives and so on [Miyaki, 1996; Miyaki and Iwasaki, 2000; Morofuji, 2007] (Table 1-2-2).

Leaders of women farmers value couple-based living patterns, but also multigenerational living. They also seek ways of self-realization. Many women farmers try to manage the divergent life vectors of family balance, couple-based living patterns, and individualism in order to live empowered, subjective lives. The rural family has developed into one with unaltered stem family morphology and the individual forefronted. These women emphasize and promote family management agreements along with supporting organizations. "Farm Management Agreements" [Gojo, 2003; Kawate, 2005], now also promoted under the support of the Ministry of Agriculture, Forestry and fishery and local governments, seek intragenerational and intergenerational lifestyle balance with the lifestyle of the individual, and simultaneously promote a shift to new farming family relations, and equal partnership among family members [Rural life Research Institute, 1999; Kawate, 2000].

Many leaders of women farmers try to send their representatives to an agriculture committee or assembly in cities, towns, and villages with the aspect of the empowering women farmers.

Leaders of women farmers have overcome tremendous difficulties and have

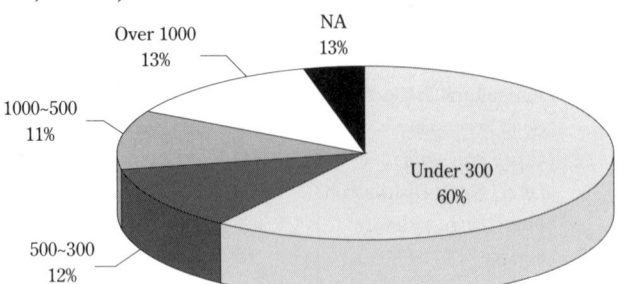

Figure 1-2-2 Rural Women Entrepreneurial Activities by Year Proceeds (Gross Sales), 2005 (Unit: 1,000Yen)

- Over 1000: 13%
- NA: 13%
- 1000~500: 11%
- Under 300: 60%
- 500~300: 12%

Source : The Division of Agricultural Extension and Women, MAFF, 2007

become the most important key persons to develop agriculture and rural life in Japan. Their actions change agriculture and rural society gradually and steadily, though they are still in the minority.

After World War II, various support, including having seminars and organizing women farmers, has been provided for improvement of the abilities and social position of rural woman. Promotion of these activities by the Ministry of Agriculture, Forestry and Fishery, local governments Agricultural Cooporatives. Especially Agricultural Improvement Extension Centers located in each prefectural government throughout the nation has played a central role.

5. A Case of One of the Leaders of Women Farmers

Mrs. Kanae Uwano, one of the representative leaders of women farmers in Japan, lives in Takizawa, a village adjacent to Morioka, the capital of Iwate Prefecture, and located about 500km north of Tokyo. She runs a farm whose main products are apples. Takizawa is not only a bedroom community of Morioka but also a farming district blessed with abundant land resources. Farmers in the village are mostly engaged in multiple cropping, combining paddy rice cultivation or dairy farming, which are the main industries in the area, with the growing of apples or vegetables. Recently, the production of flowers is increasing, too.

Kanae's family has six members, including her, of four generations: her husband (65), mother-in-law (86), her eldest son (35) and his wife (34) and their daughter (Kanae's granddaughter).

Kanae and her husband are the main workers at the farm. While her husband is responsible for crop management and work plans, Kanae takes charge of customer service, sale of apples and bookkeeping. In April 2004, her eldest son resigned as a teacher and joined his parents as a farmer. The son's wife mainly does housework and childcare, and the mother-in-law (mother of Kanae's husband) manages the family's premises.

The family's farm is composed of 2.3ha (23,000m^2) of apple orchards and 0.2ha (2,000m^2) of vegetable fields, which are used partly as a farm for learning by experience for visitors and partly as a farm for growing vegetables for the family's own consumption. A total of 19 apple varieties are planted. The most important is Fuji, which occupies 40 percent of the orchards' total area, followed by Orin, Yoko, Hokuto, Kio and Jona Gold. When apples became the farm's main product, the family began to call their apple orchards "Uwano Apple Orchards." Besides apple production, the family manages tourists' apple orchards and carries out other green tourism activities, such as orchard ownership plans and learning by experience programs in farming. The tourists' orchards have about 2,000 visitors a year. The family owns a direct sale store of farm produce, and its combined sales at the store and of home delivery service account for about 50 percent of the total sales. The owners of the orchards total about 200, and 20 percent of the sales come from these owners. Other business includes sale at the district's joint sale store (10% of the total sales), the tourists' apple orchard (10%), participation in community events (5%) and shipment to the local JA agricultural cooperative (5%).

Kanae, now 60, was born in 1946, just after World War II ended, as the seventh child of eleven brothers and sisters in a farmer family in Kuzumaki, a mountainous area 60km northeast of Takizawa. After graduating from a junior high school, she worked as an employee at the local agricultural cooperative for five years. At 20, she married and moved to Takizawa and joined her husband and his parents as a farmer. In those days, the family's farm consisted of 1.8ha (18,000m^2) of paddy fields and 1ha (10,000m^2) of apple orchards. Two years after the marriage, Kanae and her husband started pig farming, and they gradually increased the number of pigs. Also, at about the same time, the road in front of their house was reconstructed to prepare for a national athletic meet to be held in the prefecture, and taking this occasion, Kanae played the central role in promoting the direct sale of apples to consumers. The purpose was to increase the value of their apples as much as possible. At present, the direct sale of apples is commonly observed, but at that time, it was regarded as a folly by most farmers in the district. In 1980, Kanae established her own permanent store for direct sales. As a result of these activities, her apple production increased gradually. In those years, she had four children, and while engaged in housework and childcare, she continued pig farming and the cultivation of apples and other crops together with her husband.

When he graduated from a university, Kanae's eldest son said to her: "I will join you two as a farmer ten years from now. So please continue to improve and expand the apple orchards." These words were an important turning point for her. The son chose to work as a high school teacher first. Kanae and her husband selected apples as a crop that could be cultivated throughout life without too much labor and could give hope to their son, and discontinued pig farming and paddy rice cultivation to concentrate on the development of their apple orchards. At the same time, they started green tourism activities, including farm ownership plans, in an effort to further enhance the value of their apples. Kanae took the initiative in planning and establishing an easy-to-use apple warehouse, a warehouse of farm implements, a direct sale store, a room for learning by experience, a break room and a multi-purpose hall. According to Kanae, one of the reasons for introducing the farm ownership plans was the fact that a friend, with whom she became familiar with though childcare, said to her that the apple orchards were wonderful and envied her. Kanae says: "Whenever I have applicants for owners, I always ask them to come to the orchards and to walk in them. While showing them around the orchards, I talk with them about everything. I encourage them to feel like they became the owners of the orchards. If they became the owners, I hope they understand the feelings of apples growing here and the process of their ripening. I tell them I hope those who sympathize with my wishes become the owners. This may be a little selfish, but I think I can get along well with them in the apple orchards if what I can offer them and their wishes are in agreement. We will try to treat the owners of the apple orchards just as our family members, calling them 'apple family members'." In fact, the owners can enter and visit their orchards any time of the year, and can take a rest at the owners' break room "Gororian," helping themselves to a cup of tea or coffee. Kanae is also committed to the provision of barrier-free facilities, and has constructed a toilet and paths in the orchards for wheel-chair users.

In doing these activities, Kanae signed a "family management agreement" with her husband. This agreement lays down the agreed matters about farm work and life in the family as regards to role sharing, decision making, remuneration and holidays, working hours and other working and daily life conditions. "Though I have not dared to tell this to even my husband, I have strongly felt women married to farmers are disadvantaged and have many problems. I cooperated with my husband, who said to me his dream was to work as a full-time farmer, and worked hard as a wife and a daughter-in-law to help the family "Uwano" out of difficulty, but the life of my own as an individual and my efforts were never officially recognized. So, when I decided to start new forms of agriculture, I thought I would sign a family management agreement with my husband so that I may work harder and become a model as a community leader," said Kanae. After the agreement was concluded, she first came to know the amount of her remuneration. Loans of funds and their repayment plans were also made clear as a result of the bookkeeping started under the agreement, and the share of farm and other work was clearly defined.

After Kanae introduced green tourism plans, other farmers in the area began to work on a variety of activities for the same purpose, too. About three years ago, the "Flower Festival" was started in Uwano Apple Orchards. In this event, the "Network of All Good Products from Yanagisawa village," the group created by Kanae and her friends, established a section for selling farm products and has continued interchanges with many people. In addition, on the basis of this network, the "Group on the Foot of Mt. Iwate" was also formed. To offer young people opportunities for study on many subjects, Kanae is positively providing them with part of her farm, meeting places and tools. Her dream is endless; she cultivates and harvests buckwheat, the traditional food in the area, and studies new cooking methods for this crop. She also plans to establish a rural restaurant and a confectionary factory as well as to expand the direct sale store. According to Kanae, "The Group is mainly composed of relatively young people, and I hope its members will become leaders in the community in the future."

As a representative of rural women groups and as a leader of farmers approved by the Governor of Iwate Prefecture, Kanae is also making many contributions to the promotion of gender equality and to the revitalization of rural agriculture, including giving lectures about her experiences to farmers [Kawate, 2004].

6. Problems for Women Farmers

Whether new forms of social cohesion based on families respecting individuals and the independence of local communities is possible or not will greatly affect the future lifestyles of Japan's farming communities. If this proves impossible, the crises facing agriculture and rural farming villages will only deepen. In either case, a new form of cohesion will be possible and diversified farming orientated to consumers will also be possible. And then the role to be played by rural farming women is critically important, just like Mrs. Kanae Uwano.

Recently, especially since the 1990s, women's role in agriculture has finally begun to be recognized gradually. In order for farm management to improve and develop, the positions and roles of both heirs and women must be clarified, efforts must be made to improve productivity, and family members must respect each other's individuality and learn to see each other as partners. The stem family is capable of flexibly responding to these new management and lifestyle changes to support contemporary society's diverse family structures and lifestyles. The further development of agriculture and farming lifestyles will depend on the creation of new relationships within the rural family.

The rural family will likely remain centered on the stem family structure. As agriculture itself has become a matter of choice, so has the stem family systems.

Table1-2-3 Participation in Agricultural Committees and Agricultural Cooperatives

Year	1985	1995	2005
Nunber of Members in Agricultural Commitiees	64080	60917	45379
Number of Female Members	40	203	1869
Ratio of Women (%)	0.06	0.33	4.1
Number of Managers in Agricultural Cooperative	77490	68611	22797
Number of Female Managers	39	70	438
Ratio of Women (%)	0.1	0.2	1.9

Source : The Ministry of Agriculture, Forestry and Fisfheries, "2007 White Paper On Agriculture" 2008

Table1-2-4 Average Daily Hours Spent on Work and Housekeeping in Farming and Fishing Villages

	Work	House-keeping, Nursing, Child care				Total
		House-keeping	Nursing	Child care	Sub total	
Males	6.04	0.13	0.02	0.02	0.17	6.21
Females	4.45	2.54	0.09	0.09	2.72	7.17
Female Ratio vs. Male	74%					115%

Note : The ratio has been caluculated by percentage.
Source : Management and Coordination Agency "Basic Study Report on Social Life " (Year 1996)

Moreover, systems of farmland inheritance must be developed that simultaneously respect individual rights and ensure secure, stable transitions. The "modernization of family relationships" is proposed in agricultural administration without any discussion of appropriate management transfer/inheritance. What must be problematized now is that despite advocating the establishment of modern family management practices, nothing has been done to change the pre-modern patriarchal stem family practices of management transfer and inheritance. This exceptionally difficult issue is, in fact, already being addressed in communities around Japan. Systematic support is needed to solve the bevy of problems this implies.

Recently the number of rural families who try to clarify each others positions and roles and respect each other as partners is increasing and the contemporary stem family is capable of flexibly responding to these new management and lifestyle changes.

But there are still many problems remain for women farmers in Japan. The level of gender equality is not adequate. For example, in a survey about 90% of women farmers take part in farm management it some manner, about 70% receive compensation in some way, but only 40% receive on a monthly basis. Ratio of possession of farmland by women farmers is very low. Even leaders of women farmers are still excluded in the decision making process on regional agriculture and revitalization. The daily work hours of women farmers are longer compared to those of men.

It is very useful to promote "Farm Management Agreement" and "Rural Women Entrepreneurial Activities" in the light of not only empowerment of women farmers but also development of farm management and regional agriculture.

As a premise, in rural families and farm village communities, it goes without saying that it is necessary to push forward gender equality in all aspects.

The "Basic Law for a Gender-equal Society" was publicized and enforced in June 1999 in Japan, so as to 'maintain equal opportunities for both men and women to participate in various activities in all social fields according to the intentions of each individual as equal constituent members of the society'. In addition, the "Basic Law on Food, Agriculture, and Farming Village" was established in 1999, stipulating that 'maintenance of an environment shall be promoted so as to provide fair evaluation on womens roles and maintain opportunities for women to take part in the management of farming, as well as to maintain opportunities for women farmers to take part in the management of farming according to their own intentions as well as to take part in related activities.

The Ministry of Agriculture, Forestry and Fisheries in Japan presented "the Vision" in order to create and systematize new agricultural policy for women farmers before these 2 basic laws in 1999. It was first time for women farmers to be officially recognized as important key persons in farming. The goals for women farmers were described clearly. Agricultural policy for women farmers has been promoted based on "the Vision". Promotion of Family Management Agreement and Rural Enterprise were held as very important positions [Yagi, 1999; Tsutsumi ed., 2000]. At any rate governmental and social support for women farmers should be strongly provided in promoting women farmers' activities based on "the Vision" and the 2 basic laws[2].

References
Gojo, Miyoshi, 2003, *Kazokukeieikyoutei no Tenkai* (Promotion of Family Management Agreement)," Tokyo: Tsukuba Shobo. (in Japanese)
Kawate, Tokuya, 2000, "Nousonseikatsu no Henbou to 20 Seiki Sisutemu (A Study on Change in Rural Life in Japan and Influence of "20th Century System")," *Annual Bulletin of Rural Studies,* 36:118-151. Tokyo: Noubunkyo. (in Japanese)
―――, 2004, "Kanae Uwano, Women Owner of Uwano Apple Orchards," *Farming Japan,*

---

[2] This paper was presented at 12th World Congress of Rural Sociology: International Rural Sociology Association, on July 6-11, 2008 in Republic of Korea. This edition include, the most recent revision.

38(3) : 50-55.

―――, 2005, *Gendai no Kazokukeieikyoutei* (Contemporary Significances of Family Management Agreement), Tokyo: Tsukuba Shobo. (in Japanese)

Miyaki, Michiko, 1996, *Nouson de Hajimeru Josei Kigyo*, Tokyo: Rural Women Empowerment and Life Improvement Association. (in Japanese)

Miyaki, Michiko and Yumiko Iwasaki, 2000, "Seikousuru Nouson Joseikigyo (Succesful Rural Women's Entrepreneurship)," Tokyo: Tsukuba Shobo. (in Japanese)

Morofuji, Kyoko, 2007, "Nouson Seisaku toshiteno Nouson Joseikigyo ("New Work by Rural Woman Entrepreneurs" as Rural Policy)," *Journal of Rural Planning*, 26(1): 33-38. (in Japanese)

Rural Life Research Institute, 1999, Tasedaidoukyo no Kazokukankei to Josei no Jiritsu (Relationship of Family in Which Many Generation Live Together and Independence of Rural Women) Rural life Research Series, 48. (in Japanese)

Tsutsumi, Masae ed., 2000, *Women and Families in Rural Japan,* Tokyo: Tsukuba-Shobou.

Tsuru, Rieko, 2007, *Noukajosei no Shakaigaku* (Sociology of Women Farmers), Tokyo: Komonzu. (in Japanese)

Yagi, Hironori, 1999, "Strategies for Improving Women's Roles in Farm Management in Japan," Resource Paper for APO Seminar on Strategies for Improving Women's Role in Farm Management.

3
The Characteristics and the Challenges of Rural Women's Entrepreneurial Activities in Japan
Kyoko Morofuji

1. Introduction

Rural women's entrepreneurial activities (RWEAs here in after) in Japan have been looked upon positively as the objects of policy support, and both the number and the variety of these activities are increasing.

According to the Ministry of Agriculture, Forestry and Fisheries (MAFF here in after), RWEAs are defined as activities by rural women related to agriculture, forestry, or fisheries. They use local products, are managed mainly by rural women, and generate income for women. Major areas for RWEAs include farmers' markets, processing of agricultural products, restaurants using local products, and rural- urban interchange.

RWEAs are economic activities, but they prioritize the improvement of quality of life and community over profit. With these characteristic, RWEAs enabled various social effects such as sustaining food security, maintaining rural culture, environmental preservation, mental empowerment of women and elderly people in addition to economic achievements such as stabilizing the farm-household economy, empowering women's economic status, stimulating the local economy, and the promotion of local agriculture. Recently, "Chisan-chisho" (local production for local consumption), and "shokuno-kyoiku" (food and agriculture education) have also been attracting the attention.

Morofuji (2007) proposed that the communal and public role of rural women's entrepreneurial activities should be re-evaluated, and their meaning should be reconsidered in the context to agricultural and rural policy. Based on this standpoint, in this paper, the characteristics of RWEAs in Japan will be explained and then, the challenges faced by RWEAs will be discussed.

2. Characteristics of Rural Women's Entrepreneurial Activities
2-1. History of Rural Women's Entrepreneurial Activities

RWEAs in Japan can be characterized by its inclusive participation (including non-farm households) by all women, not only pioneering women farmers (Figure 1-3-1). This is

Figure 1-3-1 The Key Map of Women who Participate in RWEA

Rural women		A position in RWEA

1. Women engaged in agriculture both in farm households and non-farm households

   The support target of the agricultural policy

   ①Women engaged in agriculture as main job in farm households
   women farmers [Manager / Family employee]

   ②Women who have connection with society and market through agriculture
   family employees in agriculture as side job
   employed laborer in the agricultural corporation (outside own family farm).

   ③Women engaged in agriculture only for self supply

2. Women who are not engaged in agriculture both in farm households and non-farm households

A position in RWEA:
- Manager
- Business partner
- Member
- Employed laborer

Support targets of RWEAs

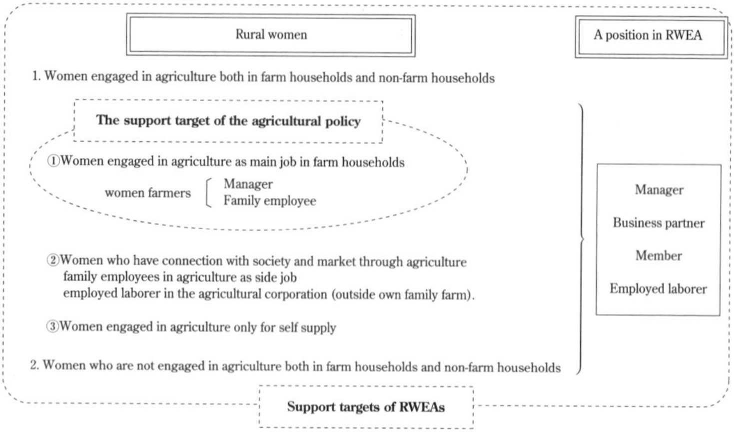

Source : made by author

one of the reasons why RWEAs have contributed to activating the local communities and stimulating the economies. Since the 1990's, agricultural policy in Japan has limited its attention to group① in Figure 1-3-1, but all rural women who participate in RWEA activities have been given support.

Such inclusive participation by rural women is rooted in the history of the emergence of RWEAs. RWEAs have decades of history starting from small, group activities such as agricultural production and processing by Agricultural Cooperatives Women's Clubs or Life-Improvement Practice Groups for providing healthy and safe food for their families (Table 1-3-1).

The origin of RWEAs can be traced to the self-sufficiency movement in the 1970's. This movement aimed at family health management and increasing production to compensate for the loss of farm-household income. Gradually, various agricultural products and processed foods came to be sold at casual events and open-air markets. In the 1980's, the regional-development movement became active, and at the same time, positive promotion of the "One-Village-One-Product" Movement began. In these activities, women were important actors for the creation and production of local special identity products. In the 1990's, the increase of farmers' markets, the construction of "Michi no Eki" (Roadside establishments), and the promotion of Green-tourism expanded the markets, and women's activities expanded from only production to also include marketing.

With regards to gender policy, various plans for encouraging rural women were

Chapter 1: Changes of Women, Families and Agriculture in Rural Japan

Table 1-3-1 Historical Background of RWEA in Japan

	Activities of Rural women in Japan	Rural women's policy in Japan	Trends of the agriculture and rural community in Japan
1950	Rural Life Improvement Activities	Starting of Rural Life Improvement Extension Program	
1960	*By the experience of Rural Life Improvement Activities, such as participation in the cooking course and vegetable gardening activities, participating women mastered agricultural produce processing skill, as keepable foods-making	Organizing of Life improvement Practice Group	Basic Agricultural Law enactment
1970	self-sufficiency movement		Starting of Acreage Allotment Program in Rice Production
1980	open-air market/morning market Making local special identity products	"Rural Women's Houses" establishment Starting of Relief program for the rural women	One Village One Product Movement, Regional development Movement
1990	Development of RWEA		Roadside Station establishment
2000		Official announcement Goals for Rural Women in the 21st Century and a Mid-to Long-term Vision for Achieving Goals Starting of Projects to encourage rural women entrepreneurs to formulate Guidelines to promote gender equality in rural areas	Official announcement of the forthcoming Basic Law Concerning Food, Agriculture and Rural Areas Rural Leisure Law (The law on the promotion of staying type leisure activities in the rural area) Basic Law on Food, Agriculture and Rural Areas enactment

source: Morofuji (2007)

stipulated in a National Action Plan after the First World Conference on Women was held in 1975. Through construction of "Nouson Fujin no Ie" (Rural Women's Houses) since the late 1970's, and support programs for rural women since the 1980's, women's opportunities to acquire skills and to process products by themselves expanded, and various rural special-identity products were created.

In the 1990's, agricultural policy changed corresponding to changes of socio-economic conditions. MAFF itself reorganized, and in 1991, the Home Life Improvement Division of the Agricultural Production Bureau was re-organized into the Women and Life Division. With this reorganization, support for rural women became systematized for the first time. "The forthcoming Basic Law Concerning Food, Agriculture and Rural

Areas" (The forthcoming Basic Law here in after) was announced in 1992, and rural women were considered to be important in the support of agricultural production and management, and it was declared necessary to assist women in exercising their abilities. Based on "The forthcoming Basic Law", "Goals for Rural Women in the 21st Century and a Mid-to-Long-term Vision for Achieving Goals" ("Vision" herein after) was planned. Policy support for RWEAs was first stipulated in this vision.

2-2. RWEAs as Realizing "An Alternative Working Style"

"A middle and long term Vision in 2001", presented a shift from a masculine society placing too much emphasis on profit to a gender-equal society paying respect to life. RWEAs were expected to take the lead in a shift towards a society paying respect to the quality of life through realizing "alternative working styles". "Alternative working styles (New working styles)" refers to working styles that are economic activities, which do not prioritize profit but put an importance on the improvement of the quality of life. Rural women living in rural areas, make use of and conserve rural resources that are unique to the locality. These RWEAs are based on such rural life practices as characterized by the "alternative working style" [Kanamori et al., 1989].

Rural resources include various tangible and intangible resources. Preservation of traditional foods, rural women's activities to conserve them, and rural women's entrepreneurial activities themselves are intangible rural resources.

2-3. Influence of RWEAs on Women and the Community

Table 1-3-2 shows the characteristics of RWEA from three aspects, "economy", "rural life/culture" and "community". Based on this table, the influence of RWEAs on participating women and communities will be examined from the results of a questionnaire survey of the representatives of RWEAs conducted in 2006[1].

Table 1-3-2 Characteristics of RWEA

	Women's empowerment	The activation of rural society
Economy	Woman's economic independence/ The stability of the farm management	The promotion of the local agriculture/ The activation of the local economy
Rural life/Culture	Women's self-actualization/The reevaluation of farmer's, rural life	The reevaluation of rural life, rural culture
Community	Women's socialization/Womenn's inclusive participation in the local agriculture, community	The activation of the community/Encouragement of the community power

Source: by author referring to Miyaki (1996)

---

1) Data is based on 89 respondents of a questionnaire survey in "Follow-up research on Food-Amenity Competition prize winner" by Rural Development Planninng Commission administered in 2007.

Chapter 1: Changes of Women, Families and Agriculture in Rural Japan   39

Figure 1-3-2 Influence of RWEA on Women (MA)

Horizons were broaden through interchanging with other people
Got deep understanding on local traditional food
As the source of income generation
Got a traditional cooking skill
Got understanding on my work by family
Could realizing personal interest in business
Could increase their voices on community management
Others

0   10   20   30   40   50   60   70   80   90 %

Source : Rural Development Planning Commission "Follow-up research on Food-Amenity Competition prizewinner", n:82

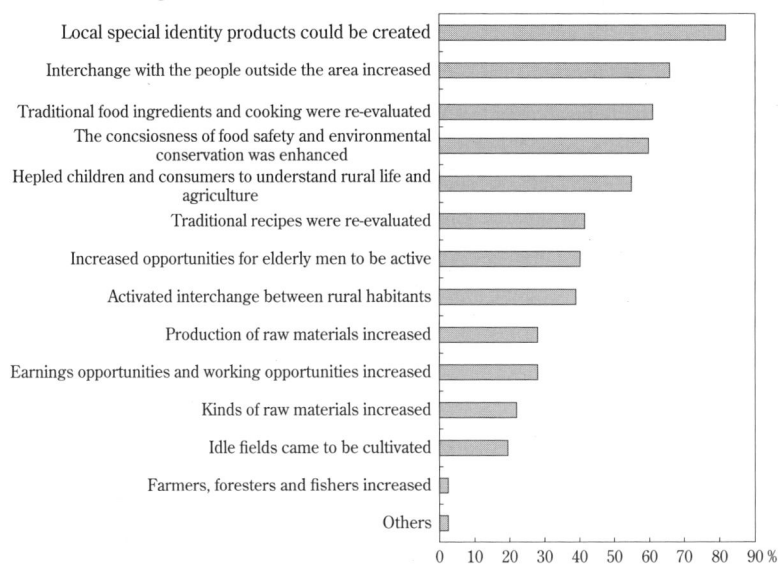

Figure 1-3-3 Influence of RWEA on Community (MA)

Local special identity products could be created
Interchange with the people outside the area increased
Traditional food ingredients and cooking were re-evaluated
The concsiosness of food safety and environmental conservation was enhanced
Hepled children and consumers to understand rural life and agriculture
Traditional recipes were re-evaluated
Increased opportunities for elderly men to be active
Activated interchange between rural habitants
Production of raw materials increased
Earnings opportunities and working opportunities increased
Kinds of raw materials increased
Idle fields came to be cultivated
Farmers, foresters and fishers increased
Others

0   10   20   30   40   50   60   70   80   90 %

Source : Rural Development Planning Commission "Follow-up research on Food-Amenity Competition prizewinner", n:82

Figure 1-3-2 shows the evaluated influences of RWEAs on participating women. About 80% of respondents answered that they could broaden their horizons through exchange with other people within and outside the community through activities. This result shows that RWEAs could provide women a chance to socialize. About

60% of participating women evaluated that they "got deep understanding of local traditional food" and "attained a traditional cooking skill" through activities. About 60% of respondents evaluated RWEAs "as a source of income generation" and it can be understood that RWEAs contributed to the economic independence for women. As shown above, RWEAs have a positive influence on empowerment of women. In contrast, only 39% of the women answered that they "could better voice their opinions on community management". Participation in management of local agriculture and community through RWEAs is not sufficient.

Figure 1-3-3 shows the influences of RWEA on the community. About 80% of respondents agreed that "local special identity products could be created", and it can be said that RWEAs encouraged participants to re-evaluate rural life and culture and activated the local agriculture, economy, and community. They also agreed with such statements as "interchange with the people outside the area increased" (66%), "traditional food ingredients and cooking were re-evaluated" (61%), "the consciousness of food safety and environmental conservation were enhanced" (60%) "helped children and consumers to understand rural life and agriculture", and "traditional recipes were re-evaluated". Through interchange between outside consumers and through "shokuno-kyoiku" (education on agriculture and food) with children, traditional food and recipes were re-evaluated, and the consciousness on food safety and environmental conservation were enhanced. As shown above, RWEAs had positive influences both on re-evaluation of rural life and culture, and activating communities. RWEAs have contributed to activating rural society in this way.

2-4. Typical Cases of RWEAs

For a concrete understanding of RWEAs in Japan, three aspects of some typical cases (1. economic, 2. cultural, and 3. social aspects) will be shown as below[2].

2-4-1. RWEA for Encouraging Local Agriculture

Group S started activities in 1996, and presently has 30 group members. They work three times a week. This group is mainly managed by wives of full time farmers who are engaged in their own farm management, as well. They manage the RWEA, equally distributing the total workload. Their main activities are the processing of agricultural products such as products made of local soybeans, and other sweets and side dishes. The products are sold by direct marketing and at local supermarkets and farmers markets.

---

2) Cases are based on interview surveys which the author participated in and were conducted by the Japan Agricultural Development and Extension Association.

Chapter 1: Changes of Women, Families and Agriculture in Rural Japan   41

In the district where S group is working, a cooperative for joint procurement and the use of machinery was set up to increase the soybean production. Through cooperative activity, increasing the yield of soybeen produce was encouraged, and it increased from 1.05ha (10,500m^2) in 1995 to 5ha (50,000m^2) in 2005. Group S purchases all the soybeans at a constant price to encourage production. Group S also supplies locally produced ingredients for school meals, and also endeavors to build interchange with local consumers.

2-4-2. RWEA for Passing on Traditional Food Culture

Group H started their activities in 1998, and presently has 14 group members. It is managed by elderly women (averaging 65 years of age). The group's main activity is to produce soybeans and soybean paste in the traditional way, and other traditional, locally-unique sweets. Products are sold at a local exhibition center.

H group gained its basic skills through involvement in earlier rural-life improvement activities, and members hope to pass on these skills and the traditional food culture. Members teach these skills at several local schools, and they are acknowledged as skillful people in that area. Encouraged by the activities of group H, other elderly people have also started to produce and sell agricultural produce. This has led to income generation and revitalization. As a result, fallow lands (0.7ha (7,100m^2) paddy fields and 0.3ha (3,000m^2) upland fields) have come to be cultivated again.

2-4-3. RWEA for Activating the Local Community

Corporation D was founded in 1989, and registered as a corporation in 2006, and presently has 9 member workers. In corporation D, women from both on-farm and off-farm households are engaged in producing and selling locally produced traditional sweets, box lunches, and side dishes. Corporation D owns a factory and a shop combined with some table and chairs, where they serve meals and drinks besides selling the above mentioned foods. This activity started about 20 years ago, when young mothers got together and started to produce traditional sweets made from locally-produced materials.

Of the materials used, 40% are made by participating members, and 40% are made by local farmers. Artificial ingredients are not used, with the goal of producing safe and authentic food. Products are used in seasonal events and as gifts by local people. The sound management and cheerful atmosphere of the corporation attracts many employee candidates. Members teach at high schools, are involved in PTAs, and also accept visits by students of a local primary school. The shop also sells products from other RWEAs, it also functions as a hub for networking and dispatching information.

3. Present Status of RWEAs and Policy Support

3-1. Present Status of RWEAs

According to the Ministry of Agriculture, Forestry and Fisheries (2007), the number of RWEAs is increasing year by year, reaching 9,444 in 2006. The main activities are food processing, but they are diversifying into other areas. RWEAs are managed mainly in two ways. One is private management with a single owner, and the other is jointly managed. Only 4% are incorporated. About 60% of RWEAs earned less than 3,000,000 yen a year (about US$30,000), more than half the participating members were over 60 years old, and half the RWEAs jointly managed had less than 10 members. Small size and aging (particularly with jointly managed types) are critical issues regarding sustainability of these activities. As mentioned above, jointly managed RWEAs, occupying about 60% of all RWEAs, have originated mainly from Life-Improvement Practice Groups, and they put emphasis on social contribution and self realization. Therefore, it often happens that they lack in managerial concepts and knowledge. It is critical to form a robust corporate structure as well as improve management technique.

3-2. Present Status of Policy Support

The contribution of rural women's activities are highly evaluated in the "Basic Plan for Food, Agriculture and Rural Areas" executed in 2005. Currently, MAFF takes measures to encourage RWEAs in the following areas: 1) training and providing information for processing skills and management, 2) Equipment for facilities for processing and sales, and 3) skill instruction. As mentioned in 2-(1), development of RWEAs is largely due to policy support. In particular, support by rural life-extension workers has been critical, but the number of rural life-extension workers is decreasing, and at present there are only 1000 staff members in the whole country. In addition, the main source of the budget for supporting RWEAs has shifted from the national government to local governments (prefectures), and specific support has become dependent on local government. With dwindling personnel and budgetary support, many local governments cannot afford to adequately subsidize RWEAs.

4. Challenges for RWEAs

RWEAs have inclusive participation by various groups of rural women, contributing to the empowerment of rural women and activating the local communities supported by national and local governments. But now, with the weakening of the support system, RWEAs have several problems. Problems regarding management, small size of the businesses, age of members, and managerial weakness have been observed. Women's participation in local agriculture and the community is not enough.

We conclude this paper by proposing some possible measures to manage the problems faced by RWEAs.

1) Problems with management; small size of the businesses, age of members, managerial weakness.
Participating women themselves should have their objectives clear in their minds and share the duties or responsibilities of each activity, and the management system should be consistent with these objectives. Except for groups that are ending their activities with no new members or that limit their activities to a hobby level; it would be better for RWEAs to become incorporated. Present voluntary groups cannot handle risk management for securing the safety and quality of food, and the responsibility for this tends to be too much for a volunteer representative to take. If the groups prioritize on economic profit, they should re-organized into corporate organizations. If they prioritize on social contribution, they can become non-profit organizations.

2) Problems with women's social participation; insufficient participation by women in local agriculture and community
It should be remembered that in RWEAs, not only pioneer women farmers, but many rural women, including non-farm households, participate. In particular, with jointly managed activities, representatives may be appointed to managerial posts in the community, but it is rare that members are recruited. But as mentioned above, participation by women itself is participation in community activities. Thus, supporting RWEA policy also leads to support for rural women's social participation.

What is important is to have non-hierarchical social participation of rural women and the characteristics of RWEA as an economic activity leading to social contribution should be understood and shared by the local people. Further interchange and cooperation with various viewpoints between producers and consumers, local people and outside people needs to be promoted, to help local agriculture and community understand the importance of RWEAs.

This paper was presented at the 12th World Congress of Rural Sociology: International Rural Sociology Association, on July 6-11, 2008 in Republice of Korea. This edition includes the most recent revision.

References
Kanamori, Toshie, Masako Amano, Fusako Fujiwara and Yoshiko Kuba, 1989, *Josei Nyuwaku Ron,* Tokyo: Yuhikaku. (in Japanese)
Ministry of Agriculture, Forestry and Fisheries, 2007, "The Outline of the Research on the Actual Condition of RWEAs," (http://www.maff.go.jp/j/press/keiei/kourei/071102.html,

September 25, 2008). (in Japanese)

Miyaki Michiko, 1996, *Nouson de Hajimeru Josei Kigyo,* Tokyo: Rural Women Empowerment and Life Improvement Association. (in Japanese)

Morofuji, Kyoko, 2007, " 'New Work by Rural Woman Entrepreneurs' as Rural Policy," *Journal of Rural Planning Association,* 26(1): 33-38. (in Japanese)

Chapter 2

Network and Socioeconomic Activity of Women

In Chapter 2, the current condition and challenges of support networks for New Farmers, and female entrepreneurship in communities will be discussed. The environment that allows women to participate in social activities without being bound with traditional rules and consciousness will also be investigated. Based on a field survey, female newcomers will be explored, their attitude, networking, life satisfaction level will be compared to those of men, and political measures will be probed. How the entrepreneurial activities of women in rural areas are organized and how they are supported will be noted. The significance of roles played by rural life study groups and the women's department at the Agricultural Cooperative will be discussed, and future tasks of support activities will be proposed. Many rural families are still fettered by "Ie" or tradition consciousness, but women are changing the age-old social norm and participating in community management, thanks to their family's cooperation and their own ingenuity. They resolve social tension and improve gender empowerment.

Chapter 2: Network and Socioeconomic Activity of Women 47

1
Network of Female New Farmers in Japan Who Come from the Non-agricultural Sector
Juri Hara-Fukuyo

1. Introduction

In the late 1980s, a public support system for New Farmers[1] in Japan has been organized. Due to decline in population and aging in farming villages, the number of people engaged in farming has decreased and more land is being left unfarmed. In some regions, it is even feared that the community may not continue to exist much longer. The situation as such has promoted support policies for New Farmers.

The main function of the support system is to give support by providing information through counseling centers for New Farmers, by helping them financially with various low-interest financing and such, and by providing training opportunities. Such support is given on the prefectural and municipal levels as well as on the national level. There is a wide range of programs according to the particular circumstances of the region, such as referring farmers who can provide training, establishing a contact window for securing farmland, providing information about housing, providing low-interest financing for acquiring housing, and supplying cash[2].

Thanks to these programs, it seems to have become less difficult to enter the farming industry. But the process of actually taking up farming in a new environment is still not easy [Uchiyama, 1999: Hara-Fukuyo, 2002]. In most cases, a New Farmer has to tackle the challenges of a new job and a new life in a new community. The kind of network New Farmers form in the community and the kind of support they receive is a

---

[1] "New Farmer" refers to someone who is not from a farming family and acquires a business base to start farming. This term is defined in various ways, and sometimes includes those who find work at an agricultural cooperation, but it is not adopted in this paper.

[2] During the 1970s and 80s, many attempts to enter the farming industry were made as a counterculture movement. That movement cannot be covered in this paper, but there was a stronger ideological background; the modern urban society was criticized and living in a village was seen as countercultural. Because of such background, many lacked enough knowledge of farming, customs of the rural area, and traditions related to social relationships, and could not settle in the rural area. On the other hand, the New Farmers who settled in a farming society and became self-sustaining as farmers became one of the reasons for the increase of other New Farmers coming into the area.

very important issue for their success in settlement [Akitsu, 1998].

The same can be applied to women who are referred to in many cases by the term a "New Farmer's wife." The support organization and preceding researchers point out the importance of the "wife's" cooperation. But women's own problems in this area have not been studied with much interest. However, even though the farming management is done by men in most cases, women often play a very important role in their starting their family life in a new community. It is necessary to investigate the often overlooked opinions and satisfaction of the women who have entered the farming industry. How a network is formed is also an important point of issue.

Regarding the influence the region's factor (how urbanized it is) has on social networks, studies have shown that people living in rural areas tend to form networks less selectively [Fischer, 1982: Boissevain, 1974]. Studies in Japan have also suggested a tendency that "non-selective" networks, which are often in traditional patterns with a lot of kin [Akitsu, 1998], tend to be formed in rural areas [Matsumoto, 1995; Otani, 1995; Morioka, 2000]. At the same time, other studies made it clear that women often have a limitation in forming networks [Allan, 1989] and women receive more support from kin than men do [Fischer, 1982: Otani, 1995]. This leads to the question: When a woman who has formed selective networks in an urban area moves to a farming village to start farming, what kind of network will she be incorporated into, and what kind of network will she form?

As a sample for this study, how women actually enter the farming industry will be examined based on the questionnaire conducted in the Doo region in Hokkaido, Japan. Women's attitudes toward entering a new industry, network formation in the community and the degree of stress and life satisfaction will be investigated in comparison with the attitudes of men.

2. Method and Respondents

The result of questionnaires conducted at four branch governmental offices in Doo, Hokkaido (Central Hokkaido area) will be analyzed in this paper[3].

---

3) Hokkaido has a relatively short history of agricultural development which started in the late 19th century. Thus farming villages in Hokkaido have short traditions of communities compared to other areas in Japan. Its identity is rather weak in social relations and community regulations. Due to relatively high mobility, it lacks strong integration, and it is characterized by "functional system of territorial bonds" based upon the agricultural union.

   Hokkaido is now called Japan's food base. Various products such as milk and wheat have the number 1 share. There have been many New Farmers in Hokkaido because of the advanced and substantial support system, and also because of the relatively low price of the land.

   As for the female farmers in Hokkaido compared to that in other prefectures, there are many young farmers whose working hours are long.

Chapter 2: Network and Socioeconomic Activity of Women 49

The questionnaires were mailed to new farming families in the jurisdiction of the four branch offices (subprefectures) in Doo (September 2001). Investigation subjects were chosen with the cooperation of the Agricultural Improvement Division and Agricultural Extension Centers and 200 people were asked to participate. When a chosen subject was married, his or her spouse was also asked to participate. Care was taken so that there would be about the same number of men and women. As a result, 106 people responded, 65 of which were male and 41 were female.

To give a brief description of the respondents, 5 of them started farming in the 1970s, 6 started in the '80s, 52 in the '90s, and 43 in 2000 or later, which means about 90% of the respondents started farming during or after the 1990s. Men's ages ranged from 26 to 67, making the average 42.9 years old. Women's ages ranged from 25 to 59, making the average 40.3 years old. 92.5% of the respondents were married and 80.2% had a child or children.

65% of the respondents were from a city, whereas 24% were from a farming village. About 40% were from Hokkaido and 60% were from outside Hokkaido. There was not distinct difference between the sexes regarding this matter.

There were various ways that the farms were managed. The main products were vegetables and flowers cultivated in greenhouses. Some combined greenhouse cultivation with outdoor cultivation. 82% of the respondents were engaged in farming with their spouse. In 71% of the cases, both the husband and the wife were engaged in farming for more than 150 days a year. More than 50% employed labor from outside the family. 40% of the respondents practiced organic farming or used a reduced amount of chemicals.

3. Process of Taking up Farming

First, the process that leads up to taking up farming will be examined. Who had the leadership role in deciding to start farming? When presented choices "Myself", "Spouse", "Together with the Spouse", 81.5% of the men chose "Myself" and 18.5% chose "Together with the Spouse", while 63.4% of the women said "Spouse", 26.8% said "Together with the Spouse", and 9.8% said "Myself". This was based purely on the respondent's subjective view, and therefore, the husband and wife did not always share the same opinion. In any case, 100% of the men thought that they had led to the decision or participated in making the decision, but only 36.6% of the women said so. More than half of the women just followed or accepted their spouse's important decision of starting farming in a completely new environment. In this paper, the women were divided into two groups, based on whether or not they had participated in the decision making. The women who selected "Myself" or "Together with the Spouse" for the answer to the question will be referred to as "Co-leader"(36.6%), and the women

Table 2-1-1 Location and Institution of the Training

(%)

		Total	Male	Female Total	Co-leader	Follower
location	inside the community	20.8	21.5	19.5	19.2	20.0
	in the municipality	30.2	38.5	17.1	33.3	7.7
	in the subprefecture	10.4	13.8	4.9	0.0	7.7
	inside Hokkaido	25.5	26.2	24.4	40.0	15.4
	outside Hokkaido	14.2	18.5	7.3	20.0	0.0
	no experience	29.5	18.8	46.3	20.0	61.5
institution	farming family	52.8	60.0	41.5	60.0	30.8
	farming corporation	18.9	23.1	12.2	13.3	11.5
	organization for organic farming	2.8	3.1	2.4	6.7	0.0
	college of agriculture	8.5	12.3	2.4	0.0	3.8
	preparatory school for farming	2.8	4.6	0.0	0.0	0.0
	others	8.5	9.2	7.3	13.3	3.8
	no experience	27.4	16.9	43.9	20.0	57.7

(M.A.)

who chose "Spouse" will be referred to as "Follower"(63.4%).

Next let us examine the preparation of farming techniques before starting to farm. In the questionnaire, the last school they graduated from and whether their major was related to agriculture were asked. The result was that only 26.8% majored in agriculture, 34% of the men and only 13.8% of the women. This shows the respondents became interested in farming relatively late.

On the other hand, many said they had received training in farming before becoming a farmer. Table 2-1-1 shows the result of the question about the location of the training and the institution involved (more than one answer could have been selected). About 30% of the respondents had taken training at the municipality where they started farming, followed by "inside Hokkaido" and "inside the community". As for the institution of the training, "farming family" was the top response from both men (60.0%) and women (41.5%). In all cases, men had more experience. Less than 20% of the men did not have any training experience, whereas more than 40% of the women did not. This is because about 60% of the female "Followers" did not receive any training. Female "Co-leaders" had about the same amount of training as the men.

Thus, as the support system in Hokkaido has become more organized, many people have received some kind of training before becoming a farmer. While men have more various agricultural training, women who were enthusiastic about the decision to start farming have training experience which is in no way inferior to the men's.

Table 2-1-2 Motive for Becoming a Farmer

(%)

	Total	Male	Female Total	Female Co-leader	Female Follower
Wanted to live in nature	49.5	50.8	47.5	64.3	38.5
Wanted to be in charge of my own work	36.9	47.6	20.0	42.9	7.7
Liked farming	33.0	38.1	25.0	35.7	19.2
Wanted to spend more time with family	31.1	25.4	40.0	42.9	38.5
Found farming as a business attractive	25.2	36.5	7.5	14.3	3.8
Wanted to produce safe food	23.3	25.4	20.0	50.0	3.8
Wanted to discontinue city life	21.4	28.6	10.0	21.4	3.8
Others	18.4	7.9	35.0	7.1	50.0

(M.A.)

When a woman in search for a new world with her spouse chooses farming as her own profession, opportunities of training are there, as the data indicate.

The most common motive of taking up farming for both sexes was they "wanted to live in nature." Almost half of the respondents chose this answer (Table 2-1-2). The next popular answers among the men were: "wanted to be in charge of my own work", and "found farming as a business attractive". Women chose "wanted to spend a lot of time with family" and "others". Many explained the answer "others" as "the husband's wish".

When the women were divided into two groups based on whether they participated in deciding to start farming, 50% of the "Co-leaders" said they "wanted to produce safe food", which was more than the men. The percentage of the female "Co-leaders" who said they "liked farming" and "wanted to be in control of my own work" was about the same as the men's. On the other hand, 50% of the "Followers" chose "others". This indicates that not only their spouse was in charge of deciding to start farming, but also many followed their spouse even though they did not sympathize with their spouse's motive for farming.

These results suggest the difference between the sexes: men tend to take the professional appeal seriously, while women tend to attach greater importance to the family environment. But moreover, the women who have participated in the decision making regard farming and family life both important. They regarded living in nature and producing safe food as important more than the men did.

4. Personal Network in the Community

Let us now consider how the respondents to this questionnaire who started farming in a new environment were incorporated into the community and who has been supporting

Table 2-1-3 Joining Organizations in the Municipality

	Total		Male		Female Total		Co-leader		Follower	
	Frequency (person)	Percent		%		%		%		%
neighborhood association	81	78.6	51	81.0	30	75.0	10	71.4	20	76.9
agricultural union	45	43.7	35	55.6	10	25.0	3	21.4	7	26.9
agricultural cooperative	57	55.3	42	66.7	15	37.5	5	35.7	10	38.5
agricultural cooperative's production section	45	43.7	35	55.6	10	25.0	5	35.7	5	19.2
agricultural cooperative women's/youth department	29	28.2	14	22.2	15	37.5	6	42.9	9	34.6
producting organization	13	12.6	10	15.9	3	7.5	2	14.3	1	3.8
farming-related study sessions	15	14.6	14	22.2	1	2.5	1	7.1	0	0.0
organic farming group	8	7.8	5	7.9	3	7.5	1	7.1	2	7.1
new farmers'group	10	9.7	8	12.7	2	5.0	1	7.1	1	3.8
PTA	19	18.4	8	12.7	11	27.5	6	42.9	5	19.2
hobby groups	12	11.7	4	6.3	8	20.0	2	14.3	6	23.1
administrative monitors	4	3.9	4	6.3	0	0.0	0	0.0	0	0.0
study groups for PC.	7	6.8	6	9.5	1	2.5	0	0.0	1	3.8
others	7	6.8	5	7.9	2	5.0	1	7.1	1	3.8

(M.A.)

them. In this section, how the respondents joined organizations, how they have been receiving various support in everyday life, and how networks, which are considered important to farmers, have been formed will be examined.

Joining Organizations

This table (Table2-1-3) shows new entries to various organizations in municipalities. While men usually join farming-related organizations in the local community (within the municipality), not as many women do, regardless of their participation in the decision-making. They join the women's department of agricultural cooperative or organizations that are related to everyday life such as PTA and hobby groups, but in any case, the percentage of women who participate is not so high.

It is quite natural that greater percentage of men join agricultural related organizations than women because the membership of some of them such as the agricultural cooperative used to be for each household. But the fact that the same condition exists at the production section that has individual membership, indicates that men are often considered to take the leadership in the farm management.

It is therefore indicated that the formation of social relations through organizations is mainly done by men.

Incidentally, few men and women join organizations outside their municipality.

Chapter 2: Network and Socioeconomic Activity of Women   53

The most popular type of organization among the respondents was "organic farmer's organization", which 12.5% of men and women joined, followed by farmer's organization, 8.9%, and environmental organization, 6.9%.

Support and Network for Everyday Life
Twelve questions were asked about support in everyday life. There were four categories: practical support, companionship support, support through counseling and opinion exchange, and support through recognition of self value. Three questions were asked about each category[4]. Then, who provided the support was asked. The respondents were asked to select one or more answers from: kin (parents, siblings, etc.), farmers whom they trained with, New Farmers, other local farmers, local friends who are not farmers, friends from outside the community, technical organizations, and others (Table 2-1-4).

The first question was whether the respondents were able to receive such support from outside their immediate family, and many answered yes. Regarding practical support, 48.1% said they "can ask someone to care for their children or aging parents when busy or sick. 76.4% said they "can ask someone for a ride", and as much as 67.9% said they "can get help with the farming". Many men selected "local farmer" as the support provider, while many women selected local friends (non-farming) and friends from outside the community. Many from both sexes selected kin as someone who cares for their children or aging parents.

Many said they received companionship support; 83% said they had someone with whom they "visit each other and spend some good time together". 84.8% said someone cares about them and sometimes calls them to encourage them. 63.9% said they had someone to share a hobby with. Regarding each item, more women received support than men. More than 50% of the men said they "visit each other" with local farmers, while many women selected local friends (non-farmer) and friends from outside the farm. Kin was the highest answer of both men (40%) and women (67.5%) as someone who "cares about me and encourages me". Many women also mentioned local friends and friends from outside the community.

About counseling and opinion exchange, the tendency of responses varied depending on the issue. The women received more support for their "personal issues", but the men had people to talk to about "ideas and dreams about farming" and "local traditions and organization management" in more cases. The women talked to kin and friends inside and outside the community for their "personal issues", and the men

---

[4] Questions were organized based on the issues pointed out during the interview with New Farmers, often referring to previous studies [Fischer, 1982; Kimura, 1997].

Table 2-1-4 Support Gained

(Response Ratio: %)

Category	Support Details	M	F	Kin (parents, siblings, etc.) M	Kin F	Training Farm M	Training Farm F	New Farmers M	New Farmers F	Local farmers M	Local farmers F	Non-farming friends in community M	Non-farming friends in community F	Friends from outside community M	Friends from outside community F	Technical Agency M	Technical Agency F	Others M	Others F
Practical	Can ask for a ride	78.5	73.2	18.5	22.0	10.8	9.8	16.9	12.2	41.5	22.0	23.1	36.6	6.2	22.0	0.0	2.4	1.5	0.0
	Can ask to take care of children or elderly when busy	50.8	43.9	26.2	22.0	4.6	0.0	7.7	7.3	10.8	12.2	10.8	17.1	3.1	9.8	3.1	2.4	1.5	0.0
	Can ask for help when farming is delayed	70.8	63.4	13.8	12.2	7.7	9.8	10.8	7.3	35.4	22.0	16.9	26.8	10.8	14.6	0.0	0.0	1.5	2.4
companionship	Visit each other and spend fun time	80.0	87.8	20.0	17.1	23.1	14.6	29.2	29.3	50.8	36.6	30.8	46.3	24.6	41.5	4.6	2.4	1.5	0.0
	Enjoy and talk about the same hobby	60.0	67.5	1.5	7.5	3.1	2.5	9.2	17.5	16.9	15.0	30.8	45.0	20.0	35.0	0.0	0.0	1.5	0.0
	Cares about me, calls me, and encourages me	83.1	87.5	40.0	67.5	16.9	12.5	16.9	17.5	30.8	25.0	30.8	47.5	36.9	55.0	3.1	5.0	3.1	0.0
Counseling	Can consult and discuss personal issues such as family and children	67.7	85.0	29.7	45.0	4.7	2.5	15.6	17.5	20.3	17.5	25.0	45.0	17.2	42.5	0.0	0.0	1.6	0.0
	Can talk about ideas and dreams about farming	78.5	60.0	10.8	17.5	18.5	10.0	30.8	30.0	44.6	20.0	20.0	12.5	24.6	22.0	3.1	0.0	3.1	2.5
	Can talk about local customs and organization management	72.3	51.3	1.5	5.1	15.4	10.3	10.8	10.3	47.7	30.8	10.8	15.4	3.1	5.1	6.2	0.0	1.5	0.0
Self-values	Respects my opinion and advice	56.3	53.8	7.8	12.8	4.7	0.0	20.3	12.8	26.6	15.4	10.9	15.4	12.5	28.2	1.6	0.0	1.6	2.6
	Listens to me talk about farming and life in village with interest	69.2	69.2	15.4	20.5	7.7	2.6	9.2	10.3	21.5	15.4	27.7	28.2	36.9	48.7	1.5	0.0	1.5	2.6
	Listens to me talk about previous job and knowledge with interest	55.4	46.2	6.2	5.1	7.7	0.0	13.8	10.3	30.8	25.6	20.0	28.2	15.4	17.9	3.1	0.0	1.5	0.0

talked to kin, local friends, and local farmers in this order. Most of the men chose "local farmers" to talk to about "ideas and dreams about farming", but New Farmers was the number one answer of the women. This is the only item where the female "Co-leaders" and "Followers" differed significantly. 85.7% of the female "Co-leaders" had someone to talk to about the "ideas and dreams about farming", while only 46.3% of the female "Followers" did. 42.9% of the former talked to "New Farmers" and 28.6% to local farmers, local friends, and friends from outside the community, while only 23.1% of the latter talked to "New Farmers", the highest answer.

Let us now look into the questions regarding the recognition of self value. These questions were asked to find out how much psychological support New Farmers receive when they might lose sight of their self value and become depressed as they try to tackle the new profession with not much experience. The result was that more than 50% of the respondents received support, even though the numbers were a little lower than other questions. As it was expected, people who would "listen to me about farming and living in a village" were local non-farmers and friends from outside the community. Local farmers and local friends would "listen to me about previous work experience". The male respondents said local farmers and New Farmers would "count my opinions and advice", while the highest answer of the female respondents was friends from outside the community.

Thus, it was made clear that there was a high level of dependence on local farmers and non-farmers, whom the respondents presumably met after they started farming, for various support. At the same time, dependence on friends from outside the community, whom the respondents met before they started farming, was also strong. This was particularly the case among women. Many men chose "local farmers" as a provider of support in general, which indicates that the men were incorporated into the farming community more deeply. On the other hand, the women were more dependent on non-farmers among local friends, and also on the relationship they had had before starting to farm such as kin and friends from outside the community. This tendency was stronger in the psychological support such as companionship, counseling, and recognition of self value.

Network

Table 2-1-5 shows geographical locations of people that are important to the respondents including those who provide support to them. It is a result of asking them about the number of "important people who provide support for farming and living" among "kin", "farming-related", and "others" by the place of residence (inside the community, inside the municipality, adjacent municipality, inside Hokkaido, and outside Hokkaido). The total number of network members was smallest in "kin" in both men and women. The

Table 2-1-5 Network of "Important People" —Averge Number of the Members—

(average:person)

		inside the community	in the municipality	adjacent municipality	inside Hokkaido	outside Hokkaido	Total
kin	Male	0.03	0.19	0.49	0.49	2.75	3.95
	Female	0.03	0.18	0.24	0.58	2.77	3.80
	Co-leader	0.00	0.18	0.09	0.09	1.10	1.46
	Follower	0.05	0.18	0.32	0.82	3.57	4.94
Farming-related	Male	1.95	3.40	1.21	1.25	0.94	8.75
	Female	1.44	0.94	0.88	0.97	0.28	4.50
	Co-leader	1.27	1.18	1.00	1.09	0.73	5.27
	Follower	1.52	0.81	0.81	0.90	0.05	4.10
Others	Male	0.62	1.05	1.40	1.56	2.16	6.78
	Female	0.56	1.22	3.59	3.56	2.84	11.78
	Co-leader	0.45	1.27	7.00	2.55	2.73	14.00
	Follower	0.62	1.19	1.81	4.10	2.90	10.62

biggest network members among the men was "farming-related", among the women "others". As for the place of residence, both men and women said most "kin" live "outside Hokkaido". Most men said their "farming-related" friends live "inside the municipality". Many women said their "other" network members live "outside the municipality".

On the whole, the men's personal network mostly consisted of farming-related friends inside the municipality (including the community), while the women's network was often made up of members outside the municipality who are neither kin nor farming-related acquaintances.

Thus, the respondents received various support for their everyday life and had important network members living in various places. Compared to the men whose networks were created mostly through joining farming-related organizations inside the community, many of the women had a network which was not farming-related and was outside the community. This is probably due to the fact that the support needed was different between men and women because the life domains they value are different. It is also thought to be related to the fact that more men had received training inside the municipality where they started farming and that more men joined agricultural organizations inside the municipality. What the data indicate is that these differences in the support and networks are not only because of the respondent's attitudes towards farming and life, but also because of the fact that the community had prepared different assistance and social structure for men and women.

5. Problems in Daily Life and Degree of Satisfaction

Lastly, let us examine the stress and the degree of satisfaction in everyday life of men

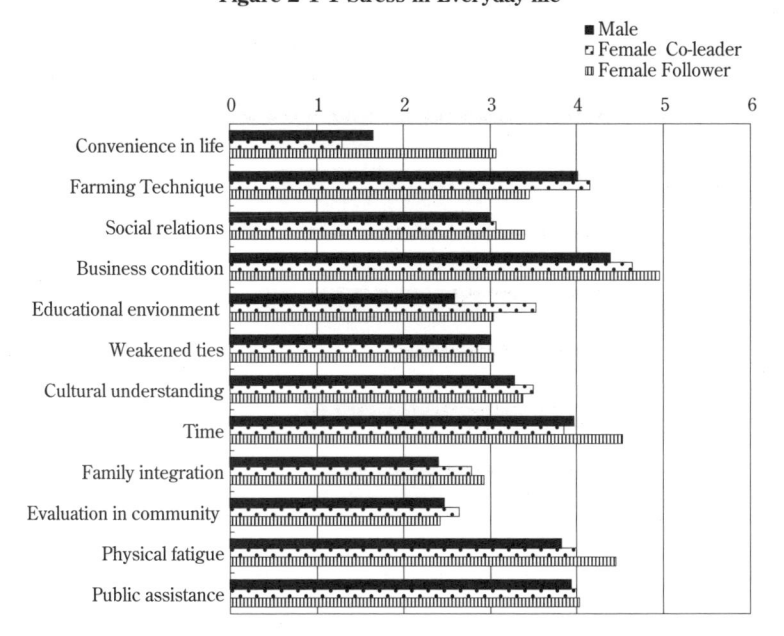

Chapter 2: Network and Socioeconomic Activity of Women   57

Figure 2-1-1 Stress in Everyday-life

■ Male
▫ Female Co-leader
▥ Female Follower

Categories (top to bottom): Convenience in life, Farming Technique, Social relations, Business condition, Educational envionment, Weakened ties, Cultural understanding, Time, Family integration, Evaluation in community, Physical fatigue, Public assistance

Scale: 0 to 6

and women.

Whether a respondent had felt stressed for the last year was asked in 12 items. Figure 2-1-1 shows the average points that indicate the degree of stress; the respondents were asked to give points from one to seven, from "Does not bother me" to "Bothers me very much". On the whole, the respondents were found to be stressed more than "usual" in the item "Financial worries because of slow improvement of business" ('Business condition' in the figure). The next items in which stress was felt were: "No time to relax or think" ('Time'), and "Physical fatigue from farming" ('Physical fatigue'). There was not much difference between the sexes, but the women tended to score slightly higher, which means they felt more stressed. When asked whether they missed convenient urban life ('Convenience in life'), the female 'Followers' stress point was considerably higher than the 'Co-leader's'. The 'Followers' also tended to feel some stress regarding time and physical fatigue. This result may mean that the female 'Followers' who did not make the decision to become a farmer were feeling more repulsed by life in a farming village than the men and the 'Co-leaders.'

The respondents were also asked about the degree of satisfaction in six fields and in general. They gave points from 1 to 7, from "Totally unsatisfied" to "Very satisfied"

Figure 2-1-2 Degree of Satisfaction

■ Male
□ Female Total
▨ Female Co-leader
▥ Female Follower

[Bar chart with categories on y-axis: Starting farming, Location of farming, Local social relations, Family relations, Business, Experience after becoming a farmer, overall satisfaction; x-axis scale 0 to 7]

(Figure 2-1-2). The men showed a higher degree of satisfaction in many issues, but a considerable difference between the sexes was found in only one issue, "Decision to become a farmer" ("Starting farming"). When the women are divided into two groups depending on whether they participated in making the decision to become a farmer, the "Followers" naturally had a lower degree of satisfaction about this decision. The female "Co-leaders" showed the same level of satisfaction as the men. The "Followers" 'degree of satisfaction in other issues was often slightly lower than that of the "Co-leaders". There was no distinct difference in overall satisfaction between the sexes or "Followers" and "Co-leaders."

As for the correlation between the overall satisfaction and satisfaction in each field, the men showed a high correlation in business and in the experience after becoming a farmer. While the women showed a high correlation in family relations and in becoming a farmer (Table 2-1-6). Therefore, it can be inferred that the factors which determined satisfaction in life in general were different between the sexes. In the case of the women, whose participation in making the decision to become a farmer varied, satisfaction in becoming a farmer was more closely related to the satisfaction in overall life.

6. Discussion

There are distinct differences between the sexes in the process of taking up farming and forming networks in a community. In many cases, women are led by their spouse to

Table 2-1-6 Correlation of Satisfaction Points in 6 Fields and Overall Satisfaction

	Overall satisfaction	Starting farming	Location of farming	Local social relations	Family relations	Business	Experience after becoming a farmer
Male	1	0.321	0.342	0.319	0.278	0.489	0.467
Female	1	0.460	0.358	0.187	0.566	0.299	0.425
co-leader	1	0.513	0.515	0.437	0.643	0.220	0.739
follower	1	0.500	0.282	0.053	0.542	0.383	0.234

become a farmer. That leads to many differences shown between the sexes. On the other hand, the women put more importance in family life regardless of their participation in the decision-making. They have a life with strong connections (networks) outside farming and outside the community than the men do.

The important fact is, however, there are certain differences among women in terms of training, stress, and the degree of satisfaction, depending on how they participated in making the decision to become a farmer. While women's attitudes vary, local organizations and assistance for women tend to be the same. They do not accommodate their differences; therefore, women's enthusiasm is often not put to good use.

Depending on the attitude of female New Farmers toward farming, the necessary support before and after they start farming may vary. Support for smooth communication and activity in life domains other than farming is considered necessary as well as support for cultivating enthusiasm toward farming. In this study, it was shown that the women who did not participate in making the decision to become a farmer had more problems. What are the important factors and what kind of measures can be taken in order for women to fully participate in such decision making? This is only one of the questions that needs to be further investigated. Although the support system for New Farmers has been well organized, this system may actually increase the possibility of leading the female spouses into farming against their intentions. Further study focusing on women is greatly needed.

References
Akitsu, Motoki, 1998, *Nougyo Seikatsu to Nettowaku* (Farming Life and Social Network), Tokyo: Ochanomizu Shobo. (in Japanese)
Allan, Graham, 1989, *Friendship: Developing a Sociological Perspective,* Hemel Hempsted: Harvester-Wheatsheaf.
Boissevain, Jeremy, 1974, *Friends of Friends: Networks, Manipulators and Coalitions,* Oxford: Basil Blackwell and Mott.
Fischer, Claude S., 1982, *To Dwell among Friends,* Chicago: University of Chicago Press.
Hara-Fukuyo, Juri, 2002, "Shinki Sannyusha no Sapoto Nettowaku (Support Network for

Agricultural Newcomers from Non-agricultural Sectors)," *Journal of Rural Studies*, 16:24-35. (in Japanese)

Kimura, Mariko, 1997, *Bunka Henyou Sutoresu to Sosharusapoto* (Acculturative Stress and Social Support), Tokyo: University of Tokai Press. (in Japanese)

Matsumoto, Yasushi ed., 1995, *Zoushokusuru Nettowaku* (Propagating Network), Tokyo: Keiso Shobo. (in Japanese)

Morioka, Kiyoshi ed., 2000, *Toshi Shakai no Pasonaru Nettowaku* (Personal Networks in Urban Society), Tokyo: University of Tokyo Press. (in Japanese)

Otani, Shinsuke, 1995, *Gendaitoshijumin no Pasonaru Nettowaku* (Personal Network of Modern City Residents), Kyoto: Minerva Shobo. (in Japanese)

Uchiyama, Tomohiro, 1999, Nougai karano Shinkisannyu no Teichakukatei ni Kansuru Kousatsu (Settling Process of New-comer Farmer from Non-agricultural Sector)," *Journal of Rural Economics,* 70(4): 184-192. (in Japanese)

This paper was presented at the 11th World Congress of Rural Sociology in 2004 in Tronheim, Norway.

Chapter 2: Network and Socioeconomic Activity of Women 61

2
How Rural Women's Entrepreneurship drawn from Life Improvement Practice Group Developed: A Case Study on Tochigi and Nagano, Japan
Kumi Sawano and Tomoko Ichida

1. Introduction
This section concerns rural women's entrepreneurship activities (RWEAs) in Japan, especially how it was developed from a kind of rural women's group, that being the Life Improvement Practice Group (LIPG)[1].

First, we will explain to you the purpose of this study, review recent statistics and some early studies on this topic. Then, we will show you 4 case studies. In conclusion, we will summarize and make some comments.

2. Purpose and Research Issues
2-1. Purpose of This Study
The purposes of this study are as follows: first, to verify the meaning of a rural women's group organized by the governmental extension service after the end of World War II, second, to clarify the development process from the organized rural women's group, that being the LIPG, to today's RWEA.

2-2. Recent Statistics and Early Studies on RWEAs
In Japan women increasingly play important roles in agricultural management in rural areas. According to a MAFF (Ministry of Agriculture, Forestry and Fisheries)'s survey, the number of RWEAs was 9,444 in 2006. Of these, over half, 5,845 were managed by groups of women. The average age of the members in group managed activities was 60 to 69, older than those members who individually managed the activities (they averaged 50-59).

Regarding RWEAs, there were two early studies.
One concerns the objectives of RWEAs . According to Iwasaki [Iwasaki, 1995]

---

[1] In this section we use the term 'LIPG' mainly in the meaning of LIPG on the municipal level, in order to distinguish from LIPG on the village level, which we call 'unit-group'.

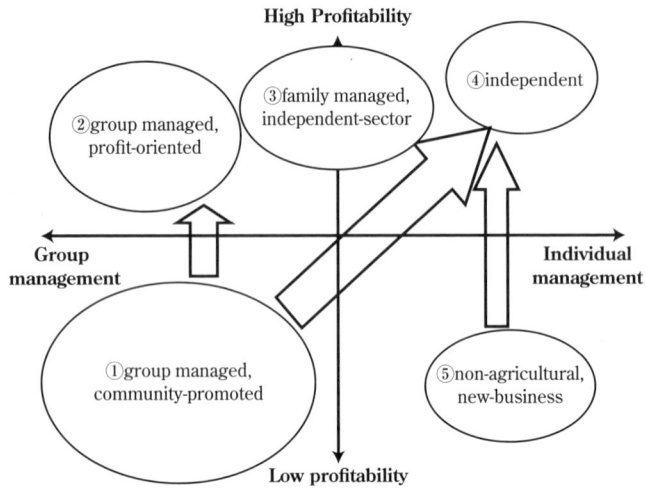

Figure 2-2-1 Classification of RWEAs and their Development

```
                    High Profitability
                            ▲
        ②group managed,   ③family managed,    ④independent
        profit-oriented   independent-sector

   ◄────────────────────────────────────────────► 
   Group                                        Individual
   management                                   management

        ①group managed,                ⑤non-agricultural,
        community-promoted             new-business
                            ▼
                     Low profitability
```

source: Fujimoto, 2004

and [Miyaki and Iwasaki, 2001], RWEAs are classified into two types: one is business-oriented and another is ambition-oriented.

In another point of view, Fujimoto [Fujimoto, 2004] puts more emphasis on business profitability of RWEAs. She analyzed the reasons why and the ways in which their activities developed, and then classified the RWEAs into five types: (1) group managed and community-promoted, (2) group managed and profit-oriented, (3) family managed and independent-sector, (4) independent, and (5) non-agricultural, new-business (Figure 2-2-1).

According to Fujimoto's study, Type 1 & Type 2 are gradually decreasing because of rural women's aging. She points out development to Type 4 from Type 1 and states that Type 4 and Type 5 play a key role in the future of RWEAs.

However, our opinion is different from Fujimoto's hypothesis. We focus on Type 1, especially those initiated from the LIPGs. There are two reasons. First, RWEAs are still being managed by groups. Second, according to a survey done in 1994, about 60% of these group managed were initiated from LIPG. Besides, we suppose that Type 1 RWEAs are able to be classified based on two indices as Figure 2-2-2: 1. The LIPG members came from villages (community) or were individuals, 2. Participation in RWEAs is required or voluntary.

Here let us add a brief explanation about the LIPG. The LIPG was originally promoted by the Home Life Improvement Division, MAFF while under GHQ occupation just after

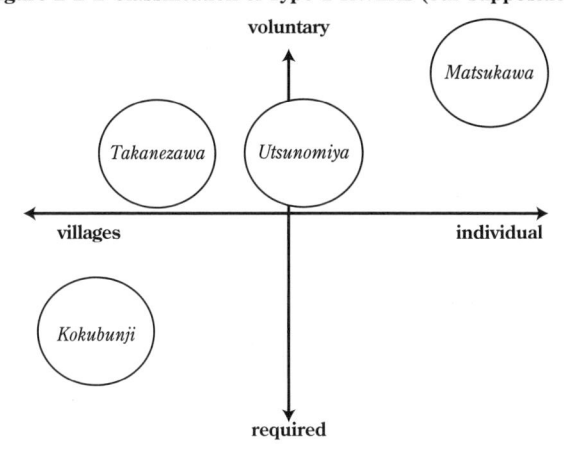

Chapter 2: Network and Socioeconomic Activity of Women   63

Figure 2-2-2 Classification of Type 1 RWEAs (our supposition)

```
                    voluntary
                       |
                       |         ( Matsukawa )
    ( Takanezawa )  ( Utsunomiya )
                       |
  villages ←───────────┼───────────→ individual
                       |
    ( Kokubunji )      |
                       |
                    required
```

the end of WW II. It was distinct from the local Women's Association (*Fujinkai*) and the Agricultural Cooperative Women's Association (*Nokyo Fujinbu*). Both the associations are affiliated with their nation-wide body which requires women from the associations to become their members as well.

On the contrary the LIPGs were voluntarily organized and mainly composed of young farm wives, mostly daughters-in-law (*Yome*), who were willing to learn rational, practical, and economical ways of life, through using improved stoves, preserving food and later food processing.

From 1950's membership in LIPGs increased up to the 20 thousand groups to the beginning of 1980's, but from then on it has been decreasing due to the aging of members[2].

2-3. Research Issues

On the grounds of 1) and 2), we focus on RWEAs drawn from LIPG and in particular we are going to clarify following 4 issues:
1. How / In which way women established RWEAs drawn from LIPGs.
2. In what way RWEAs developed.
3. How rural women themselves and the rural community were influenced.
4. How they are going to solve the problem of aging members and lack of successors.

---

[2] For more information about the LIPG and the home life improvement extension services see Ichida-Iwata [Ichida-Iwata, 2000].

3. Case Study
3-1. Characteristics of Cases

The cases for this study were selected from *Tochigi* Prefecture and *Nagano* Prefecture. The reason is because *Tochigi* Prefecture is in the *Kanto* region and *Nagano* Prefecture lies next to the *Kanto* region, so that both were relatively easy for us to access. Moreover the LIPG are active in these prefectures.

According to the MAFF's survey, the percentage of RWEAs managed by groups in *Tochigi* Prefecture is 63%. It is just in line with the national average, but the LIPGs are very active.

On the other hand in *Nagano* Prefecture the percentage is 77% and significantly higher than the national average. *Nagano* Prefecture is distinctive by having women's colleges promoted by the agricultural extension office and these women became the base for the LIPG.

In *Tochigi* prefecture the number of LIPGs peaked in 1970 and has declined slowly in recent years. Membership peaked in 1965. The major programs of the LIPGs have been changing from dietary improvement around 1960, to improving family vegetable gardens and keeping household accounts; and from around 1990, the processing of agricultural products, to make effective use of and raising the value of agricultural produce cultivated in former rice paddies. Women in agricultural communities who were trained at the agricultural extension office became the leaders of the programs, helping to promote the communities.

In *Nagano* prefecture the number of groups peaked in 1985 and has been in continuous decline since then. Membership peaked in 1975 and continues to decline, with significant drops in 1980 and 1989. Major programs included making the improved cooking stoves be widely used in Japan around 1950, production of paper for the gift wrapping of agricultural products, and holding the Shinshu Region Food Culture Exhibition in or around 1980. In recent years, the LIPGs have been particularly active in promoting dietary education.

3-2. Analyses of Cases

Before analyzing 4 cases let us briefly show you the location. In *Tochigi* prefecture *Utsunomiya* is the capital city. *Takanezawa* and *Kokubunji* are near the capital city (Figure 2-2-3). In *Nagano* prefecture *Matsukawa* is located in the northwest (Figure 2-2-4).

3-2-1. Kokubunji

The *Kokubunji* LIPG was established in 1960. In 2007 8 unit-groups (49 members) are

Chapter 2: Network and Socioeconomic Activity of Women   65

Figure 2-2-3 A Map of *Tochigi* Prefecture

Utsunomiya
(prefectural capital)

Takanezawa

Kokubunji

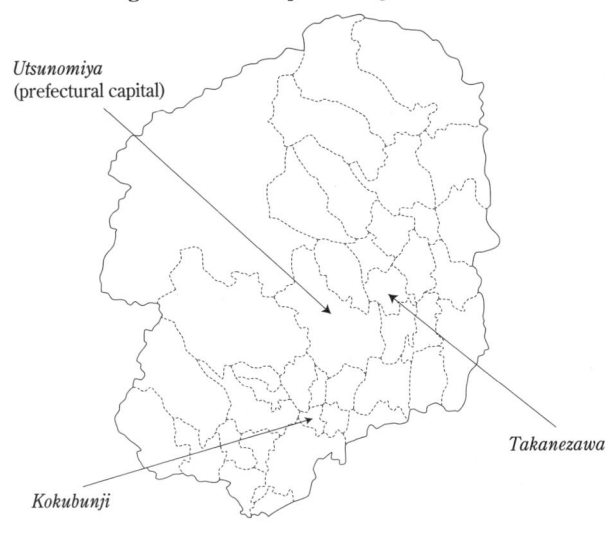

Figure 2-2-4 A Map of *Nagano* Prefecture

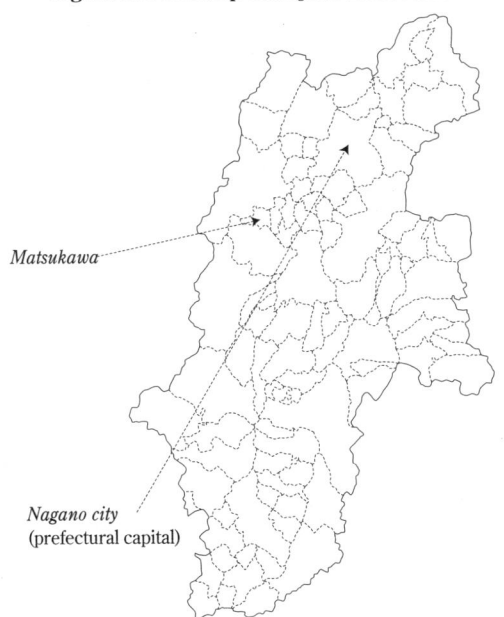

Matsukawa

Nagano city
(prefectural capital)

Figure 2-2-5 Structure of *Kokubunji* LIPG

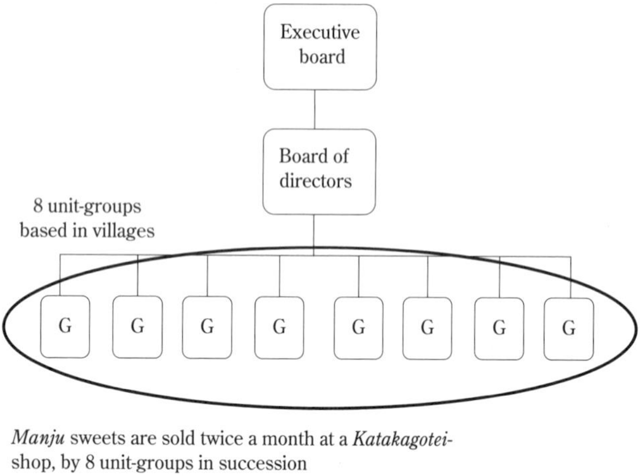

```
                    ┌───────────┐
                    │ Executive │
                    │   board   │
                    └─────┬─────┘
                          │
                    ┌───────────┐
                    │  Board of │
                    │ directors │
  8 unit-groups     └─────┬─────┘
  based in villages       │
     ┌──────┬──────┬──────┼──────┬──────┬──────┬──────┐
   ┌─┴─┐  ┌─┴─┐  ┌─┴─┐  ┌─┴─┐  ┌─┴─┐  ┌─┴─┐  ┌─┴─┐  ┌─┴─┐
   │ G │  │ G │  │ G │  │ G │  │ G │  │ G │  │ G │  │ G │
   └───┘  └───┘  └───┘  └───┘  └───┘  └───┘  └───┘  └───┘
```

Manju sweets are sold twice a month at a *Katakagotei*-shop, by 8 unit-groups in succession

still engaged in activities. On average members are in their early 50's. The main activity of *Kokubunji* is the sale of *Zeniishi Monogatari Manju,* a kind of Japanese sweet bun. The sweets are sold at *Katakagotei*-shop twice a month and at events such as the *Tenpyo-no-Oka* Park Flower Festival in April. Their annual sales are over 10 million yen, most of them during the Flower Festival. Each person working either in production or in sales is paid 10,000 yen per day.

Figure 2-2-5 is the structure of the *Kokubunji*. 8 unit-groups are respectively based in the villages. *Manju* sweets are sold twice a month at shops by 8 unit- groups in succession. A board of directors is formed by selecting one director from each unit-group.

3-2-2. Takanezawa

The *Takanezawa* LIPG was established in 1963. In 2007 2 unit-groups (*Sakura* group and *Nanohana* Group) and individual members are still engaged in activities. There are 27 members in total. In 1999, they established an entrepreneurship named *Mame Mame Club* and constructed a direct selling shop named *Kirazu*. *Mame Mame club*'s main activity is processing of agricultural products, such as *Tofu*. The amount of annual sales is about 20 million yen. The members receive 760 yen per hour for their work, rising to 860 yen per hour on Saturdays, Sundays and holidays, and an additional 100 yen for work before 7:00am. Working hours are flexible, depending on members' childcare and so forth.

Figure 2-2-6 is the structure of the *Takanezawa* LIPG. As in the case of *Kokubunji*,

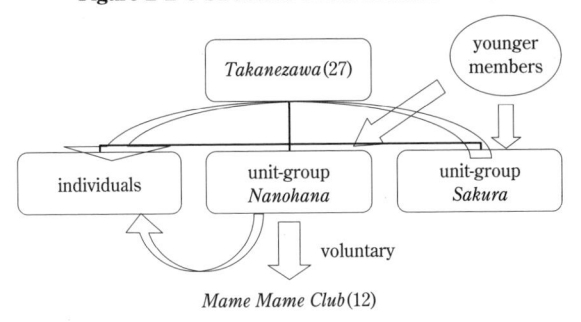

Chapter 2: Network and Socioeconomic Activity of Women   67

Figure 2-2-6 Structure of *Takanezawa* LIPG

```
     Takanezawa(27)           younger members

  individuals    unit-group         unit-group
                 Nanohana           Sakura
                          voluntary
                 Mame Mame Club(12)
```

unit-groups are based in the village. It is quite characteristic, however, that old members become 'individuals' after they retired from the unit-group and were replaced with younger members. At the time of establishment of the *Mame Mame Club* all of the *Takanezawa* members were invited to participate in that club, only 12 members volunteered. Presently, only the members of *Takanezawa* group are allowed to participate in the *Mame Mame Club*.

3-3-3. Utsunomiya
The *Utsunomiya* LIPG was established around 1955. Now 18 unit-groups in five areas and some individual member, totaling 114 members are engaged in activities. In 1985 they had a chance to participate in a direct delivery products market held by a *Seibu* Department Store in the center of the city. It was so successful, that they started a

Figure 2-2-7 Structure of *Utsunomiya* LIPG

```
              Utsunomiya(114)

  individuals(9): not belong
  to any unit-group              18 unit-groups
                      voluntary
              Agri-land city shop (ACS)
```

19 regular members+10 sub-members+1 processing group (=unit group)
* Those sub-members who don't belong to the *Utsunomiya* group have no voting rights for ACS.

regular shop called *Agri-land City Shop* in 1991. *Agri-land City Shop* sells mainly handmade *Udon* and *Soba,* Japanese noodles and buckwheat noodles, and many other products, such as traditional food and fresh vegetables. The annual sales of just the agricultural products and processed products are about 46 million yen. The shop workers, including an employed worker, are paid 800 yen per hour.

Figure 2-2-7 is the structure of the *Utsunomiya* LIPG. 18 unit-groups are respectively based in villages. *Agri-land City Shop* is presently composed of 3 categories; 19 regular-members, who are all *Utsunomiya* LIPG members, 10 sub-members, who are not originally from the *Utsunomiya* LIPG and have no voting rights for *Agri-land City Shop,* and one processing group, which is a unit-group.

3-3-4. Matsukawa

Matsukawa LIPG was established in 1964. Now 16 unit-groups and a total of 72 members are engaged in activities. Many unit-groups of *Matsukawa* consist of members who graduated from 'women's colleges' (promoted by the agricultural extension office) in the same academic year and who wanted to learn more. That is a distinctive feature of *Matsukawa.*

After the construction of a facility for rural women's meetings (*Nouson Fujin no ie*) in 1984, *Matsukawa* LIPG began with the production of *Miso* paste and it was the start of their entrepreneurship. Later, mothers-in-law of unit-group members set up a mature women's group (*Jukunenkai*) and they both jointly hold open markets.

Then they gradually set up various kinds of businesses and expanded their activities

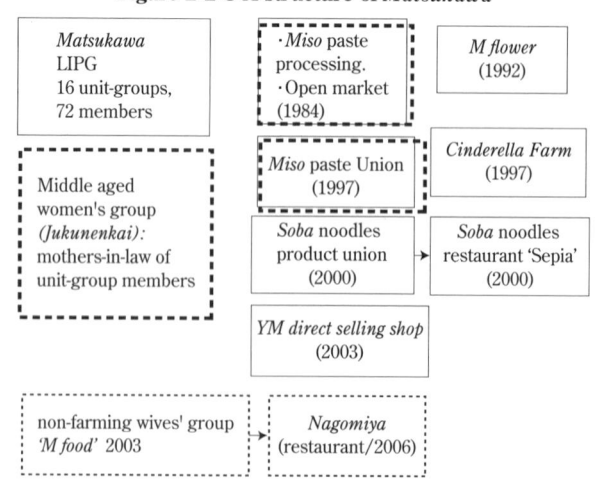

Figure 2-2-8 A structure of *Matsukawa*

Matsukawa LIPG 16 unit-groups, 72 members	·*Miso* paste processing. ·Open market (1984)	*M flower* (1992)
Middle aged women's group (*Jukunenkai*): mothers-in-law of unit-group members	*Miso* paste Union (1997)	Cinderella Farm (1997)
	Soba noodles product union (2000) →	*Soba* noodles restaurant 'Sepia' (2000)
	YM direct selling shop (2003)	
non-farming wives' group '*M food*' 2003 →	*Nagomiya* (restaurant/2006)	

as in Figure 2-2-8: *M Flower* (selling potted-flowers), *Miso* paste union, *Cinderella farm* (farming experience), *Soba* noodles product union, *Soba* noodles restaurant and YM direct selling shop.

From 2003, agricultural committee members who are also members of *Matsukawa* began to provide classes on cooking local traditional meals and using rice powder, for married women of non-farming families. The municipal government assisted in drawing in such women. This was the start of *M Food*. Some *M Food* members opened a restaurant in 2006 called *Nagomiya*, which serves meals using rice powder.

Now their main activity is running the *Soba* restaurant 'Sepia' and the annual sales from 'Sepia' is about 7.5 million yen. The wage per hour is from 650 to 700 yen. 'Sepia' is opened from 11:00 to 17:00, except for Tuesdays.

It is quite characteristic that every member of *Matsukawa* can freely participate in more than one activity, according to their purposes and interests.

4. Summary and Comments

4-1. How Rural Women Established RWEAs Drawn from the LIPG

First, let us compare 4 cases concerning the LIPG member composition (Table 2-2-1). The first case, *Kokubunji* LIPG is drawn from villages. Second case the *Takanezawa* LIPG and third case, *Utsunomiya* LIPG are both in principle drawn from villages, but partly include individual members. The *Matsukawa* LIPG is drawn from women who graduated from women's colleges in the same year.

As for participation of LIPG to rural women's entrepreneurship, only in the *Kokubunji* case, all LIPG members and all unit-groups were required to join the entrepreneurship activity and they all actually did. In the other 3 cases, all LIPG members were invited to participate in entrepreneurship, but actually only a part of them did.

Within these 3 cases there are some differences. In the case of *Takanezawa*, only the LIPG members are allowed to participate in entrepreneurship (*Mame Mame Club*), in other words entrepreneurship members have to be LIPG members.

In the case of *Utsunomiya,* non-LIPG members are allowed to be engaged in

Table 2-2-1 Establishment of Entrepreneurship Drawn from LIPGs

	LIPG drawn from...	participation to entrepreneurship
Kokubunji	village	required
Takanezawa	village and individuals	voluntary
Utsunomiya	village and individuals	voluntary
Matsukawa	graduates from women's college	voluntary

entrepreneurship activity as sub-members, unlike *Takanezawa*, but they have no voting rights concerning *Agri-land City Shop* management. It is commonly found both in *Utsunomiya* and *Takanezawa* that entrepreneurship members run various activities together.

In the case of *Matsukawa*, each activity is managed by the members who wish to participate regardless of their original unit-groups. Members can freely participate in the business they themselves have chosen.

4-2. In What Way Has RWEAs Developed?

To summarize the results of the 4 case studies and to explain the process of development as entrepreneurship, we show you 2 important points:

1. Who proposed the content of activity?

At the beginning of entrepreneurship, the activity was proposed mainly by an agricultural extension office adviser who had been involved in the LIPG since the early stages, but gradually women tried to take the challenge of starting new activities by themselves.

2. What kind of activities are they engaged in?

At the beginning they were engaged exclusively in agricultural product processing, such as *Tofu* or *Miso*. But now their activities expand to exchanges with visitors from cities and providing farming experience such as rice-planting and so on. In other words, their activities have changed from those based on the agricultural extension programming to those based on the rural women's own ideas.

For instance, *Matsukawa* expanded its activities from processing and sales of agricultural products such as *Miso* paste to exchanges with visitors from cities, providing farming experience and starting a restaurant.

4-3. How Rural Women Themselves and the Rural Community Were Influenced?

Here we show you 4 steps and a successful cycle. First, rural women wish to attract interest in and restore local traditional food. Then they begin to sell food they have made themselves which becomes so successful that their products become well-known as local food. Second, they gain self-confidence, become more enthusiastic, have more fun selling their own products, and can generate income of their own. In all four cases, people receive an income for their work similar to wages paid to part-time workers in each area. Third, they can get understanding of their families. Their motivation to join activities grows more. Fourth, they become to be acknowledged by the community, as in the case of *Kokubunji,* where a former director was elected as a town assembly person. Consequently it returns to the first step and causes willingness to search for another local food or to expand on their activities.

4-4. How are They Going to Solve the Problem of Aging and Lack of Successors?

Presently, in all of the four cases, the ages of each unit-group and the LIPG members are about fifties. And their main activity is food processing. For younger generation or newly-participated-members, especially those coming from non-farmer households, however, food processing is sometimes too difficult to begin with, as we saw in the case of *Kokubunji*. For them direct-selling is supposed to be easier to begin with. In other words, where each member is allowed to choose activities as in the case of *Matsukawa*, they have more possibilities to involve the younger generation and to solve the problem of aging.

In conclusion, the development from Type 1 to Type 4, as stated by Fujimoto, was not seen in the 4 cases. The LIPGs take a role as the basis of rural women's entrepreneurship. With regard to the 4 cases, the meaning in continuing group activities based on the LIPG is as follows: to make friends, to have fun while working with other people, to exchange information, and to have the possibility to expand activities. Especially multi-business structures such as *Matsukawa* could increase profitability and attract the younger generation.

Adding some more information on another type of rural women's entrepreneurship, the author (Sawano) has recently analyzed 6 cases based on the Agricultural Cooperative Women's Association in *Akita* prefecture, and 3 individually managed cases in *Yamagata* prefecture. Being a part of JA (Japan Agricultural Cooperative Association) business, the women's associations have more difficulties than the LIPG in starting entrepreneurship unless there is an agreement by the mostly male-dominated committee members. In the individually managed cases, rural women used various sorts of networks effectively and dealt with the lack of resources and information.

Through these case studies, we suppose that the main role of rural women's entrepreneurship is to be changed from the original one, which fulfills the need to release themselves from the familial restraints, as the social relationship of rural women is generally expanded into other than family, relatives and village.

This paper was presented at the 12th World Congress of Rural Sociology: International Rural Sociology Association, on July 6-11, 2008 in Republic of Korea. This edition in cludes the most recent version.

References

Fujimoto, Yasue, 2004, *Nihon no Nougyo*, 228. (in Japanese)

Ichida-(Iwata), Tomoko, 2000, "Gender Issue in Home Life Improvement Extension Service in Postwar Japan," Masae Tsutsumi ed., *Women Families in Rural Japan*, Tokyo: Tsukuba Shobo, 57-74.

Iwasaki, Yumiko, 1995, Nousonniokeru Joseikigyo no Igi to Houkousei (Aspects of the Promotion of Women's Own Business in Japanese Rural Communities), *Annual Bulletin of Rural Studies,* 13:169-190. (in Japanese)

Miyaki, Michiko and Iwasaki Yumiko eds., 2001, *Seikousuru Nouson Joseikigyo* (Successful Rural Women's Entrepreneurship), Tokyo: Tsukuba Shobo. (in Japanese)

Ministry of Agriculture, Forestry and Fisheries, 2007, Heisei 18 nendo Nouson-Josei ni yoru Kigyokatsudo Jittaichousa no Gaiyo (http://www.maff.go.jp/j/press/keiei/kourei/071102.html, June 14, 2009). (in Japanese)

3
Issues and Characteristics of the Economic Activities by Women in Japanese Farming Villages: From the Examination of a Business Establishment Process
Miki Shibuya

1. Introduction

In recent years, there has been an increase in businesses that involve agricultural products processing, agricultural products sales and restaurants, etc., run by women in Japanese farming villages. Most of these economic activities make use of home-grown agricultural products and skills that women have learned in their daily lives. Such activities have been drawing attention to the fact that they have a potential ripple effect on the regional economy by creating jobs and furthering the development of special local products.

Among these businesses run by women in farming villages, this report will focus on the group management structures by middle-aged women and examine the characteristics and issues concerning support for such entrepreneurs. To do so, the report will first explain the general characteristics of businesses run by women and illustrate their life-course, and the transition of the group management structures starting from the pre-conventional regional organizations. Second, a business establishment process model is extracted by comparing case examples of businesses run by middle-aged people and by the elderly.

2. General Characteristics of Economic Activities

Two points can be noted as general characteristics of economic activities by women in farming villages. The first point is about management style. Group management exceeds individual management; its ratio is 60%. Most of the group-managed business activities were generated from conventional regional organizations such as the agricultural co-operative women's group and home life improvement group. Farming women are the main members of these organizations. Because there are many women who gained skills through working together to grow and process various agricultural products, most of such businesses are group-based.

The second point is about the age of the entrepreneurs. The average age of the

Figure 2-3-1 The Average Age Ratio of Entrepreneurs

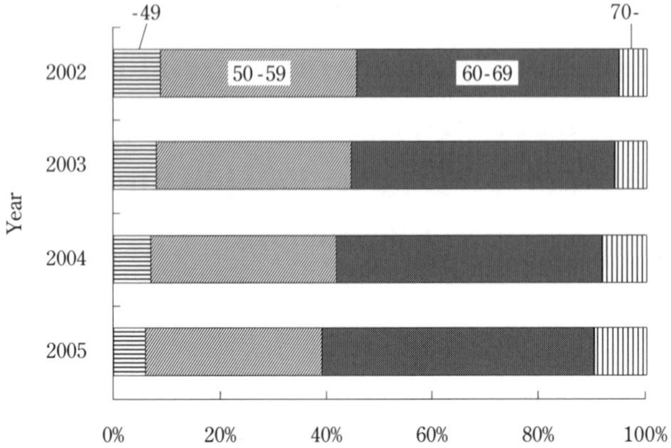

Source: Ministry of Agriculture and Fisheries

members of group management is mostly between their 50s and 60s. However, since 2002, the ratio of people in their 50s has been decreasing, while the ratio of those in the 60s has been increasing (Figure 2-3-1). If we define those in their 50s or under as middle-aged and over 60 years old as the elderly, we can say that the average age of entrepreneurs is rising slowly but steadily. The main farming for the rising age is the change in the course of the lives of the women living in farming villages (herein described as life-course) and the number of member who belong to conventional organizations.

To start with, we will explain the change of life-course. Figure 2-3-2 illustrates the transition of job conditions of women in farming villages according to their generations. The left figure shows the life-course of women born between 1941 and 1945, who are categorized as the elderly; the right figure shows the life-course of women born between 1946 and 1950, who are categorized as middle-aged. Looking at the job conditions of women in farming villages born between 1941 and 1945, we can see that the proportion of people involved in agriculture and those not involved in agriculture are almost the same for each age. In Japan, due to the rapid economic growth since the late 1950s, the number of people not involved in agriculture has been increasing. In such a social climate, the life-course of women born between 1941 and 1945 has changed from agricultural to non-agricultural work. Although no data are shown here, people born before 1935 who are in the higher age range bracket had a life-course focused on farming. On the other hand, among the women in farming villages born between 1946 and 1950, the ratio of non-agricultural work was high for every age, and they had a life-course focused on non-agricultural work. We can conclude that older

Chapter 2: Network and Socioeconomic Activity of Women   75

Figure 2-3-2 Job Conditions of Women According to Each Generation

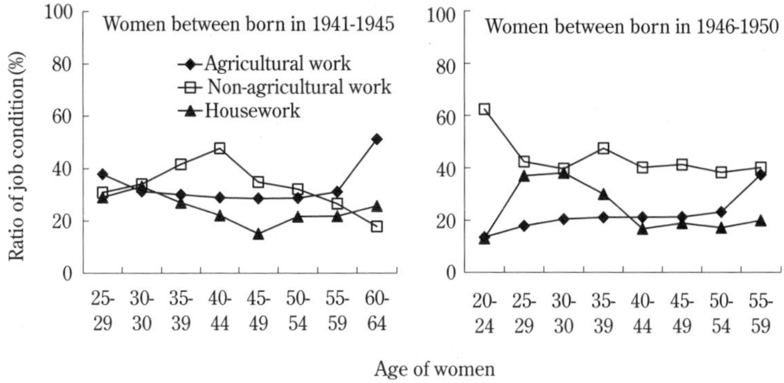

Source: Ministry of Agriculture, Forestry and Fisheries: (Census Agriculture and Forestry)

Table 2-3-1 Changes of Number of Members in Conventional Organizations

Year	Women in farming village	Agricultural co-operative women's group	Home life improvement group
1985	100.0	100.0	100.0
1990	88.1	87.6	85.3
1995	80.5	70.6	60.9
2000	73.1	52.8	47.0
2005	46.1	37.3	33.3

Source: Ministry of Agriculture, Forestry and Fisheries, National Council of Agricultural Co-operative Women's Associations, Rural Women Empowerment and Life Improvement Association

women are farming more, whereas middle-aged women are hardly farming as much.

Explained next is the number of members of conventional organizations. Table 2-3-1 illustrates the transition of the number of members that belong to agricultural co-operative women's groups and home life improvement groups by indexes. If we set the numbers of 20 years ago as 100, women in farming villages is -54 points, whereas agricultural co-operative women's group is -63 points and home life improvement group -67 points. The number of members of conventional organizations is significantly decreasing compared to the population of women in farming villages. Because the life-course of middle-aged people has changed from agriculture to non-agriculture employment, and there are fewer new members from middle and young age groups who join the conventional organizations, it can be concluded that the average age of entrepreneurs is rising slowly but steadily.

In the past, related organizations such as local government offices took measures to support such entrepreneurship by approaching leaders of the conventional organizations. However in recent years, there are fewer middle aged women farming and actively participating in such conventional organizations, in effect decreasing the number of women eligible for such support. Thus a new support strategy targeted to middle-aged people is now needed to support entrepreneurship.

3. Business Establishment Process Models

Examined next is the process of establishing a business by middle-aged people in comparison to that by the elderly. Regardless of business descriptions and management styles, there are five conditions required for starting a business. The first one is the motivation for starting one's own business. The second is gaining skills that are core to the economic activities and ideas which are the seeds of a business. The third is acquiring knowledge needed for dealing with tax and accounting matters. The fourth is securing business partners to consult with concerning management and making decisions, that is, a parenting business body. The fifth is preparing facilities such as farm stands, spaces for processing products, and procuring funds. We will compare business examples of middle-aged people and the elderly, and aim to extract business models by sorting out the processes they took to meet the requirements mentioned above.

Here is an example of production and sales of sweets made of *mochi* by Ms. A who belongs to "the elderly" age range bracket. This business group consists of 8 members, whose average age is in the 60s. The total amount of annual sales was 13 million yen. After marriage she had a non-agricultural job, but she retired in 1980 and became totally engaged in home farming. In 1994 she was the district leader of an agricultural co-operative women's group and she established a cooperative of local produce with other members of the cooperative. In those days she was not thinking of starting a business involving processing agricultural products. After participating in observation-study programs on progressive businesses run by women, planned by the agricultural cooperative or the town, and after hearing about offers made by the agricultural cooperative to provide facilities for those hoping to start a business, she became interested in starting a business of producing and selling sweets made of *mochi* in order to carry on the tradition of local food. Since she was young, she had opportunities to make sweets made of *mochi* and so naturally had those making skills. She asked other members of the agricultural co-operative women's group and made a voluntary processing group. She gained management skills such as tax and accounting knowledge after starting the business under the guidance of the agricultural cooperative.

Next is a case example of millet food restaurant by Ms. B from the middle-

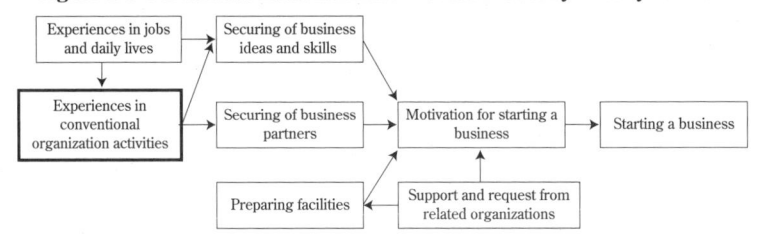

Chapter 2: Network and Socioeconomic Activity of Women   77

Figure 2-3-3 Business Establishment Process Model by Elderly Women

```
Experiences in jobs ──→ Securing of business
and daily lives            ideas and skills
      │                            │
      ▼                            ▼
Experiences in                                                           
conventional      ──→ Securing of business ──→ Motivation for starting a ──→ Starting a business
organization activities    partners                business
                                                     ▲
                                                     │
                           Preparing facilities ←── Support and request from
                                                    related organizations
```

Figure 2-3-4 Business Establishment Process Model by Middle-aged Women

```
                        Experiences in jobs and daily ──→ Securing of business
                        lives                              ideas and skills
                                                                  │
                                                                  ▼
Motivation for    Cultivation of human       Experiences in new
starting a    ←── resources/ establishment of ←── organization    ──→ Securing of business ──→ Starting a
business          a business organization       activities           partners                  business
                                                     ▲
                                                     │
                           Support and request from ──→ Preparing facilities
                           related organizations
```

age group. This restaurant is also group-managed and there are 4 members. The average age is 54. The total amount of annual sales is 20 million yen. Ms B had non-agricultural employment after marriage, except during her child-raising period. She was thinking about becoming involved in food-related activities since she was young, and had a cooking license. While working at a government-related office, she came to know about local millet food and became interested in carrying on that tradition. With the help from the city, she called upon voluntary members to join a class on millet in 1996. After that they developed their skills and menu through study and work, and researched consumer needs. In 2002, they had a proposal from the chamber of commerce and industry, and as a subsidiary project of the national government, they prepared a facility to start their own restaurant. The members of this business are the ones who agreed to start the business during their group study period. They gained management skills such as tax and accounting knowledge after starting the business under the guidance of the chamber of commerce and industry.

Based on these case examples, we made Figure 2-3-3, which shows the process model of businesses run by elderly women. For this age group, women who had been leaders in conventional organizations such as an agricultural co-operative women's group and had gained skills and trust from others decided to start their businesses after receiving support and suggestions from their related organizations. On the other hand, for the middle-aged group, women who did not belong to conventional organizations but were motivated to start a business, directly approached appropriate organizations on their own to receive support and start their business activities (Figure 2-3-4).

4. Conclusion

As mentioned before, the life-course of middle-aged women is different from that of elderly women. Middle-aged women were mainly engaged in non-agricultural work, and they do not have much experience in activities in conventional organizations such as an agricultural co-operative women's group. It is getting more difficult for them now than before to become leaders in conventional organizations and acquire business skills or partners, which are essential to business activities. Instead, new organizations formed to promote businesses are playing an important role in the businesses run by middle-aged women. A systematic process is needed for middle-aged women to establish a business organization with similarly-motivated members, and they need to acquire business ideas and partners through activities in such organizations.

From these points, we can conclude that for elderly women, who start their economic activities in conventional organizations and use them as parental structures, traditional support measures such as approaching conventional organization leaders is more effective. But middle-aged women, with less agricultural work experience and involvement in conventional organizations, need different types of support measures. One of the features of the middle-aged women is that they gain business partners and business skills through activities in newly established entrepreneurial organizations. The following two points are raised as issues on support measures. One is to cultivate human resources among women in farming villages who do not belong to conventional organizations and want to start a business, and to help them establish a business structure. The other is to come up with support measures for leaders in newly established organizations to supplement their inexperience in their new vocation. Leaders of newly established organizations lack experience which could have been gained in conventional organizations, where resources such as business partners and business can easily be obtained. It is considered necessary to promote organizational activities to supplement the farmers' inexperience by offering opportunities such as observing other business facilities and preparing classes on local food materials.

This paper was presented at the 12th World Congress of Rural Sociology Association, on July 6-11, 2008 in Republic of Korea. This edition includes the most recent revision.

References
Iwasaki, Yumiko, 1995, "Nouson ni okeru Joseikigyo no Igi to Houkousei (Aspects of the

Promotion of Women Owned Business in Japanese Rural Communities)," *Annual Bulletin of Rural Studies*, 31: 169-190. (in Japanese)

Shibuya, Miki, 2007, "Nouson Josei no Sedaiteki Tokuchou kara mita Kigyo no Sokushin Youin (General Features of Rural Women and the Promotion of their Own Business)," *Journal of Rural Plannig Association*, 26(1): 13-18. (in Japanese)

4
Background and Factors Promoting the Empowerment of Women in the Rural Society of Japan

Rieko Tsuru

1. The Purpose and Method
1-1. Review and Issues

In the field of research about Japanese rural women, Hideko Maruoka (1937) is a pioneer. At about the same time, Mieko Ema, a folklorist completed an excellent study on traditional large Japanese families in Hida-Takayama area. They had a common viewpoint that many of the social problems of rural women were in their daily family and societal life. In the late 1950's Yasuko Mizoue, a philosopher, researched rural women's voice in the Sanin area. Akiyoshi Takahashi, a rural sociologist, studied the changes of the rural family and the social status of women in the post World War II era caused by the development of capitalism in Japan.

These studies clarified rural women's social problems and created an analytical framework that the social status and social role of rural women should be linked to their social norms or social customs that they belonged to. But afterwards, later studies on rural Japan didn't focus on this framework. On the other hand Takahashi's framework to study the process of capitalism in rural Japanese society and the changes of rural society and agriculture has become the mainstream in Japanese rural studies. There were few about women farmers.

Since the late 1980's, rural sociologists started to focus on women farmers as an object of study again. This was the theme of the 42nd session of the Japanese Rural Studies Association in 1994. Sonoko Kumagai took part as the chair and was a symbol of that tendency. The book edited after that session presents the level of studies of women farmers. Afterward, there were many studies, Tokuya Kawate wrote about the actual conditions and issues of the agreement of rural family management and the changes of rural families, Wasa Fujii focused on the role of regional leadership of women farmers, Tomoko Ichida focused on the agent promoting agricultural policies, Yukiko Nagano studied women independent from Ie. Since the mid 1990s I have studied some issues, i.e. the relationship between the changes of the structure of a farmer's household economy, the process of getting their own personal income, and the meaning and effects of having one's own personal income to themselves and the family and community.

Through these studies we have certainly recognized an expansion in the field of women farmers displaying their capabilities. But there are some unsolved questions; how can such women farmers extend these fields? What is the background and what are the factors relating to women farmers empowerment? When preparing this report I received many suggestions from Maruoka, Ema and Mizoue therefore I have researched some cases of women farmers empowered through their participation in some organizations and social networks. I think the process of expanding their activities is the adjustment to many tense relationships, which were caused by gaps between women farmers' social action and the former social norms of rural society.

I will present these tense relationships and how they made adjustments or solved their problems and I will try to show the background and factors promoting women's empowerment.

In this report I define empowerment as "the process that women who have no social power and no right to participate in household management, become the agents in the changing of society, politics and the economy through many activities."

2. Framework
2-1. The Definition of Some Words: Ie, Mura, Tense Relationship

First I will definite these words, "Ie", "Mura" and "The Tense Relationship". I define Ie as "the household management style, which seeks the final goal of guaranteeing the household members necessities of life". I think "Ie is made up of many components", the eternity of Ie, ancestral rites, maintaining and managing the family's property, the management of the family business, the shares of the village and the issue of the right of the master of the household. Even if one of these components is lacking, Ie is still existant. I define Mura as "an organized village". I define a tense relationship as a social relationship involving many conflicts arising from the gap between social norms in the social group and social action of the members.

Tense relations within Ie arise from the gap between the activities of women farmers and the social norms of Ie. For example, the significant others for women farmers are her husband, her father-in-law, mother-in-law and children. Sometimes tension is generated by the significant others, and other relationships are resolved by them.

The tense relationships within Mura arise from the gap between activities of women farmers and the social norms of Mura, such as community management, events and projects of community groups.

2-2. Two Pairs of Social Norms and the Hypothesis of This Report

At present in Japanese rural society there are two contrasting pairs of social norms and people in rural society choose these behavior principles based upon relevant circumstances.

The first norm has existed since before World War II up to present and is widely deep-rooted. 1-(1) "men belong to the public, women belong to the individual" (here in after written as "The Private Norm"), 1-(2) "men are the leaders, women are the assistants (subordinate to the husband)", (written as "The Assistant Norm"). 1-(1) "The Private Norm" and 1-(2) "The Assistant Norm" are related to the idea of the predominance of men over women. So they were suited to the former Ie and Mura. In households, these two norms plus 1-(3) "men work, women work and do housework, (the senses of the new division of labor [1-(3)]" (written as "The New Division of Labor Norm") justifies the reasons why women undertake all housework. 1-(1) "The Private Norm" and 1-(2) "The Assistant Norm" have been considered as if they essentially connected Ie and Mura, but it is not true logically. If circumstances around Ie as household management style, and Mura as an organized village and each social situation surrounding them change, each suitable social norm might change. For example it is evident that after rapid economic growth, women's activities have been gradually reevaluated on a continuing basis.

The second norms are 2-(1) sexual equality (written as "The Sexual Equality Norm") and 2-(2) the achievement principle norm estimate by achievement principle or ability principle (written as "The Achievement Principle Norm"). These have spread all over Japan since World War II, people know them well but it is not the social norm that has not fully penetrated our daily lives. Because they are considered politically correct, it is impossible to deny the value of the sexual equality norm and the achievement principle openly. So when a person chooses to take 2-(1)"The Sexual Equality Norm" and (2)"The Achievement Principle Norm" seriously, the response depends on the relevant circumstances. Frequently in women's only activities they might be accepted positively. On the other hand when men and women are in the activities they might be targeted by open refusal or denial and they maybe derided and mocked due to their limited knowledge of the society, or negative comments maybe spread behind their backs.

In the field applied 1-(1) "The Private Norm" and 1-(2) "The Assistant Norm" as far as women farmers are concerned, when taking a role in the private area and not taking a role in the public area, there might not be any tense relationship on them. But if the women farmers had internalized both 1-(1)"The Private Norm"/(2)"The Assistant Norm" and 2-(1) "The Sexual Equality Norm"/(2) "The Achievement Principle Norm" she might feel the gap and might experience serious conflict. On the other hand in the same field, when she chooses to participate in her household agricultural management and community management on an equal position as men, she will have a tense relationship from the gap between 1-(1) "The Private Norm" and 1-(2) "The Assistant Norm" and 2-(1) "The Sexual Equality Norm"/(2) "The Achievement Principle Norm".

So if women farmers are in such a double binded situation where there are two pairs of contrastive social norms, how have they acted and how have they expanded their activities? I think if the gap between social norms and social action is diminished, then the tense relationships might be solved. As long as they have fear of the generation of tense relationship because of the social norm gap, they might restrict their actions to something suitable to 1-(1) "The Private Norm"/(2) "The Assistant Norm". And they can not expand their acting field. But in fact, they could take action in many areas, I think there must be some background and factors promoting women's activities and in the situation, they might have chosen action against 1-(1) "The Private Norm"/(2) "The Assistant Norm" and they might have continued and gradually changed the social norms and actions.

I think there are three types of relations of norm and action. One the power of norm 1-(1) "The Private Norm"/(2) "The Assistant Norm" has decreased because for some reason(s), family members or the community doesn't follow the norm. Secondly the power of norm 2-(1) "The Sexual Equality Norm"/(2) "The Achievement Principle Norm" has increased because for some reason(s) family members or the community has come to support the norm. And third it seems that they follow norm 1-(1) "The Private Norm"/(2) "The Assistant Norm" on the surface, but in fact, they support norm 2-(1) "The Sexual Equality Norm"/(2) "The Achievement Principle Norm" through a steady accumulation of actions to that effect relatable to norm 2-(1) "The Sexual Equality Norm"/(2) "The Achievement Principle Norm".

2-3. A Summary of Cases and These Characteristics

I have been researching rural Japan for over 10 years starting in 1997. I have chosen some groups and networks that have been active for several years, or in some cases, for over ten years and accumulated undeniable results. Almost none of them have shrunk from the tense relationship in Ie and Mura. Furthermore they seem to only act in a few limited circumstances. Many times I have done fieldwork with such women farmers and groups or networks for a few years. The objects of this research were leaders of women farmers and other members in the same group or network, husbands, and formal institutions of agriculture including city hall, or other prefectural governmental offices. These research areas are located in western Japan, i.e. Okayama, Tottori, and Shimane prefectures, with exception of one area, Iki-island at which I have continued fieldwork since the mid. 1980's. I think it is important to visit research areas many

Table 2-4-1 Outline of Cases

	Area	Group Name	Starting Period	Activity Content	Member Ascription	Result
1	Whole Iki-island, Nagasaki-pref.	Nokyo Fureai-ichi (JA Market Network)	1985~	Farm and fishing products, processed goods	40~70s females in farm cooperative	Economic power, pride as a farmer
2	Ishida-town, Nagasaki-pref.	Ishida Fureai -ichi (Ishida Market Network)	1991~	Farm and fishing products, processed goods	40~70s females in farming and fishing	Economic power, pride as a farmer
3	Y. village, Gonoura-town, Nagasaki-pref.	Coin Operated Vegetable Stand	1985~	Farm products	40~70s females of farming	Economic power, pride as a farmer
4	Kayo-town, Okayama-pref.	T. Organic Farming Group	1992~	Organic products	40~70s females of farming	Economic power, pride as a farmer
5	Kamitake-area, Kayo-town, Okayama-pref.	K. Himawari (Sunflower) Group	1996~	Food life improvement, holding events	30~80s rural women	Enjoy life, community revitalization
6	Nagato-village, Okutsu-Town, Okayama-fref.	N. Women Processing Group	Mid. 1980's~	Farm products, processed goods, rural-urban exchange	30~80s rural women	Economic power, community revitalization
7	Miyo-village, Kofu-town, Tottori-pref.	M. Women Processing Group	1996~	Farm products, processed goods, rural-urban exchange	30~70s rural women	Economic power, community revitalization, self confidence
8	O. area, Koge-town, Tottori-pref.	Mikado House	1996~	Farm products, processed goods	40~80s rural women	Economic power, self confidence
9	Masuda-city, Shimane-pref,	Masuda Women Farmer Forum	1999~2000	Conferences, lectures, workshops	40~70s women farmers	Sharing problems, self confidence, making friends
10	All over Japan	Female Ladder Group	1969~	Handing on reading notebooks, conferences	Female readers of "Nihon Nogyo Shinbun (Japan Agriculture Newspaper)"	Sharing problems, making friends
11	All over Japan	Exciting Network for Rural Heroins	1993~	Conferences, lectures, workshops	10~80s women farmers, consumers, etc.	Making friends, excogitating problems on food and agriculture

Notes: Made based on fieldwork.

times and I decided to study areas that are not far from my residence, I live in Tottori prefecture. At first, I considered taking a case where they are active in some small area, mainly in their village and the surrounding villages (I call them "grass-root activities"). But as I continued my research I discovered that two nationwide networks (I call them "Nationwide Activities") had been tremendously influencing many women farmers, so I changed my course of research and added those two networks.

In this report I use 11 cases and I summarize each case on Table 2-4-1. Some cases started in the mid 1980's but the majority of the cases started in the 1990's with the exception of case 10. They are focused in the direction of generating the revival of the kitchen gardens, and developing new agricultural products for sale under the auspices of JA (Japan Agricultural Co-operatives) and Agricultural Improvement and Promotion Centers in the prefecture. The main imputation is that the members are over 40 years of age and although their child raising has come to the end of the first stage, they have little time for women farmer's activities. They don't work regularly or full-time in a non-agriculture job. They work at their household agriculture management. There are many effects from their activities. For example, they are gaining economic power by having their own personal income, becoming proud of their agricultural work and revitalization of their community.

Chapter 2: Network and Socioeconomic Activity of Women   85

Table 2-4-2 Characteristics of Cases

	Area	Degree of Voluntary Participation	Activity Social Norm	Tense Relationship in "Ie"	Tense Relationship in "Mura"	Notes
1	Whole Iki-island, Nagasaki-pref.	high	2 − ① · ②	high→low	low	Activities of women farmers co orperative
2	Ishida-town, Nagasaki-pref.	high	2 − ① · ②	high→low	low→high→low	Independent→city, Chamber of Commerce and Industry
3	Y. village, Gonoura-town, Nagasaki-pref.	looks low, but is high	looks 1, but is 2	low	low	Independent→Y. village
4	Kayo-town, Okayama-pref.	high	2 − ① · ②	high→low	high→low	Started as a prefecture project
5	Kamitake-area, Kayo-town, Okayama-pref.	high	2 − ① · ②	low	high→low	Started as a reconstruction of community female group
6	Nagato-village, Okutsu-town, Okayama-pref.	looks low, but is high	looks 1, but is 2	low	low	Started as a prefecture project
7	Miyo-village, Kofu-town, Tottori-pref.	low	1 → 2	low→high→low	low→high→low	Started as a prefecture project
8	O. area, Koge-town, Tottori-pref.	looks low, but is high	1 , 2	high→low	high→low	Started as a prefecture project
9	Masuda-city, Shimane-pref.	high	2 − ① · ②	high→low	low	Started as a prefecture and city project
10	All over Japan	high	1 , 2	high→low	low	Nihon Nogyo Shinbun (Japan Agriculture Newspaper)
11	All over Japan	high	2 − ① · ②	high→low	low (→high→low)	Supported by Ienohikari (Britenning up the Hosehold) Association

Notes: Made based on fieldwork.

Table 2-4-2 presents each characteristic based on Table 2-4-1. The criteria are a degree of voluntary participation, activity norm, tense relationship from Ie and tense relationship from Mura. A degree of voluntary participation is judged whether participation in the group or network is voluntary or automatic (compulsory). Activity norm means that they apply the standards of action in the activity. I identified which norm they apply to through numerous narrative data in my fieldwork. I think that there is almost no relationship between grass-root activities and the degree of voluntary participation.

Members in activities of which the degree of voluntary participation is high (cases 1, 2, 4, 5, 9, 10, and 11) are not only in villages but also cities all over Japan. So if a woman participates in an activity, she will drastically increase the number of her relationships. The customer behavior is almost 2-(1) "The Sexual Equality Norm" and 2-(2) "The Achievement Principle Norm".

On the other hand I can find that activities of which the degree of voluntary participation is low are organized by existent social groups and they might participate with a unit within the village. So at the beginning of the activity, behavior patterns were 1-(1) "The Private Norm" and 1-(2) "The Assistant Norm". But during their activities the behavior began changing to 2-(1) "The Sexual Equality Norm" and 2-(2) "The

Achievement Principle Norm".

Thus, at the beginning of on activity, the degree of voluntary participation is related to the difference of the social norm in many cases. But as they continue, activity norms might change gradually from 1-(1) "The Private Norm" and 1-(2) "The Assistant Norm" to 2-(1) "The Sexual Equality Norm" and 2-(2) "The Achievement Principle Norm", and the degree of voluntary participation is not related to the difference of social norm. I will describe in section 3.

In cases 3, 6, and 8, the degree of voluntary participation seems low, but actually it is high. The reason is that they chose a common strategy when they recruit new members for the group. They recruit from all houses in the village. They aim to impress that the activity is not done by a limited number of members and has the approval of the Mura. I will describe in section 3.

At first the tense relationship against Ie is usually high, but it gradually begining low. However, there are some cases where the tense relationship against Ie is low from the beginning. What is the mechanism to change these tense relationships? I will describe in section 3.

The tense relationships in Mura, in one case, remained low from the beginning, and in another case, decreased overtime. For example, cases 9, 10, and 11 are activities beyond Mura. The people in their village seldom heard the news about the activity and didn't know about nor were they concerned with the activity. So we could not see if in such cases, tense relationships were generated.

In the notes you can find that some women farmers activities are related to some public organizations, farmers' cooperatives, municipalities and prefectures. I will state in section 5 if they use these organizations effectively, this is one of the factors promoting women's activities.

3. Experience of Tense Relationships by Women Farmers and Their Responses

3-1. Tense Relationships in Ie and the Responses

Tense relationships within Ie are generated by a gap between the social norm applied to Ie and women farmer actions. Most tense relationships that women experience at the beginning when they start on activity are caused by the gap among 1-(1) "The Private Norm", 1-(2) "The Assistant Norm", 1-(3) "The New Division of Labor Norm", and their actions. At first, when a woman decides to participate, she has to ask to her husband, father-in-law and mother-in-law. There are many women in such situations. Generally it was common for them to act suitably to 1-(1) "The Private Norm"/(2) "The Assistant Norm"/(3) "The New Division of Labor Norm". So except when they act with their husband they can't decide on their own. During my research I often heard that many women said they couldn't make a decision without asking their husbands.

In case 9, in spite of the fact that time was so short in the forum, there were quite a few women who couldn't decide by themselves. Ms. I .W. she is the leader of the network, said that if/when women wanted to allocate time in their everyday life they had to express their reasons to their family, especially to their husband and they also had to manage the farm work and housework properly.

After the decision to participate, with their husband's permission, the next problem was how to proceed with 1-(3) "The New Division of Labor Norm". A lot of women farmers don't want to change the norm. So they choose a way of not changing the social norm and overcoming it by their own efforts so as to avoid conflict with surrounding people. In many cases, they first talked about their activity with their family, they didn't ask for any changes of their role in the family structure. It is very difficult for them to try to take on two roles, the conventional role, i.e. farming, housework and mothering and the new activities. Before they would go out, they would finish doing their ordinary housework. They didn't think that it would be okay if someone else would have to do their work. Except in case 6, all cases completed their housework.

After women started an activity and became busier but more satisfied because of the appropriate economic rewards, most family members gradually changed their consciousness and attitudes. They recognized and began to show more and more cooperation. For example they tried to help her with the housework or do it themselves. As the result, though women farmers didn't strongly express their opinions, the family role structure started to reorganize "naturally". Women farmers say that the cause of change was her efforts and how the results effected her family and community.

In cases 1, 2, 3, 4, their activities are all concerned with morning market participation and management. So they are usually very busy from pre-evening to night or from evening to midnight in preparation. At first, after they complete all their work, both farming and housework, they prepare for the morning market. But after a while her husband, son and daughter-in-law undertook a part of her role or helped her. There are various tasks, for example, gathering vegetables from the field, cleaning them, sorting them by size, packing, labeling, delivering, cooking and doing the dishes.

In case 7 there are some members who are in their 30s and mothering is their main role. At first, it was a big problem how young mothers could participate in the activity, because mothering is different to other housework, it is a continual task. Initially, members of the group helped each other, gradually most husbands and mother-in-laws began to help.

Thus at the beginning there is a tense relationship in Ie, in many cases the tense relationship gradually diminishes. As a result of women farmers and their family members changing the family role structure, 1-(1) "The Private Norm", 1-(2) "The

Assistant Norm", 1-(3) "The New Division of Labor norm" have lost that power, have been modified a little, and 2-(1) "The Sexual Equality Norm" and 2-(2) "The Achievement Principle Norm" have been applied. Because Women farmers know all too well how difficult it is to change social norms, they themselves seldom choose strategies that change social norms.

3-2. Tense Relationships within the Mura and the Responses

Tense relationships within the Mura is generated by the gap between social norm 1-(1) "The Private Norm" 1-(2) "The Assistant Norm" and women farmers actions. In some cases we find that they have two choices to respond to tense relationships.

One is that they try to hide the gap. They don't seek to directly change the applied social norms from 1-(1) "The Private Norm"/(2) "The Assistant Norm" to 2-(1) "The Sexual Equality Norm"/(2) "The Achievement Principle Norm" and they behave as if they obey 1-(1) "The Private Norm"/(2) "The Assistant Norm". In case 6, Ms. K .Y. the leader of the group, says that she thinks if women only try to jump the gun they will fail. It is better to accumulate results and show them to men. Women are changing, men are changing and the community is changing. In N village, people have a division of labor where men work at non-farming, women work at farming and housework. So most of the women in N. village have had to take the initiative in house farming management and most men have taken an assistant role. The women processing group was established in the mid. 1980's when N village accepted a county project. From the beginning, the men were very cooperative and by themselves built a processing place for women to work in. Through these activities a sense of solidarity amongst the group members become stronger and therefore it gave them satisfaction to live in N village. It gave them energy. Men have no choice but to support women's activities.

The second choice is to use male community leaders. Women have already built up a cooperative relationship with their husbands within the families, so they ask their husbands and neighbors to do public relations work for many people in various situations, Especially the husband of a female leader who is usually a male leader in the community and has a strong influence in the community.

In case 5, women in rural society, both farmers and non-farmers, have tried to revise their own eating habits. They have also reconsidered family relationships, daughter-in-law and mother-in-law family role structure, and community planning. Men have been influenced by a wife and mother who took action and actually changed. They began to help and support those women's activities. For example one of the male area leaders said that members of Himawari-Kai looked happy and he envied them, so we should try to do something, too. This positive comment encouraged and supported women's activities.

Thus not only women but also men work to change social norms in the village to reduce 1-(1) "The Private Norm"/(2) "The Assistant Norm" and diminish or shut out tense relationships in the village.

4. Background of Promoting Empowerment

4-1. The Creation of an Atmosphere Fitting to the Social Norm 2

From all 11 cases we can find some social atmosphere which is suitable to 2-(1) "The Sexual Equality Norm"/(2) "The Achievement Principle Norm" and promotes women farmer activities widely. It is becoming common for women farmers to participate in their own farm management now, to work on production, processing and sales with social groups or networks. In interviews, I have often heard these words or phrases, proper, natural, times have changed, and women's abilities are being estimated properly. We don't have to struggle any more, it is old-fashioned to be concerned about gender.

One of the main factors generating such a social atmosphere is local government policy, specifically, approval of the Basic Law on Gender Equality, that has been promoting agreement on family management since the 1990's. Case 11 is a typical example. Ms. I.W. is the leader of that forum and has served on the agricultural committee since 1999. She is the first female committee member in Masuda city in Shimane pref. In case 2, Ms. K. N. and in case 3, Ms. A.Y. are both female directors of farmer's cooperative.

The second factor is that past results built on many years of committed activities through the women farmer's cooperative section and farmers' life improvement movement. Up to cases 1-11with the exception of a representative, Ms. I. W. in case 9, not only all case leaders but also members had a history of empowerment through activities of JA (Japan Agricultural Co-operation) and the Prefectural Center for Agricultural Expansion and Improvement. In each activity most women farmers obtained their own bankbook for the first time and they gradually developed and improved their abilities. These facts are conspicuous but they are great results.

The present social atmosphere expects and encourages women farmers' activities and is one of the social backgrounds promoting these activities. Women make the most of the many chances they come across, such as, the enthusiastic introduction of various projects, tactical usage of family management agreements, etc.

4-2. The 6th Industrialization of Agriculture and Reevaluation of Women's Roles

The 6th industrialization of agriculture means agricultutal business diversification and integration. It reevaluates women farmers' roles and it is one of social backgrounds promoting their activities. The recognition that farmers do not only plant crops but also do many things has become widely known and that fact further motivates women farmers and their activities have dramatically increased. Now, women farmers' activities vary. They include production, processing and sales, exchanges between rural-urban communities, and making groups or networks for close and direct relationships. So it is impossible to do all this without women in rural life. Men can't cover these responsibilities.

For a long time women farmers have steadily done the housework but it was unpaid work and was not properly evaluated. Recently, through these other activities their housework is now evaluated as high and useful. It gives them confidence. Women's ability to farm is now a very attractive way to increase family income, and revitalize the community.

4-3. Contribution to Continuance of Ie by Women Farmers

Ie is the household management style and it is an important matter for each member including the women farmers' continuance of Ie. I found that social factors promoting women farmers' empowerment is changing the way of Ie is continued. Figure 2-4-1 provides details on the changes in income and changes of social norms, the period of pre-rapid economic growth to the present shown in three periods.

The first period is pre-rapid economic growth. At that time, Ie was a free labor system and the head of family directed other family members. The social norm 1-(1) "The Private Norm"/(2) "The Assistant Norm" applied to that situation. But since rapid economic growth there has been a modernization in agriculture and an increasing number of farmers have side jobs. The social norm changed from 1-(1) "The Private Norm"/(2) "The Assistant Norm" to 2-(1) "The Sexual Equality Norm"/(2) "The

Figure 2-4-1 Details of Household Income and Changes of Appropriate Norms

First Period
　farming income + non-farming income = one purse
　↓
Second period
　farming income + non-farming income = household purse + each member's purse
　↓
Third period
　farming income + non-farming income + each member's income
　　= household purse + each member's purse

```
                        First period   →   Second period   →   Third period
Appropriate norm    1 — ①·②              1 — ①·②              1 — ①·②
                                           2 — ①·②              2 — ①·②
```

Achievement Principle Norm".

The second period is rapid economic growth. There is a spreading of increasing farmers with a side job, as well as mechanization and modernization in farming. The household structure is becoming organized complex income of Ie and personal income of member. In a part of farm management it has remained that Ie is a free labor system and the head of family directs other family members. The social norm 1-(1) "The Private Norm"/(2) "The Assistant Norm" applied to that situation. But in a part of non-farm jobs depend on each member's ability, so it applies to 2-(1) "The Sexual Equality Norm"/(2) "The Achievement Principle Norm". In more households, the ratio of income from non-farm jobs is increasing therefore family power structure and role structure has been changing.

The third period is the activity that women farmers have gotten her personal income since the mid 1980's. In household economics, the ratio of income from non-farm job is increasing more and more.

Thus the whole society it has been changing radically surrounds agriculture and farmer. Each farmer tried to change the principle of house management and social norm to survive. As the result of those it is promoting background women farmer activity.

4-4. Contribution to Continuance of Mura by Women Farmers

Mura is an organized village. Previously according to the 1-(1) "The Private Norm" and 1-(2) "The Assistant Norm" it has been acknowledged that men manage Mura and the management of the community are men's roles. Men are leaders, women are assistants; planning, proposal and actions are all done by men, and women obey men's directions.

But in underdeveloped, aging and mostly rural societies, a new situation has arisen, men can't disregard the number of women. We have already described the 6th Industrialization of Agriculture and reevaluation of women's Roles. Not only quantity, but also the women farmers' abilities are highly evaluated, so for the prosperity of the village, men and women came to the conclusion pretty easily that they had to work together.

In this way, women farmers' activities are one of the ways to continue the existence of the village. The fact that it promotes the social background and evolution of women farmers' activities.

5. Promoting Factors of Women's Empowerment
5-1. Increasing of the Social Resources of Women Farmers

Women farmers have increased their social resources and it makes it easier for them to respond to some problems incurred during the activities and it has influenced the family power structure and promoted those activities.

I define social resources as educational background, life experience, and economic power. In increasing social resources there are two circumstances. One is dependent on the course of life and the other is relative when comparing generation or gender.

Most women I interviewed were born post World War II and were educated under a democratic and sexually equal society. Their educational background is the same as their husbands. In the case of women born before the war, the leader had graduated from a girls' high school, which was superior at that time. So in comparing with the husbands' high educational background, education has not influenced the family power structure.

For women there were some opportunities to gather life experiences, such as; working at non-farming jobs, commitment to farming management, and participation in women's activities of a farmers' cooperative. These opportunities might introduce them to another world except that is world tantamount to traveling between house and field. They could have a relative perspective of farming life and farm management. They realized the double binding situations and gap between two different norms and discussed those situations with their companions to solve their problems. Thus they understood their situation clearly and changed their attitude towards farming more subjectively.

It is important for women farmers to have economic power. As we found the increasing of the member's income means not only a plus for management of Ie but also an enlargement of the member's power to manage Ie from Figure 2-4-1.

Thus women have much social recourse that makes family relationships change. First, the relationships of couples change so that the wife does not have to obey one-sidedly and they respect each other. This decrease of social resources difference makes couples construct equal or close to equal relationships. There is a reverse relationship between father-in-law and mother-in-law and women, they regard that it is possible to have an equal relationship with them. In relationships among mother and child and grandmother and grandchild, women farmers prefer to be seen as lively workers and respectable mothers or grandmothers.

5-2. Empowerment through the Activities of Women Farmers

The increasing of social resources makes it easier for women farmers to participate and continue in activities and promotes more women's empowerment. I think that there are two types of empowerment. One is at an individual level, and the other is at a group member level. They help and stimulate each other. In 11 cases I found that women leading activities have distinguished talents as leaders. They are of high educational background, intelligent, have a sense of humor, are positive thinkers and have a high sense of responsibility. These qualities are attractive to many people and people will follow her intently. They have changed their lives applicable to the conservative norm 1-(1) "The Private Norm"/(2) "The Assistant Norm" to added 2-(1) "The Sexual Equality Norm"/(2) "The Achievement Principle Norm". As a result of the practice of responsible tasking, they studied and learned how to consider things, state their opinions, and cooperate with many people. And while growing up, they are changing social relationships among members. In many cases, I have heard that most of women have become proud of their associates, in spite of the fact that the other members are the same.

First women get experience performing at only women's groups for a few years or so, they become able to collect their thoughts and state their opinions in public. After that, in a situation that is composed of men and women they can speak without hesitation. They have confidence because they have been maturing and the people around them have changed their views of them. I often have heard in research "the bigger the position that women farmers have been given and performed the more she is empowered." "People admit they are inferior to her". In community or regional societies making fellowships and acting together makes it possible to increase women's empowerment.

5-3. Effective Use of Public Agents and Organizations

From table 2-4-2, I found that most activities are interrelated with some public agents and organizations. It varies on the relationship but there is a similarity among them; the prestige of it, funds, wisdom, technique, the place for activity, paperwork support system, and so on are important social resources for their activities. If they use them effectively, the activities might advance smoothly. For example, when women start the activities and say as in the phrase, "The specialists at the center for the promotion of agriculture improvement are encouraging," they are a big influence to the family and the village, and the large amount of money for these activities really helps them. Advice from the staff of the public agencies and organizations efficiently support these activities.

Recently, women farmers are aware of the fact that they are being vigorously appealed to promote policies, such as the family management agreement, exchange projects between rural and urban communities and the promotion of a gender equal society, etc. Although I think we have to carefully study their influence and results. It is obvious to women farmers that such dependable public agencies and organizations exist and they can use them accordingly, upon their request, when necessary.

5-4. Mobilizing Resources from Other Activities

From research I found that there is a mutual complementary relationship between "Grass-root Activities" and "Nation-wide Activities". What grass-root activities get from nation-wide activities are connections with various people beyond their area and receive information about the widespread problems about women farmers, agriculture, food, modern society, etc. They could always confirm the meaning and validity of these activities through these connections. In case 11 I heard that a member Ms. K. N. who is a cattle farmer from Hokkaido, said at a Committee meeting, in preparation for a nationwide conference, "Have you ever experienced, when you try to talk about serious topics among your neighbors, they give you a odd face. In my neighborhood there is no one I can talk to about what I have in my mind. Therefore, when I come here, I am energized and regain my confidence."

Conversely "Nationwide Activities" must get many findings and be fully aware of "Grass-root Activities". In case 11, in general, while each member engages in her household farming, she is also busy in participating in grass-root activities. Through these activities, problems occur and they bring them to study groups held several times a year or to the national conference which is held once every few years. They are always generating a movement of women farmers who can think and act by themselves.

5-5. What do Women Farmers Realize about the Society and Their Actions?

They realize that if they want to change society the way they'd like to, it would be necessary for them to recognize the framework of the existing society and change it. They are becoming aware of politics and sometimes help assembly members. There is a new wave that women farmers who aim to become assembly members or committee members and try to change their social situation.

In case 2 and 3 each leader has become a female director of a farmer's cooperative. In case 9, the leader became the first female agricultural committee member in 1999 in Masuda city in Shimane Prefecture.

In case 11, in a national conference once every few years, there was a subcommittee for increasing female assembly members. After those discussions some women farmers became candidates of city assemblies and a few won elections. Women farmer's consciousness of politics has been changing.

In this context I define politics as meaning not only the local assemblies and diet (national legislature) but also power relationships developed by various groups and organizations related to farming and farm life. In my view, this includes agricultural committee members, Japan Agricultural (JA) directors, assembly members of local government and national government. Nothing can be changed if you only complain about this being a male dominated society. The appeal is for "let's start obtaining

6. Conclusion

I focused how women farmers could extend their areas of activity. Women farmers have experienced tense relationships in activities from gaps between their actions, 1-(1)"The Private Norm", 1-(2) "The Assistant Norm" and 1-(3) "The New Division of Labor Norm". But they have tried to overcome by pretending to obey these norms on the surface but actually they continued based on 2-(1) "The Sexual Equality Norm" and 2-(2) "The Achievement Principle Norm". As a result, their activities have contributed to the continuance Ie and Mura. They succeeded in changing social norms from 2-(1) "The Sexual Equality Norm" to 2-(2) "The Achievement Principle Norm".

From the 11 cases we found some social backgrounds that are creating an atmosphere fitting to the social norm 2, changes of agriculture, evaluation of women farmers, and the continuance Ie and Mura. The factors promoting women's empowerment are increasing the social resources of women farmers, effective use of public agents and organizations, mobilizing resources from other activities, and changing attitudes in society. Thus these social backgrounds and factors have made women farmers expand their fields of activity.

Finally, I would like to describe some problems. One is, in farmer's life, is sexual division of labor right or wrong. The second is, how to construct systems to distribute labor payment in family farming, including agreement of family management. The third is how to make women farmers' activities successful in aging, rural societies. Now, many women farmers groups or networks have a common problem that they don't have any successors.

This paper was presented at The 12th World Congress of Rural Sociology: International Rural Sociology Association, on July 6-11, 2008 in Republic of Korea. This edition includes the most recent revision.

References

Akitsu, Motoki, Wasa Fujii, Miki Shibuya, Kazuo Oishi and Tamaki Kashio, 2007, *Nouson Jenda* (Gender in Rural Society), Kyoto: Showado. (in Japanese)

Ema, Mieko, 1942, *Hida no Onnatachi* (Women in Hida), Mikuni Shobo. (in Japanese)

―――, 1943, *Shirakawamura no Daikazoku* (Big Families in Shirakawa Village), Mikuni Shobo. (in Japanese)

Ichida, Tomoko, 1995, "Seikatsukaizenjigyo nimiru Jendakan: Seiritsuki kara Genzai made (View of Gender in Rural Life Improvement Project: from Formation to Present)," *Annual Bulletin of Rural Studies,* 31:112-134. (in Japanese)

Kawate, Tokuya, 1998, *Nihon no Nougyo*, 206. (in Japanese)

Kumagai, Sonoko, 1995, "Kazoku Nougyo Keiei ni okeru Josei-Roudou no Yakuwari-Hyouka to sono Igi (The Appraisal of Women's Work in Farm Family Enterprise)," *Annual Bulletin of Rural Studies*, 31: 7-26, 245. (in Japanese)

Maruoka, Hideko, 1937, *Nihon Nouson Fujin Mondai* (Women Farmers'Problems in Japan), Koyoshoin. (in Japanese)

Nagano, Yukiko, 2005, *Gendai Nouson ni okeru "Ie" to Josei* (The Ie and Women in Contemporary Rural Communities), Tokyo: Tousui Shobou. (in Japanese)

Takahashi, Akiyoshi, 1969, "Nousonkazoku no Henka to Fujin no Chii (Change of Rural Agricultural Families and Women's Social Status)," Kiyoshi Oshima and Hideko Maruoka eds., *Gendai Fujinmondai Koza* (Course of Women's Problems in Modern Era), 3: 105-130. (in Japanese)

Tsuru, Rieko, 2007, *Noukajosei no Shakaigaku* (Sociology of Women Farmers), Tokyo: Komonzu. (in Japanese)

Yamazaki, Yoko, 1995, *Inakagurashi ni Yumenosete: Onnano Nettowaku Tanjomonogatari* (Life in Rural Society having Dreams: About the Story of the Birth of Women's Network), Tokyo: Ie no Hikari Association. (in Japanese)

Chapter 3

Women Balancing Family and Farming

Chapter 3 will zoom in on young couples' trying to balance work and life. How farming women work, how they feel about pregnancy and child rearing, mother and child health, and support for balancing children and work will be examined. Today with a serious decline in birthrate and a shrinking population, what kind of environment do farming women want for rearing children for the next generation? What are the problems with child rearing in rural areas? What kind of support is needed? Answers to these will be sought based on field surveys, while the child rearing potential in rural regions' and the work methods will not be overlooked. The internal structure of rural Japan's stem family will be investigated from a relationship between the mother-in-law and the daughter-in-law, showing the significance of a family management agreement. There will be some issues proposed such as career support for women, family management agreements, and financial aid so that farming women may have children without worries and keep working while raising them.

1
Maternity Leave for Farmers and the Potentiality of the Family Management Agreement in Japan
Chie Katayama

1. Introduction

For women to continue to work through the period of childbirth and child rearing, first off, rest and consideration for the strain on a mother's body, both ante- and postpartum as well as during pregnancy is vital from the aspect of the mother's safety and health. Financial problems also arise for the period when the mother cannot work, and the problem of personnel shortages occurs at the workplace due to maternity leave. Furthermore, when the mother wishes to return to work after giving birth, can she continue her career and who will take care of the child rearing while both parents are working.

In Japan, ways of working and resting both before and after the employed person gives birth, and laws aimed at harmonizing work and family life during the child-rearing period (the so-called "work-life balance") are currently being developed. These are based on the existing laws such as: *Roudou-kijyun-hou* (the labor standards law), *Danjyo-Koyoukikai-kintou-hou* (the law for equal employment opportunity of men and women) or *Ikuji-Kaigo-kyugyou-hou* (the law for workers who take care of children or other family members including child care and family care leave), etc. These laws were not originally intended to be applied to self-employed workers, including farmers. However, considerations regarding how to work and how to rest during this time period are very important for the self-employed, including farmers. Naturally, measures for this is not just a matter of setting up a similar system as that for the regularly employed, but must take into account the special nature of farm management and farm labor.

We have considered the issues and current situation that allows for the creation of an environment which permits Japanese farmers to safely take leave through the birth and the child-rearing periods and also keep working. Among these, this report focuses on maternity leave, and looks first at the framework surrounding maternity leave for farmers from an international point of view. Following that, we offer an arrangement for maternity leave based on a Family Management Agreement as one solution for Japan, a country which does not legally apply maternity leave to farmers.

2. Support Frameworks for Farmers in Birth and Child-rearing Periods from an International Point of View

First, we will examine the financial support systems and maternity leave in the current social security programs in Japan and in various countries, mainly in Europe. Along with that, we will confirm the situation in international organizations [Öun and Parad, 2005] and in France, where maternity leave for farmers is being positioned in the social security program.

2-1. Maternity Leave and Leave Support in Japan and Selected Overseas Nations

Japan's maternity leave is a total of 14 weeks for the employed, with 6 weeks coming before birth and 8 weeks after. While on leave, two-thirds of the standard daily remuneration is paid from the health insurance program as a maternity allowance. This is based on the Labor Standards Law. Aside from this allowance and the maternity leave, there are provisions for the guarantee of health checkups and reduction of working hours while pregnant, and certain forms of work are forbidden. Also, there is guarantee of a child-rearing period after birth, and, as a basic rule, child-rearing leave is until the child is one year old (to a maximum of 18 months). However, this law does not cover the self-employed. For birth expenses, the employed and the self-employed both receive a one-time birth payment from their health insurance program.

Next, looking at the application of maternity leave in various countries in Europe, based on a summary of the literature, we can see that there are two major types of countries: those that include all residents, including farmers, in the system, and those that only include those who qualify under certain conditions in the system. In many cases of the latter sort, like Japan, only the employed are eligible, and farmers are not. Among these, France, for example, has a specific system for farmers.

2-2. The International Labor Organization (ILO)

In the International Labor Organization, maternity leave is taken up in recommendations (R) or in conventions (C) concerning maternity protection. Child-rearing leave and paternity leave are seen differently, and considered as covered under the Workers with Family Responsibilities Convention.

First, provisions for maternity leave were made according to the 1919 "Convention concerning the Employment of Women before and after Childbirth" (C3), and then in the 1952 "Convention concerning Maternity Protection (Revised 1952)" (C103) and the Recommendation of the same (R95), an additional item was added to Convention 3. The same year, a provision for a maternal benefits package was included in the "Convention concerning Minimum Standards of Social Security" (C102). Additionally, in 2000, the "Convention concerning the revision of the Maternity Protection Convention (Revised), 1952 (C183)" and the "Recommendation concerning the revision of the Maternity Protection Recommendation, 1952 (R191)" were adopted. These were aimed at the employed, in principle, but with the 2000 revision, the phrase "including those in atypical forms of dependent work" was added to Article 2.

In agriculture, the 2001 "Convention concerning Safety and Health in Agriculture (C184)" and the same Recommendation (R192) were adopted as the first comprehensive international standards dealing with safety and hygiene. In these, considerations towards farm laborers regarding the protection of women were taken up.

2-3. The European Union (EU)
The European Union has the Council Directive of 11 December 1986 on the application of equal treatment between men and women engaged in an activity, including agriculture, in a self-employed capacity, and on the protection of self-employed women during pregnancy and motherhood. It is considered that it was instituted from the view point of equal treatment between men and women, not of the health of mothers and children.

2-4. France
In France, due to its historical background, social security systems have developed on a per-occupation basis, and there is an agricultural social security system with compulsory membership for farmers. When we look at the support for birth and for employed farm laborers there is the same sort of system as for employees in other industries including, for example, paid leave at the time of birth, benefit in kind for delivery costs and consultations regarding pregnancy and birth. On the other hand, for managers and their families there is a system whereby they can be sent substitute workers to cover the personnel shortages caused by women taking leave and receive subsidies to cover the costs of hiring them. This system was set up in 1977, before the EU directive.

As a prerequisite to this French system, the definition and positioning of farmers is made individually clear without any reference to sex, and there is commensurate treatment and obligations. At the same time, the goals of these systems were gradually achieved through the efforts to raise the position of women that began in the 1970s, and their financial position as well as the position of women gradually ensured consistency with other domestic systems [Harada, 2003].

Additionally, as a social background, a lifestyle based on a household of husband and wife, the high awareness about getting leave, and the lowness of the psychological barriers regarding accepting social support can also be offered [Katayama et al., 2006].

3. The Status of Farming Women during the Period when They Give Birth in Japan

3-1. The Working Status of Young Farm Household Women

Figure 3-1-1 shows the working status of young women in farming households. It is based on extracting and re-totaling ages of birth and child-rearing among women aged 20 to 39, according to the Farming and Forestry Census 2005.

The total number of women in farming households in Japan is 4,254,764, of which women aged 20 to 39 are 726,388, or 17% of the total. When we consider the status of work engagement among women family members aged 20 to 39, the most common is "Did not engage in work," and "Only engaged in non-farming," with a total of 424,000 people. The next most common is "Engaged in both farming and non-farming work, with the non-farming work being most significant," with 195,000 people. The "Population mainly engaged in farming," consisting of both those "Engaged only in self-operated farm work," and those "Engaged in both farming and other work, with farming work being most significant," is 108,000 people. Of the population mainly engaged in farming, those whose "Normal main situation" is "Mainly work" (Core persons mainly engaged

Figure 3-1-1 Status of Work Engagement of Young Women (from 20 to 39 years old) in Farming Households

		Working condition				
		Engaged only in self-operated farm work	Engaged in both farming and non-farming work		Only engaged in non-farming work	Did not engage in work
			with Farming work being most significant	with Non-farming work being most significant		
Normal main situation	Mainly work	Core persons mainly engaged in farming 34,899 (4.8%)		194,746 (26.8%)	423,711 (58.3%)	
	Mainly did housework and child-rearing	73,032 (10.1%)				
	Other					

| Population mainly engaged in farming 107,931 (14.9%) | Persons engaged in farming 302,677 (41.7%) | The total number of women in farming households 726,388 (100%) |

Source: calculate from the census of Agriculture 2005

in farming) is no more than 35,000, and those who "Mainly did housework and child-rearing" or "Other" were 73,000 people, or two thirds of the total. Note that the ratio of 20 to 39 year old women among the core persons mainly engaged in farming is 3.4% of the total age ranges, or the equivalent of one in thirty.

In other words, among women aged 20 to 39 almost 60% do no farm work at all, despite being in farming families, and if we included those that do some farm work, but mainly work in other industries, then the percentage rises to over 80%, indicating that few farm household women of this age bracket are involved in farm work. And of the 110,000 that are mainly engage in farming, there are about 35,000 people in the entire country who are mainly involved with farm work as opposed to housework or child rearing, or less than one in twenty among farm household women of the same age group. Since unmarried or childless women are included in this, we can assume that the number of women who do farm work while raising children is even lower.

3-2. The Status of Systems Concerning Maternity Leave for Farmers

As noted earlier, in Japan various systems, starting with maternity leave, are set up for employed people. For this reason, farmers, most of whom are self-employed, do not have legally guaranteed maternity leave, child-raising leave, or the assurance of baby feeding time. Among this, in agriculture, the following approaches are used.

In the 2000 "A New Vision for Rural, Mountainous and Coastal Societies to Solve the Problem of Declining Births," was formed. The basic direction shown for low birthrate measures, "regarding the proper condition of pre- and post-natal pregnancies, from the point of view of protecting the mothers' body, and work and leave while the child is an infant .[in short], we need to ensure that it is not less than that comparable to working women in other industries." "Setting up a support system that allows balancing both work and child-rearing" was pointed out as being important.

Also, though in the dairy husbandry field only, the dairy farm relief service system (provision for substitute workers) applied to maternity leave starting in 1997, and has been used to good effect.

Other than this, the Rural Women Empowerment and Life Improvement Association works on educating "child-raising support counselors" and their networking.

3-3. Status of Farmers Pre- and Post-Partum

Problems related to the practice of working before and after giving birth and the health of the mother and child in farm households have existed for years and have been continually noted as problems that farming villages must solve.

While there are limits due to the selection of objects and survey methods, there is a certain amount of data on women in Japanese farming households in the 21st century, in terms of the way of working and leave before and after giving birth. In our study [NIRE, 2005], we were able to confirm the actual existence of women who were not able to take sufficient maternity leave. Also, as a reason for why farmers find it hard to take maternity leave, the following points are suggested. First, there is the point that women are concerned about how their parents or neighbors view maternity leave. Also, in family run farms, the lack of the total operational labor force due to the reduction in the volume of labor related to the woman's pregnancy and birth must often be mainly covered by an increase in the volume of labor of the other family members. Thus, we can note that though the woman herself is resting, there is concern about the increase in the family's labor load, and about the costs and assurance of a substitute labor force.

In this situation, from our preliminary case study [RLRI, 2004], it can be suggested that, in terms of the need for a maternity leave system and its form, there must be adaptability to the diverse working methods of farmers or individual management, there must be a guarantee of "ease of leave," and there is a need for a system to compensate for the lessened labor force (readiness and cost subsidies for substitute workers). In particular, in terms of the ante- and post-partum period, it is important to connect it to the fact that "if there was a specific system then it would be easy to take leave." In these cases, we saw examples where understandings towards pregnancy situations conflicted even within a family, and among the parents' generation, the ideas that "giving birth is not a disease," and "when I was pregnant I worked right up to the last minute" still remain. These facts cannot avoid adding psychological stress to ante- and post-partum women, and to alleviate it, we need to set up a system where it is "easy to take leave."

Thus, in the current situation in Japan, where the social security system does not guarantee maternity leave for farmers, it is considered effective to set up a way to take leave from work before and after childbirth as well as balance child-raising and work in the Family Management Agreement, which is a relatively simple approach to ensure farming women's maternity leave.

3-4. Status of the Conclusion of Family Management Agreements

Modern Family Management Agreements are arranged based on full and complete discussions among family members regarding working environments that are easy for family members to work in, the division of roles and direction of management, and that the aim for an attractive farm management where each member of the household involved in family agriculture management can express their desires and wish for challenges to its management. There is no legal restrictive power.

The number of Family Management Agreements signed in Japan as of March 2007 is 37,721 [Ministry of Agriculture, Forestry and Fisheries, 2007]. Among the

Chapter 3: Women Balancing Family and Farming   105

extent of the arrangements, the most common is between the farm manager and the spouse, with 50.2% of the total, followed by between the farm manager, the spouse, and the children (16.0%). There is a high chance that women who are pregnant or raising children are included in the cases where more than two couples are connected, such as farm manager - spouse - child - child's spouse (10.3%), or parents - farm manager-spouse (10.3%), and three-generations of couples (0.6%), which together make up over 20% of the total.

The most common details of the arrangements (multiple answers were possible) were "deciding the direction of farm management," (86.0%), "working hours and days off," (85.9%), with "child-raising role division" at a mere 9.3%. There were no survey questions about maternity leave, and we are not aware of any national-level cases who realize maternity leave supported by Family Management Agreement.

4. The Possibilities of Gaining Maternity Leave Utilizing a Family Management Agreement

Here, we look at prior cases of where there has been actual expressed provisions of maternity leave in Family Management Agreements, and consider their details, and their evaluation and issues [NIRE, 2006].

4-1. Methods

We looked for appropriate cases from existing reports and information from related organizations, taking regionality into account, and conducted surveys from six cases who agreed to cooperate with our survey and participate in interviews (2005).

These cases consisted of farming women (mothers of pre-school children) and their families from farm households with pre-school children who had clear provisions for maternity leave in signed Family Management Agreements. In the contents were the details of the maternity leave, its background and evaluation, and the status of work ante- and post-partum and the current state of changes in the amount of labor.

We chose two prefectures from the North-East (Tohoku) region of Japan, "A" and "B", and two from the southern Kyushu region, "C" and "D". When we look at the labor situation of young farming women in terms of the ratio of "Population mainly engaged in farming" and "Core persons mainly engaged in farming," of women aged 20 to 39 among the entire farm family members, we see that A, C, and D are, as of the year 2000, above the national average (18% and 5.1%, respectively). Also, the number of cases which had signed Family Management Agreements, and where we could determine that maternity leave was clearly specified, was 474 and 3 for Prefecture A, 407 and 2 for Prefecture B, 1,090 and 3 for Prefecture C, and 927 and 5 for Prefecture D (at the time of the survey). Therefore, we can say that cases where maternity leave is part of the agreement are exceedingly rare.

4-2. Findings
4-2-1. Outline of the Farm Households
In the six cases, farm households were all dedicated farming households, and the main items managed were rice, flowers and ornamental plants, vegetables, and fruits. The labor structures were of three types: family only, employed workers during busy periods, and employed workers throughout the year, with there being no particular limit on the type of management.

4-2-2. Special Points Seen in the Agreements
The limits of the signees to the Agreements included both two generations and just the husband and wife. Maternity leave was positioned as part of the labor conditions such as "leave or rest," or "labor conditions" in some cases, and as part of the lifestyle items such as "child-raising and education" in other cases. Phrases used to describe maternity leave included some cases where it was made clear that time could be taken off from work, and cases where the time to be taken was specifically spelled out. In this way, the contents of the Agreements were diverse, reflecting the needs and ideas of each family and farm households.

4-2-3. Background to Bringing about Maternity Leave and Evaluations by the Principals
Regarding the background of bringing about maternity leave, we found that a common theme was, the mother of the parental generation not wanting her daughter or daughter-in-law going through the same hardships that she had. Also, from the male members (father and husband), we could see concerns for the new member of the household by marriage. Similarly, as in general Family Management Agreements, there were many cases where they said that the Agreement was merely writing down of promises and customs that had already existed in the family. In our evaluation of the farming womens' comments, it was noted that, when specifics were written down in the agreement, it was easier to take a leave of absence from work. Though not taking the total amount of time as promised, they said it was easy to take leave and there was a sense of "written promises were better than verbal promises." Also, there were people who positively evaluated the clarification of roles saying "the timing and the limits of my duties when I returned to work were made very clear." Furthermore, they positively evaluated the fact of working on a farm before they got married.

4-2-4. Labor Force Changes and Supplementation Resulting from Leave
Finally, we will analyze how the limited labor force caused by maternity leave taken by

women was taken into consideration and dealt with based on cases when the women worked both ante- and post-partum.

In the farm household cases, the effects of leave due to childbirth were divided into two opinion groups, those who thought that labor was insufficient, and those who thought that there was no or minimal effect.

Those that considered that the labor force was insufficient due to women's leave were in cases where the woman had been involved in farm work for a certain period of time before giving birth, and were dealt with by increasing the amount of work of each family member, or by hiring workers (increasing wage costs), and many people pointed out the need for substitute workers. For example, in one case a couple running a farm said there was no room for a decrease in the amount of labor needed to do the job, but the wife was given maternity leave. The husband felt the loss of one person's share of work, but found it preferable to increase his own working hours in light of the fact that it would cost him a lot to hire a replacement. The wife couldn't bear to see how hard her husband worked, and resumed farm work three months after giving birth.

On the other hand, for those who considered that there was no effect, there were cases where this period was seen as a time when the woman could not work, and had already prepared for the effects from the loss of the labor force by restricting management expansion, or by adjusting the amount of work in anticipation of the fine when the child was several years old.

4-3. Discussion

We have confirmed that under the current system in Japan, making an express provision for maternity leave in Family Management Agreements is one realistic method for making an environment where it is easy to take leave. In particular, it is considered effective in assuring a psychological "ease of leave" state.

However, we also found that in the current situation families and farm households must be ready to adapt to changes in the labor force. Therefore, provisions for substitute workers while mothers are on maternity leave and subsidization of expenditures as in France may be an option.

In addition, we feel it is necessary to clarify the position of women in farm management. Even if we construct a support system, and we do not clarify who can use it, and who supports it, it will become difficult to run.

5. Conclusion

In this report, we have focused on maternity leave, giving a quick sketch of the state of maternity leave for farmers in various countries. We have considered arrangements for maternity leave in Family Management Agreements as one solution for Japan, a country which does not apply maternity leave in a legal form for farmers.

Finally, this report has focused on maternity leave, on how women can safely and comfortably give birth. However, These are among the many issues that remain to be resolved. For example raising children, continuing to work and their careers, and on individual financial problems if personal income is made clear to begin with, then it will be possible to calculate leave subsidies in the same manner as for other industries.

In terms of setting up conditions where farming women in Japan can easily take leave, and also in terms of developmental support for women who are responsible for farm work from an early stage, and furthermore looking at it from the direction of supporting birth and child-raising throughout society as the low birth rate continues, we believe that it is necessary to consider further support measures.

This paper was presented at the 12th World Congress of Rural Sociology: International Rural Sociology Association, on July 6-11, 2008 in Republic of Korea. This edition includes the most recent revision.

References

Harada, Sumitaka, 2003, "Furansu no Shin Nougyo no Houkouzuke no Houritsu no Naiyou to Tokuchou (Contents and Characteristics of New Agricultural Basic Law in France)," *Nousei Chousa Jihou*, 550: 2-35. (in Japanese)

Katayama, Chie, Yasue Fujimoto and Kiyomitsu Kudo, 2006, "Furansu no Josei Nougyosha ni miru Shussan-Ikujiki no Seikatsu to Shien-Kankyo (The Work, Lifestyle and Support Environment for Female Farmers during the Period when They Give Birth to and Raise Their Children in Rural France)," *Journal of the Rural Life Society of Japan*, 50: 47-57. (in Japanese)

Ministry of Agriculture, Forestry and Fisheries, 2007, *"Kazoku-Keiei-Kyoutei ni kansuru Jittaichousa Kekka nitsuite* (Report of Circumstance of the Family Management Agreement)." (http://www.maff.go.jp/danjo/19kyoutei.pdf, June 30, 2008) (in Japanese)

National Institute for Rural Engineering (NIRE), 2005, "Nougyosha no Shussanzengo no Hatarakikata Yasumikata (The Circumstances of Work and Maternity Leave of Women and Farm Households)," *Heisei 16 nendo Nouson-Seikatsu Sougou Chousa Kenkyu Jigyou Houkokusho 3*, Tsukuba: NIRE, 1-40. (in Japanese)

――――, 2006, "Shussanzengo no Nougyosha heno Shien (The Support for Working Women through Pregnancy, Giving Birth and Child-rearing in Agriculture)," *Heisei 17 nendo Nouson-Seikatsu Sougou Chousa Kenkyu Jigyou Houkokusho 3*, Tsukuba: NIRE, 1-50.(in Japanese)

Öun, Ida and Gloria Parad Trujillo, 2005, *Maternity at Work: A Review of National Legislation*, Geneva: ILO.

Rural Life Research Institute (RLRI), 2004, *Rural Life Research Series*, 60. (in Japanese)

2
Mother and Daughter-in-law Dyads in Farming Families Executing the Family Management Agreement[1]

Yukiko Otomo

1. Introduction

In Japan, the farming unit has been a family, which is to be succeeded by the first son of the farm manager. Following the traditional stem-family system, the farm successor was supposed to continue living with his parents even after his marriage.

In traditional stem-family households based on the Ie institution, there was a hierarchy. The male household members were more dominant than that of the females and the senior household members were more dominant than that of the junior members. Thus, it has been necessary for the successor's wife to obey her parents-in-law in terms of farm work and daily family life.

There was a woman in a stem-family household who exercised headship as a housewife, and this status was transferred from the mother to her daughter-in-law some years after the daughter-in-law's marriage. Before the succession the daughter-in-law had to learn the family traditions and communal duties under the guidance of her mother-in-law. The complicated relationships between the mother and daughter-in-law in stem families have been one of the classical issues for family studies in Japan.

However, the stem-family system is being replaced by the conjugal-family system in current Japan. Although the composition ratio of stem-family households is still relatively high in rural areas, the inner structure of the stem-family household has acquired several new aspects, deviating from the tradition. In an aged society, the prolonged life-expectancy extends the period that a married couple lives together with the parents. Therefore, each married couple needs to be more or less independent in order to avoid any conflicts. Moreover, declining birthrate decreases the number of siblings, sometimes leading to a lack of a brother among the successors in the family. A female successor is therefore not unusual nowadays[2].

---

1) This paper was presented at the 12th World Congress of Rural Sociology: International Rural Sociology Association, on July 6-11, 2008 in Republic of Korea. This edition includes the most recent revision.
2) According to the National Survey on Family in Japan, in rural areas the more traditional institution based on paternal family line is still dominant. In spite of this tendency, more than 10% of married

The change in the inner structure of the stem-family household shifted the mother and daughter-in-law dyad from dominance of the mother-in-law to equality between the mother and daughter-in-law or dominance of the daughter-in-law[3]. In this study, current mother and daughter-in-law dyads in farming families are analyzed according to semi-structured interviews with farming families executing the Family Management Agreement.

The Family Management Agreement had been introduced for establishing the personal position in a farming family, especially women's status, and modernizing farm management by carrying out a partnership among family members. The mother and daughter-in-law dyad within a farming family, pioneering in the Family Management Agreement, shows a partnership and that they are able to fulfill their needs complimentarily. This mutual relationship between the mother and daughter-in-law involves integrated family-ties.

2. Methods

The relationships between the mother and daughter-in-law can be seen from a life course perspective. The course of one's life is a chain of events dependent on age and determined by when and what events one experiences. The mother and daughter-in-law have passed across a different life course according to historical and social conditions. Women's life course patterns are deeply related to family career as well as occupational career; i.e. whether her occupational career has been consistent or interrupted considering her family career. In order to compare life course between the mother and daughter-in-law, the early life stages of the mother-in-law are focused on.

The Family Management Agreement is contributing to the career formation of farming women. Most of the farming families executing the Family Management Agreement have signed an agreement on the field of farm management such as decision-making policies in farm management, working hours and holidays, farm labor allocation and remuneration for farm work. Moreover, half of them have made an agreement about their family life covering issues such as family life allocation, farm management rights transfer, sanitary cleanliness, working conditions, health care, etc.

---

women are living with their own parents even in rural areas. Behind this figure, we can assume that the bilateral family line is rising deviating from tradition [The National Institute of Population and Social Security Research, Japan, 2000].

3) The following factors advanced the status of the daughter-in-law within the stem-family: conjugal-family system taking the place of the stem-family system, farm successors having a disadvantage in finding a partner, farm managers having much difficulty keeping their successor within the agricultural sector, the younger generation of farming women having more chances to manage their own accounts, and the parents expecting to receive care from their daughter-in-law [Sato, 2007, 173-174].

Chapter 3: Women Balancing Family and Farming   111

Each Family Management Agreement is composed of several clauses which cover issues from farm management to family life, according to the family condition.

This study is based on the nationwide survey of farming households executing the Family Management Agreement[4]. The interviewed were introduced by the local Extension Service Centers, which were evaluated as regions with well-promoted Family Management Agreements by the Regional Agricultural Administration Offices staff in charge and by the Expert Extension Workers at the prefectural level. In this study, in order to examine the generational relationships between the mother and daughter-in-law, three model cases are shown where the mother and daughter-in-law are present, the latter still engaged in childbirth/child-raising, and the data from semi-structured interviews both with mother and daughter-in-law were obtained.

The role allocation in farm work and in family life concerning the manager's wife and the successor's wife is analyzed in addition to their life course. Moreover, in order to indicate the generational relationships in stem-family households, the degrees of generational integration and separation in a co-residence were measured in terms of housing, facilities, i.e. kitchen and bathroom, and living expenses[5].

3. Cases of Mother and Daughter-in-law Dyad

Table 3-2-1 shows basic information about three comparative farming families executing the Family Management Agreement, from which data from semi-structured interviews both with mother and daughter-in-law were obtained.

These three cases for this study are located in various regions in Japan: Hokkaido, Miyagi and Aichi. The type of farm management is different in all these cases: dairy, rice and vegetable, and horticulture. However, these stem-families are almost on the same life-stage, i.e. on the childbirth/child raising stage, because these successors' wives are of the same generations (b.1970, 1970, 1973) and these managers' wives

---

4) Thanks to the generous support of the Japan Society for the Promotion of Science and their 2005 and 2006 Grant-in-Aid for Scientific Research, I conducted an authorized interview with the staff at the Regional Agricultural Administration Offices Agricultural Extension Service, Women and Youth Affairs in different locations throughout Japan: Sendai, Saitama, Kanazawa, Nagoya, Kyoto, Okayama, Kumamoto and Sapporo [Otomo, 2007]. The main purpose of this interview was to find out the regional trends with regards to the Family Management Agreement and its specifics, and development in each area under consideration. Although the access to original documentation of the Family Management Agreement became difficult after the enactment of the Act on the Protection of Personal Information in 2005, we could still see some valid samples, obtainable, thanks to the Extension Worker's collaboration and assistance.

5) The former studies on the incidence of the co-residence of parents and the married child referred to the concept of 'family solidarity' used by Vern L. Bengtson [Morioka ed., 1985] [Sugaya, 1985] [Sato, 2007].

are also of the same generations (b.1947, 1944, 1941). These mother and daughter-in-law dyads reflect some aspects relating to career formation of farming women and development of partnership among family members.

3-1. Family A in Aichi
3-1-1. Family Management Agreement
The first document was signed in 1996. The manager's wife was a rural-life advisor certified by the local government, and because of that this farming family was the first to sign the agreement in this region.

The following year the successor got married, and therefore the agreement was revised among four family members, i.e. the manager, the manager's wife, the successor and the successor's wife.

3-1-2. Farm Management
This family farm has 4ha of cultivated land for horticulture. Its sales amount was 100 million yen per year in 2006. There are 17-18 part-time workers.

Table3-2-1 Basic Information

	Location	Aichi	Miyagi	Hokkaido
	Interview	March 7. 2007	February 23. 2006	September 7. 2006
	Number of family members	7	8	8
	Family composition	3 Generations	4 Generations	4 Generations
	Family members	Manager (b.1938)	Manager (b.1941)	Manager (b.1946)
		Manager's wife (b.1941)	Manager's wife (b.1944)	Manager's wife (b.1947)
		Successor (b.1971)	Successor (b.1968)	Successor (b.1972)
		Successor's wife (b.1973)	Successor's wife (b.1970)	Successor's wife (b.1970)
		Successor's son (b.1997)	Successor's daughter (b.1996)	Successor's son (b.2004)
		Successor's son (b.1999)	Successor's daughter (b.1997)	Successor's son (b.2005)
		—	Successor's daughter (b.2000)	—
		—	Manager's mother (b.1920)	Manager's mother (b.1920)
		Manager's daughter (b.1972)	—	Manager's daughter (b.1977)
	Agreement signing	1996	2002	2002
	Agreement revision	1997	—	2005
	Farm management	4ha of cultivated land for horticulture. Sales amount 100 million yen per year in 2006.	1.3ha of rice fields, 70a of cultivated land for around 40 kinds of organic vegetables, processing and selling handmade box lunches and apartment management when the agreement was signed in 2002. The cultivated land under management area for the rice planting had expanded to ten hectares when the interview was conducted in 2006.	90 milking cows and 35 heifers, milk production 660t per year in 2006.

Chapter 3: Women Balancing Family and Farming   113

In 2007, the manager and the successor were engaged in planting seedlings for flower beds, and the manager's wife was engaged in planting Hydro culture.

In the document, it was stated that book-keeping and personal management are allotted to the manager's wife and her working hours are from 9 a.m. to 18 p.m., matched with the working hours of the part-time workers.

The successor's wife was not engaged in farming and felt isolated from the other family members, and she let this frustration out on her children. The manager's wife noticed some unusual behavior in her grandchildren's actions. Therefore, she assigned sowing as farm work to the successor's wife, which she could begin easily. In 2006, the manager was hospitalized due to an injury, and currently the successor's wife is in charge of sowing independently.

In 2006, the manager's wife handed over her accounting tasks for the wages of the part-time workers to the successor's wife exactly as scheduled. When the interview was conducted, a year had passed. The successor's wife needed one more year to take over accounting tasks completely.

It is written in the document that the income was 200,000 yen for the wife, 170,000 yen for the successor and 50,000 yen for the successor's wife per month. However, currently their salary has gone up.

In the document, it was planned that the farm management transfer would be when the manager turns 63 and his wife turns 60. The manager actually handed over his management right to his son when he was 65 years old because of the farmer's pension[6].

3-1-3. Family Life
There is a detached building on the premises for the successor, his wife and children. However, it has neither a bathroom nor a kitchen. The bathroom and the kitchen in the main building are shared by all family members.

In the document it is stated that the successor's wife is the main person in charge of cooking, washing, cleaning and kitchen gardening, and the manager's wife assists her. In 1997, the manager's wife fractured her hand and it caused some difficulties for her to perform household chores. She determined this occurrence to be a good opportunity to hand over her domestic role to the successor's wife.

The manager's wife hands the successor's wife between 150,000 yen and 200,000 yen to cover household expenses every month. In the manager's wife's opinion, household expenses should be given to the successor's wife independently from

---

6) Although the management right was transferred in 2003, we call here the former manager "the manager" and the current manager the successor.

her own salary because the successor's wife has to learn how to save for household expenses.

There is no information in the document about child care because it was signed before the children were born. In fact, overall child care is allotted solely to the successor's wife.

3-1-4. Life Course of the Manager's Wife

The manager's wife was born as the fourth daughter of a school teacher in a neighboring district. Her father was sick, and therefore her eldest brother engaging in family farming supported her economically. She went to an agricultural high school to help her eldest brother's work. However, after graduating from high school, she worked as a telephone operator that was one of the prestigious jobs at that time.

Her current husband was a salesman of an agricultural machinery company before their marriage. Her eldest brother was one of her husband's customers. Her eldest brother helped with setting her up with her current husband. In the 1960s, more full-time farm households converted to part-time farm households in which husbands were engaged in off-farm work and wives were engaged in farming with her parents-in-law. To avoid working in the family farm with only her parents-in-law, she asked her husband to resign from his company. She began to engage in farming with her husband right after their marriage in 1963.

Because her mother-in-law died four years after this, she has been engaged in book-keeping and personal management since the beginning of her marriage. At that time, her husband's three siblings lived with them and there were always more than two interns working on her family farm. She had been in charge of their meals in addition to household chores.

She gave birth to her children in 1968, 1971 and 1972. Her three children entered the day nursery around the age of three. She raised her first daughter on her own but she asked her father-in-law to take care of the other two. He was a man of strict morals and inflexibility. However, grandparents generally find that their grandchildren are very pleasant to be with, and therefore he became a gentle person to his daughter-in-law.

3-1-5. Life Course of the Successor's Wife

The successor's wife was born as the first daughter of an office worker in this district. She went to high school, where she learned home economics and achieved licenses for cooking and sowing.

After graduating from high school, she worked as a medical office worker for five years. One of her colleagues asked her to attend an event organized by a group of

Chapter 3: Women Balancing Family and Farming   115

farm successors, where she became acquainted with her current husband. In 1996, she resigned from her job to get married at the age of 23. She had no anxiety in living with her husband's family and in engaging in family farming in the future because her father's family ran a vegetable farm.

Right after her marriage, she undertook overall domestic chores from her mother-in-law. She gave birth to two sons in 1997 and 1999. Overall child care is allotted solely to her.

In the greenhouse, the manager's wife regularly held a tole painting class inviting an instructor, and the successor's wife attended as a student. The manager's wife offered her daughter-in-law a chance to obtain the qualification to teach tole painting. She spent three years preparing for the exam and attained a license in 1999. She teaches tole painting monthly in her class.

In 2006, she began to engage in farming as mentioned above (3-1-1).

3-1-6. Characteristics of this Mother and Daughter-in-law Dyad
The mother-in-law was born and brought up in a large farm family; therefore, it was easy for her to live with her husband's parents and many siblings right after her marriage. However, the daughter-in-law grew up in a small nuclear family. This difference between their home environments before their marriage has driven the mother-in-law to give her daughter-in-law extra consideration. Because of that the daughter-in-law has concentrated on housework and child care, and has not engaged in family farming. The degree of generational integration in this co-residence is high, and this is supposed to cause more conflicts. Division of labor between the mother and daughter-in-law is one of the measures against conflicts. For example, the manager's wife could be in charge of farm work and the daughter-in-law in charge of housework. However, this causes the daughter-in-law to be isolated from the other family members. In general, the manager's wife's duties in farming tend to be handed over to the successor's wife earlier than the farm management right is handed over to the successor. However, it is not clear when and how the manager's wife's duties should be transferred, since it depends on the mother-in-law's decision.

3-2. Family B in Miyagi
3-2-1. Family Management Agreement
This farming family signed the agreement in 2002 because the manager's wife was a core member of the Women's Department of the Agricultural Cooperative in the city. The manager's wife was the main person to sign it and she focused on the decision-making policy for farm management.

3-2-2. Farm Management

When the agreement was signed in 2002, the farm management of this family was as follows: 1.3ha (13,000m^2) of rice fields, 0.7ha (7,000m^2) of cultivated land for around 40 kinds of organic vegetables, processing and selling handmade box lunches, and apartment management. The cultivated land under management for the rice planting had expanded to ten hectares when the interview was conducted in 2006.

The manager and the successor are engaged in rice farming, the manager's wife is engaged in planting organic vegetables and the successor's wife is in charge of processing and selling handmade box lunches.

In the document, it is stated that the monthly salary amounts to 50,000 yen and the bonus amounts to 80,000 yen twice a year, which are paid to each family worker, i.e. the manager, the manager's wife, the successor and the successor's wife. However, each person is drawing their own income from the apartment management. Therefore, only the successor's wife receives her monthly salary and her bonus from her mother-in-law. The profit from the direct sales store is deposited into the manager's wife's account because the seller's name belongs to her, while the producer's name belongs to the successor's wife.

There is no information about farm management transfer in the document. The current manager will not retire on a pension at 65. He has not set up his farmer's pension[7].

3-2-3. Family Life

The successor and his wife started to share a residence and its facilities with his parents since right after their marriage. This is the traditional co-residence of parents and the married child. The manager said that the result of too much democracy would fall into individualism, and therefore a three generation family was the best, even if there was some degree of hierarchy within the family. Moreover, the manager's wife added that it was the way of her family to have the eldest son live with his parents even after his marriage.

House-keeping is allotted to the successor's wife and the manager's wife is a helper.

It was written in the document that taking children to and from the day nursery was allotted to the successor and his wife, and the manager's wife helped them in addition to taking charge of the house cleaning. However, the successor's wife became busy at her new business cooking and selling handmade box lunches. Therefore, currently the manager is in charge of taking the children to and from the day nursery and their piano

---

7) The farmer's pension system is private in Japan.

lessons, and the manager's wife of having the children eat breakfast.

3-2-4. Life Course of the Manager's Wife

The manager's wife comes from a farming family in a neighboring town. She studied home economics in high school, and then before her marriage, she learned sewing in a private class while working part-time in a bookstore.

When she was 21 years old, her marriage was arranged. Her husband was the eldest son of a farm manager; therefore, she began to live with her parents-in-law, three sisters-in-law and a brother-in-law right after her marriage. Soon after, she gave birth to the eldest daughter at the age of 22 and the eldest son at the age of 24.

Her husband's family introduced sericulture at that time in order to improve cash earning. The sericulture needed more labor forces. The current manager's wife had to be engaged in family farming as a young diligent unpaid worker. She could not get her own account, although it was common in this community that young farming women earned their pocket money by peddling vegetables cultivated by themselves.

Around 1995, the manager's wife set up her vending counter of packed bags offering 30 kinds of vegetables. Her unique vending counter rose to fame in the region.

The family changed its main farm products from silkworm cocoons to rice with a large management scale under the contract with other landowners around 2005.

She is very satisfied that she can have her own account thanks to the direct sales store and she can contribute to her family's income.

3-2-5. Life Course of the Successor's Wife

The successor's wife was born as a daughter of an office worker in this region. She graduated from a commercial high school, and was working in a company. One of her friends asked her to attend a party organized by young farm successors, and there she got acquainted with her current husband.

In 1994, she resigned from her company in order to get married at the age of 24, which was the standard age to marry in this rural area at that time. It was unusual for young women to willingly marry a farm successor, and thus her marriage received a lot of attention. She had no hesitation in getting married with a farm successor and living with his parents because she was brought up in a three-generation household.

Following her marriage, she gave birth to three daughters in 1996, 1997 and 2000. Her family role has been household chores and childcare. Thus, she doesn't have any knowledge of agriculture.

In 2002, the Agricultural Cooperative in this region opened a direct sales store. The manager's wife advised her daughter-in-law to cook and sell her handmade box lunches by using organic vegetables cultivated by her. In the manager's wife's opinion, her daughter-in-law was skillful at cooking. The manager built a kitchen for her. The successor's wife was willing to begin taking part in the processing and selling division of her family farm. Currently, she occasionally serves as the lecturer in the cooking school in her community. She found her new talent.

3-2-6. Characteristics of this Mother and Daughter-in-law Dyad
The farm work of this family is divided by gender, i.e. the males are engaged in rice farming, and the females are engaged in planting, processing and selling organic vegetables. Therefore, the mother and daughter-in-law are cooperative, and they fulfill their needs complimentarily. This generational relationship between the mother and daughter-in-law is due to their new business in the direct sales store. They could achieve their own personal position in a family farm. Moreover, the parents-in-law came to be more helpful to the daughter-in-law in taking care of her children, and the degree of generational integration in this co-residence developed.

However, the profit from the direct sales store is deposited into the manager's wife's account. The daughter-in-law cannot achieve a legitimate position in family farming just yet. It depends on the timing of the farm transfer from the manager to the successor, although the manager has no specific plans for retirement.

3-3. Family C in Hokkaido
3-3-1. Family Management Agreement
This dairy farming family signed the first agreement in 2002 because the manager was the chairman of the City Chamber of Agriculture. In 2004, the successor's wife gave birth to the first son, and therefore the agreement was revised.

3-3-2. Farm Management
The founder of this dairy farm is the grandfather of the current manager. He settled in Hokkaido and started dairy farming with a milking cow in 1934. When the current manager married in 1970, the management scale had been enlarged as follows: 60 cows including 40 milking cows, and milk production of 200t per year. The current management scale has reached as follows: 90 milking cows and 35 heifers, and milk production of 660t per year in 2006. Its working force consisted of the manager, his wife, the first son and his wife. However, currently the successor's wife is on child-care leave. There is no special information about farm work allocated to the manager's wife in the document, because she is engaged in farming almost as much as the manager and the successor.

In the document, it was planned that the farm management transfer would be in 2009 when the current manager turns 62.

3-3-3. Family Life

Each couple has its own independent residence on the same premises. However, before the birth of the successor's first child in 2004, they shared the bathroom and the kitchen of the manager's residence. In the manager's wife's opinion, the young mother would benefit from this independence by acquiring better domestic skills.

The agreement provides that all family members cooperate in the child care. However, it is also added that the successor's wife is the main person in charge. According to the manager's wife's suggestion, the child care is allotted mainly to the successor's wife, i.e. the child's mother.

Monthly salary for the young couple is 150,000 yen. It is for their pin money, food, commodities and child-care expenses. The expenses for electricity, heating, insurances, gasoline and automobile inspection are excluded.

3-3-4. Life Course of the Manager's Wife

The manager's wife is from the same district. Although her parents ran a small-scale dairy farm, she disliked helping with the farm work. Because her younger brother was a farm successor, she had lived in a store as a salesgirl away from her parents since she was a junior high school student.

After graduating from high school, she worked at a shoe store and took charge of accounting for 5 years. She grew tired under the strain of daily overtime work, and assumed that farmers would be able to work in their family farm at their own pace. She was introduced to her current husband who was a graduate from the same high school by a friend and she got married at the age of 23.

Her husband entered the agricultural technical college after graduating from high school, and following this he went to the U.S. and studied dairy farming under large management scale for a year. He married at the age of 25, three years after he returned from abroad and began to engage in family farming.

Her marriage, co-residence with the parents-in-law, initiation into the dairy farm and giving birth to the eldest son almost coincided. She had never worked in her father's farm before her marriage, and therefore she left the child care to the mother-in-law, and made an effort to learn dairy farming under her husband's guidance. The farm work was hard enough for her to have a miscarriage twice. Five years after the birth of the eldest son, the eldest daughter was born when she was 29 years old.

She has not taken care of children. The daughter-in-law said that she was a so-called sandwich-generation woman, i.e. her mother-in-law brought up her children, and her daughter-in-law is bringing up her grandchildren.

In spite of her lack of childrearing, she has secured her personal position in producing more than 30 kinds of vegetables for her family and friends independently.

She prefers vegetable farming to child care.

3-3-5. Life Course of the Successor's Wife

The successor's wife was born as office worker's daughter in Osaka. After studying English in a two-year college, she worked in a company in Osaka. However, she gradually realized that she was not suited for office work and she did not want to marry an office worker.

She had a dream to marry a fruit farm successor because peaches were her favorite fruit. When she was 26 years old, she participated in an excursion in Hokkaido which was organized in order to introduce single women to farm successors to consider marriage. During the excursion she saw cows nearby for the first time. She was overwhelmed by their huge size and attracted to dairy farming. The next time, she tried to stay at a dairy farm in Hokkaido. There, a calf sucked her fingers and she was enchanted by its charm. This occurrence made her determined to change her occupation. The day after getting back from this farm stay, she resigned from her company.

At the age of 27, she began to work on a dairy farm in Hokkaido as a live-in temporary worker for 6 months, and then looked for a dairy farm successor as her partner. A principal of an elementary school in the region introduced her to her current husband. She got married at the age of 30 in 2000.

Right after her marriage, she began to engage in family farming. Due to hard work in the dairy farm, she had a miscarriage 3 times and at last gave birth to the first son at the age of 34 in 2004. Following this, she gave birth to the second son at the age of 35, and she is currently on child-care leave.

It is written in the document that the successor's wife will be engaging in farming again after her children enter nursery. She intends for them to enter a pre-school after they turn 4.

3-3-6. Characteristics of this Mother and Daughter-in-law Dyad

In this case, the degree of generational integration in farming is high. The manager, the manager's wife, the successor and the successor's wife are all engaged in dairy farming, although the successor's wife is currently on child-care leave. The successor's wife selected dairy farming as her occupation after engaging in office work. The manager's wife was also engaged in office work before her marriage and she recognizes that farming is preferable to office work. This mother and daughter-in-law share an occupational preference. In addition to this, both of them suffered a miscarriage two or three times. Their similar life experiences made them closer.

The degree of generational separation in the co-residence is nevertheless high because the manager's wife wishes her daughter-in-law to be independent within the family as well. Furthermore, the manager's wife prefers vegetable farming to child care because of her lack of childrearing skills. She has established her personal position in planting vegetables. This mother and daughter-in-law keep a moderate distance.

4. Comparison and Conclusion

The aim of this study was to clarify the generational relationship of farming women within a stem-family household focusing on the mother and daughter-in-law dyad in current Japan, according to a case study of farming families executing the Family Management Agreement.

In this study, the current mother and daughter-in-law dyads in farming families were analyzed based on the nationwide survey of farming families executing the Family Management Agreement. The Family Management Agreement had been introduced for establishing the personal position in a farming family, especially women's status, and modernizing farm management by carrying out partnership among family members.

In order to examine the generational relationships between the mother and daughter-in-law, three model cases were shown where the mother and daughter-in-law were present, the latter still engaged in childbirth/child-raising, and the data from semi-structured interviews both with the mother and daughter-in-law were obtained.

The relationships between the mother and daughter-in-law can be seen from a life course perspective. The course of one's life is a chain of events dependent on age and determined by when and what events one experiences. The mother and daughter-in-law have passed across different life courses according to historical and social conditions. Besides their life course, the degrees of generational integration in a co-residence and in farming were analyzed.

The main findings from the comparison of these three families are as follows:

1) These mothers-in-law had achieved their personal positions in farming[8]. Their daughters-in-law should also be able to follow them.

2) In a traditional stem-family household, the mother-in-law was expected to keep her commodity management right until her retirement even though other household chores were handed over to her daughter-in-law right after her marriage [Kamiko &

---

8) Based on the interviews with farm families executing Family Management Agreement, Nishiyama stated as follows. In the traditional integrated stem family, married women, especially young women, could not state their own opinion, they had to repress their desires and be tolerant of collective views, and they had neither free time nor free space, i.e. they could not go out freely because they had to dedicate all of their time to their family life and farm work under the patriarch. However, farming women are able to keep and to join a wide range of social activities in the community, and they achieved freedom and independence in terms of money, time and space have currently [Nishiyama, 2004].

Masuda, 1976]. However, these three daughters-in-law have been in charge of domestic duties including the commodity management right after their marriage.

3) When the mother and daughter-in-law do not share home environments before their marriage like Family A, the mother-in-law is expected to give her daughter-in-law extra consideration. In the case of Family A, the mother-in-law is engaged in farming and her daughter-in-law is in charge of domestic duties. This division of labor between the mother and daughter-in-law isolates the daughter-in-law from the other family members.

4) The daughter-in-law of Family C is one of the new types of farming women who selected farming as their occupation. In this case, the mother and daughter-in-law are able to share an occupational preference.

5) Even though the mother and daughter-in-law do not share an occupational preference, it is possible for them to be cooperative in their farming and fulfill their needs complimentarily like Family B. In the case of Family B, the daughter-in-law's domestic skills contributed to the development of a new business in their family farming and generational integration in their co-residence.

References

Kamiko, Takeji and Koukichi Masuda eds., 1976, *San-Sedai Kazoku* (Three-Generation Families), Tokyo: Kakiuchi Shuppan. (in Japanese)

Kawate, Tokuya and Mima Nishiyama, 1998, "Kazoku Keiei Kyoutei no Kouka ni kansuru Kousatsu (Family Management Agreement and Its Effect to Establish a Partnership for Farming and Household within a Rural Family in Contemporary Japan)," *Journal of Rural Studies,* 9: 21-32. (in Japanese)

Morioka, Kiyomi ed., 1985, *Family and Life Course of Middle-Aged Men.*

Morioka, Kiyomi and Kazuo Aoi eds., 1987, *Gendai Nihonjin no Raifukosu* (Life-course of the Modern Japanese), Tokyo: Japan Society for the Promotion of Science. (in Japanese)

Nagano, Yukiko, 2005, *Gendai Nouson ni okeru "Ie" to Josei* (The Ie and Women in Contemporary Rural Communities), Tokyo: Tousui Shobou. (in Japanese)

Nishiyama, Mima, 2004, "Nougyo Keiei Tenkai to Kazoku Kankei no Henyou Katei (Change in the Agricultural Management and Changing Process of Family Relationships)," *Wakate Kenkyu-Sha Nouson Josei to Kenkyu Ronbun Shu,* (Collection of Study Thesis about Rural Women by Young Researchers), Tokyo: Yaguchi Mitsuko Kinen Kenkyu Syourei-Kai, 175-207. (in Japanese)

Otomo, Yukiko, 2003, "Kagyo Keiei-Tai no Sonzoku-Senryaku (A Strategy of Family-business Succession)," *Shakaijouhou Ronsou,* 7: 89-110. (in Japanese)

―――, 2006, "Generational Change in Career Formation of Farming Women and Agricultural Policy in Postwar Japan: A Case of Katsunuma Town," *Shakaijouhou Ronsou,* 10: 33-59.

―――, 2007, *Kazoku Keiei Kyoutei Teiketsu-Jirei ni miru Kazoku Kankei no Sedai Henka*

Chapter 3: Women Balancing Family and Farming 123

(Generational Change in Family Relationships of Farming Families Executing the Family Management Agreement), Report of Grant-in Aid for Scientific Research. (in Japanese)

Sato, Hiroko, 2007, *Kazoku no Hensen Josei no Henka* (The Change of Farm Family and Farm Women from 1980's to 1990's), Tokyo: Nippon-Hyoron-Sha. (in Japanese)

Sugaya, Yoshiko, 1985, "Doukyo-Seikatsu no Sedai-teki Henka (Generational Change in Living Arrangement: A Rural Three-Generation Family Study)," *Journal of Miyagi College for Women,* 62: 29-56. (in Japanese)

The National Institute of Population and Social Security Research, Japan, 2000, *The Second Survey of Japanese Family Households Report.*

Tsutsumi, Masae, 1999,"A Lifecourse Study of Stem Family Women in Rural Japan: A Comparison of the Changes over Three Generations," *International Journal of Japanese Sociology,* 8: 117-140.

―――ed., 2000, *Women and Families in Rural Japan,* Tokyo: Tsukuba Shobo.

3
Experimental Study on Work Life Balance of Women Farmers in Japan
Michi Tsutsumi

1. Introduction
1-1. Purpose and Assumption
1-1-1. Purpose
This paper is aimed at considering the necessary conditions in different cultures and systems. Recently, Japan is facing an era of undeniable population decline with declining birthrates, a growing proportion of elderly people, and the rapid spread of globalization. It is said that the trend of the falling birthrate is a prevailing condition in advanced countries including Japan. However, there are countries that improve this condition by creating support plans for women and families at the stage of childbearing and child-rearing. These measures have become key national policies in present Japan. To achieve a society where positive energies exist, creating an environmental situation is needed, in which the individual can voluntarily select various possibilities and his/her abilities can be demonstrated to its maximum. However, in the current state of Japan the situation of exists for which where an individual cannot lead a hopeful life, because of the problems of long working hours, less flexible working environments, and unstable job situations. This influences problems the home, the local society and it is related to labor force, problems.

In such a situation's, there has been research done into worker's work life balance but, there is no research on individual proprietors including agriculture and especially farmers. It is important that farmers straighten out their work life balance in each stage of their lives.

1-1-2. Assumption
I have the hypothesis that farmers in Japan still have the sexual divisions of labor that comes from the role division of labor. When there is a sexual division of labor, I would like to examine reasons and the degress of satisfaction or dissatisfaction that exist for farmens wives. The type of balancing is not 50/50 (work/ child-rearing), but how life fits someone's needs that is the most important thing.

From a point of their life time, I want to examine how women farmers, who are in the child-rearing age, satisfy both work and child-rearing by the allocation of their time, and the "decision-making" is appropriate for needs in their these instance. It is acknowledged that the balance between work and life is based upon the ability to do the decision making.

1-2. Viewpoints of Analysis

The actual situation at the country level can be understood from statistical material. In addition, from research subjects, i.e. women farmers, the family, and a regional system, I want to examine some case studies. I want to clarify the various concrete conditions for women farmers to have and raise children work and participate' in each stage of their lives social activities. I aim to examine what various conditions are necessary in different cultures and systems.

1-3. Literature Overviews

The major researches are Oshima 1992, Katayama 2004, 2005 and 2006. These research papers investigated the support plan for women farmers who give birth and raise a child. Moreover, it investigates the support environment centering on both before and after birth in Japan and France. The realities of the women farmers of the EC and the investigation into the degree of legislation are shown in these research papers. The system in France serves as a useful reference for a case in an advanced country. The balance befween how wonen farmers in Japan work and raise their children and how it becomes the background of the declining birthrate is exanined.

1-4. Characteristics of this Research

The trend of the falling birthrate in advanced countries has already been clarified by statistical material. Moreover, countermeasures to the falling birthrate and the family support plans also are a feature in each country associated with a social security system. It is difficult for independent enterprises including agriculture, to adjust though the key measure in the background of the falling birthrate deals with the workers.

Agriculture protects nature, supports health, and bears a multipronged function. Therefore, this research has the feature of farmer's countermeasures to the falling birthrate to make an empirical analysis.

1-5. Subject Area

The questionnaire survey was done through out Japan. For the respondent selection, the researcher asked the Agricultural Extension Center and JA[1] for assistance. A total

---

1) Japan Agricultural Cooperatives

of 24 people were targeted, focusing on the women agricultural workers. The case study is as follows.

2007 October 25th	Yamanashi Prefecture Katsunuma City (6)
2007 October 26th	Yamanashi Prefecture Minami Alps City, and, Kofu City (4)
2007 October 29th	Kanagawa Prefecture Isehara City (1)
2007 December 10th	Hokkaido Hokuto City (2)
2007 December 13th	Wakayama Prefecture Kinokawa (2)
2007 December 14th	Wakayama Prefecture Hidaka (2)
2007 December 17th	Hokkaido Wakkanai City (1)
2007 December 20th	Aichi Prefecture Kariya City (1)
2007 December 21st	Aichi Prefecture Nagoya City Moriyama Ward (1)
2008 January 7th	Kumamoto Prefecture Kamoto (1)
2008 January 18th	Kumamoto Prefecture Koushi City (1)
2008 January 21st	Chiba Prefecture Yachimata (1)
2008 January 22nd	Chiba Prefecture Tomisato City (1) Total: 24 people

1-6. Survey Contents

The investigation targeted the women farmers in the child bearling or child rearing who are in their twenties, thirties, and forties. The following were understood.

(1) Women farmers' actual work, managerial participation circumstances, change in the way of working and the aspects were understood.

1) The actual work and way of working: ①The subject is chiefly engaged in the child care and housework. ②She is chiefly engaged in agriculture. ③She is chiefly engaged in work other than agriculture. ④Others. The investigation items were divided into these four categories, and the researcher tried to determine to which category a respondent belonged to.
2) The managerial participation situation was divided into the following four categories and the researcher tried to determine to which category a respondent belonged to.
   ① There is no discussion concerning farm management, and other familiy members decided on their own.
   ② There is a discussion concerning the farm management however, the respondent does not present a case.
   ③ The subject sits in on the discussion concerning the farm management however, the respondent does not present a case.
   ④ The subject sits in on the discussion concerning farm management and the respondent speaks her opinion.
3) The role and the standpoint in the labor for farming were divided into the following

four categories and the researcher tried to determin which category a respondent belonged to.

①The subject is engaged only in farm labor as directed by the husband and parents or others. ②In the same standpoint as the husband and parents, she is engaged in firm labor based on her own intentions. ③In the standpoint directed the husband or parents; she is engaged in the labor for farming. ④She is not engaged in the labor for farming.

4) In the questionnaire survey, presentation of a case, and the reason for 1) was understood. At that time, the period was set for the future. About 2) and 3), the hopes in the present and for the future was understood.

5) During the interviews: About 1), the change of the content between the marriage and present was understood. ①, ②, ③, ④ each contents change was understood. ⑤When, ⑥what reason (factor), ⑦how it changed or whether it had been maintained was understood.

About 2) and 3), the change in the way of working was understood at the marriage time and present time.

6) During the interviews, the realities of the child care: "How did you take care of a child?" was understood.

7) In the questionnaire survey, about the attributes of the women farmers and the household; ①age, ②cohabitation family, ③child of cohabitation or separation, ④farm produce revenues, ⑤most two title goods and amount of sales, ⑥cultivation area, were understood.

8) During the interviews, about the attributes of the women farmers and the household: ①date of birth, ②birthplace is a farmhouse or non-farmhouse, ③marriage date, ④prenuptial career or experience of famer, ⑤marriage, change, and present, and two high-ranking commodities of sales amount and area and breeding numbers, ⑥transition and factor of social participation from marriage, ⑦method of acquiring agro technology and management technology, ⑧transition and factor of life management from marriage time, ⑨ascertain presence and content of agreement of family management were understood.

2. Dynamic Trends in Population, Agrarian Labor and Way of Working in Japan

2-1. Dynamic Trends in Population of Japan

In 1966, the population of Japan was 99 million 36 thousand people, and it exceeded 100 million people for the first time in 1967. The overall population of Japan reached 127.77 million people in 2006. However, it is forecasted that the population of Japan will decrease in the future (Table 3-3-1).

2-2. Agrarian Labor

In 1975, total population of farmers in Japan was 23.19 million people, but it rapidly decreased to 8.37 million people in 2006. The ratio of the population of farmers to the overall population was 6.6% in 2006 a decrease from 21.0% in 1975. It is understood that the male/female agricultural work force has decreased especially in the 15-59 (Table 3-3-2).

The male population of agricultural work force, in the 15-59 year old age bracket, was 1 million 835 thousand people in 1975 but, it decreased 885,000 people, dropping below one million people in 1990. In the statistical data in 2006, it decreases to 465,000 people (about 1/4). There were 3 million 574 thousand female farm workers who held the majority in 1975. However, the population of women farmers in 2006 shows a sharp decline to 572,000 people (1/6). However, male farmers of 65 years or more hardly had any change from 1.14 million people in 1975 to 1.1 million people in 2006, between 1975 and 2006, the number of women farmers has decreased by about 142,000 people. It is not clear why the population of the agricultural work force is not different with men.

The level that exceeds the majority of the farmers consists of employed farmers of

Table 3-3-1 Overall Population of Japan: 2006 from 1966

Year	Population (Unit: 1000 people)		
	Total	Male	Female
1966	99,036	48,611	50,425
1970	103,720	50,918	52,802
1975	111,940	55,091	56,849
1980	117,060	57,594	59,467
1985	121,049	59,497	61,552
1990	123,611	60,697	62,914
1995	125,570	61,574	63,996
2000	126,926	62,111	64,815
2001	127,316	62,265	65,051
2002	127,486	62,295	65,190
2003	127,694	62,368	65,326
2004	127,787	62,380	65,407
2005	127,768	62,349	65,419
2006	127,770	62,330	65,440

Source: Ministry of Internal Affairs and Communications: Statistical Resarch and Training Institute

Table 3-3-2 Population of Farmer

Unit (1,000 people)

Year	Total	Population of agricultural work force	Male			Female			Ratio of population of farmer to overall population (%)
			Total	15–59 years	60 years old or more	Total	15–59 years	60 years old or more	
1975	23,197	7,907	2,975	1,835	1,140	4,932	3,574	1,358	21.0
1980	21,366	6,973	2,674	1,532	1,142	4,300	2,943	1,356	18.4
1985	19,839	6,363	2,478	1,227	1,252	3,885	2,369	1,515	16.5
1990	17,296	5,653	2,249	885	1,364	3,404	1,758	1,646	14.0
1995	12,037	4,140	1,767	608	1,159	2,372	1,053	1,320	9.6
2000	10,467	3,891	1,721	533	1,187	2,171	793	1,378	8.3
2002	9,898	3,751	1,667	495	1,172	2,083	731	1,352	7.8
2003	9,647	3,684	1,645	485	1,160	2,039	706	1,333	7.6
2005	9,400	3,622	1,621	471	1,150	2,000	679	1,321	7.4
2006	8,370	3,353	1,564	465	1,100	1,788	572	1,216	6.6

Source: Ministry of Internal Affairs and Communications

60 years or more. From this tables, it shows the decrease of young workers who forge the future and this can be perceived to be remarkable.

2-3. Transition of Japanese Women Farmer's Way of Working

Recently, hope and circumstances have changed greatly, for example in the relationships men and women's approach to their work and domestic life. From figure between 3-3-1, the number of both double income and lone income exceed, since the ratio of both male and female people who think, "Women should keep working even if they have children" has risen. The number of double-income households in Japan increases every year after 1980. Double income households exceeded single income households in 1997. The margin of increase is a growing phenomenon. Double-income households numberd is 9.88 million, and single income households, numberd 8.63 million in 2005. Households consisting of six year old children or above for the youngest child in the double-income household occupies more than half.

From the Figure 3-3-1, it indicates that the number of double-income households are increasing today. A proposal that parents can have the number of desired children, are to be provided with support to families raising children, especially, support to ease financial strain, on increase in educational allowance, and an increase in the amount of the child allowance is required.

A proposed measure focus on reducing an economic cost or a aguaranteed wage at the bearing and child-rearing period. However, from the time the child is born, there is a reality of the extravagantly amount of child support or educational expenses needed to be covered until advanced education ends. The high expense of education is one of

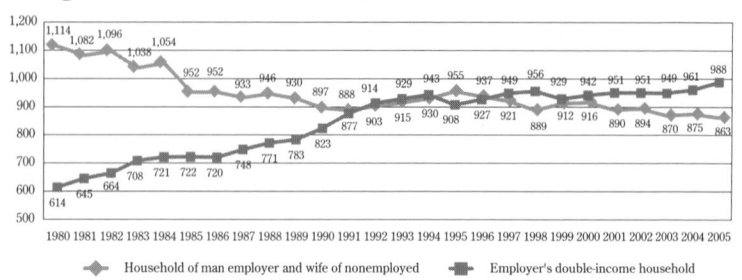

Figure 3-3-1 Transition of the Number of Double-Income Household

Source: Cabinet Office, Government of Japan 2008

the factors behind the falling birthrate.

3. Result of Research Analysis

Initially a survey was taken all over Japan. 276 were distributed to married couples of which 248 (97%) responded. From among those, an intensive hearing survey of 19 cases was carried out. Hereafter, two results of the surveys are described[2].

3-1. Analysis of Japan Wide Questionnaire

1. Respondent to a Questionnaire's Attribute

(1) Response Situation According to Wife and Husband

Information married couple farmers who answered the investigation are shown Figure in 3-3-2, A high percentage of both husband and wives were between the ages of 30 and 34 years of age. In comparison, the percentage wives in the younger ratios was high and there were a lot of husbunds in the over 40 group.

Figure 3-3-3, it shows 49.4% of wives are chiefly engaged in housework and child care, and 41% are engaged in the agrarian labor, while 85.1% of husbands are mainly engaged in agricultural work.

(2) Response by each Household's Circumstance

Household attributes are shown in Figures 3-3-4, 3-3-5, 3-3-6, and 3-3-7. We were able to receive a lot of answers from formers who owned and cultivated land under the category of 4.0~10.0 ha, followed next small scale farmers 1.0 ha to 2.0 ha and larger scale farmers in the 10.0 ha to 20.0 ha group.

As is shown in figure 3-3-5, the management crops of "Poultry farming" is 0.4%,

---

2) The data investigated with Dr. Yotaro Arima who belongs to Japan Agricultural Development and Extension Association, is used.

Figure 3-3-2 Age of Married Couple Respondents

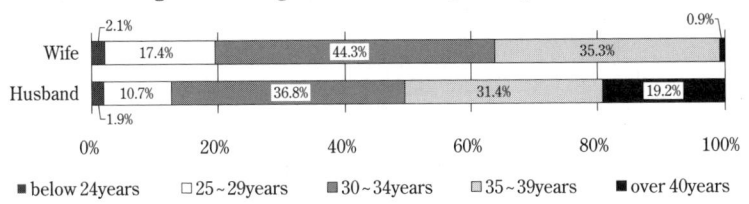

	below 24years	25~29years	30~34years	35~39years	over 40years
Wife	2.1%	17.4%	44.3%	35.3%	0.9%
Husband	1.9%	10.7%	36.8%	31.4%	19.2%

Figure 3-3-3 Task allocation Among Married Couples in Their Daily Lives

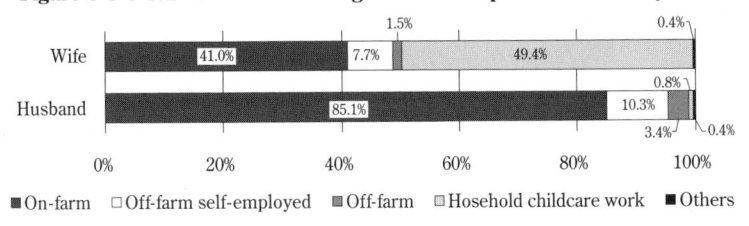

	On-farm	Off-farm self-employed	Off-farm	Household childcare work	Others
Wife	41.0%	7.7%	1.5%	49.4%	0.4%
Husband	85.1%	10.3%	0.8%	3.4%	0.4%

"Facilities vegetable", and "Fruit" are about 20% respectively.

Figure 3-3-6 and 3-3-7 shows, Family Management Agreement is concluded in 71.3% of farms, and the recongnition farmer exists in most farms.

Figure 3-3-8 shows that extended family of the third generation (46.4%) and the fourth generation (33.0%) has a high proportion of way of living. The nuclear family composition is 19.2%.

Figure 3-3-9 shows that with the exception of child in an elementary school, the rest of the data was roughly, equally distributed.

Figure 3-3-10 shows that more than half of the respondents and extended families live in the same house, moreover, it accounts for about 80% when residing on the same site was included.

It linked to these "Status of Living Situation" and "Presence of Family Management Agreement" is related to the child care, housework, and the agrarian labor of the women farmer who is in a birth or raising children period. It is an attribute for which the answer population parameter is secured.

3-2. Result of Case Study Interviewd

The author took 19 people (13 women and 6 men). These 19 subject people were selected from the respondents of a nation wide survey. In this study, we examined how their work/life balance was kept fased on their daily life schedules. Women famer's result of analysis is presented here. These 13 cases were classified by farm management for

Figure 3-3-4 Cultivation Area

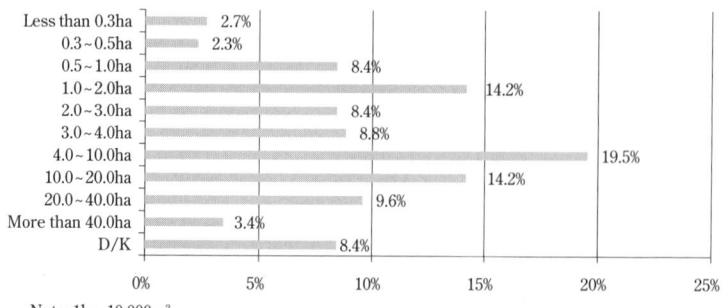

Cultivation Area	Percentage
Less than 0.3ha	2.7%
0.3~0.5ha	2.3%
0.5~1.0ha	8.4%
1.0~2.0ha	14.2%
2.0~3.0ha	8.4%
3.0~4.0ha	8.8%
4.0~10.0ha	19.5%
10.0~20.0ha	14.2%
20.0~40.0ha	9.6%
More than 40.0ha	3.4%
D/K	8.4%

Note: 1ha=10,000m^2

Figure 3-3-5 Cultivated Crops

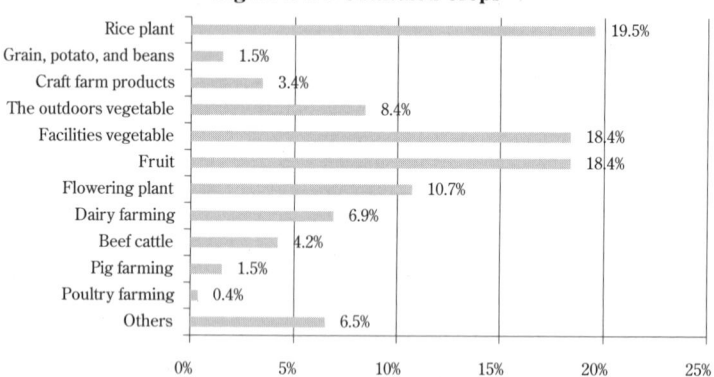

Crop	Percentage
Rice plant	19.5%
Grain, potato, and beans	1.5%
Craft farm products	3.4%
The outdoors vegetable	8.4%
Facilities vegetable	18.4%
Fruit	18.4%
Flowering plant	10.7%
Dairy farming	6.9%
Beef cattle	4.2%
Pig farming	1.5%
Poultry farming	0.4%
Others	6.5%

Figure 3-3-6 Presence of Family Management Agreement

	Conclusion	Non-Conclusion
Presence of Family Management Agreement	71.3%	28.7%

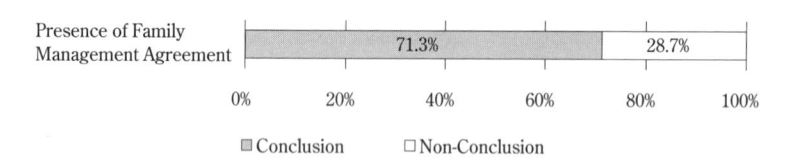

Figure 3-3-7 Presence of Recognition Farmer

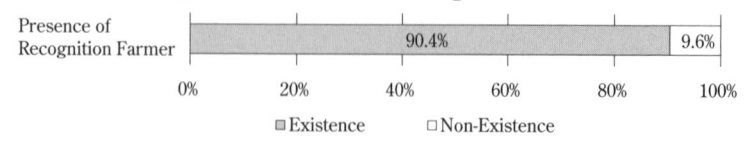

	Existence	Non-Existence
Presence of Recognition Farmer	90.4%	9.6%

Figure 3-3-8 Family Structure

- Nuclear family: 19.2%
- 3rd generation extended family: 46.4%
- 4th generation extended family: 33.0%
- D/K: 1.5%

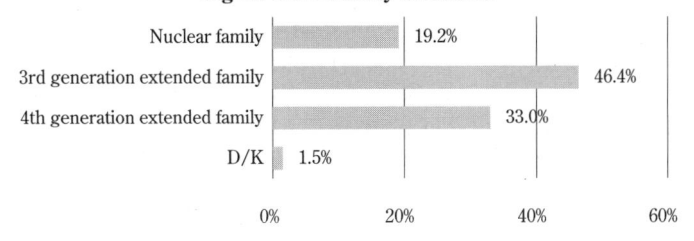

Figure 3-3-9 Number of Households According to Child's Life Stage

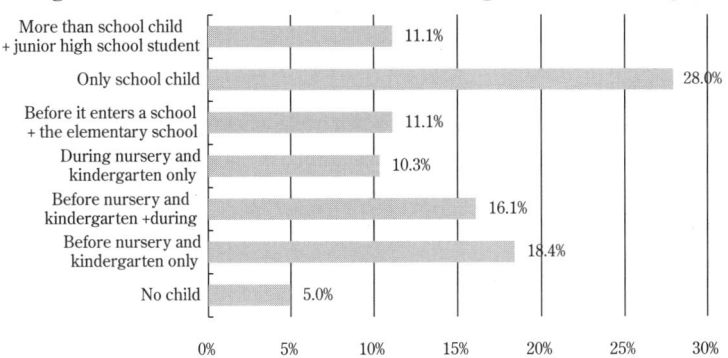

- More than school child + junior high school student: 11.1%
- Only school child: 28.0%
- Before it enters a school + the elementary school: 11.1%
- During nursery and kindergarten only: 10.3%
- Before nursery and kindergarten +during: 16.1%
- Before nursery and kindergarten only: 18.4%
- No child: 5.0%

Figure 3-3-10 Status of Living Situation

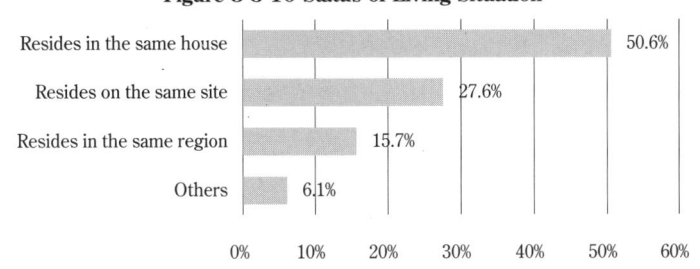

- Resides in the same house: 50.6%
- Resides on the same site: 27.6%
- Resides in the same region: 15.7%
- Others: 6.1%

relations and position of doing agriculture work. The results of five of these case are (1) 6 of 13 subject women "sit in on the discussions concerning the farm management, and give their own opinion" and "In the same standpoint as other families, and engaged in the farming based on their own intentions." They are occupied in an independent position of both the home and the labor for farming.

6 wives (Cultivation of cucumbers, tomatos, mini tomatos, rice, alley vegetables, asparagus, peanuts, mandarin oranges, and grapes)
As for the tendencies to the common features of this 6 people, it is given that their child has already gone to kindergarten, a day nursery, elementary school, junior high school, or high school.

All these 6 people are registering "Management income and expenditure and labor for farming" therefore, they understand the total sales of farm products in 2006.

5 people are suggested by the member of agricultural popularize and have signed a Family Management Agreement. The reason why the 1 person did not sign with the Family Management Agreement is that there is no necessity because management is steady.

Work life balance
All 6 people focus their lives on their children while engaging in farming. There are 3 wives who do not have so many differences during farming season on a busy day and during the off season of when they are not busy.

The reason these three people were without a difference was their life pattern

Characteristics of life time: 1 of 6 subject women
Case 1   A3's Daily Routine

Farming season (December)		Farmer's leisure season (July)	
4:50	Wakes up and does preparation of her. The manages the field in front of the house, does washing and cleaning.	7:00	Wakes up
		7:30	Breakfast, dress up of children and cleanup
		8:30	She drops off her children at the nursery
6:30	Children get up, she makes children's breakfast.	9:00	
		9:20	Returns home
7:30	Breakfast, dress up of child	9:40	Dry clothes in the sun
8:30	She drops off her children at the day case center.	12:00	She goes to fresh farm center
9:00	She goes to the office and 5 places of fresh farm center	13:00	Lunch
			It takes about 1hour delivering to fresh farm center (two places).
12:30	She returns to the office (On the way, have lunch in the car.) Irrigation of the rice field in a different location is seen.	15:00	
		15:30	Returns to the office
13:00			
14:00	She returns to work. Begins harvest of mini tomato and cucumber	17:30	Work ends and picks up children
17:30		18:00	Goes back home, and prepares dinner, runs hot water for a bath,
18:00	Picks up her children	18:30	
	She returns to home once, goes back to the office again. *Maintenance and harvest of garden farming	19:00	Gives children a bath
19:00		20:00	Dinner (While watching TV.)
19:20		21:00	Cleans up with husband
	Runs hot water for a bath, prepares dinner, and takes a bath with the children.	21:30	Reads book or play with children
19:45		22:00	Child going to bed
20:45	Eats dinner. (30 minutes)		
21:00	Plays with children and watch TV/DVD She sleeps with children.		Going to bed

could not be changed because the attending school and going home time of the child set.

The bedtime of the child is not changed. Therefore, their husband or the cohabiting family lend a hand with household duties
- Three wives get up earlier than usual during the farming season; they return to the house before the child goes to school interrupting the in agricultural work. They return to the agricultural work again after handling the cooking washing, and sending off their child.
- When the child comes home, they return to the home and prepare their dinner. Two of three wives are shortening work hours more than the husband. They change the content of work and, they live as much as possible around the child.
- One wife's child is already a high school student therefore; she is engaged in the agrarian labor as much as her husband. The housework has been allotted within the family.
- All six wives are pressed by work during the busy farming season, but they try to live around the child. They are also working at the farmer's off season, though they take time for their child and lead an easygoing way of life. For that reason, it was not possible to be around their family, especially their child during the farming season.

They can hardly have any private time during the farming season. Nevertheless, while the child was in to school, or after the child went to sleep, they cut down sleeping time occasionally and made their own time for relaxing, some private time.

Regarding the evaluation of housework and the child care, all six people did not seem to feel dissatisfied very much. The reason comes from the great factor that their families allotted housework and child care. (Child care, cooking, cleaning, washing, grocery shopping, and bathing, and putting out the garbage.)

(2) Farm management, involvement and status of doing agricultural work: The subject wife sits in the discussions concerning the farm management, and gives her opinion. She is engaged only in the agricultural work as directed by her husband.

<u>Works at a Lily Garden</u>
She is working while watching one year old child and two years old child on the premises. Therefore, she cannot get a responsible job yet. Because the husband is recording the management revenue and expenditures, and the agricultural work list, she only roughly understood the total sales of the farm products in 2006. She doesn't remember the content so much though she knows that she signed a Family Management Agreement. Her husband has employed the mother-in-law and her.

<u>Work life balance</u>
Her life pattern changed into the child center after the child began to go to the day

nursery.
- She helps at work selecting lilies between 1 and 5 p.m. because there are an insufficient number of people during the busy farming season.
- There is no agriculture work during farmer's off season, and she is spends her time with her child or doing house work.
- During both the busy and off seasons, she make time for herself when her children are sleeping. During the off season she sometimes leaves the children in the care of her parents (at their home) and she is slowly spending more time by herself (private time).

She doesn't especially have any dissatisfaction with house work or childcare. She takes care of the cooking, cleaning, washing, child care, grocery shopping, dropping of and picking up her children at the nursery and cares for her child when he/she is sick. Her husband is in charge of the children's bath and taking out the trash. This he does in cooperation with his wife. She hopes to take charge of the housework with more assistance from her husband in the future. She occasionally experiences mental irritation with the housework and childcare, however, she hardly feels any physical overload. She can not take part in many outside activities besides her agricultural work

Characteristics of life time: Subject woman
Case 2   KC1's Daily Routine

Farming season (May)		Farmer's leisure season (July)	
6:00	Wakes up and gets dressed Breakfast and dress her children	6:00	Wakes up and gets dressed Breakfast and dress as her children
8:30	drops off children at school, then starts work	9:00	Drops off children at the day nursery by car
9:00	(separate lily)		Washing, cleaning and cleanup Prepares lunch (take care the youngest child)
12:00	Lunch is taken with mother	12:00	Lunch time
13:00	Starts work (separate lily) Picks up her children at 5pm	13:00	Cleans up, go to shopping
17:00	Prepares	14:00 15:00	Works while playing with the children (sorts the pay slips.)
17:30	Takes bath with the children		
18:00	Dinner is taken	16:30	Picks up children
20:00	Prepares children for bed.		
		17:00	Goes back home. Prepares supper Takes care children
21:00	Bed time for children		
23:00	go to bed	18:00	Take bath with the children
		19:00	Dinner time
	*children is playing there when they are working in the warehouse.	20:00	Bed time for children, and cleanup
		21:00	
			Goes to bed
		23:00	

Chapter 3: Women Balancing Family and Farming   137

because she is still busy at raising children. She relieves her stress by playing with her children and taking care of her fish in her fish tank.

(3) Farm management involvement and status of doing agricultural work. The subject sits on the discussions concerning farm management, and doesn't give her opinion. She is in the situation of being engaged only in the agricultural work directed by her husband.

One wife (works at a lily garden)
She started to help doing agricultural work when her children went to Kindergarten. She doesn't know the total sales of farm products in 2006, and she doesn't know whether to sign the Family Management Agreement.

Work life balance
Her pattern of life changed after her child started going to Kindergarten. Because her child is still young, her working house are shorter than her husbands because she gives priority to child-rearing.

In February, which is the farmers off season, the amount of lilies decreases and she is

Characteristics of life time: Subject woman
    Case 3   CB's Daily Routine

Farming season (June)		Farmer's leisure season (February)	
6:00	Wakes up and gets dressed, makes breakfast laundry	6:00	Wakes up and gets dressed, make breakfast Laundry
7:30	Eats breakfast	7:30	Eats breakfast
8:30	Takes children to bus terminal	8:30	Takes children to bus terminal
9:00	Go to workplace		
12:00	Lunch	9:00	Goes to workplace
	Washes the dishes (after a meal)	12:00	Lunch
13:00	Starts working		Washes the dishes (after a meal)
		13:00	Starts working
15:30	Picks up children, and goes to shopping	15:30	Picks up children, and goes shopping
		16:30	Makes dinner, takes in the laundry
17:00	Takes children to workplace (selection of lily, and pack in a box)	18:30	To supper 19:30
17:30	Makes dinner	20:00	Takes bath with the children
18:00			
	Dinners time	21:00	Bed time for children Cleans up and, Preparation for breakfast on the next day Prepares for next days breakfast
18:30	Takes bath with the children		
20:00	Bed time for children		
21:00	Cleanup and, Prepares for next days breakfast	23:00	Goes to bed
23:00	Goes to bed		

not busy. She centers her life around her child and the pace of her life slows down.
- During the busy farming season in June when the collection of cargo of cut flowers is bustling, she picks up her children at 3:30p.m. At 5p.m. she takes her children to the workplace and selects flowers or packs them in cases.
- During the busy forming season and the off season, she makes time for herself when her children are sleeping.

Presently, she doesn't have any dissatisfaction with the housework or childcare. She is taking charge of everything, i.e. dropping off and picking up her children at extracurricular actives, cram school, and Kindergarten or when they have a fever, giving the children a bath and overall childcare. Her husband also helps with the children's care in some ways. She is also taking charge of all the housework, i.e. cooking, laundry, house cleaning, taking out the trash, cleaning the garden and around the house. It is not necessary to get assistance from her husband now. She thinks that she wants her husband to do his part in the future when that time comes.

She often has mental irritation or stress with the housework and childcare. She also, sometimes feels physical fatigue. As a method to relieve her stress, she vents her stress by rearing her children at home and going shopping alone.

(4) Farm management involvement and status of doing agricultural work: They sit in on discussion concerning the farm management, and don't give their her opinions, and they are not engaged in agricultural work.

Two wives (cattle farmers)
A common feature of the two wives is, their children are still young (less than 1 year old) like a pre-Kindergarten or before nursery school child. It is given that they have to take care of their newborn babies.
Another family member is keeping records of all revenue and expenditures and the agriculture work list, therefore, they did not know the total sales of farm products in 2006.

Work/life balance
They have no connection with agricultural work now and are mainly taking care of housework and caring for their children. In the future, they plan to help with the agricultural work as soon as it becomes unnecessary to take care of their children on a fulltime basis.
- They are taking care of their children 24/7 because their kids are still young. Their are not so many changes in their daily routine during the busy farming season or the off-season.

Chapter 3: Women Balancing Family and Farming   139

Characteristics of life time: 1 of 2 subject women
Case 4   W1's Dirly Routine

Farming season		Farmer's leisure season	
6:00	Wakes up and gets dressed	8:00	Wakes up and gets dressed
6:30	Makes breakfast	8:30	breakfast
		9:00	Washing /cleanup and domestic duties
8:30	Breakfast		
	Washing /cleanup, and cleaning	11:00	End time of domestic duties
11:30	Preparation for lunch	11:30	Prepares lunch
		12:30	Lunch
12:30	Lunch		
13:00	Washes the dishes (after a meal) (takes care the children)	13:00	Washes the dishes (after a meal)
17:30	Free period		
	Makes dinner	17:30	Takes care of children
	Eats with the husband		Makes dinner (It takes time because there are two young children.)
20:00	Dinner		
20:30	Gives a bath to children with husband		
	Bed time for children	19:00	Dinner
21:00		20:30	Gives a bath to children cooperate with husband.
	Prepares the bed		
		21:30	Watches TV, and gets settled
22:00	Goes to bed		
		23:00	Goes to bed

Their schedule differs between 3 and 4 p.m. on busy days when they have to deliver sweets and tea to the cowshed and the hour of rising and bedtime are also different on busy days.

· During both the busy farming season and the off season, they do not have any time for themselves. When their children are asleep they are able to make a little private time for themselves.

They take charge of almost all the housework, childcare, cooking and washing at both homes. Their husbands and mothers and fathers-in-law cooperate a lot. However, they sometimes feel the mental burden of taking care of the children 24/7. they are occasionally physically fatigued when they can not get enough rest. Although they almost never have any private time, they really enjoy raising their children.

(5)Farm management, involvement and status of doing agricultural work: There is no discussion concerning the management of the farm, parents or father-in-low decide everything.

Three wives (work at a rosary/peach and grape orchard)
One person works at the Japan Agricultural Development and Extension association although she is on maternity leave now. Her husband is managing the rosary with the mother and father in law. During the busy season and when she is off from work, she

helps out at the rosary. However, she did not know the total sales of farm products for 2006 and she has not signed the Family Management Agreement.

The second person helps out at her parents' fruit (peach) farm. Although the parents are notion agreement that she and her husband will be successors to the orchard, she is preparing to do so, she does not know the total sales of farm products for 2006.

The third person is now working part time at a food company which she was working at prior to her marriage. Regarding her participating in agricultural management, she only helps out with the farm work during the busy season.

Work/life balance

The three wives basically concentrate on childcare, housework and only help with the agricultural work during the busy farming season. We were asked about their Sundays and weekdays when they were not busy. Two said that they take care of the children and do the housework so the others in the family can concentrate on the agricultural work. One wife is newly wed and doesn't have a child yet. She is learning how to make an internet homepage and participates in a course of study on how to sell farm products on the internet.

- All three do household chores on not so busy days.
- During both the busy farming season and off season, two of the wives do not have much private time because their children are still young. Their mother's and father's

Characteristics of life time: 1 of 3 subject women

Case 5 KG1's Daily Routine

Not busy day on Sunday		Not busy on Weekday	
7:30	Wakes up	6:00	Wakes up
7:30	Prepares breakfast	6:30	Prepares breakfast
8:00	Eats breakfast, takes care of children	7:00	Eats breakfast, takes care of children
8:30	8:00~9:00 Watches TV	8:00	Washing /cleans up, and personal affair
12:00	Lunch	10:00	cleanup/washing, takes care of children
13:00	washes the dishes (after the meal) Takes care of children	11:00	10:00~11:15 Watches TV 11:00~11:15 Takes a break
14:00	15:00~15:30 Take break Washing /cleanup	11:15	Prepares the lunch, and takes care of children
17:00	Makes dinner	12:00	Eats lunch and washes the dishes (after the meal)
17:30	Eats dinner	15:00	Watches TV or a DVD, takes a break
18:45	Cleans up	17:00	Domestic duties, makes dinner
19:30	Takes care of children	19:30	Eats dinner
21:30	Domestic duties	23:45	Takes care of children
22:00			
22:15	Goes to bed	24:00	Goes to bed
24:00			
	*Almost 24 hours taking care of children who are unclear 1 years old.		*Almost 24 hours taking care of children who are unclear 1 years old.

in law sometime take care of their children giving them a rest once in a while. One wife does not have any children so she lives a slow life based around housework.

They are not dissatisfied because their lives are based around their children and taking charge of the housework. In the future, they would like their husbands to help with the housework a little more.

4. Conclusion

The way of life has become diversified because women remain single, marry late and have children later in life. These life style changes have income generalized today. Women may often get married, get pregnant, raise a child, work and spend leisure time all in a balanced way, taking into consideration the life designs of the individual, help from the family or social system and the sexual division of labor and how it relates to her life.

Moreover, satisfaction of both work and domestic life becomes a problem not only for the women but also the men. Today, the number of women entering the agricultural industry is decreasing while the number of women who start other work is increasing. Men's participation in parenting is more common in today's society. However, for women who take care of children, working as a farmer becomes difficult if community support is not given.

As a result of this investigation, a point that we were able to find was, women farmers, during the period of time when they were caring for their children, were only able to secure some personal time for themselves when their children went to bed. During the busy farming season, they became too busy to evenly distribute their own time. In their rural communities, child-support services are minimal and nobody takes care of their children besides themselves. They have a hard time making private time. For women farmers, it is difficult to achieve a balance between housework and agricultural work while being confronted with the responsibilities of child-rearing every day.

As for agriculture, due to the advancement of mechanization, the sexual division of labor has been disappearing in recent years. Two income families will increase in the future, in farming households, the traditional division of labor is still widespread. Why is farmers work life balance a problem? The sexual division of labor accomplishes a conventional role in business. Heavy labor has decreased because of information and technology progressed recently, but the work of a man and women is still fixed. The situation is one that the sexual division of labor is fixed as it is in the family role. In the hypothesis, women famers are not dissatisfied with it though they want to improve the traditional sexual division of labor. It's interesting to note how they see this gap. Moreover, there are two ways to effect balance, such as responded balance of each life stage, and balances for the long term. The women farmers tried to effect the balance for the long term.

In Japan, the M-shaped starting work pattern is still a general tendency. However, it is hoped that the women farmer who makes all commodities becomes a trapezoid type starting work pattern for the balance of work and life.

The following needs exist when the nation, the community, and for society consider what kind of support is necessary for young women farmers. As future tasks, it is a necessary matter of course to support training in housework and the child care for husbands. And also, it is necessary to support training of married couple participation, companion and network making, technological training as employment support to farmer, secure enough helpers during child-rearing and nursing care, and the training of technology and IT.

This paper was presented at the 12th World Congress of Rural Sociology: International Rural Sociology Association, on July 6-11, 2008 in Republic of Korea. This edition include, the most recent revision.

Reference
Cabinet Office, Government of Japan, 2008, *Shoshika Hakusho,* Tokyo: Saeki Insatsu. (in Japanese)
―――, 2007, *Kokumin Hakusho,* Tokyo: Jijigahosha. (in Japanese)
Japan Statistical Association, 2008, *Sekai no Toukei.* (in Japanese)
Katayama, Chie, 2004, "Nougyousha no Shussan Zengo no Hatarakikata Yasumikata: Furansu no Seido no Jissai to Nihon no Jirei kara," *Kosodate shiyasui Kankyo Zukuri ya Chiikikan no Tayou na Kouryu Katsudou nado wo tsujita Chiikizukuri,* 1-40. (in Japanese)
―――, 2005, "Shussan Zengo no Nougyousha heno Shien-Furansu-Japanizu Shussan Kyuka wo Chushinni-," *Kosodate shiyasui Kankyo Zukuri ya Chiikikan no Tayou na Kouryu Katsudou nado wo Tsujita Chiikizukuri,* 1-50. (in Japanese)
―――, 2006, "Ikujiki ni aru Joseinougyousha heno Shien," *Kosodate shiyasui Kankyo Zukuri ya Chiikikan no Tayo na Kouryu Katsudou nado wo Tsujita Chiikitsukuri,* 31-71. (in Japanese)
Maruo, Naomi, Hiroyuki Kawanobe and Yasuko Matoba, 2007, *Shusshoritsu no Kaifuku to Waku Raifu Baransu,* Tokyo: Chuohoki. (in Japanese)
Oshima, Masako 1992, "Kaigai niokeru Joseinougyousha no Tachiba," Nouson Josei Mondai Kenkyukai ed., *Mura wo Ugokasu Joseitachi,* Tokyo: Ie no Hikari Association, 203-228. (in Japanese)
Rural Life Research Institute, 2002, *Rural Life Research Series,* 55. (in Japanese)
―――, 2004, *Rural Life Research Series* 60. (in Japanese)
Rural Women Empowerment and Life Improvement Association ed., 2007, "Nouka Josei no

Hatarakikata no Henka to sono Youin," *Shussan Ikujiki Josei Nougyousha Katsudo Shien Jigyo Houkokusho*. (in Japanese)

Chapter 4

The Roles of Female Farmers

In Chapter 4, community activities of farming women, women's roles, social norms and worries about others that hinder social activities, gender equality and family management agreement will be discussed. Farming women's activities play an important role in forming and reviving a community. Today food safety and security has become a social issue. People now pay more attention to the food system. But most consumers are concerned with just their own food and not the system or the environmental problems. Even though increasing attention is now paid to the food issue, it has not reached fundamental levels. Also, the convention, social norms, and worries about others that prevent the realization of a gender-equal society will be explained. The importance of cooperating and sharing tasks such as caring for children or the elderly for promoting equal relationships will be pointed out. How the family management agreement influences family relations and role sharing will be discussed, based on an experimental study in three regions.

1
Can Farm Women's Activities Reconstruct the Community?*

Mima Nishiyama

1. Introduction

Agricultural Globalization is progressing all over the world, and global competition leads to unfair situations and social insecurity all over the world [Stiglitz 2006; Oxfam 2006]. It also leads to a greater distance between food production and consumption and unawareness about local food. The increased distance between food production and consumption is one of main reasons for the food problems and food company scandals, purposeful mislabeling of food products, falsification of expiration dates, chemical contamination and so on. A lack of awareness about local food leads to an unconsciousness of local issues and a disappearance of traditional local activities.

On the other hand, many new activities related to food have emerged in rural areas, for example, farmers markets, farm stays, restaurants, cooking classes, conduction of rural-community food events and so on. Many of them are conducted by women farmers because women farmers have learned useful skills and acquired knowledge to produce and process food for a long time [Negishi 2000, Ichida 2005]. Then, I focus on the issue that women farmers have played dual roles as producer and consumer of foods because they have engaged in agriculture both as a producer and they have taken daily meals as a consumer. These skills and knowledge have been handed down from generation to generation for a long time. Women farmers' knowledge and experience in agriculture, for example, appeal to urban people at farmers' markets. At the same time, farm women can share some of their interests and sense of life with urban people as a consumers. Farm women's knowledge and experience of being both a producer and a consumer helps them communicate with urban people.

We know various problems exist in our society, such as environmental, agricultural and social justice issues, and some of these are closely related to the food system because the characteristics of the society reflects on the form of food supply and consumption,

---

* This Paper was based on the presentation at the 12th World Congress of Rural Sociology: International Rural Sociology Association, on July 6-11, 2008 in Republic of Korea. This edition includes the most recent revision.

as Lappe (1991) expresses by her notion that "food is good entry point". But I point out that the local food movement, "Chisan-chisho (produce locally, consume locally)", has not been developed to solve or control various problems in our society, although Chisan-Chisho is the first movement that is aware of the concept of local region. We conclude that local food movements are recognized as movements related only to food. The area of Chisan-chisho activities do not expand from food to other local issues. Then, we expect the emergence of a new channel to sell domestic agricultural products for producers [Nishiyama and Kimura, 2005, Kimura and Nishiyama, 2008]. We also pointed out that, judging from the results of hearing investigations, consumers are conscious only of food safety, and not so interested in the food system, even though they are taking part in the Chisan-chisho movement. They are also interested in issues related to their own issues, that is, mainly their own health and global issues that are expressed through global warming, they responded when we asked about their area of interests related to food and the food system (Nishiyama *et al.*, 2007). We can point out that both producers and consumers don't have any sense of connection between their daily lives and local issues.

I would like to analyze the activities of women farmers in order to examine the reconstruction of the community. When I examined the reconstruction of the community, I focused on the expansion of the area of interests of the community members. I believe that the community members can manage and solve their problems by themselves in a developed community. I expect that farm women's activities related to "local" food leads to better communication and connection between community members. Subsequently, they can solve other problems via their network within their community. At the same time, the area of interests of community members expands gradually in the process. We analyzed two cases of rural activities by women farmers. The reasons why I choose these two cases are as follows: the first reason is that they are typical activities related to local food. The second reason is that the activists are women farmers. However, their activities involve not only rural but also urban people.

2. Objectives

I investigated two activities: "Kusunoki (camphor tree)" is located in the Kamimihara district of Minamiboso-city of Chiba prefecture in central Japan and "Okamisan Ichi (Women's market)" is the women farmers' network association located in the town of Shimanto-cho in Kochi prefecture, in western Japan.

The "Kusunoki" building had been used a public elementary school. When the city authority decided to close the school due to the decrease and lack of students, the community residents discussed and decided to re-use the building as an accommodation to lodge visitors. They also decided to manage it by themselves. The reason they decided to re-use of the school building is that almost all the residents had graduated from that school, and they all are familiar with the building; a big camphor tree in the schoolyard at the entrance of the school is a major symbol of their community. Activity at "Kusunoki" started in December 1997. I interviewed two key people of "Kusunoki" in December, 2006. One person is the leader of the women's group. The other is the administrator of "Kusunoki". Both of them are residents of this community.

About 200 women farmers who lived in 18 communities in Towa-village are members of "Okamisan Ichi". Towa-village merged with other villages and became a part of the city of Shimanto in 2006. Towa-village consisted of 18 communities and was located in a mountainous area. "Okamisan Ichi" has three main activities. The first is a farmer's market in the Towa-village. The second is their farmers' market in capital city of Kochi prefecture 2.5 hours from Towa-village. The third is an event that takes urban residents to Towa village where they are served regional and seasonal meals. Their activities have become more and more active year by year. For example, they are starting to serve local meals at a restaurant in the village, inviting school students in the village, eating together and so on. I interviewed 6 people who were taking part in the Okamisan Ichi activities in September 2007 and in March 2008. The leader of this activity was included in the interviews.

3. Results—The effect of the activities to the community—
3-1. "Kusunoki" (camphor tree)

Almost all of the community members participate either in directing or managing this accommodation. A group of women work to cook and to provide meals for guests at the accommodation. A group of older women clean up the rooms after guests. A group of elderly men prune the trees and maintain the garden around the building. A group of men serve as security guards during the nighttime. It is mainly the women who manage the accommodation because men are farming or earn money via an off-farm job during the daytime.

A potluck party was held with the people who live next to their community as a part of an event called "Let's talk about food in Chiba," held by the Satoyama-symposium in May of 2005. Each participant brought one or two homemade dishes and they ate their meals together. They talked about ingredients, cooking, the history and cultural background of local food during the party. At that party, they recognized that two customs in their local community were disappearing. One, called "Sagejyu", is a potluck party with using a traditional set of lunch box brought by members of the community and enjoyed in a community setting.

"We got to know the original taste of dishes prepared by members of the community through the custom of Sagejyu."

Residents engaged in the custom of bringing meals to Sagejyu and ate together during community meetings, traditional events, the theater and during picnics. Nowadays, catered meals are usually consumed, and the custom of Sagejyu is disappearing.

Another traditional custom is "Kou" and "Kou dishes". Historically, the local population kept "Kou" to function as a regional mutual aid and religious association for each generation. The meetings of "Kou" were held at a community member's house. The housewife prepared a big meal named "Kou dishes" for participants of the meeting. The meetings were an occasion to get to know cooking recipes and experience dishes skillfully prepared by different houses in the community.

"For example, everyone knew an experienced older lady of a particular household was skillful at pickling vegetables and an other older woman may be known for her ability to prepare dishes made from boiled vegetables." (resident A)

"Residents had appreciated dishes cooked well and the tendency of taste for every family" (resident B)

But the customs of "Kou" and "Kou dishes" have been disappearing over the last 20 years or so. Therefore, they expressed the following about this situation:

"Recently, I can't even get an image of dinner dishes prepared by my neighbors" (resident A)

"Although some elderly women were known for their cooking skills decades ago, I don't know of any elderly women with good cooking skills nowadays."(resident B)

They recognized that their own traditional dishes and customs were disappearing. Similarly, they recognized that there is a lack of communication between residents throughout their daily lives. They also understand that eating together is a very important mechanism to facilitate communications with other people.

"I realized that the experiences related to food promotes communication between people when talking about the taste and ingredients of the dishes that people brought and the cooking skills of people who made them." (resident A)

We can safely assume that everyone can communicate with each other, even though they have more or less knowledge and experiences about community events, traditional customs and local foods, and even though traditional customs are disappearing. Several

Chapter 4: The Roles of Female Farmers   151

times, parties were held with residents in the community. After that, the events called "Sagejyu party" started with urban residents, taking place regularly in Kusunoki. Traditional dishes were prepared for urban residents who visited Kusunoki for the "Sagejyu party".

When they had the chance to eat with the people of the neighboring community, they talked about ingredients, cooking, and history and cultural background of local food. Those occasions of communicating with people from nearby communities in a potluck party enabled them to recognize a sense of community.

They recognized that traditions have been disappearing, and experienced their cultural identity. They discovered the characteristic features and qualities of their own community. This discovery resulted in the revival of "Kou dishes" and the start of new activities which let urban residents experience food from their community. I can point out that the importance of understanding the characteristic features and qualities of their community on their own helps them expand on such activities. Communicating with other communities gives them an important opportunity to discover the characteristic features and qualities of their own community. I can also point out the effectiveness of "Kyoshoku (eating together)" in enabling people to communicate with other people.

The area of "Kusunoki" activities is expanding. They offer not only a chance to eat local food, but also a chance to experience farming or cooking local foods. More than 1600 people visit the Kamimihara district every year. These visitors have a positive effect on the local economy. Old people and especially women can find fulfillment in their work. But it is not clear how this effects depopulation.

3-2. "Okamisan Ichi" (Women's market)

Before the establishment of "Okamisan Ichi", women farmers' activities were based only in their own communities, and consisted only of minor activities. The establishment of "Okamisan Ichi" was led by village authorities who aimed to initiate the Chisan-Chisho movement in this village. Small women farmers' activities in the village were combined into "Okamisan Ichi," and some activities were newly started as a part of "Okamisan Ichi". Every activity is performed by the group, and not by any individual. Hence, "Okamisan Ichi" is a network of group activities covering the whole village.

After organizing "Okamisan Ichi", the people were able to effectively execute these activities. They were able to do this because they could make use of more local resources, local facilities, as well as special products and other things. However, the bigger the size of the organization, the weaker the bond of the participants tended to be. They have some systems to promote their bonds. One is a cable TV system. They use this system to inform a variety of its members. I addition, many meetings are held between each of the group's leaders which leads to good communications between the members.

Second are the ISO initiatives. They started ISO initiatives in order to have their way of farming recognized and the goal of farming by themselves. Much time and many meetings were needed to understand the necessity of the ISO initiatives before starting.

"When I first heard the word "ISO", I thought, what is ISO? It looked very hard." (member A)

"When I first heard the word "ISO", I thought, it was none of my concern." (member B)

Also, much time and many meetings were needed to study how to practice ISO initiatives after starting. But after meetings about studying of ISO, they could answer what ISO is and understand what they should do about ISO initiatives.
"I understood that ISO initiatives enable me to express my daily farming goals in writing. It is not difficult for me." (member C)

These meetings facilitated communication between members and strengthened their bonds. They also talked about their local resources after starting the ISO initiative, and their thoughts about their farming changed.

"We want to know what the roles of our activity are in our society" (member D)
"We want Shimanto River to be preserved clear for next generation" (member E)
"We want to produce safe vegetables for consumers" (member F)
"I recognized that the ISO initiative leads me to live in nature harmoniously." (member A)

Through their activities, they discovered two systems. One is a system that attaches people to their community. Simultaneously, the system establishes bonds between members. The other system recognizes the identity of their community. From their statements, we can understand that their area of interests and activities are expanding. Furthermore, they have become conscious of their responsibilities to consumers and the environment around them.

There was one 80 years-old woman who was participating in "Okamisan Ichi", who, because her community is deep in a mountainous area, had never been outside her community. The community was enlarged to village scale due to the establishment of "Okamisan Ichi". Now, she sometimes commutes to sell her vegetables at the farmer's market in Kochi city. The expansion in the area of their activities gives them an important opportunity to understand their own tradition and culture. The deepened sense of community led to the development of their activities. In addition, they very much understood the identity of their local community and themselves. But the change did not happen overnight.

4. Discussion
—The role of farm women for reconstruction of community—

The two activities let us reconfirm the effectiveness of using suitable, local food and dishes to stimulate the local community. Women farmers cooked local dishes in their homes and for community events. Women farmers also produced ingredients for local dishes, and they are very skillful at producing them. Women farmers support the concept of local food and local meals both as producers and as consumers. I believe women farmers can contribute to the development of the community and to further develop people's quality of life by using this characteristic of being both producer and consumer.

These two cases show that the evaluation of the people's own community and the understanding of its value are absolutely needed in order to use their skills to develop their community. The potluck party in the "Kusunoki" case-study and the formation of a combined community in the "Okamisan Ichi" case-study were important opportunities for them to evaluate their own culture and to find the identity of their community. These two cases also show that it is necessary to communicate with people outside of the community.

It is necessary to understand the values of their own culture, tradition and resources to use local food and to prepare local meals effectively. In order to do so, they need some system that allows them to share the changes in their perception of each other. Furthermore, they should change and develop these activities based on the impact of their change in perceptions. In "Kusunoki," the chance of eating together with people outside of the community became a way for them to spread their impact on other people in the community (Table 4-1-1). In "Okamisan Ichi", there is an ISO initiative. This initiative gave them the power to change their perception. People changed the area of their interests from family and community to a wider area, for example the watershed of the Shimanto River (Table 4-1-2). According to the results of this analysis, we realized that these activities widen both the area of activity and the interests of both activists and participants.

I would like to set forth the results of our research again. I illustrate how the extent of the regional influence by their action corresponds to the area of their interests as an ideal type (Figure 4-1-1). According to the results of our research, we pointed

Table 4-1-1 The Transition of Area of Activity and Interest —Case of Kusunoki—

Key Affairs	Area of the activity	Area of their interest
Closing elementary school Establish lodge "Kusunoki"	Community	Own, Coomunity
Pot luck party "Eating together"	Inter community	Community and inter community

Table 4-1-2 The Transition of Area of Activity and Interest —Case of Okamisan Ichi—

Key Affairs	Area of the activity	Area of their interest
Individual activity in each community	Community	Own, Coomunity
Establish of "Okamisan ichi"	Inter community=village	Community and inter community
Starting Exchange program and ISO initiatives	Wider area, ex: watershed of shimanto river	Community and wider area

Figure 4-1-1 Schematic of Relations between Interests and Activities (Nishiyama et al., 2007)

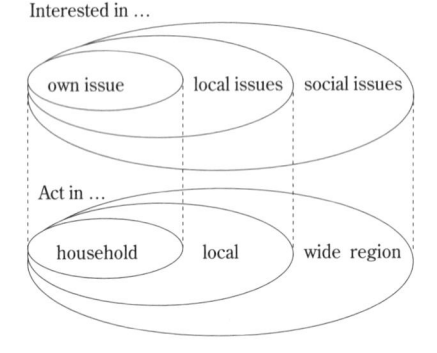

Interested in …
own issue / local issues / social issues

Act in …
household / local / wide region

out that there is no group of informants that is interested in local issues, and no one has some community -based activities voluntarily [Nishiyama et al., 2007]. We can say that their level of interest in local issues and local activities is very low, even though the number of local food movements like Chisan-Chisho movement are increasing all over Japan. Even if people know, not only the slogan of "Chisan-Chisho" but also the meaning of it, they do not understand why local food is important. This shows that they are not interested in their local food or the local food issue itself. The lack of people's interest in local issues may be one of the reasons for why the Chisan-Chisho (local food) movement generally functioned only as a market for consuming local food.

We need to make people realize that their regional food or cuisine can help them solve their problems on their own. We believe that good connections within the community are one of the best ways to develop the community, the society and the people themselves. We point out that it is important to connect local production, how food is prepared and consumed, and their local lifestyle because some of these things are related to their daily problems. We believe that it is one of the best ways to connect local production and local consumption, and that it helps to ensure safe food in a sustainable manner. In the process, it is important to combine people from the producers side to the consumers side to solve food problems, people in the community communicated and formed a link with each other. Hence, I can say that the processes to solve food issues lead to the solution of other problems and issues in the community. The key person to communicate and combine people in the community is a farm woman.

The analysis of farm women's activity showed that their area of activity and interest is expanding from their community or their own issues to a wider area or local issues. We can recognize that farmwomen contribute to the reconstruction of the local community. Further, I believe that their activities have the potential to change and to reconstruct the community.

References

Ichida, Tomoko, 2005, "Sengo Henkakuki to Nouson Josei (Rural Women in Transition of After World War II)," Tabata Tamotsu and Ouchi Masatoshi eds., *Nouson Shakaishi,* Tokyo: Association of Agriculture & Forestry Statistics, 37-62. (in Japanese)

Kimura, Aya Hirata and Nishiyama Mima, 2008, "The Chisan-Chisho Movement: Japanese Local Food Movement and its Challenges," *Journal of Food, Agriculture and Human Values,* 25(1): 49-64.

Lappe, Moore, 1991, *Diet for a Small-Planet 20th Anniversary Edition,* New York: Ballantine.

Negishi, Hisako, 2000, "Noukyo no Joseikigyo Sien-Saki," Mamoru Okabe, Nousonjosei ni yoru Kigyo to Houjin-ka, Tokyo: Tsukuba Shobo, 35-50. (in Japanese)

Nishiyama, Mima and Kimura Hirata Aya, 2005, Alternative Agro-food Movement in Contemporary Japan, *The Technical Bulletin of Faculty of Horticulture, Chiba University,* 59: 85-96.

Nishiyama, Mima, Shinpei Shimoura, Atsushi Maruyama, Shinichi Kurihara, Makito Hirose and Tomoyoshi Matsuda, 2007, "The Analysis of Consumers' interests for Construction of Local Agri-food System," *Japanese Journal of Farm Management,* 45(2): 141-146.

Oxfam, 2002, *Rigged Rules and Double Standards: Trade, Globalization, and the Fight against Poverty,*= Tatsuya Watanabe trans., 2006 *Hinpu-Kousei Boueki-NGO: WTO ni Idomu Kokusai NGO Oxfam no Senryaku,* Tokyo: Sinhyouron. (in Japanese)

Stiglitz. Joseph E., 2006, *Making Globalization Work,* New York: W.W. Norton & Company.= *Sekai ni Kakusa wo Baramaita Gurobalizum wo Tadasu. (Making Globalization Work).* Tokyo: Tokuma Syoten. (in Japanese)

This research was supported by Grant-in-Aid for Scientific Research(C) of Japan Society for the Promotion of Science from 2006 to 2007. Research representative was Mima Nishiyama.

2
The Social Norm and the Awareness of the Constraints of Rural Women in Japan
Masashi Yamashita

1. Introduction

Some of the explanations proffered by the rural population to explain the lack of female participation in social activities include the lack of time due to women's full-time responsibilities on the farm and in the household.

Under the surface, there is awareness among rural women of the constraints that are placed on them due to a systemic barrier, the prescriptive social norm by which their social activities are prohibited, and which governs their existence as women.

It is necessary to clarify the realities of the social milieu in which these women live, the understanding of which can help promote women's participation in the decision-making of the policies that affect them.

This research aims to enhance the understanding of the prescribed social norm that is persistent in the customs and practices of rural society and imposes a barrier to the achievement of equality between the sexes in the rural villages. Moreover, this research clarifies the mechanism by which the barrier to the rural women's social participation is maintained.

2. Method

X City in Akita Prefecture was selected as the location for the case study based on the purpose of the research. Furthermore, the realities of the self-control demanded of women to perform the actions sanctioned by society and the prescribed social norm that imposed a barrier to the achievement of a gender-equal society in the rural village were revealed. This promoted a better understanding of the mechanisms that enable the preservation of the barriers preventing the rural women's social participation.

In November 2003, a survey was conducted among the female members of an

Table 4-2-1 Distribution and Collection of the Surveys

Number of houses	Number of distributions	Number of collections	Collection rate (%)
165	330	137	41.5

agricultural cooperative to assess the awareness of rural women who felt constraints and a survey was initiated to investigate the social participation of two generations of women (mothers and daughters) completed by approximately 300 people in 164 households. The distribution and collection of the surveys were accomplished by mail. Table 4-2-1 presents the number of distributions and collections.

3. Findings and Implications
3-1. Criticism and Slander and Social Sanction at that Time

Figure 4-2-1 presents the generational differences in terms of criticism and slander.

There are clear differences between generations in terms of their reactions to the actions of others; however, there are also commonalities between each generation. One of the commonalities is that judgments are based on appearances rather than on the knowledge of the person.

On the other hand, 25% of the 65 years and above age group thought that "appointment to an official position in the community regardless of the social hierarchy." would be criticized. Along with 21% of the young generation of 20~49 years, who thought the same of "working on the farm in flashy clothing and conspicuous makeup."

The level of social sanction or disapproval received for certain actions is shown in Figure 4-2-2. Many among the 50~64 years and 65 years and above age groups (approximately 25%) felt that it was difficult to go out or to be seen going out.

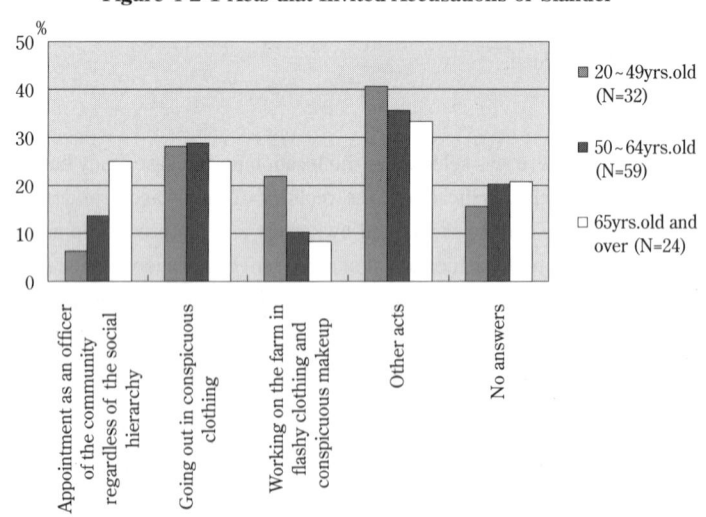

Figure 4-2-1 Acts that Invited Accusations or Slander

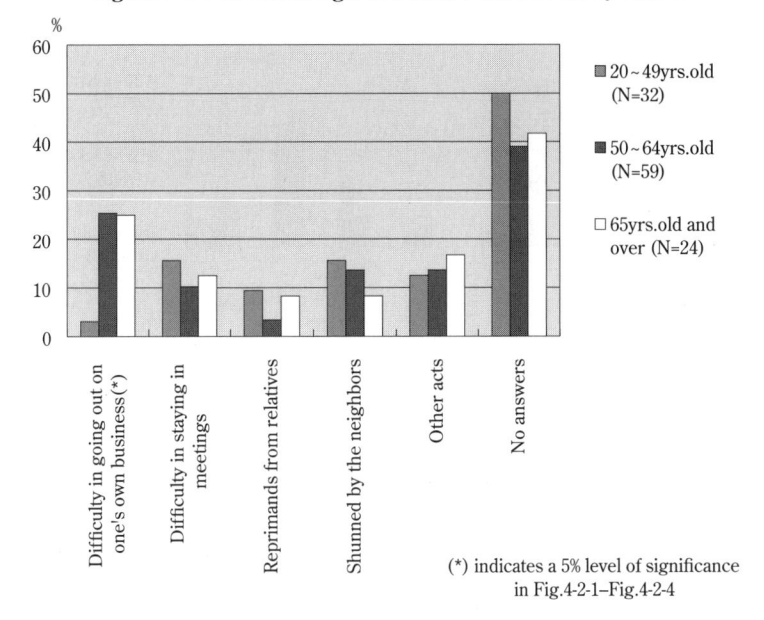

Figure 4-2-2 Sanctions Against Acts in the Previous Question

[Bar chart with categories: Difficulty in going out on one's own business(*), Difficulty in staying in meetings, Reprimands from relatives, Shunned by the neighbors, Other acts, No answers. Legend: 20~49yrs.old (N=32), 50~64yrs.old (N=59), 65yrs.old and over (N=24).]

(*) indicates a 5% level of significance in Fig.4-2-1–Fig.4-2-4

On the other hand, the younger generation, the 20-49 age group, felt ostracized by people from the local community, uncomfortable at regional meetings, and are warned about their behaviors by their relatives. The fact that rural women control their own behavior is evident in the manner in which a woman dresses among the 20~49 age group, and it is evident that there is a difference between the views of the two older generations in terms of defining social order.

Altogether, people of the younger generation are given advice directly from their relatives, while the older generation tends to govern themselves by trying not to go out.

3-2. The Other Parties who Rural Women Feels Impose Constraints on their Public Behavior

Figure 4-2-3 represents the rural women's beliefs about other parties who impose constraints on them when they go out in public, such as to attend meetings and to go to school. There are generational differences in terms of the reaction to women going out. Among those in the 20~49 years age group, the awareness of the constraints imposed is high for mother-in-law (34%) and much lower for father-in-law (19%).

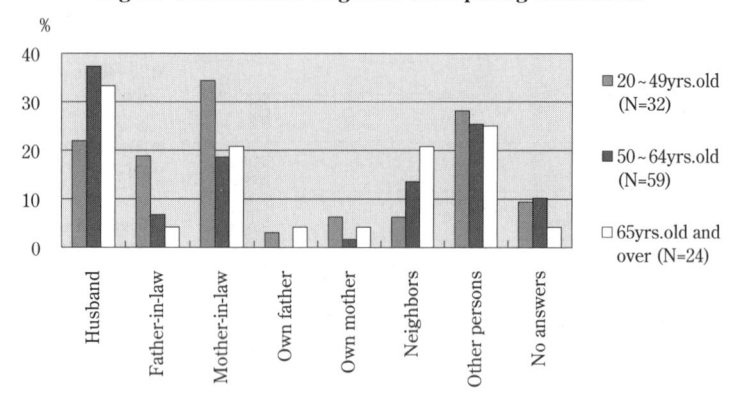

Figure 4-2-3 Persons Regarded as Imposing Constraints

- 20~49yrs.old (N=32)
- 50~64yrs.old (N=59)
- 65yrs.old and over (N=24)

Categories: Husband, Father-in-law, Mother-in-law, Own father, Own mother, Neighbors, Other persons, No answers

However, those in the 50~64 years age group recognize most of the constraints to be imposed by the husband (37%). The 65 years and above age group feels constraints from neighbors more than the other age groups (21%).

Next, we examine the reason for the awareness of constraints being imposed on women to venture out in public. Among the age group of 20~49 years, 22% selected child care and the nursing of their elderly relatives. On the other hand, for the respondents in the 50~64 years age group, agricultural work and housework were found to have high significance (32%). Among the 65 years old and above age group, there was clear anxiety about others watching them and judging their behavior (Figure is omitted).

3-3. The Formation of the Awareness of the Constraints Experienced by Rural Women

It is considered that actions representing gender discrimination, for example the phenomenon where "Only the girl child is compelled to help in the household chores" is related to the formation of the experience of constraints.

Here, a rural woman who was subject to gender discrimination in the home as a child is considered one of the factors that cause the experience of feeling the imposition of constraints. Figure 4-2-4 presents the generational differences in the experience of gender discrimination during childhood. The majority (72%) in the 20~49 years age group reported that "There was no gender discrimination."

On the other hand, many responses such as "Only the girls were compelled to help with the household chores" (63%) and "Punishment for mistakes committed by the boys and the girls was different" (42%) indicated that the respondents in the 65 years and above age group experienced gender discrimination. Specifically, 72% of the 20~49

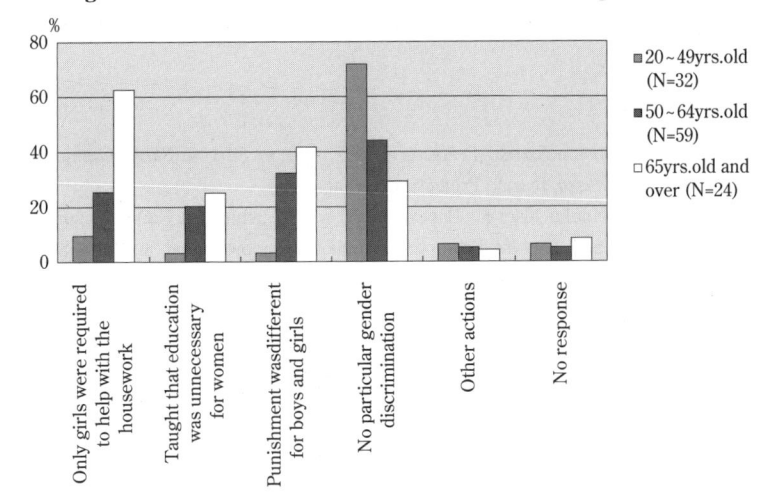

Figure 4-2-4 Gender Discrimination in the Home during Childhood

A bar chart with three series:
- 20~49yrs.old (N=32)
- 50~64yrs.old (N=59)
- 65yrs.old and over (N=24)

Categories (x-axis): Only girls were required to help with the housework; Taught that education was unnecessary for women; Punishment was different for boys and girls; No particular gender discrimination; Other actions; No response.

year age group replied "There was no particular gender discrimination" and yet the 50~64 year age group also had a rather high response rate for "Only girls were required to help with the housework," which indicates the experience of gender discrimination during childhood.

This suggests that there has been a reduction in gender discrimination during childhood, which is regarded as one of the factors of the awareness of constraints experienced by rural women.

4. Conclusion

This paper examined the prescribed social norm in the rural society, which results in the curtailment of the social activity of rural women in Japan based on the results of the questionnaire survey conducted in X city in Akita Prefecture. The survey was conducted among rural women, and it investigated the restraints that rural women felt were imposed on them. It was clarified that each generation of rural women restricts its own actions due to the awareness of the imposition of constraints. More specifically, it was clarified that there is still a persistent prescribed social norm with regard to "Working on the farm wearing flashy clothing and conspicuous makeup" among the youngest generation. Moreover, it was evinced that women feel that they must not go out because their parents-in-law feel that this has an adverse effect in terms of child care and providing nursing to the elders in the family.

The youngest generation especially thought that child care, care for the elders of the family, and cooperation between the family concerning the roles that the younger generations play is indispensable to the future advancement of equality between the sexes in rural society.

References

Life Social Affairs Division Ibaraki Prefecture, 1992, *Josei ni Furi na Shakaikankyo to Jirei Chousa Houkokusho,* Ibaraki Prefecture. (in Japanese)

Tsuru, Eriko, 2003, "Nouka Josei no Enpawamento wo Sokushinsuru Haikei to sono Youin (Background and Factors Promoting Women's Empowerment in Rural Society)," *Journal of Rural Studies*, 9(2): 49-60. (in Japanese)

Yamashita, Masashi, Kiyomitsu Kudo, Youhei Doi and Sumiko Abe, 2006, "Nouson Josei no Shakai Katsudou wo Kobamu Shakai Kiban to Kigane Ishiki (The Social Norms and Sense of Constraint that deters Rural Women's Social Activities)," *Journal of the Rural Life Society of Japan*, 50(2): 18-27. (in Japanese)

3
Career Formation of Farming Women and Agricultural Policy in Postwar Japan: A case of Katsunuma Town[1]

Yukiko Otomo

1. Introduction

The aim of this study is to clarify the influence of agricultural policy on the career formation of the farming women in postwar Japan, according to the life-course analysis of panel data in Katsunuma Town. It is located in Yamanashi, a neighboring prefecture of the capital Tokyo.

The postwar Japanese government improved the institution of independent family farming. From 1947 farmlands were opened for each farm family from pre-modern large farm owners, because of democracy. This agrarian reform made a lot of small-scale family farms in current Japan [Sugioka, 2001]. In 1961 the Basic Law on Agriculture was established and it contributed to the improvement of modernized independent farming families.

In this institution of independent family farming, farming women were expected to be the labor force in their farm operations and thrifty housewives in their family life. Besides Land Reform, Agricultural Cooperatives and the Cooperative Agricultural Extension Service were inaugurated as three big reforms in the field of agriculture, promoted by the General Headquarters of the Allied Armies (GHQ) to democratize Japanese rural society [Ichida, 2000, 58]. Since 1948 the Home Life Improvement Extension Service (HLIES) had been conducted by the Ministry of Agriculture, Forestry and Fisheries. In rural communities many kinds of associations for farming women were established under the direction of governmental Extension Advisors. Moreover, Agricultural Cooperatives also began to promote the improvement of farm-families' daily life in 1970, when they drafted the Basic Plan for Farm Life [National Central Union of Aglicultural Cooperative, 1990]. And the institution of Farm Life Advisors was set up. Extension Advisors and Farm Life Advisors had contributed to

---

[1] This paper was presented at the 21st European Society for Rural Sociology Congress, on August 22-27, 2005 in Keszthly, Hungary. This edition includes the most recent revision.

Table 4-3-1 Family Life Course, School Education Level and Career Pattern of Farming Women in Three Generations

Age, Actual number, Composition ratio

		First generation	Second generation	Third generation
	Total	108	108	36
Family life course	Birth	1882-1913	1921-1942	1947-1967
	Marriage	22.9	24.8	25.6
	Number of children	5.9	2.6	—
	The first birth	24.3	26.1	26.7
	The last birth	37.4	30.9	—
	Birth interval	13.1	4.8	—
School education level	0. No education	3 (2.8%)	0 (0.0%)	0 (0.0%)
	1. Elementary school completed	48 (44.4%)	7 (6.5%)	0 (0.0%)
	2. Junior high school completed	46 (42.6%)	40 (37.0%)	1 (2.8%)
	3. High school completed	10 (9.3%)	56 (51.9%)	13 (36.1%)
	4. Junior college	1 (0.9%)	4 (3.7%)	16 (44.4%)
	5. University level or higher	0 (0.0%)	0 (0.0%)	4 (11.1%)
	6. Unknown	0 (0.0%)	1 (0.9%)	2 (5.6%)
	7. Total	108 (100.0%)	108 (100.0%)	36 (100.0%)
Career patterns	1. Farming and farming	74 (68.5%)	40 (37.0%)	0 (0.0%)
	2. Office and farming	27 (25.0%)	60 (55.5%)	18 (50.0%)
	3. Office and office	0 (0.0%)	2 (1.9%)	1 (2.8%)
	4. Office and housewife	0 (0.0%)	0 (0.0%)	9 (25.0%)
	5. Non-working and housewife	6 (5.5%)	2 (1.9%)	0 (0.0%)
	6. Others	1 (0.9%)	4 (3.7%)	8 (22.2%)
	7. Total	108 (100.0%)	108 (100.0%)	36 (100.0%)

Notes: This table extracted data of stem-family members from collective data of by Tsutsumi (Tsutsumi,1999). The career patterns were simplified from 12 types by Tsutsumi to 6 types.
Source: Tsutsumi, 1999.

the vocational education of farming women and improvement of women's farm-family livelihood. However, at the same time, such a tendency emphasized that the domestic work is for women and the farming work is for men. The gender division of labor in the farm family was thus extended [Otomo, 2000].

In this paper, a panel from the longitudinal study of family change in Katsunuma Town[2], census data and official documents from several sources, such as town office records, central public hall (*Chuo Kominkan*) records and personally kept documentation, were used for the interpretation of generational change in career formation of farming women and agricultural policy in postwar Japan.

---

2) For more details, see pp.211-212.

Chapter 4: The Roles of Female Farmers 165

2. Generational Change in Career Formation of Farming Women
2-1. Life Course Patterns of Farming Women

The number of farming women belonging to the first generation is 108, born from 1882 to 1913, the second generation is 108, born from 1921 to 1942, and the third generation is 36, born from 1947 to 1967. The number of farming women belonging to the third generation is small. However, by comparison mainly between the first generation and the second generation, we can see the generational change in life course pattern of farming women after World War II.

The life course pattern of the first generation is that after having completed compulsory education, they helped their on father's farm, and after their marriage they were continuously engaged in their farming. Their average life course involved marriage at the age of 22.9, and giving birth to an average of 5.9 children, the first childbirth being at the age of 24.3, and the last at the age of 37.4.

However, the life course pattern of the second generation is that after their graduation from high school, they found employment but some years later discontinured their employment to marry (Table 4-3-1). Their average life course involved marriage at the age of 24.8, and giving birth to an average of 2.6 children, the first childbirth being at the age of 26.1, and the last at the age of 30.9 [Tsutsumi, 1999].

2-2. Career Patterns of Farming Women

There is a variety of career patterns of farming women, in terms of their career continuity before and after their marriage. One of the patterns shows uninterrupted engagement in farming or office work disregarding the change in their marital status, while other patterns show a combination of office work before marriage and engaging in farming after marriage. In other cases we have a pattern of women not engaged in any work outside of their family before getting married and after their marriage they normally become housewives.

The farming women of the first generation represent 68.5% of the farming and farming pattern, 25.0% of the office and farming pattern, and 5.5% of the non-working and housewife's pattern.

On the other hand, the farming women of the second generation represent 37.0% of the farming and farming pattern, 55.5% of the office and farming pattern, 1.9% of the non-working and housewife's pattern, and 1.9% of the office and office pattern.

Here we can find that farming women of the second generation have a special feature in their career formation. They began to engage in farming after their marriage and dedicated their lives to their farming labor, because of their shorter birth intervals. They worked as salaried women after their graduation from high school. But they gave up their career at the time of their marriage and after giving birth to their children they began to get engaged in farming as helpers of their husbands. They did not have any farming skills and were instructed by skillful family members.

Concerning the farming women of the third generation, the actual number is really small, but they represent 50.0% of the office and farming pattern, 25.0% of the office and housewife's pattern and 2.8% of the office-office pattern. Some of them had to interrupt their work for a while because of giving birth and bringing up their children.

3. Working Status of Farming Women
3-1. The Number of Women Engaged in Farming

In Japan, the majority of people engaged in farming are women. As shown in Table 4-3-2, "the share of female labor in agricultural labor power has remained at 60% during these fifty years" [Kumagai, 1995, 245]. In 1946, just after World War II, the ratio of females engaged in farming was 54.6% of the total farming population. This composition ratio grew and reached its peak of 62.4% in 1975, after which it began to decrease slightly. In the latest agricultural census (2005) it was 53.3%. Nevertheless, it can be said that the major part of agricultural labor power in Japan has been provided by women.

This nationwide tendency also applies to the Katsunuma area. According to the agricultural census in 2005, full-time farm households in Katsunuma Town occupied 37.8% in farm households. This composition ratio has remained high when compared to that of the national ratio (2005, 22.6%). The composition ratio of males in this town is also a little higher (47.6%) than that of the national ratio (46.7%). Accordingly, the composition ratio of females is 52.4%, which is a bit lower than that of the national figure (53.3%).

The composition ratio of females mainly engaged in farming in Katsunuma Town has been kept generally stable, within 53-55%, since 1970. By observing Table 4-3-3 in more detail, we can recognize three special features.

Firstly, the composition ratio of younger females mainly engaged in farming has diminished. In 1970, the actual number of persons was 148, and the composition ratio was 3.7%. In 2005, the actual number was 17 persons, and the composition ratio was 0.7%, in spite of the age range being increased in the youngest age-group to 15-19 years of age in 1995.

Secondly however, the composition ratio of older females mainly engaged in farming increased rapidly. The elderly, by definition in Japan, are the group of persons aged 65 and over. However, the agricultural census data of 1970 used only one age-group to classify persons aged 60 and over, as shown in Table 4-3-3. From 1970 to 2005, the actual number increased by 1.6 times, from 460 in 1970 to 737 in 2005. On the contrary, the total number of people mainly engaged in farming in this town diminished

Chapter 4: The Roles of Female Farmers 167

Table 4-3-2 The Share of Female Labor in Agricultural Labor

Actual number: Persons, Composition ratio: %

Year	Persons engaged in farming		Population (of householed members) mainly engaged in farming	
	Actual number	Composition ratio of females	Actual number	Composition ratio of females
1920	14,208,500	44.9	—	—
1930	14,131,000	45.3	—	—
1940	13,842,600	52.2	—	—
1946	18,486,206	51.7	16,320,822	54.6
1960	19,320,925	56.0	14,541,624	58.8
1965	15,443,345	51.5	11,513,989	60.4
1970	15,618,169	50.9	10,451,956	61.2
1975	13,732,215	49.9	7,907,487	62.4
1980	12,539,197	48.8	6,973,085	61.7
1980*	11,628,692	48.1	6,363,228	61.0
1985*	9,427,734	47.9	5,428,438	59.4
1990*	8,492,968	47.7	4,818,921	59.0
1995*	7,397,594	46.5	4,139,809	57.3
2000*	6,856,469	46.9	3,891,225	55.8
2005*	5,562,030	46.5	3,352,590	53.3

Notes: 1) 'Persons engaged in farming' means the total of farm household members who were engaged in farming at least a day in a year
2) 'Population mainly engaged in farming' means the total of farm household members who were engaged in farming only, and those who were engaged in both of farming and other jobs; the days worked for farming outnumbered those of other jobs.
3)* is in accordance with the new definition among commercial farm households.
Source: Figures in 1920, 1930 and 1940 are taken from the results of the National Census.
Figures in 1946 are from results of the Census of Farm Population.
Figures from 1960 are from results of the Census of Agriculture.

considerably, from 4,009 to 2,269. Therefore, the composition ratio of females aged 60 and over mainly engaged in farming increased from 11.5% in 1970 to 32.5% in 2005, a total increase of 2.8 times.

I would like to discuss now the third special feature. If we mark the age-groups which reveal the highest composition ratio in every year, we can recognize a special group of women, born in the years from 1921 to 1935. In the 1970's, this group, then in their forties, was the highest. There had been two surveys, one in 1970 and the other

Table 4-3-3 Number of Females Mainly Engaged in Farming (Katsunuma Town)

Actual number: Persons, Composition ratio: %

	Age-groups	1970	1975	1980	1985	1990	1995	2000	2005
Actual number	Total	4,009	3,726	3,580	3,244	3,090	2,696	2,485	2,269
	Females Total	2,139	1,994	1,945	1,745	1,664	1,472	1,318	1,189
	16-19	148	79	37	25	16	**18	**37	**17
	20-29	287	195	190	96	54	14	24	19
	30-39	368	343	341	263	226	153	82	40
	40-49	471	461	371	326	307	236	208	143
	50-59	405	421	467	427	353	316	272	233
	60-64	—	187	206	209	226	192	150	156
	65-69	—	131	155	175	207	216	163	148
	70 and over	—	177	178	224	275	327	382	433
	60 and over*	460	495	539	608	708	735	695	737
Composition ratio	Females Total	53.4	53.5	54.3	53.8	53.9	54.6	53.0	52.4
	16-19	3.7	2.1	1.0	0.8	0.5	**0.7	**1.5	**0.7
	20-29	7.2	5.2	5.3	3.0	1.7	0.5	1.0	0.8
	30-39	9.2	9.2	9.5	8.1	7.3	5.7	3.3	1.8
	40-49	11.7	12.4	10.4	10.0	9.9	8.8	8.4	6.3
	50-59	10.1	11.3	13.0	13.2	11.4	11.7	10.9	10.3
	60-64	—	5.0	5.8	6.4	7.3	7.1	6.0	6.9
	65-69	—	3.5	4.3	5.4	6.7	8.0	6.6	6.5
	70 and over	—	4.8	5.0	6.9	8.9	12.1	15.4	19.1
	60 and over*	11.5	13.3	15.1	18.7	22.9	27.3	28.0	32.5

Notes: 1)* In 1970, the ages 60 and over were classified as just one age-group only. A total figure for '60 and over' has been included in future years

2)** The age range was increased to 15-19 years of age.

Source: Census of Agriculture

in 1975. In 1970 the group occupied 11.7%, and in 1975 it was 12.4%. In the 1980's, the group, then in their fifties, was the highest, with 13.0% in 1980 and 13.2% in 1985. Lastly, the group, then in their sixties, marked the highest in the 1990's, with 14.0% in 1990 and 15.1% in 1995. In every survey, the same group of women born in the years from 1921 to 1935 was top.

In Katsunuma Town, this group of farming women, aged 70-84 in 2005, has contributed the most to farming and the women have played extremely important roles. They are just farming women of the second generation of our panel.

3-2. Specialization in Grape Farming and Women's Labor

Why have so many women born during the years 1921 to 1935 dedicated themselves to farming, and why has this period of commitment to farming increased so much? It has been already discussed in a former paper [Otomo, 2000], that one of the reasons is the shortage of farm labor which occurred when young men in farm households started to work in other fields. Women were naturally expected to make up for the shortage.

The shortage of farming labor in Katsunuma Town was caused not only by this, but also by the increased labor demand by the technological innovations in grape

Table 4-3-4 Area of Cultivated Land under Management (Katsunuma Town)

Actual number: ha, Composition ratio: %

		Total	Paddy fields	Normal upland fields	Orchards and Vineyards	Mulberry fields	Others
Actual number	1953	842.4	—	250.4	374.5	81.8	3.7
	1960	911.0	106.0	64.0	687.0	54.0	—
	1965	904.3	48.0	28.4	805.2	15.4	7.0
	1968	916.5	22.0	20.6	871.1	2.8	—
	1970	922.4	15.3	20.7	884.9	1.5	—
	1975	894.7	2.3	19.6	872.8	—	—
	1980	885.0	0.0	10.0	875.0	—	—
	1985	900.0	0.0	3.0	897.0	—	—
	1990	885.0	0.0	2.0	883.0	—	—
	1994	861.0	0.0	5.0	855.0	—	1.0
	2000	830.0	0.0	11.0	818.0	—	1.0
	2004	813.0	0.0	4.0	808.0	—	1.0
Composition ratio	1953	100.0	15.6	29.7	44.6	9.7	0.4
	1960	100.0	11.6	7.0	75.4	5.9	—
	1965	100.0	5.3	3.1	89.0	1.6	7.0
	1968	100.0	2.4	2.1	95.2	0.3	—
	1970	100.0	1.7	2.2	95.9	0.2	—
	1975	100.0	0.2	2.2	97.6	—	—
	1980	100.0	0.0	1.1	98.9	—	—
	1985	100.0	0.0	0.3	99.7	—	—
	1990	100.0	0.0	0.2	99.8	—	—
	1994	100.0	0.0	0.6	99.3	—	0.1
	2000	100.0	0.0	1.3	98.6	—	0.1
	2004	100.0	0.0	0.5	99.4	—	0.1

Source: Industry Department of Katsunuma Town Office

cultivation. In Japan, the size of cultivated land is not so large and farmers must therefore produce better quality farm products by using various technological systems, such as machines, equipment and chemicals in order to make a profit. To implement such systems, Katsunuma grape farming requires a lot of manual labor, and this manual labor is supplied by women. The paradox of the grape production is that its technology requires a lot of manual labor. Besides, according to this generation, the idea that women are more suited to the delicate work of grape producing is commonly accepted.

Table 4-3-5 Area of Cultivated Land for Fruit (Katsunuma Town)

Actual number: ha, Composition ratio: %

		Total	Grapes	Peaches	Persimmons	Japanese plums	Ume apricots	Kiwifruits	Apples	Japanese pears	Others
Actual number	1958	609.7	496.6	102.0	5.9	1.3	0.5	—	—	—	3.4
	1960	687.0	569.6	106.8	4.8	2.0	1.2	—	—	—	2.6
	1965	805.2	643.9	147.3	4.4	3.9	3.8	—	—	—	1.9
	1968	871.1	676.2	174.0	3.6	5.4	6.7	—	—	—	5.2
	1970	884.9	684.4	173.2	3.7	10.3	6.4	—	—	—	6.9
	1975	872.6	731.8	120.0	3.1	10.5	5.6	—	—	—	1.6
	1980	875.0	730.0	110.4	2.0	11.0	3.0	—	—	—	19.0
	1985	897.0	749.0	100.0	5.0	17.0	3.0	—	2.0	—	21.0
	1990	883.0	714.0	125.0	2.0	20.0	3.0	—	3.0	—	16.0
	1994	855.0	696.0	114.0	2.0	18.0	3.0	16.0	4.0	1.0	1.0
	2000	818.0	672.0	104.0	3.0	13.0	3.0	16.0	5.0	1.0	1.0
	2004	808.0	667.0	114.0	5.0	10.0	2.0	6.0	2.0	0.0	2.0
Composition ratio	1958	100.0	81.4	16.7	1.0	0.2	0.1	—	—	—	0.6
	1960	100.0	82.9	15.5	0.7	0.3	0.1	—	—	—	0.5
	1965	100.0	80.0	18.3	0.5	0.5	0.5	—	—	—	0.2
	1968	100.0	77.6	20.0	0.4	0.6	0.8	—	—	—	0.6
	1970	100.0	77.3	19.6	0.4	1.2	0.7	—	—	—	0.8
	1975	100.0	83.9	13.8	0.4	1.2	0.6	—	—	—	0.1
	1980	100.0	83.4	12.5	0.2	1.2	0.3	—	—	—	2.4
	1985	100.0	83.5	11.1	0.6	1.9	0.3	—	0.2	—	2.3
	1990	100.0	80.9	14.2	0.2	2.3	0.3	—	0.3	—	1.8
	1994	100.0	81.4	13.3	0.2	2.1	0.3	1.9	0.5	0.1	0.1
	2000	100.0	82.2	12.7	0.4	1.6	0.4	2.0	0.6	0.1	0.1
	2004	100.0	82.5	14.1	0.1	1.2	0.2	0.7	0.2	—	0.2

Source: Industry Department of Katsunuma Town Office

Chapter 4: The Roles of Female Farmers   171

The area of cultivated land under management in Katsunuma Town began to enlarge gradually since 1953 (Table 4-3-4). In 1953, the composition ratio of cultivated land area for fruit farming was only 44.6%. However, in 1965 it almost doubled to 89.0%. Since 1968, this ratio has constantly reached 95% and over. Table 4-3-5 shows that about 80% of cultivated land for fruit farming has been occupied by grape farming. The grape production industry in Katsunuma Town has grown in the last 50 years by converting cultivated land to grape farming.

Farming women born between 1921 and 1935 began to engage in farming during this period, in which Katsunuma Town industry began to specialize in grape farming and the shortage of farming labor became a problem. It means that farming women of the second generation of our panel began to engage in their family farming when grape farming became the main industry in this town.

4. Social Activities and Career Formation of Farming Women

An old farming woman of the first generation, born in 1905, told me her life history [Otomo, 1993]. "When I was young, there wasn't a variety of local groups for farming women, except the National Defense Women's Association during the war. I gave birth to ten children and I was really busy with bringing them up. Because of that I could hardly take part in any social activities." She was 86 years old when the interview was conducted in 1992. Her case is typical for her generation. On the other hand, the farming women of the second generation gave birth to 2.7 children on the average. Because of their shorter birth intervals (between first and last child), they were able to participate in a variety of social activities in addition to their family farming. The majority of them were engaged in the office work before their marriage and began to engage in farming after their marriage. Their school education and career before their marriage were not consecutive with their farming. Social activities for farming women of this generation had to function as a vocational education. After the war many kinds of residents' associations were settled all around the country to democratize Japanese society. Table 4-3-6 summarizes women's groups and associations in postwar Katsunuma Town. There are a lot of small groups for rural women. Even then, we can find that the main fields of their activities had remained in their home life, welfare, cultural and environmental events.

4-1. The Women's Association (*Fujin-kai*)

After World War II, around 1955 due to the trend of spreading the idea of democracy and woman's emancipation, four Women's Associations came into existence in four blocks of Katsunuma Town forming a union. In this town every woman representing her household had obligation to participate in the association.

Table 4-3-6 Women's Groups and Associations in Katsunuma Town

	Groups and Associations	Period		Main Activities					
		Establish	Dissolve/Separate	Home life	Welfare	Culture	Environment	Occupation	Community
	The Women's Association	1955	about 1975	○	○	○	○	○	○
2	The Department of Mother-Child Health and Welfare	1961	1973		○				
3	The Department of General Education	?	about 1975			○			
4	The Women's Department of the Agricultural Cooperative	?	about 1975	○	○	○	○	○	
5	The Department of General Affairs	1966-1971	about 1975		○				○
6	The Department of Physical Education	1966-1971	about 1975			○			
7	The Department of Service for the Japanese Red Cross	?	1966-1970		○				
8	The Department of Fire-fighting	?	1966-1970						○
9	The Association of Home Life Improvement Practice Groups	1967	2005	○			○		
4	The Women's Department of the Agricultural Cooperative in Iwai Block	1972	—	○			○		
10	Katsunuma Town Liaison Council of Women's Groups	1987	2005	○	○	○	○	○	○
2	The Mother-Child Health and Welfare Society	1961	—		○				
7	The Branch of Japanese Red Cross Society	1955	—		○				
11	The Food Balance Improvement Promotion Committee	1960s	—	○					
12	The Association of Study Groups on Ecological Home Life	1970	—	○			○		
13	The Association of Study Groups on Expenditure	?	2004	○					
14	The Social Support Network for Single Parents	?	—		○				
15	The Association of Volunteer Societies for Social Welfare	1985	—		○	○			
9	The Association of Home Life Improvement Practice Groups	1967	—	○			○		
16	The Women's Department of the Union of Merchants and Craftsmen	1961	—					○	○
1	The Women's Association in Katsunuma Block	1955	1992	○	○	○	○	○	○
17	The Mothers' Volleyball Clubs' Association	?	1991			○			
18	The Association of Women-leaders of the Public Hall	?	1989			○			○

Source: See the list of primary sources pp.181-182.

The aims of these associations were to elevate the standard of women's lives by the power of organization, which could never achieved by an individual effort. It became legitimate for housewives to go out of town on their own for shopping, travel or spend their free time away from their family duties by participating in some social activities of these groups.

The official documents of the Union of Women's Associations were almost lost, except for a few scraps of records from 1965 to 1971 and from 1990 to 1992, which were kept personally or stored in the central public hall of Katsunuma Town.

According to the official record of its annual meeting in 1965, the Union had been managed by the following five departments at that time: the Department of Mother-Child Health and Welfare (*Aiiku-bu*), the Department of General Education (*Kyouyo-bu*), the Department of Service for the Japanese Red Cross Society (*Nisseki Houshi-bu*), the Department of Fire-fighting (*Syoubo-bu*) and the Women's Department of the Agricultural Cooperative (*Noukyo Fujin-bu*).

However, the official record of its annual meeting in 1971 shows that the following five departments replaced the above-mentioned: the Department of General Affairs (*Soumu-bu*), the Department of General Education (*Kyouyou-bu*), the Department of Mother-Child Health and Welfare (*Aiiku-bu*), the Women's Department of the Agricultural Cooperative (*Noukyo Fujin-bu*) and the Department of Physical Education (*Taiiku-bu*). It means that during 1966 and 1970 the Department of Service for the Japanese Red Cross Society (*Nisseki Houshi-bu*) and the Department of Fire-fighting (*Syoubou-bu*) became independent societies. Moreover, in 1973 the Department of Mother-Child Health and Welfare (*Aiiku-bu*) followed them.

During the period of the Japanese hyper-economic growth, from 1955 to 1973, standards of living were elevated. Indeed, vital activities of the Women's Association accomplished improvement in rural life. But at the same time they had to put up with rising costs of living by profitable grape farming. The activities chained farming women to many duties because there were a lot of roles in the organization. Many farming women left the association willingly because the association-related duties became a burden on them. In early 1970's three Women's Associations were dissolved, and only one local association had continued its activities until the beginning of 1992.

4-2. The Association of Home Life Improvement Practice Groups (*Seikatsu-kaizen Kenkyu-kai*)

The Home Life Improvement Extension Service (HLIES) has been administered by the Ministry of Agriculture and Forestry since 1948, just after World War II. A lot of practice groups for home life improvement were formed all around the country under the directions of governmental Extension Advisors.

Table 4-3-7 Number of Home Life Improvement Practice Groups (Katsunuma Town)

Number of group members

	Group name	Area	Establish	1981	1982	1983	1984	1985	1986	1987	1988	1989	1991	1993	1995	2002	2003	2004	2005
1	Katsunuma group	Katsunuma Uwa-machi	1981.4	8	8	8	8		7	7	7	7	6						
2	Yoko-machi group	Katsunuma Yoko-machi	1981.4			14	18	18	18	18	18	18	17	17	17	16	16		
3	Niju-go nichi Kai	Katsunuma	?	7	7	7	7												
4	Himawari Kai	Katsunuma	1994.4													4	4	4	4
5	Sumire Kai	Katsunuma	2004.4															6	6
6	Todoroki group	Todoroki 12	1967.2	26	28	28	28	28	29	29	27	24	19	16	15	12	12	11	7
7	Himawari Kai	Todoroki Shita machi	?	17	7	7													
8	Ayame Kai	Todoroki	1991.4											2	3	3	3	3	3
9	Sumire Kai	Osade	1977.4		20	18	16	5	5	5	5	5	4	5	5				
10	Mutsumi Kai	Osade	?	22	22														
11	Hinode group	Watazuka	1983.4					4	4	4	4								
12	Kyusoku group	Kyusoku	1980.4	9	9	7	10	10	9	9	9	9	8						
13	Katatsumuri Kai	Kyusoku	1982.4			9		9	10	9	9	9							
14	Asunaro group	Kyusoku	1981.4		5	5	5	5											
15	Sakura Kai	Kyusoku	?					5											
16	Satsuki Kai	Yama	1980.4	8	9	9	9	9	9	9	9	9							
17	Yotsuba Kai	Yama	1982.2			12		12	12	12	12								
18	Hishiyama group	Hishiyama	1980.4		48	34	31	30	29	28	25	27	21	25	23	15	15	14	13
19	Syowa group	Simo-Iwasaki	?	5	5	3		7											
20	Sarubiwa Kai	Simo-Iwasaki	1984.4					4	4	4	4	4							
21	Suehiro Kai	Simo-Iwasaki	?	9	9	10	10	10	10										
	Total number of group members			103	171	171	137	168	151	139	129	112	84	65	67	50	50	38	29
	Total number of groups			8	11	14	9	14	13	12	11	9	7	5	6	5	5	5	4

Source: See the list of primary sources pp.181-182.

According to official documents of the Katsunuma Town Office, the first practice group in this town was decided in 1967. At that time their purpose was to improve living standards by reforming the sanitary conditions in homes, e.g. kitchen, bathroom and toilet. The members saved one coin per day for this reform [Katsunuma Town, May 2001, 9]. However, during the period of high growth of the Japanese economy, its goals had changed to the establishment of a more comfortable, affluent home life by personal budget management and income generation. For example, they produced and sold homemade grape jam, recycled garbage for compost instead of spending on fertilizer [Katsunuma Town, May 2000, 7].

During the 1980's many small farming women's groups, seeking to improve the living conditions, were set up (Table 4-3-7). These small practice groups gathered voluntarily through the farming women's network. In the early 1980's, at the most there were 14 groups in this town. In 1986 a National Athletic Meeting was held in Yamanashi prefecture. This big national event also aimed at promoting the development of regional

Chapter 4: The Roles of Female Farmers 175

industry. These small farming women's groups worked for the event as a receptionist committee and they welcomed athletes with special homemade grape juice [Higashi-Yamanashi Chiku Seikatsu-Kaizen Kenkyu-Kai, 1987, 12]. They contributed to the advertising of Katsunuma grapes and to the development of the local industry. After the event, the number of the groups decreased and by today, in 2005, there are only four groups. There is no generational change among these group members, thus the members have aged, most of them, second generation representatives.

4-3. The Women's Department of the Agricultural Cooperative (*Noukyo Fujinbu*)

The origin of Agricultural Cooperatives goes back to Agricultural Associations that were established in 1900 [MAFF]. In 1947 Agricultural Cooperatives were founded all over the nation by democratizing reform of Agricultural Associations. As mentioned above, it was one of the three big reforms in the field of agriculture that was promoted by the GHQ for democratizing rural society in postwar Japan.

According to official documents of Katsunuma Town, in the early years the Women's Department of the Agricultural Cooperatives belonged to each Women's' Association in four blocks of Katsunuma Town. However, the disappearance of Women's Associations meant the disappearance of the Women's Department of the Agricultural Cooperatives. Along with dissolving of Women's Associations in three blocks in early 1970's and in one block in 1992, the Women's Department of the Agricultural Cooperatives were also dissolved except the one in Iwai block where the composition ratio of farming households was high and the office of Agricultural Cooperatives was located there. Since 1972 the Women's Department of the Agricultural Cooperative has belonged to the Agricultural Cooperative in Iwai block.

As mentioned above, Agricultural Cooperatives have been promoting improvement of farm-families' daily life, especially after 1970, when they drafted the Basic Plan for Farm Life, otherwise profitable farm management [National Central Union of Agricultural Cooperative, 1990]. And the institution of Farm Life Advisors (*Seikatsu Shidou-in*) was set up. Farm Life Advisors are almost exclusively women who are trained in home economics. In Iwai block there has been a Farm Life Advisor in the office of Agricultural Cooperative, who has been working for the improvement of the farm family life in this block instead of Extension Advisors for HLIES. Because of that there are no Home Life Improvement Practice Groups in this block.

In this block all farming families are members of the Agricultural Cooperative, and one farming woman per family has been acting in its women's department under the directions of the Farm Life Advisor, e.g. a group providing daily supplies, seminars for healthy family life and farm operation, etc.

Since 1987 a producers' price for grapes has hovered for a long time. In order to make profit by grape farming and because of the greater number of women engaged in farming, farming women were emphasized and empowered to run grape farms. Before a farming woman was only a helper of her family farming, but later on she had to acquire skills to manage it. The Women's Department of the Agricultural Cooperative in Iwai block has held farming women's basic seminars since 1988. Its purpose was to make farming women skillful enough in managing their farms. It was the first step in the empowerment of farming women.

Farming women of the second generation of the panel have benefited by participating in the above-mentioned social activities, and it improved their family lives. However, after continuously working as assistants to their husbands, they were required for the first time to become skillful workers in grape farming and it was a difficult transition for them.

4-4. The Katsunuma Town Liaison Council of Women's Groups (*Josei Dantai Renraku Kyogikai*)

In Katsunuma Town, a lot of small women's groups have been acting in each block and united in several associations. From 1987 to 2005 these associations had formed a liaison council, the Katsunuma Town Liaison Council of Women's Groups (KTLCWG). Each association of the KTLCWG had been officially registered in the central public hall and subsidized by the town authorities. The Liaison Council's official records of the annual gathering in 2004 shows its business plan, which consisted of the year-end charity bazaar, activities for recycling improvement, seminars on ecological problems and gender equality, study tours, a New Year's party for companionship, etc.

When the KTLCWG was set up in 1987, its members were participating in the following 12 associations:

(1) The Mother-Child Health and Welfare Society (*Aiiku-kai*)
(2) The Branch of Japanese Red Cross Society (*Nisseki Houshi-dan*)
(3) The Food Balance Improvement Promotion Committee (*Syoku-seikatsu Kaizen Suisin Iinkai*)
(4) The Association of Study Groups on Ecological Home Life (*Seikatsu Gakkou*)
(5) The Association of Study Groups on Living Expenditures (*Syouhi-seikatsu Kenkyu-kai*)
(6) The Social Support Network for Single Parents (*Boshi Kafu Fukushi Rengou-kai*)
(7) The Association of Volunteer Societies for Social Welfare (*Borantyia Gurupu Rengou-kai*)
(8) The Association of Home Life Improvement Practice Groups (*Seikatsu-kaizen*

Kenkyu-kai)
(9) The Women's Department of the Union of Merchants and Craftsmen (*Syou-kou-kai Fujin-bu*)
(10) The Women's Association (*Fujin-kai*)
(11) The Mothers' Volleyball Clubs' Association (*Mama-san Barei Renraku Kyougikai*)
(12) The Association of Women-leaders of the Public Hall (*Jichi Kominkan Renraku Kyougikai*)

In 1989 the Association of Women-leaders of the Public Hall separated from the Liaison Council and in 1991 the Women's Association and the Mothers' Volleyball Clubs' Association followed next. It was because they were dissolved at that time though each local group kept active status. Only nine associations were left by March 2005. In 2004 the Association of Study Groups on living Expenditures withdrew from the Liaison Council. In 2005 the Liaison Council decided to end its activities with an intention to form larger units, after a period of municipal consolidation[3].

From 1999 to 2001 the articles on these associations were published in the Katsunuma Monthly Town Bulletin (*Kouhou Katsunuma*) in 22 consequent parts. Here we can see briefly what kind of activities was conducted by the nine associations.

4-4-1. The Mother-Child Health and Welfare Society
The headquarters was founded in 1934 for celebrating the birth of the Emperor's heir, i.e. currently the Emperor of Japan. In 1961 the Mother-Child Health and Welfare Society was set up in the Women's Association of Katsunuma Town. Its activity contributed much to decrease the infant mortality of this town [Katsunuma-chou Aiiku-Kai, 1991]. During those days infant mortality in the town was 17.3%. Four years later it decreased to 7.9% because of this society's effort. Lastly, in 1966 this town was honored by the Ministry of Health and Welfare, due to the results of the excellent work done by the society. Just in 1960's there was an advanced growth in Japanese economy and the standard of living in rural areas was prosperously elevated.

In 2001 its main activities were as follows: promotion of bringing up babies on mother's milk, seminars for childcare, baby's dental check-ups, promotion of gynecology medical checkups and prevention of osteoporosis, etc.

---

3) On November 1, 2005, the city of Enzan merged with the towns of Katsunuma and Yamato to form the new city of Kōshū.

4-4-2. The Branch of Japanese Red Cross Society
The Japanese Red Cross Society was established in 1877 and one of the branches was established in Katsunuma Town in 1955. In this town the membership of the Japanese Red Cross Society is obligatory for all households and sequentially, taking turns at each household. However, in reality, housewives of each household are working accomplishing tasks.

The main activities of this branch are as follows: a blood donation campaign, a fund-raising campaign, seminars for first aid, volunteer work at home for the aged, etc.

4-4-3. The Food Balance Improvement Promotion Committee
This committee provided new members training courses for 30 years or more up until July 2000. There had been 113 women who had completed these courses and at that time 40 members among them were consigned as a committee by the town.

When this committee was set up, it acted to improve the living standards of each family in this town. However, through the period of high growth of the Japanese economy, its aim had changed to the improvement of nutritional balance, especially the spread of the low-salt dishes. And now its activity reaches even the health care during the farmer's leisure season.

4-4-4. The Association of Study Groups on Ecological Home Life
This association was formed in 1970 by 60 women for the purpose of making a handmade additive-free 'Miso", soybean paste, which is an indispensable seasoning for Japanese daily dishes. Besides this 'Miso' making, they made soap from used cooking oil. In 2000 the number of its members decreased to 20, they were studying Post-harvest Application, the Genetically Modified Foods, safe-detergent, etc.

A member described in an official bulletin the following, "We are busy for farming, and occasionally we use convenient food to supplement our daily meals. However, sometimes we cook healthy handmade dishes with plenty of love," [Katsunuma Town, August 2001, 11].

4-4-5. The Association of Study Groups on Living Expenditures
The members of this association held study meetings because of being well-educated consumers themselves. They made efforts to get enough knowledge of commodities and had done some activities, e.g. making soap from used cooking oil, making compost from raw garbage, recycling of water, saving rain water for the trees in their garden, etc.

There was no information on when they first started their official bulletin.

4-4-6. The Social Support Network for Single Parents
This is a mutual self-help group of the single parent families. The members study the social-welfare system and enjoy travel and sports together. Moreover, sometimes they are involved in volunteer work in homes for the aged.

4-4-7. The Association of Volunteer Societies for Social Welfare
In 1985 this association was established for community care in terms of the aging society. There were eight groups of 45 members in 2000. The following group was introduced in the official bulletin. It was an amateur puppet-show group of farming women. At that time, the average age of its members was 60. They wrote the scenario by themselves in the local dialect, and presented the puppet show mainly in homes for the aged. The main themes of the performance were family problems of the elderly, bride shortage in farm families, problems about farm successors, etc.

4-4-8. The Association of Home Life Improvement Practice Groups
See above pp.173-175.

4-4-9. The Women's Department of the Union of Merchants and Craftsmen
This union is one of the Public Service Corporations under the Law of Commerce and Industry Association. The women's department was set up in 1961 with main activities such as volunteer work, study tours, seminars, etc. Since 1997 the Union has campaigned to beautify the town. As a part of this campaign the members planted a lot of flowers along the streets and gleaned the empty cans thrown away on the roadside.

Even though there were several kinds of associations, the contents of activities were quite similar and their main themes were home life, culture, welfare and ecology. These were still gender-oriented activities. In the last article on the Katsunuma Monthly Town Bulletin in 2001, a women's advisor of the town office wrote that she hoped, each women's group would continue these activities with a women's touch and sense of female nature. According to this dialog, it is obvious that these activities of women's associations has promoted the feminine gender.

5. Conclusion and Discussion
The aim of this study was to clarify the influence of agricultural policy on the career formation of the farming women in postwar Japan.

After World War II, Japanese government improved the institution of independent family farming. The agrarian reform from 1947 made a lot of small-scale family farms and in 1961 the Basic Law on Agriculture was established. It contributed to improvement of modernized independent farming families.

In this institution of independent family farming, farming women were expected to be the labor force in their farm operations and thrifty housewives in their family life. According to the census data, farming women born during the years 1921 to 1935 contributed the most to family farming in Katsunuma Town.

One of the reasons was the generational change in life course pattern of farming women. Our panel showed that farming women of the second generation, born between 1921 and 1942, began to engage in farming after their marriage and dedicated their lives to their farming labor, because of their shorter birth intervals. However, the majority of them were engaged in the office work before their marriage. Their school education and career before their marriage were not consecutive with their farming. Though several social activities for farming women elevated their status in their communities and in their family lives, the main fields of those activities had remained in their home life, welfare, cultural and environmental events. The gender role division in farm-family lives was thus extended.

Japanese traditional division of labor in a family is gender-oriented: the domestic work is for women and the farming work is for men. Comparing with farming women of the first generation, farming women of the second generation could achieve their career in their family farming, and also take part in social activities. However, most of activities were also gender-oriented.

In 1992 the Goals for Rural Women in the 21st Century and a Mid-to Longterm Vision for Achieving these Goals was formulated, according to the ILO Convention (No.156) Concerning Equal Opportunities and Equal Treatment for Men and Women Workers, Workers with Family Responsibilities. It has led to promoting more vigorous activity for establishing equal opportunities in the decision-making of family farming and communal affairs. In 1999 the Basic Law for a Gender-equal Society went into effect in Japan, according to the Beijing Declaration and Platform for Action of 1995 Fourth World Conference on Women. At the same time the Basic Law on Agriculture was changed into the Basic Law on Food, Agriculture and Rural Areas. Article 26 was developed to promote women's involvement in agriculture. In 2001, the Council for Gender Equality and the Gender Equality Bureau were established within a Japanese Cabinet Office. Every local government in Japan was required to draw its own action plan for a Gender-equal Society. The Katsunuma Human Plan drafted in 2002 emphasized on the following four main fields: promotion of Gender-equality in the family, in the community, in education and in the working conditions. The number of farming women belonging to the third generation of our panel was small, thus we could not discuss them in this study. However, they are standing at the turning point of agricultural policy nowadays.

Chapter 4: The Roles of Female Farmers 181

References

Ichida, Tomoko Iwata, 1995, "Seikatsu Kaizen Fukyu Jigyo no Rinen to Tenkai (How the Home Living Improvement Extension Service was Born and Developed in Post-war Japan)," *Nougyo Sougo Kenkyu*, 49(2): 1-64. (in Japanese)

―――, 2000, "The Gender Issue in the Home Life Improvement Extension Service of Postwar Japan,"Masae Tsutsumi ed., *Women and Families in Rural Japan*, Tokyo: Tsukuba Shobo, 57-74.

Kumagai, Sonoko, 1995,"Kazoku Nougyo Keiei ni okeru Josei-Roudou no Yakuwari-Hyouka to sono Igi (The Appraisal of Women's Work in Farm Family Enterprise)," *Annual Bulletin of Rural Studies*, 31: 7-26, 245. (in Japanese)

MAFF, 1973, *Nourin Gyousei Shi* (The Agriculture and Forestry Administrative History), 11. (in Japanese)

National Central Union of Agricultural Cooperative ed., 1990, *Noukyo no Seikatsu Katsudou* (Activities of the Agricultural Cooperative for Farm Life), Tokyo: Ie no Hikari Association. (in Japanese)

Otomo, Yukiko, 1993, "Sonraku Shakai ni okeru Sapoto Nettowaku no Kenkyu (Ge) (A Study on Support Networks in Rural Community, 2)," *Jomin Bunka*, 16: 1-19. (in Japanese)

―――, 2000, "Women's Status in Agricultural Households," Masae Tsutsumi ed., *Women and Families in Rural Japan,* Tokyo: Tsukuba Shobo, 101-120.

―――, 2003, "Kagyo Keiei-Tai no Sonzoku-Senryaku (A Strategy of Family-business Succession)," *Shakaijouhou Ronsou*, 7: 89-110. (in Japanese)

―――, 2006, "Generational Change in Career Formation of Farming Women and Agricultural Policy in Postwar Japan: A Kaso of Katsunuma Town," *Shakaijouhou Ronsou*, 10: 33-59.

―――, 2008, "Chiiki Shakai ni okeru Josei no Kurashi to Roudou no Henka (The Changes in Life and Work of Rural Women)," Masae Tsutsumi, Sadao Tokuno and Tsutomu Yamamoto eds., *Chihou kara no Shakaigaku* (Sociology from Local Region), Tokyo: Gakubunsha. (in Japanese)

Sugioka, Naoto, 2001, *Kazoku Keiei Kyoutei no Kazoku-Moderu no Tenkan ni kansuru Shakaigaku-teki Kenkyu* (A Sociological Study of Shift in Family Farm Agreement), Report of Grant-in Aid for Scientific Research. (in Japanese)

Tsutsumi, Masae, 1999, "A Lifecourse Study of Stem Family Women in Rural Japan: A Comparison of the Changes over Three Generations," *International Journal of Japanese Sociology*, 8: 117-140.

Primary Sources

Higashi-Yamanashi Chiku Seikatsu-Kaizen Kenkyu-Kai, 1981, 1982, 1983, 1984, 1985, 1987, 1988, 1989, 1990, 1991, 1992, 1993, 1994, 1995, *Hohoemi* (Annual Bulletin of the Home Life Improvement Practice Groups in the East Block of Yamanashi Prefecture). (in Japanese)

Iwasaki Noukyo Fujin-Bu, 1972, *Soukai Shiryo* (The Women's Department of the Iwasaki

Agricultural Cooperative General Assembly Hand-outs). (in Japanese)

———, 1974, 1975, *Seikatsu Dayori* (Annual Bulletin of the Women's Department of the Iwasaki Agricultural Cooperative). (in Japanese)

———, 1976, 1977, 1978, 1979, 1980, 1981, 1982, 1983, 1984, 1985, 1986, 1987, *Fujin-Bu Dayori* (Annual Bulletin of the Women's Department of the Iwasaki Agricultural Cooperative). (in Japanese)

Katsunuma-Cho Aiikukai, 1991, *Aiiku 30 nen no Ayumi* (The Chronicle of Mother-Child Health and Welfare Society in Katsunuma Town 1961-1991). (in Japanese)

Katsunuma-Cho Fujin Dantai Renraku Kyogi-Kai, 1995, 1996, 1997, 1999, *Soukai Shiryo* (The Katsunuma Town Liaison Council of Women's Groups General Assembly Hand-outs). (in Japanese)

Katsunuma-Cho Josei Dantai Renraku Kyogi-Kai, 2000, 2002, 2003, 2004, 2005, *Soukai Shiryo* (The Katsunuma Town Liaison Council of Women's Groups General Assembly Hand-outs). (in Japanese)

Katsunuma-Cho Noukyo Iwasaki Shibu Fujin-Bu, 1988, 1989, 1990, 1991, 1992, 1993, 1994, 1995, *Fujin-Bu Dayori* (Annual Bulletin of the Women's Department of the Katsunuma Town Agricultural Cooperative Iwasaki Branch). (in Japanese)

Katsunuma-Cho Rengo Fujin-Kai, 1965, 1971, 1990, 1991, 1992, *Soukai Shiryo* (The Union of Women's Association in Katsunuma Town General Assembly Hand-outs). (in Japanese)

Katsunuma-Cho Seikatsu-Kaizen Kenkyu-Kai, 1984, 1985, 1986, 1987, 1988, 1989, 1990, 1991, 1992, 1993, 1994, *Soukai Shiryo* (The Association of Home Life Improvement Practice Groups in Katsunuma Town General Assembly Hand-outs). (in Japanese)

Katsunuma-Cho Seikatsu Kenkyu Gurupu, 2002, 2003, 2004, 2005, *Soukai Shiryo* (The Association of Home Life Improvement Practice Groups in Katsunuma Town General Assembly Hand-outs). (in Japanese)

Katsunuma Town, 1999-2001, *Kouho Katsunuma* (Katsunuma Monthly Town Bulletin), 461, 464, 465, 466, 467, 468, 469, 470, 471, 473, 475, 476, 477, 478, 479, 480, 481, 482, 483. (in Japanese)

Yamanashi-Ken Seikatsu Kaizen Kenkyu-Kai, 1986, *Nakama* (Annual Bulletin of the Home Life Improvement Practice Groups in Yamanashi Prefecture). (in Japanese)

4
Effects of the Family Management Agreement on Gender Equality[1]
Yukiko Otomo

1. Introduction

The purpose of this study is to examine the effects of the Family Management Agreement on gender equality in current Japan, according to a case study of typical farming families executing the agreement.

The Family Management Agreement in Japan has been promoted by the Division of Agricultural Extension Service, Women and Youth Affairs in the Ministry of Agriculture, Forestry and Fisheries (MAFF) since 1995. It aims not only to improve the technical and management skills of farmers but also to carry out partnership within farming families and to empower farming women under the policy toward developing a gender-equal society.

Traditional division of labor within a family is gender-oriented: the domesic work is for women and the farm work is for men, but in reality farming women have a great deal contributed to agricultural production. Thus, the Family Management Agreement should be practical for more profitable farm management and also for gaining a gender-equal family life.

Most of these farming families have signed an agreement on the field of farm management, e.g. decision-making policy in farm management, working hours and holidays, farm labor allocation and remuneration for farm work. Moreover, half of them have made an agreement about their family life, e.g. family life allocation, farm management rights transfer, sanitation, working condition, health care, etc. Each Family Management Agreement is composed of several clauses, which cover fields from farm management to family life, according to the family condition.

Over ten years have passed since the beginning of its promotion. The number of farming families executing the Family Management Agreement in 2007 reached 37,721 households [MAFF]. Does it really mean more farming women have come to participate in the decision-making process of farm management? Have women in farming families

---

1) This paper was presented at the 22nd European Society for Rural Sociology Congress, on August 20-24, 2007 in Wageningen, the Netherlands. This edition includes the most recent revision.

executing the agreement achieved their status in family farm management?

2. Gender Issues in Rural Japan

Table 4-4-1 is a chronology of basic facts regarding the change of rural women's status in postwar Japan. We can divide the development of gender issues into three major time periods: after the end of World War II in 1945, after the International Women's Year in 1975, and after the Beijing Declaration and Platform for Action in 1995.

2-1. The Period after World War II

Japan's current gender policy in the field of agriculture started at the end of World War II. The General Headquarters of the Allied Armies (GHQ) promoted three significant reforms in the field of agriculture in order to democratize Japanese rural society. These are the Agrarian Reform, the Agricultural Cooperative and the Cooperative Agricultural Extension Service [Ichida, 2000].

In 1947, the Agricultural Improvement Promotion Law (AIPL) was established and based on that, the Cooperative Agricultural Extension Service was introduced the following year. As the Cooperative Agricultural Extension Service, the Home Life Improvement Extension Service (HLIES) dealt with issues connected to the home life of farming families and women's role in rural households.

At the beginning, main goals of the HLIES were to improve the farmer's daily life, e.g. the problems generated from lack of privacy, typical Japanese-style houses, the lack of fat and protein in daily meals, and the impractical shabby farm clothing.[2] In 1949, the qualification examination of HLIES advisors was introduced and Extension advisors on home life improvement were started training. They made a great effort in rural areas toward educating farm women by promoting voluntary study groups named the Home Life Improvement Practice Group. Through various activities such as improving heating and the kitchen system and making various kinds of preserves and selling eggs, group members aimed to raise their status in the family and the rural community. However, they came to spend more time on housework in those days.

In 1961, the Agricultural Basic Law was established, which contributed to the improvement of modernized and profitable farming. The activities of the Home Life Improvement Practice Group were characterized by a modern and rational approach to the family farming issues. During the period of high economic growth between 1955 and 1970, the living standards of farmers gradually improved. The Home Life Improvement

---

[2] The first director of the Home Life Improvement Division of MAFF was Matsuyo Ohmori (Yamamoto), who was educated in the United States majoring in home economics and had an extensive experience as an editor of school textbooks for homemaking courses [Ichida, 2000, 61].

Chapter 4: The Roles of Female Farmers   185

Table 4-4-1 Chronology of Basic Facts Regarding the Change of Rural Women's Status

	Agricultural Policy in Japan	Farming Women in Japan	Gender Equality in Japan	Gender Equality in the World
1945	The end of World War II			
1946	Agrarian Reform			
1947	The Agricultural Improvement Promotion Law (AIPL)			
1948		The Home Life Improvement Extension Division The Home Life Improvement Extension Service (HLIES)		
1961	The Basic Law of Agriculture			
1970			The aging rate 7%	
1975			The Headquarters for the Planning and Promotion of Policies Relating Women	The World Conference of the International Women's Year (Mexico City) →Adoption of the World Plan of Action
1977			The National Plan of Action	
1979				The Convention on the Elimination of All Forms of Discrimination against Women
1980				World Conference of the United Nations Decade for Women (Copenhagen)
1981			The National Plan of Action and Priority Targets	ILO Convention (No.156) Concerning Equal Opportunities and Equal Treatment for Men and Women Workers: Workers with Family Responsibilities (Geneva)
1983				ILO Convention (No.156) enforced generally
1985			ILO Convention (No.156) enforced for Japan →The Law of Gender Equality in Labor Opportunities	World Conference to Review and Appraise the Achievements of the UN Decade for Women (Nairobi) →Adoption of the Nairobi Forward-looking Strategies for the Advancement of Women
1987			The New National Plan of Action toward the Year 2000	
1989			TFR fell down to 1.57.	

	Agricultural Policy in Japan	Farming Women in Japan	Gender Equality in Japan	Gender Equality in the World
1990		The Women and Life Division		
1991			The First Revision of the New National Plan of Action	
1992		Goals for Rural Women in the 21st Century and a Mid- to Long-term Vision for Achieving these Goals		
1994			The Angel Plan	
1995		Family Management Agreement	The aging rate 14.5%	The Fourth World Conference on Women (Beijing) →Adoption of the Beijing Declaration and Platform for Action
1999	The Basic Law on Food, Agriculture and Rural Areas		The Basic Law for a Gender-equal Society →Article9: Prefectural gender equality plan	
2001		The Women and Young-farmers Division	The Gender Equality Bureau	
2003			The Basic Law on Measures for the Declining Birthrate The Law toward Promoting Support for the Next Generation Upbringing	
2004	The Revised Agricultural Improvement Promotion Law			
2005		Agricultural Extension Service, Women and Youth Affairs		

Source: Gender Equality Bureau Cabinet Office, 2006, *Steps towards Gender Equality in Japan*, p.30.

Practice Group came to deal with new tasks, such as encouraging a healthy way of living and facilitating the availability of commonly used equipment. This is regarded as a sort of ecological feminism according to the feminine discourse symbolized by motherhood [Ichida, 2000, 68]. In fact from at that time, Japan became an ageing society. In 1970, the composition ratio of the elderly, i.e. people over 65, reached 7%.

2-2. The Period after the International Women's Year in 1975
The World Conference of the International Women's Year, which was held in 1975 in

Mexico City, adopted the World Plan of Action toward the following main goals: Equality, Development and Peace. In accord with the world trends, the Japanese government formulated the National Plan of Action in 1977 for raising the status of women.

The Convention on the Elimination of All Forms of Discrimination against Women was enforced in 1979. Soon after, in 1981, the ILO Convention (No. 156) Concerning Equal Opportunities and Equal Treatment for Men and Women Workers, Workers with Family Responsibilities was adopted by the United Nations. Following worldwide trends, Japan ratified the ILO Convention (No.156) and approved the Law of Gender Equality in Labor Opportunities in 1985.

In 1987, the New National Plan of Action toward the Year 2000 was enforced and the Home Life Improvement Division of MAFF became more active in promoting equal participation of both genders in rural communities. It resulted in increasing the number of women's agricultural committees and in allowing more farming women full membership in Agricultural Cooperatives.

In 1992, the Goals for Rural Women in the 21st Century and a Mid- to Long-term Vision for Achieving these Goals was formulated. It has led to promoting more vigorous activity for establishing equal opportunities in the decision-making of family farming and communal affairs[3].

Following this vision, the Family Management Agreement was introduced into farming families in 1995 in order to ensure women a fair evaluation of the roles they fulfill and to enable them to secure an income /form assets commensurate with their work contributions. In the revision of the Farmers' Pension Act in 1996[4], women were given the right to take the farmer's pension if they executed the Family Management Agreement [Nakamichi, 2000].

2-3. The Period after the Beijing Declaration and Platform for Action in 1995

In 1995, the Fourth World Conference on Women was held in Beijing and in the following year, the Japanese government issued the Plan for Gender Equality 2000, adopting the Beijing Declaration and Platform for Action. In this plan, one of the main

---

3) This vision also proposed to reconsider the "rural lifestyle" quality, which can make people feel more comfortable than in the urban life and suggested thus that rural women are superior to men in recognizing a "rural lifestyle" because of their sense of daily life. The vision was written on the grounds of both liberal and ecological feminism [Ichida, 2000, 69-70].

4) The Farmer's Pension system changed from the pay-as-you-go financing to the personal type of defined contribution pension, the so-called Japan-version 401(K) in 2001. Currently, every farmer who is engaged in farming more than 60 days per year is able to participate in the Farmer's Pension [Act on the Farmers' Pension Fund].

points is building partnerships in agriculture, forestry and fishing villages, which contributed essentially toward gender equality in rural areas.

Then in 1999, the Basic Law for a Gender-equal Society went into effect. At the same time the Basic Law of Agriculture was revised and renamed as the Basic Law on Food, Agriculture and Rural Areas. Article 26 was developed to promote women's involvement in agriculture[5].

These basic laws reinforced the institution of the Family Management Agreements. In 2003, the Japanese government introduced a system where from certified farmers can receive substantial funds. On the assumption that farming women have signed the Family Management Agreement, they can become certified farmers sharing this qualification with their husbands.

2-4. Fostering Work-life Balance for Increasing the Birthrate

At about the time of the Fourth World Conference on Women in Beijing in 1995, Japan's society faced serious population problems with lower birthrates reaching a new peak and an essential increase in the number of the elderly. The total fertility rate (TFR)[6] fell down to 1.57 in 1989. It was named "1.57 shock'" because Japan had never recorded such a low TFR. On the contrary, the aging rate[7] has been rising rapidly at the same time. In 1995, the rate had reached 14.5%, which meant that Japan was not an aging society yet but an aged society, at that time.

The reason why TFR has been getting lower is that the higher percentage of the non-married population. The population census of 1995 showed that 33% of males and 19% of females on the age group of 30 to 34 years had never been married[8] and never intended to have a child. There are two main reasons for the falling birthrate in Japan. One of them is the cost of raising a child and the other is the busy nature of full-time working husbands, which does not leave them enough time to spend at home with their family.

In 1994, the so-called Angel Plan implemented concrete steps toward overcoming

---

5) In consideration of the importance of securing opportunities for both men and women to participate in all kinds of social activities as equal members of society, the State shall promote the creation of an environment in which women's roles in farming operations are fairly assessed and women can be provided with opportunities to become involved in farm management and other relevant activities on a voluntary basis (Article 26).

6) A cumulative rates of age-specific fertility rates for women aged 15 to 49 in a given year; this corresponds to the number of births-giving per woman in her lifetime based on these age specific birthrates [Gender Equality Bureau Cabinet Office, 2006].

7) The proportion of population aged 65 years and over to total population.

8) Illegitimate children are rare in Japan.

the declining birthrate and at the same time a 5-year emergency plan for increasing the number of nurseries was drawn. This was the reason for the next step towards a second Angel Plan, which was set up in 2000.

In 2001, after the enforcement of the Basic Law for a Gender-equal Society, the Council for Gender Equality and the Gender Equality Bureau were established within a Japanese Cabinet Office. Every local government in Japan was required to draw its own action plan for a gender-equal society.

In 2003, the Basic Law on Measures for the Declining Birthrate and the Law toward Promoting Support for the Next Generation's Upbringing were enacted. These laws aim at improving work-life balance for both wife and husband with children under the school age [Gender Equality Bureau Cabinet Office, 2006].

3. Promotion of the Family Management Agreement

The Family Management Agreement in Japan can trace its history back to the Family Agreement after the 1960's. In 1961, the Basic Law on Agriculture was established and it contributed to the improvement of modernized independent farming families. In order to further its improvement, the Japanese government introduced the Family Agreement by modifying the American "father-son contract'. In 1964, the National Chamber of Agriculture published the 'Promotion Charter of Family Agreement Farming'. The Family Agreement was at that time a father-son contract for seeking a democratic family relationship and modernized farm management. However, such a contract among family members did not suit the traditional Japanese farming families and went out of use, except for some rural communities [Toshitani, 1995].

In 1992, the Women and Life Division of MAFF presented 'Goals for Rural Women in the 21st Century, and a Mid- to Long-Term Vision for Achieving these Goals'. Following the trend after the International Women's Year in 1975, this 'Vision' suggests that farming women should have more chances to participate in the decision-making process, both in family life and family farming. In 1995, the Family Agreement was renamed the Family Management Agreement, for partnership within farm families and for empowerment of farming women under the policy toward developing a gender-equal society.

The Family Management Agreement has been promoted by local Agricultural Committees and local Agricultural Extension Service Centers. Over ten years have passed since the beginning of its promotion and the number of farming families executing the Family Management Agreement reached 37,721 households in 2007 (Figure 4-4-1).

Table 4-4-2 shows that there are nine categories in the Family Management Agreement according to the combination of family members executing the Family

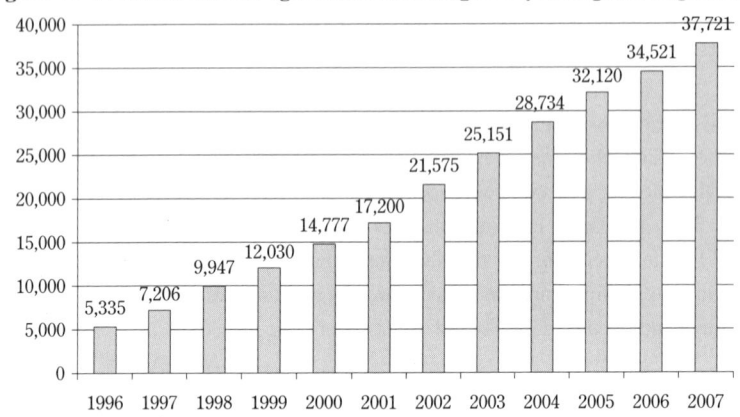

Figure 4-4-1 Number of Farming Families Executing Family Management Agreement

Year	Number
1996	5,335
1997	7,206
1998	9,947
1999	12,030
2000	14,777
2001	17,200
2002	21,575
2003	25,151
2004	28,734
2005	32,120
2006	34,521
2007	37,721

Source: Survey by the Division of Agricultural Extension Service, Women and Youth Affairs, Ministry of Agriculture, Forestry and Fisheries

Management Agreement. In 2007, half of the agreements are only between spouses (Category No.7 is 50.2%) though half of the agreements imply generational relationships, i.e. agreements including both a manager and his/her successor are 35.3% (Category No.1, No.2, No.4, No.5, No.6 and No.8.) and agreements including both a manager and his/her parent(s) are 13.0% (Category No.1, No.2, No.3 and No.4). These farming families need partnership not only between males and females but also among different generations.

The executed items of the Family Management Agreement vary from farm management to family life. According to Table 4-4-3, most farming families executing the Family Management Agreement have signed an agreement in the field of farm management in 2007, e.g. decision-making policy for farm management (86.0%), working hours and holidays (85.9%), farm labor allocation (74.1%) and remuneration for work (71.9%), etc. Moreover, half of them have made an agreement about their family life, e.g. family life allocation (41.7%), farm management rights transfer (40.1%), sanitation, working conditions and health care (35.3%), etc.

In rural Japan, the unit of farming is mainly the family household. It is an institution expected to exist over generations through a succession of headship and inheritance of the family farm from father to heir. Accordingly, farm management and family life are inseparable from each other in the rural community. The Family Management Agreement is to be useful not only for more profitable farm management but also for a democratic family life.

Chapter 4: The Roles of Female Farmers 191

Table 4-4-2 Family Members Executing Family Management Agreement in 2007

	1	2	3	4	5	6	7	8	9
Manager's father	○	○	○	○					
Manager's mother	○	○	○	○					
Manager (husband)	○	○	○	○	○	○	○	○	
Manager's spouse (wife)	○	○	○			○	○	○	
Manager's son and/or daughter	○	○		○	○	○		○	
Manager's son's and/or daughter's spouse	○			○					
Other cases									○
	0.6%	1.4%	10.3%	0.7%	10.3%	16.0%	50.2%	6.3%	4.1%

Source: Survey by the Division of Agricultural Extension Service, Women and Youth Affairs, Ministry of Agriculture, Forestry and Fisheries

Table 4-4-3 Included Items of Family Management Agreement in 2007

1. Decision-making policy for farm management	86.0%
2. Working hours and holidays	85.9%
3. Farm labor allocation (tasks per person, book-keeping)	74.1%
4. Remuneration for work (daily, monthly)	71.9%
5. Profit distribution (except remuneration)	46.3%
6. Family life allocation (household chores, family courtesy)	41.7%
7. Farm management rights transfer (succession)	40.1%
8. Sanitation, working conditions and health care	35.3%
9. Farm sector allocation (including food processing, sales and other related sectors)	23.3%
10. Community service and social activities	19.9%
11. Money support for elderly after farm management rights transfer (residency, livelihood, nursing care etc.)	15.8%
12. Child raising duties allocation	9.3%
13. Family property inheritance	8.5%
14. Others	41.7%

Source: Survey by the Division of Agricultural Extension Service, Women and Youth Affairs, Ministry of Agriculture, Forestry and Fisheries

4. Data Collecting

This study is based on the nationwide survey of farming households executing the Family Management Agreement[9]. The interviewees were introduced by the local Extension Service Centers, which were evaluated as regions with well-promoted

---

9) Thanks to the generous support of the Japan Society for the Promotion of Science and their 2005 and 2006 Grant-in-Aid for Scientific Research, I conducted an authorized interview with the staff at the Regional Agricultural Administration Offices Agricultural Extension Service, Women and Youth

Family Management Agreements by the Regional Agricultural Administration Offices staff in charge and by the Expert Extension Workers at the prefectural level. Although the access to original documentation of the Family Management Agreement became difficult after the enactment of the Act on the Protection of Personal Information in 2005, we could still see some valid samples, obtainable thanks to the Extension Worker's collaboration and assistance.

In the case of family farming, farm management and family life are inseparable. This is why in this study, we would like to emphasize on farming families with clear cases of duties' allocation not only in farm management but also in family life. In order to analyze the generational changes by sex and age, the most suitable cases for such research proved to be stem families where both the mother and daughter-in-law are present, the latter still engaged in childbirth/child-raising.

5. Cases of Farming Families Executing the Family Management Agreement

From Table 4-4-4 to Table 4-4-10 the assembled data show three comparative farming families executing the Family Management Agreement, which were derived from their valid documentation[10] and semi-structured interviews conducted with the family members. By means of these data we would like to discuss the executed items of the Family Management Agreement concerning family life and gender issues.

5-1. Characteristics of Three Farming Families

These three farming families are located in various regions in Japan: Tokushima, Niigata and Hokkaido (Table 4-4-4). The type of management is different in all these cases: carrot production, flower planting and dairy. However, they are all stem-families consisting of four generations, including the manager, manager's wife, successor, successor's wife, successor's children and manager's parent(s). These stem-families are almost on the same life-stage, i.e. on the childbirth/child raising stage, because these managers are of the same generation (b. 1946 and 1947). Moreover, the manager's wives (b.1947, 1948), successors (b.1971, 1972, 1974) and successor's wives (b.1970, 1972, 1975) are also each from the same respective generations, though their successor's children have some differences in their age, according to their consecutive

---

Affairs in different locations throughout Japan: Sendai, Saitama, Kanazawa, Nagoya, Kyoto, Okayama, Kumamoto and Sapporo. The main purpose of this interview was to find out the regional trends with regards to the Family Management Agreement and its specifics and development in each area under consideration. See Chapter 3, Section 2, footnote 3 on p.111.
10) See the primary source information on pp.195-202.

Chapter 4: The Roles of Female Farmers   193

Table 4-4-4 Basic Information on Three Farming Families

		Family A	Family B	Family C
Location		Tokushima	Niigata	Hokkaido
Interview		February 20. 2007	March 1. 2007	September 7. 2006
Number of family members		9	7	8
Family composition		4 Generations	4 Generations	4 Generations
Family members		Manager (b.1946)	Manager (b.1947)	Manager (b.1946)
		Manager's wife (b.1948)	Manager's wife (b.1947)	Manager's wife (b.1947)
		Successor (b.1971)	Successor (b.1974)	Successor (b.1972)
		Successor's wife (b.1972)	Successor's wife (b.1975)	Successor's wife (b.1970)
		Successor's son (b.1995)	Successor's son (b.2002)	Successor's son (b.2004)
		Successor's son (b.1997)	Successor's son (b.2004)	Successor's son (b.2005)
		Successor's daughter (b.1999)		
		Manager's mother (b.1923)	Manager's father (b.1915)	Manager's mother (b.1920)
		Manager's daughter (b.1970s)		Manager's daughter (b.1977)
Agreement signing		2002	2005	2002
Agreement revision		—	—	2005
Farm management		6 ha of cultivated land for carrot production	2.5 ha of cultivated land for lily planting and 20 a of rice fields Sales amount 28 million yen/year in 2006	90 milking cows and 35 heifers, milk production 660t per year in 2006
Living conditions		There is a detached building on the premises for the successor, his wife and children. However, it has no bathroom or kitchen. The bathroom and the kitchen in the main building are shared by all family members	In 2004, successor's family moved from Kanagawa Prefecture and began to live in this town independently from the manager and his wife. However, since November 2006 they reunited and currently live together with the manager and his wife. Their private spaces are located on the second floor of the main building. The bathroom and the kitchen are shared by all family members.	Each couple has its own independent residence on the same premises. However, before the birth of the successor's first child in 2004, they shared the bathroom and the kitchen of manager's residence.

years of birth: elementary school age (Family A), nursery age (Family B) and infant age (Family C).

5-2. Farm Management Transfer

These three farm managers are old enough to plan their farm transference (Table 4-4-5). The manager of Family A planned it for his 61st year of age in 2007. However, because of his successor's personal reasons, it has been postponed. The successor prefers farm operation to farm management. The manager of Family B plans it for his 65th year of age in 2012. As for Family C, it is written clearly in the documentation that in January

Table 4-4-5 Farm Management Transfer

Family A	Family B	Family C
Although planned for 2007 (current manager turns 61) it was postponed for 2008 for the successor's personal reasons. Enlargement of the management land and the purchase of a tractor belong to the current manager. The successor prefers farm operation to farm management.	There is no information about farm transfer in the document. However, the current manager plans it for his 65th year of age (2012).	In the document it was planned that the farm transfer will be in 2009 when the current manager turns 62.

after the 62nd birthday of the manager, the management rights will be transferred to the successor. In an aged society like Japan, generational change of a stem-family household is to be dilatory. The Family Management Agreement is effective for fostering young farm managers.

5-3. Women's Labor Load and Wages

Concerning wages, all three managers' wives and successors get a monthly salary (Table 4-4-6). Thanks to signing the Family Management Agreement, they secured income commensurate with their farm work contributions. However, there is no information in the document about wages of the successor's wives except in the case of Family A.

Table 4-4-7 shows women's labor load in family farming. The manager's wives are engaged in farming as full-time farm workers. However, as for the successor's wives, the successor's wife of Family A is only engaged in accounting book-keeping and overall farm labor as much as the manager's wife. During the years of raising her children, she was only required to pack vegetables in the shed in the yard of the residence. In 2004, Family A specialized its farming in carrot producing on a larger management scale with employees. At that time, the successor's youngest child turned 5 and his wife was able to be in charge of personal management.

The successor's wife of Family B began to engage in farming as a part-time worker in 2006, because her children turned 2 and 3 years old, she entrusted them to the day nursery between 9:00 and 15:00.

The successor's wife of Family C is currently not engaged in farming. It is written in the document that the successor's wife will be engaged in farming again after her children enter a day nursery. In her opinion, her children are currently too young to entering day nursery. She intends to make them enter pre-school after they turn 4.

Thus, it is clear that women's labor load on family forms is different depending on the age of their children.

Chapter 4: The Roles of Female Farmers 195

Table 4-4-6 Wages

Family A	Family B	Family C
300,000 yen for the wife, 300,000 yen for the successor and 200,000 yen for the successor's wife per month. Wages for the successor and for the successor's wife include family food expenses.	150,000 yen for the wife and 200,000 yen for the successor. These wages include family expenses. Since 2006 the successor's wife is engaged in farming as a part-time worker. However, there is no clear indication about her wages.	150,000 yen for the successor and his wife. It is for their pin money and food, commodities and for child-care expenses. However, the expenses for electricity, heating, insurance, gasoline and automobile inspection are excluded.

Table 4-4-7 Women's Labor Load

	Family A	Family B	Family C
Farm work of the manager's wife	Overall farm labor is allotted to the manager's wife.	The manager's wife is engaged in flower planting and shipping.	There is no special information about farm work allocated to the manager's wife in the document. She is engaged in farming almost as much as the manager and the successor.
Farm work of the successor's wife	Overall farm labor and accounting book-keeping are allotted to the successor's wife. However, during the years of raising her children, she was required to pack vegetables in the shed located in the residence yard.	There is no information in the document signed in 2005 about the farm work allotted to the successor's wife. However, since 2006 the successor's wife is engaged in farming as a part-time worker. Because her children turned 2 and 3 years old in 2006, she entrusted them to the day nursery between 9:00 and 15:00.	It is written in the document that the successor's wife will be engaged in farming again after her children enter nursery. In her opinion, her children are currently too young to enter day nursery. She intends to make them enter pre-school after they turn 4.

5-4. Household Chores

Even in stem-family households, their family lives are more or less separated by generations. We can see their variations in Table 4-4-4 and Table 4-4-8.

In Family C, each couple has their own independent residence on the same premises. Before the birth of the successor's first child in 2004, they shared the bathroom and the kitchen of the manager's residence. According to the manager's wife, the young mother would benefit from this independence by acquiring better domestic skills.

Table 4-4-8 Household Chores

Family A	Family B	Family C
House-keeping is allotted to the successor's wife and the manager's wife is a helper. Cooking duties are allotted mainly to the successor's wife. Manager's wife assistance is needed for lunch only. Gardening is allotted to the manager. Kitchen gardening and exterior beautification are allotted to the manager's mother.	House-keeping is allotted to the manager's wife and the successor's wife assists her. However, there is no particular role allocation after the family reunited in 2006, because of the short period (3 months only have passed when this interview was conducted).	Each couple has its own independent residence on the same premises. According to the manager's wife opinion, the young mother would benefit from this independence by acquiring better domestic skills.

As for Family B, the successor's family moved from Kanagawa Prefecture and began to live in this town independently from the manager and his wife in 2004. When the current Family Management Agreement was signed in 2005, the successor's family lived independently. In the document it is written that house-keeping is allotted to the manager's wife and the successor's wife assists her. However, in November 2006, they reunited and currently live together with the manager and his wife. Although their private spaces are located on the second floor of the main building, the bathroom and the kitchen are shared by all family members. There has been no particular role allocation after the family reunited because of the short period, i.e. only 3 months had passed when this interview was conducted.

Family A has a detached building on the premises for the successor, his wife and children. However, it has no bathroom or kitchen. The bathroom and the kitchen in the main buildings are shared by all family members. House-keeping is allotted to the successor's wife and the manager's wife is a helper. Cooking duties are allotted mainly to the successor's wife, too. The manager's wife's assistance is needed for lunch only. Moreover, in the document, it is written that the gardening is allotted to the manager, the kitchen gardening and exterior beautification are allotted to the manager's mother.

In comparison, among these three families, the household chores are allotted solely to women. Men are not concerned with domestic duties at all. At the most, men are engaged in gardening.

5-5. Child Raising Duties

On the contrary, child raising duties tend to be assisted by men in these farming families (Table 4-4-9). The agreements of Family B and Family C provide that all family members cooperate in child care. The successor of Family A is obliged to, yet willingly help parenting and the latter is clearly stated in the document.

Table 4-4-9 Child-raising Duties

Family A	Family B	Family C
Overall child care is allotted to the successor's wife. The successor is obliged to, yet willingly help her and the latter is clearly stated in the document.	The agreement provides that child care is allotted to the successor's wife and family members who are available to help her. However, the successor attends the youth training seminar for farming in this community every evening, and rarely helps her.	The agreement provides that all family members cooperate in child care. However, it is also added that the successor's wife is the main person in charge. According to the manager's wife child care is allotted mainly to the successor's wife, i.e. the child's mother.

However, overall child care is allotted to the successor's wife in all cases. The manager's wife of Family C suggests that child care should be allotted mainly to the successor's wife, i.e. the child's mother. When she was young, she was unwilling to entrust her children to her mother-in-law and worked hard on the farm. As for Family B, the successor rarely helps parenting, because he attends the youth training seminar for farming in the community every evening.

Thus, farming women are isolated from their family farming during the years of raising their children. It is caused by gender-oriented opinions of the elder generation and the busy nature of the husbands.

5-6. Young Farming Women's Social Activities within the Community

Table 4-4-10 shows training seminars and study tours to improve management skills for career development regarding farming and farm life. Here, we can see young farming women's social activities within the community in three cases, e.g. the successor's wife of Family A got driver's licenses for both tractors and large vehicles in 2006, along with other young farming women in the community.

The successor's wife of Family C is the head of a local women's group, only for house wives in farming families of ages up to 35-38. Because all 12 members of this group are the successors' wives of dairy farmers, they hold study meetings and make study tours. However, the study group for improving the raising of cattle and book-keeping study groups in the community are for young successors. Training fields for farming tend to be divided by sex.

It is written in the document of Family B that family members are actively joining training seminars, especially for youth and women. In fact, the successor goes out to the youth training seminars every evening. However, on the contrary, the successor's wife doesn't have any social contacts with women of her generation in the community. The members of the training seminars for women in this community are mostly of the

Table 4-4-10 Training Seminars for Farming within the Community

Family A	Family B	Family C
It is written in the document that family members are actively joining training seminars and study tours to improve their management skills for career development regarding farming and farm life. The successor's wife got driver's licenses for both tractors and large vehicles in 2006, along with other young farming women in the community.	It is written in the document that family members are actively joining training seminars, especially for youth and women. In fact, the successor goes out to the youth training seminars every evening. On the contrary, the successor's wife doesn't have any social contacts with women of her generation in the community. The members of the training seminars for women in this community are mostly of the manager's wife's generation.	The manager is the chair of the city agricultural committee and the manager's wife is a leader of the local women's group, too. The successor is also a chair of the study group for improving the race of cattle and a member of the book-keeping study group in the community. The successor's wife is a head of a local women's group, only for house wives in farming families of ages up to 35-38. All 12 members of this group are all successors' wives of dairy farmers. They hold study meetings and go on educational tours.

manager's wife's generation. The generational changes of farming women is slower than that of men.

6. Conclusion

In accord with the world trends after the International Women's Year in 1975, the institution of the Family Management Agreement was introduced into farming families in 1995 in order to establish each family member's personal position in a farming families, especially women's status, and to modernize farm management by carrying out partnership among family members. In this study, the effects of the Family Management Agreement on gender-equality in farming families were examined, according to a case study of typical farming families executing the agreement. The results of these comparative studies are as follows:

    1) In an aged society like Japan, the generational change of stem-family households is to be dilatory. The Family Management Agreement is effective on fostering young farm managers.

    2) Thanks to signing the Family Management Agreement, the manager's wives have secured income commensurate with their farm work contributions. However, there is little information in the document about the wages of the successor's wives.

    3) The managers' wives are engaged in farming as full-time farm workers. However, as for the successor's wives, there are not many successors' wives who are engaged in farming as much as the manager's wife.

    4) Women's labor load in family farming is different depending on the age of their

children.

5) Household chores are allotted solely to women. Whether their family lives are generationally separated or not, men are not involved in domestic duties at all.

6) Farming women are isolated from their family farming during the years of raising their children, which is caused by the gender related opinions of elder generation and the busy nature of husbands.

7) Successor's wives tend to have fewer social contacts with women of their generation in the community. The members of training seminars for women are mostly of the manager's wives' generation. Generational change of farming women is slower than that of men.

Though there are some middle-aged women who have achieved their status in family farm management, the Family Management Agreement has not been effective evenly in every generation. Younger women tend to be responsible for general household duties until their children reach school age, because housework and childcare are considered one of the tasks for family farm management. In this case, the Family Management Agreement causes career-loss for younger women.

In 2003, the Basic Law on Measures for the Declining Birthrate and the Law toward Promoting Support for the Next Generation Upbringing were enacted. These laws aim at improving work-life balance for both wife and husband with children under the school age. The Family Management Agreement should be more effective on gender-equal family life especially for the younger generation in farming families.

Primary Source Information[11]

I. Family A in Tokushima

Family Management Agreement

1. Main Goal
This is an agreement between the undersigned manager, manager's wife, successor, successor's wife and manager's mother. They all made decision to work together according to their responsiblities with the family farm management principles in order to establish modern farm management and to build a healthy, balanced and delightful family life.

2. Decision-making for Farm Management
After a thorough discussion among the undersigned family members, the following management policy was decided on loan applications, land scale for planting, farming facilities, management scale and working conditions.

3. Role Allocation
Following a discussion with respect to their needs and after carefully considering each person's ability and influence, these role allocations were decided.

Family members	Farm management	Family life
Kiyoshi Noguchi* (manager)	Overall Farm Labor, Operating big machinery, Chemical insect prevention, Main Staff in pumpkin cultivation	Gardening
Yoko Noguchi* (manager's wife)	Overall Farm Labor	Helper in housekeeping
Makoto Noguchi* (successor)	Overall Farm Labor, Operating big machinery, Chemical insect prevention, Main Staff in bitter cucumber cultivation	Childcare
Yumiko Noguchi* (successor's wife)	Overall Farm Labor, Accounting book-keeping	House-keeping, Overall child care
Fumiko Noguchi* (manager's mother)	Helper at/during busy farming seasons (Packing vegetables)	Kitchen gardening, Exterior beautification

---

11)* Names and the address here been changed.

4. Remuneration

4-1. Monthly salary is supplied as follows. However, it is subject to change in the cases of additional profit beyond our preliminary expectations and after a thorough discussion among the undersigned family members.

Family members	Monthly salary	Payday	Payment
Yoko Noguchi (manager's wife)	300,000yen	Monthly on the 30th	Bank account transfer
Makoto Noguchi (successor)	300,000yen	Monthly on the 30th	Bank account transfer
Yumiko Noguchi (successor's wife)	200,000yen	Monthly on the 30th	Bank account transfer

4-2. Income from pumpkin sales is assigned to the manager. A certain percentage of sales from bitter cucumber (*Gohya*), Chinese green leaves (*Chingen-sai*) and Japanese winter rape (*Komatsuna*) is assigned to the successor. The ratio is determined during their discussions.

4-3. Wages from the Japan Agricultural Cooperative (JA) on consignment to farm work in rice harvesting belong to the successor.

The ratio for each family member is reconsidered depending on profits and labor distribution under the planned farm labor allocation once a year.

5. Working Hours and Breaks

Season	Period	Working hours	Lunch breaks	Tea breaks
Peak season	From the end of March to the beginning of June	5:30-20:00	12:00-13:00	10:00-10:30 / 15:00-15:30
Active season	October – December	8:00-18:00	12:00-13:00	10:00-10:30
Off season	July – September	Depends on farm work requirements		

However, depending on overall housework requirements, the hours are flexible.

Attendance hours at gatherings and seminars regarding agriculture are to be included in the working hours for family farming.

6. Holidays

6-1. The day before market closure

6-2. All family members are allowed to indicate their personal appointments, hobbies and leisure plans on the family calendar.

7. Domestic Accounting
Food expenses are supplied by the manager's wife and the successor's wife. The children's education-related expenses are managed by the successor and his wife, and other domestic expenditures are supplied by the manager.

8. Training Seminars
8-1. Family members are to actively join training seminars and educational tours to improve management skills for career development regarding farming and farm life.
8-2. The family plans for leisure activities and overnight trips for their welfare.

9. Safety Precautions and Conditions for Family Members
9-1. Yearly medical checks for all family members
9-2. Observation of chemical machinery safety rules
9-3. People-friendly working environment (restrooms, relaxation spaces)
9-4. Emergency situation and accident compensation insurance

10. Clauses for Extraordinary Situations
10-1. This agreement is subject to change in the case of unforeseeable circumstances following a thorough discussion between all family members.
10-2. In an extraordinary situation, family members can make decisions out of the context of this agreement.

Addenda
1. This agreement is effective on October 9th, 2002.
2. This agreement is valid one year from the date of its enforcement. If not required by family members, this agreement is unchangeable and it is to be automatically renewed upon the date of its expiration.
3. Only one original document has been issued for all family members involved. The head of the household has been entrusted with document keeping.
    The observer of the agreement receives a copy of this document and the secretariat of the local extension service center keeps it.

October 9th, 2002
Itano-gun, Aizumi-chou, Nakano 136*
Manager : Kiyoshi Noguchi
Manager's wife : Yoko Noguchi
Successor : Makoto Noguchi

Successor's wife : Yumiko Noguchi
Mother : Fumiko Noguchi

Head of the local Extension Service Center: Masaru Yamamoto*

II. Family B in Niigata.

Family Management Agreement

1. Main Goal
This is an agreement between the undersigned manager, manager's wife, successor and successor's wife. They all made decision to work together according to the responsible family farm management principles in order to establish modern farm management and to build a healthy, balanced and delightful family life.

2. Decision-making for Farm Management
After a thorough discussion among the undersigned family members the management policy and farming plan decided mainly by the manager: buying bulbs, selection of the types of lilies, etc.

3. Role Allocation

	Manager	Manager's wife	Successor	Successor's wife
Flower production	Soil disinfection Manure Insect prevention	Assistance to assemble green houses Assistance for planting bulbs	The assembly of green houses Planting bulbs	
Shipment	Flower cutting Flower selecting	Flower cutting Flower selecting	Flower packing Shipment of flowers	
Others	Keeping a work diary	Housework	Report about daily shipments to JA by PC Report about planting to JA by PC	Child care Housework assistance

4. Profit Distribution
Monthly salary: Manager's wife 150,000 yen Successor 200,000 yen
    A bonus is payable in December based on yearly profits.

5. Working Condition
5-1.Working Hours: 7:30-17:30
Except the high season for farming from June to September

5-2. Breaks: For 30 minutes in the morning and the afternoon
5-3. Holidays: 2 days a month typically
   Except the high season for farming from June to September
   They will likely be off in cases of heavy rain or small amount of farm work.
5-4. Vacations: The Bon Festival (*Obon*), New Year and December.

6. Health and Welfare
6-1. Family members are to actively join training seminars, especially for youth and women.
6-2. The family plans for overnight trips in December.
6-3. Complete medical checkup in December.

7. Family Life Allocation
   The person who is available helps with the housework and child care.

March 25th, 2005
Manager : Hiroshi Saito*
Manager's wife : Kazuko Saito*
Successor : Kenichi Takahashi*
Successor's wife : Mayumi Takahashi*

Observers
Director of the Kita-Uonuma Agricultural Extension Service Center : Isamu Abe*
Head of the Kita-Uonuma Agricultural Cooperative Association : Akira Honma*

III. Family C in Hokkaido—The first agreement from 2002

Family Management Agreement

The Family C Ranch aims a family life and farm management which is based on mutual respect, help and improvement of all family members.

Main Goal:
The undersigned, including Minoru Sato* (manager), Kazuko Sato* (manager's wife), Takeshi Sato* (successor) and Mayumi Sato* (successor's wife), aim at ensuring mutually responsible decision-making rights in farm management and family life. They also signed this agreement for establishing a stable and efficient dairy farm management and for securing a healthy and delightful family life.

1. Secure Holidays
The undersigned take turns in taking one day holiday per month.
The day off is decided in conformitt with each family member's schedule.
Two family members are allowed to take their monthly holiday together when farm helpers are available.

2. Full Communication between Family Members
The schedule and working plan of each family member and appointments with a veterinarian for health control and artificial insemination of cows are to be written on the family announcement board.

3. Control of Breeding Cows
All management rights on half of the milking cows will be transferred to the successor next year. Therefore, this is a transitional period before the inheritance.

4. Management Transition
In January after the 62nd birthday of the manager, the management rights will be transferred to the successor.

March 28th, 2002
Minoru Sato (manager)
Kazuko Sato (manager's wife)
Takeshi Sato (successor)
Mayumi Sato (successor's wife)

Observers
Chair of the Monbetsu City Agricultural Committee : Tadashi Makino*
Representative Director and Head of the Ohotsuku-hamanasu Agricultural Cooperative Association : Kazuo Suzuki*

IV. Family C in Hokkaido—The revised agreement in 2005

Family Management Agreement

The Family C Ranch aims at a family life and farm management based on mutual respect, help and improvement of all family members.

Main Goal:
The undersigned, including Minoru Sato (manager), Kazuko Sato (manager's wife), Takeshi Sato (successor) and Mayumi Sato (successor's wife), aim at ensuring mutually

responsible decision-making rights in farm management and family life. They also signed in this agreement for establishing a stable and efficient dairy farm management and for securing a healthy and delightful family life.

1. Farm Work

Farm work is to be started at 5:00 am and end at 4:00 pm, and to be ended by the time when milking starts at 6:30 am and at 5:30 pm. However, the hours are flexible on occasion when the agricultural equipment or machinery have some trouble or a calf is delivered.

The successor's wife will engage in farming again after her children enter nursery.

2. Remuneration (Salary)

The couple, Takeshi (successor) and Mayumi (successor's wife), is paid 150,000 yen monthly for their pocket money, food, daily necessities, and child care expenses. However, the utility bill, various kinds of insurance, the gasoline fee, and the car inspection fee are excluded.

"Grants to producers of milk for processing"[12] are to be applied to the yearly bonus.

Monthly salary of the full-time worker is a subject to change when there is increased milk production due to the growing number of milking cows.

3. Control of Breeding Cows

All family members make an effort to keep track of which cow is in the mating season. The artificial insemination for cows is mainly managed by Takeshi (successor) and that for heifers is mainly managed by Minoru (manager).

4. Child Care

All family members cooperate in child care. However, the successor's wife is the main person in charge.

5. Holidays

Takeshi (successor) and Mayumi (successor's wife) are allowed to be excused from farming in the morning and at night once every two months until their child becomes one year-old.

They are allowed to make overnight trips several times a year after their child's

---

12) Market price system of milk for processing has been introduced since 2001. This producer reserves funds which depend on the producer's donation and the subsidy from the government were introduced against the price fall because of the demand fluctuation. It aims at contributing to stable dairy-farm management [MAFF].

first birthday.

6. Management Transition
In January after the 62nd birthday of the manager, the management rights will be transferred to the successor.

7. Other Clause
The above-mentioned contents are subject to review once a year when a yearly farm plan is drawn.

March 30th, 2005
Minoru Sato (manager)
Kazuko Sato (manager's wife)
Takeshi Sato (successor)
Mayumi Sato (successor's wife)

Observers
Chair of the Monbetsu City Agricultural Committee : Tadashi Makino
Representative Director and Head of the Ohotsuku-hamanasu Agricultural Cooperative Association : Yukio Nishimoto*
Director of the Monbetsu Agricultural Extension Service Center : Shigeru Nomura*

References
Gender Equality Bureau Cabinet Office, 2006, *Steps towards Gender Equality in Japan*.
Gojo, Miyoshi, 2003, *Kazoku Keiei Kyoutei no Tenkai* (Promotion of Family Management Agreement), Tokyo: Tsukuba Shobo. (in Japanese)
Ichida, Tomoko Iwata, 2000, "The Gender Issue in the Home Life Imoprovement Extension Service of Postwar Japan,"Masae Tsutsumi ed., *Women and Families in Rural Japan,* Tokyo: Tsukuba Shobo, 57-74.
Kawate, Tokuya, 2006, *Gendai no Kazoku Keiei Kyoutei* (Contemporary Significances of Family Management Agreement), Tokyo: Tsukuba Shobo. (in Japanese)
Nakamichi, Hitomi, 2000, "Current Issues on Women's Policy in Rural Areas: The Establishment of Partnerships in Farm Families and in the Rural Community," Masae Tsutsumi ed., *Women and Families in Rural Japan,* Tokyo: Tsukuba Shobo, 13-37.
Otomo, Yukiko, 2000, "Women's Status in Agricultural Households," Masae Tsutsumi ed., *Women and Families in Rural Japan,* Tokyo: Tsukuba Shobo, 101-120.
―――, 2003, "Kagyo Keiei-Tai no Sonzoku-Senryaku (A Strategy of Family-business Succession)," *Shakaijouhou Ronsou,* 7: 89-110. (in Japanese)
Toshitani, Nobuyoshi, 1995, "Kazoku Keiei Kyoutei no Riron-teki Kadai (Theoretical Problems of the Family Management Agreement)," *Nougyo-Hou Kenkyu,* 30: 56-66. (in Japanese)
Tsutsumi, Masae, 1999, "A Lifecourse Study of Stem Family Women in Rural Japan: A Comparison of the Changes over Three Generations," *International Journal of Japanese Sociology,* 8: 117-140.

Chapter 5

Family Strategy on Succession and Family Farm Management

Chapter 5 focuses on generation transfer of "Hito (people)" and "Mono (property)" and analyzes generational changes. Special attention will be given to family management agreements from the pre-war period until today. Succession from the parent to the child generation has become diverse, and living together is not enough to characterize generation transfer of the stem family. The notion that the eldest son must take over from the parents is now not as strong, but still eldest sons are aware that they are the successor. In Japan, although inheritance laws regarding "Mono (property)" cite equal distribution, in farming households the successor is given priority to receive everything. Land is seldom divided and it is inherited solely by an eldest son, the heir. Recently, some families incorporate their farming businesses and maintain the farmland collectively. How agriculture and families develop in the future is related to inheritance and farmland ownership. Family management agreement is one of the measures to realize gender-equal partnership management, and it is also important for promoting women's social activities or pursuing a career. How farming business has been passed down and how people have been encouraged to be hardworking farmers will be analyzed using generation comparison.

1
New Trends in Stem-family Succession in Rural Japan: A case of Katsunuma Town[1]
Yukiko Otomo

1. Introduction
1-1. Aim

After World War II, the Japanese family ideology has generally been viewed to have changed from the stem-family system[2] to the conjugal-family system [Morioka, 1993]. This has been observed by the changes in living condition among two successive married couples. In Japan, couples which had held the stem-family ideology continued to live with the heir's family; thus, a stem family persisted especially in the rural areas [Otomo, 2007].

Today, however, we can observe considerable changes in living arrangements between a couple and their heir in farming families. These changes make indicators of household succession quite diverse, and the succession from father to his son cannot be determined only by the son's marriage [Otomo, 1993]. Therefore we need to recognize some different patterns of succession in terms of the inter-generation relationship between father and heir.

In order to determine different patterns of succession, we shall deal with panel data taken from surveys conducted six times for a period of 31 years, observing about 100 stem-family households in Katsunuma Town. This was one of the few panels which participated over a long term, since it requires much time and resources to continue panel surveys, although panel data are generally useful to grasp social change more objectively.

1-2. Data

The panel was designed by Kiyomi Morioka (1923-, Tokyo University of Education Hon. Prof.) in 1966 when the first survey was performed. The following main criteria

---

[1] Support for this research was provided by the Institute for Household Economy. This paper was presented at the 1st International Congress of the Asian Rural Sociology Association, on January 29-31, 1999 in Bangkok, Thailand. This edition includes the most recent revision.
[2] See Chapter 3, Section 2, Introduction on pp.109-110.

Figure 5-1-1

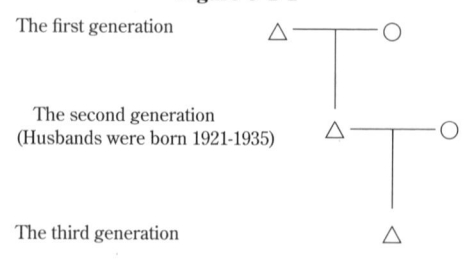

The first generation △─┬─○

The second generation
(Husbands were born 1921-1935) △─┬─○

The third generation △

for selecting about 100 family households are: (1) it had to be a stem-family household having the household head, his wife, father and mother, and (2) the householder needed to be born between 1921 and 1935 when they were from 31 to 45 years old.

These stem-family households had to be located within five areas in Katsunuma Town, which is not too far from Metropolitan Tokyo and is famous for its commercial grape production. Most of the surveyed households are running grape farms.

After the first research in 1966, these stem-family households were researched repeatedly: in 1972, 1976 (limited research), 1981, 1992 and 1997. Now, we have acquired a series of panel data on 108 stem-family households.

At the first panel, all these households contained two married couples-one from each consecutive generation. After that, during the period of 31 years, most of the parents have passed away and some new couples of the next generation were added to these households. Here we name these three consecutive generations in a family line as the first generation; the husband's parents, the second generation; the couple, and the third generation; child(ren) of the couple (Figure 5-1-1).

2. Findings

2-1. Change in Household Composition of the Stem-family Households

Table 5-1-1[3] shows the change in household composition of the 108 stem family households from 1966 to 1997. At the first panel in 1966, these 108 households all consisted of two or more married couples from different generations, and they were all classified as the family type "Other relatives households," containing relative(s) besides conjugal family members. During the period of 31 years, most of the fathers and mothers have passed away, so that many households in the family type "Other relatives households" have changed to the type "Family nuclei," conjugal family (Figure 5-1-2). After 31 years in 1997, there were more households in the family type "Family nuclei"

---

3) This classification of household composition almost applies to that of the National Census.

Table 5-1-1 The Change in Household Composition

Household(%)

		1966	1972	1981	1992	1997
	Total	108(100.0)	108(100.0)	108(100.0)	107(100.0)	107(100.0)
	Family nuclei Total	0(0.0)	5(4.6)	26(24.1)	47(43.0)	54(50.5)
	A married couple only			5(4.6)	17(15.9)	24(22.4)
	A married couple with their child(ren)		5(4.6)	19(17.6)	29(27.1)	26(24.3)
	Father with his child(ren)					2(1.9)
	Mother with her child(ren)			2(1.9)	1(1.9)	2(1.9)
	Other relatives households Total	108(100.0)	103(95.4)	82(75.9)	60(56.1)	51(47.7)
Relatives households	A couple with their parents	3(1.8)		3(2.8)	3(2.8)	2(1.9)
	A couple with their parent		1(0.9)	2(1.8)	6(5.6)	4(3.7)
	A couple with their child(ren) and parents	70(64.8)	68(63.0)	23(21.3)	21(19.6)	26(24.3)
	A couple with their child(ren), parents and parent's other child(ren)	32(29.6)	6(5.6)	1(0.9)	4(3.7)	1(0.9)
	A couple with their child(ren) and husband's or wife's father		7(6.5)	9(8.3)	4(3.7)	1(0.9)
	A couple with their child(ren) and husband's or wife's mother		20(18.5)	38(35.2)	12(11.2)	10(9.3)
	A couple with their son's wife and her child(ren)				1(0.9)	2(1.9)
	A couple with their parent(s) and grandparent(s)	3(1.8)	1(0.9)	6(5.6)	8(9.3)	4(3.7)
	Other relatives households not elsewhere classified				1(0.9)	1(0.9)
One-person households	Total					2(1.9)

Note: 1) "A couple" is the first generation couple, the second generation couple or the third generation couple
2) "Other relatives households not elsewhere classified is" couple with their parent(s), grandparent(s) and non-relative(s)

Figure 5-1-2

【Family nuclei】(examples)

【Other relatives households】(examples)

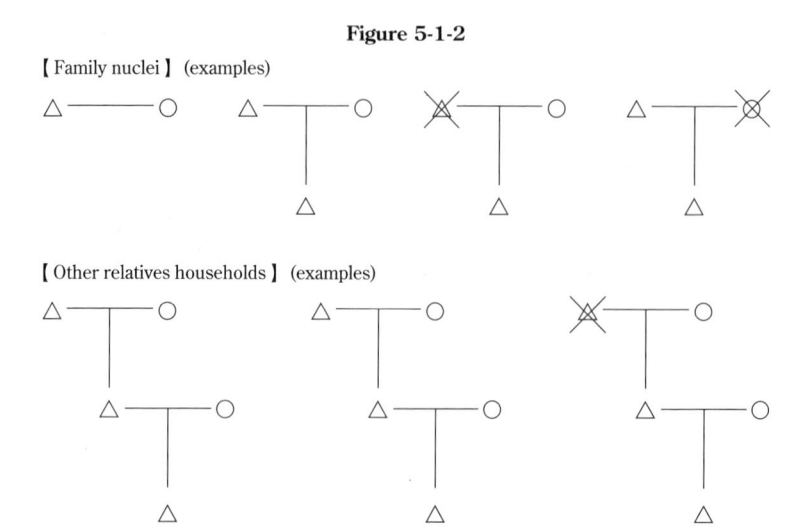

(50.5%) than households in the family type "Other relatives households" (47.7%).

The increase in the percentage of "Family nuclei" households was due to an increase in the number of households of "A married couple with their child(ren)" until 1992. But during the last five years between 1992 and 1997, the increase of "Family nuclei" was due to an increase of "A married couple only": 15.9% in 1992 (26 years later) to 22.4% in 1997 (31 years later).

As for "Other relatives households," the percentage of "A couple with their child(ren) and parents" was at the highest in 1966(64.8%) and in 1972(63.0%), but this figure dropped to 21.3% in 1981 and 19.6% in 1992, almost one third of that of the 1966-1972 period.

However, the figure rose to 24.3% in 1997 after 31 years from the first panel. We need to note here the change in generation. The couples of this family type were the second generation in the surveys of 1966 and 1972, while those in 1997 were the third generation of the stem families: eight households had the third-generation couple in 1981, 34 in 1992 and 43 in 1997[4]. These households with the third-generation couple were pursuing the typical stem-family life cycle.

The rest of the households may be considered as having "dropped out". Although all the second-generation couples had child(ren), the rest of the households have not yet had a third-generation couple. These households are either following the stem-family life cycle or may have stopped being in that cycle.

---

4) These figures are not in the tables.

Chapter 5: Family Strategy on Succession and Family Farm Management 215

In 1997, two households had become "One-person households"[5], in which the widower/widow of the second generation lived alone, or was living separately from his/her married son/daughter. This is a good example of "drop outs" of the stem-family life cycle.

2-2. Reestablishment of Stem-family Households : Stem-family Succession
As stated above, during the period of 31 years, 43 out of 108 (39.8%) households have changed to households such that married couples of the third generation live with their parent(s). These stem-family households have reestablished their household composition.

However, living together with a married son/daughter does not always guarantee that the son/daughter has succeeded his/her parental home, or the so-called Ie which is the native family institution in Japan. It is said to consist of these ideals: the family line, the family name, the status in community, the family properties (money, house, land, farm, grave, etc.), the family tradition and so on, that have been made by the ancestors and are to be passed down from generation to generation [Morioka *et al.* eds., 1993, 31-32].

A son/daughter who is the successor can inherit Ie from his/her parents, even if he/she is living separately from his/her parent(s) temporarily. On the contrary, there are cases where a son/daughter does not inherit Ie, or in other words does not succeed the family line, even while living with his/her parent(s). Before World War II, in general, the first-born son was defined as the successor by Civil Law, and he continued to live with his parents even after his marriage. After the War, there was a change in this Law, but the stem- family ideology has remained stable for a long time, so that most of the first-born sons have been regarded as heirs.

However, recently, the ideology of the stem family has gone out of date and it has become rather difficult to determine who the successor is. The living arrangement between parents and their married son/daughter is one of the useful indicators in determining who the successor is. Among the 43 stem-family households with a couple of the third generation in 1997, there were some households that had atypical successors.

2-2-1. The Third Generation of Stem-family Households who are Not Successors
For example, there was a case in which the parents, especially the father, did not recognize their married son as their successor, although the son has been living with them for over 10 years. Another example was that of a divorced daughter with her child

---

5) Strictly speaking, "One-person households" is not a family, because a family is a small group.

who was living with her parents. These are two cases of the reestablished stem-family households. The son and the daughter in each case did not succeed Ie.

2-2-2. Married Successors Living Separately from their Parent(s)
During the period of 31 years (1966-92), 48 out of 108 households have reestablished their household composition where the third-generation couples lived with their parent(s). In 1997, however, there were only 43 households of such a composition. The other five households have become a conjugal family again. This had happened during the last five years of the panel, as the couples of the third generation had started living independently. As for Japanese families which have the traditional stem-family ideology, the successors ought to continue living with their parents even after their marriage. Therefore, we may say that this is one of the new trends of stem families that married successors discontinue living with their parents.

On the other hand, 14 third-generation couples who first formed a conjugal family started living with their parents between 1992 and 1997. These two facts indicate that those who live separately from their parents can become successors.

This same behavior is observed between the first generation and the second generation, but it was regarded as atypical in those days. At that time, living arrangements between the second generation and the third generation are diverse, even in stem families. To sum up, a married son/daughter living with his/her parent(s) would not necessarily succeed his/her Ie, and a single son/daughter living separately from his/her parent(s) can become a successor. Therefore, we need to explore indicators of stem-family succession other than the successors' marital status and living arrangements.

2-3. Other Indicators of Stem-family Succession
To understand family succession more accurately, we should discuss the issue from three points of view: 1) Whether the father recognizes his son/daughter as his successor or not, 2) Whether the successor is married or not, 3) Whether the successor lives with his/her parent(s) or not. These factors are required for stem families to be succeeded from generation to generation. We shall now elaborate on these three indicators.

2-3-1. Whether the Father Recognizes his Son/Daughter as his Successor or not
In this study, this indicator comes from the attitude of husbands of the second generation. The question was, "Do you have any plans for your family succession?" There were the four choices:
    a) I have already selected a son/daughter as my successor (with his/her consent).

b) I have already selected a son/daughter as my successor (without his/her consent).

c) I have not selected a son/daughter as my successor yet (want to make a decision but cannot).

d) I have not selected a son/daughter as my successor yet (have not thought about it at all).

The husbands who had chosen a) or b) were asked to answer a sub-question: "Which son/daughter will you select as your successor?" There were 80 husbands who chose a) or b) and answered the sub-question. 14 other husbands chose c) or d). We could not interview the rest of the husbands, for 12 had passed away and two households refused to answer the question. The result is that we can identify 80 persons of the third generation as successors of the second generation.

2-3-2. Whether the Successor is Married or not

For a stem family pursuing a typical stem-family life cycle, the successor of the family must be married and have child (ren). This indicates that this stem family has performed its succession. In 1997, 69 out of 80 (86.3%) successors, who were recognized by each father, had gotten married.

There were two out of 69 married successors who were living separately from their wives. One reason of separation was due to trouble within the family. The other was the wife's preference of city life in Tokyo over rural life in Katsunuma Town. This couple had lived separately for 14 years and the husband had been visiting his wife and his child every week during that period. Such a lifestyle had seemed improbable in farming families before the third generation.

In these two exceptional cases, the successors were legally married, but their households were not in the form of a typical stem-family household.

2-3-3. Whether the Successor Lives with his/her Parent(s) or not

The stem-family ideology is intricately inked to rules of residence between two consecutive generations. Whether the successor and his/her parents live together or not is also an indicator of stem-family succession. In 1997, 52 out of 80 (65.0%) successors recognized by each father lived with their parent(s).

Moreover, there were 10 households with persons of the third generation living with their mothers, with their fathers having passed away. Nine out of these 10 households were stem-family households and one consisted of a son and his mother.

As I mentioned above, there was a married son living with his parents but his father did not recognize him as his successor.

In this study, people living in the same house number are identified as people living together, yet there were a few cases in which a married couple and their parent(s) registered one residence officially, but in reality lived separately. Whether couples of the third generation live with their parents or live separately from their parents depends on their family consciousness. The consciousness mostly comes from the actual life conditions. Recently, a lifestyle in which each married generation lives in different buildings, but on the same premises is favored by rural stem families.

2-3-4. Facts of Stem-family Succession being Performed

In 1997, there were sons/daughters who were not recognized as successors by their father, but had already inherited his/her parents' property, title and so on. The persons of the third generation whose father had passed away had already succeeded. Let us think about facts of succession of the second generation, regardless of their recognition.

There were eight households in which the title to the house belonged to persons of the third generation.

There were 22 households in which persons of the third generation were the managers of their family farming, although these managers were often only nominal managers; some of them lived separately from their parents or did not engage in farming at all. The Japanese farmer's pension required that pensioners had to transfer the title of farm manager to their successors at that time[6].

There were 16 households in which persons of the second generation mainly engaged in family farming. In seven households of the sixteen husbands of the second generation were dead, so persons of the third generation really did manage their

Table 5-1-2 Types of Stem-family Successors (Katsunuma Town in 1997)

Persons

	Living conditions between successor and parents	Marital status	Has succession been performed?	Successors	Non-Successors	Husbands of second generation who died
				N=80	N=14	N=12
Type I	separately	single	no	4		
Type II	together	single	no	12		
Type III	separately	married	no	15		
Type IV	separately	single	yes	1	1	
Type V	together	single	yes	6	1	1
Type VI	separately	married	yes	8		
Type VII	together	married	no	11	1	
Type VIII	together	married	yes	23		9
Not else-where classified					11	2

---

6) See Chapter 4, Section 4, footnote 4 on p.187.

Chapter 5: Family Strategy on Succession and Family Farm Management 219

farming. In three other households, couples of the third generation lived away from and commuted to their parental homes to work. Before the third generation, a successor lived with his parent(s) and worked together. Such a change in working style is one of the new trends in family farming in Japan.

2-4. Stem-family Succession from the Second Generation to the Third Generation

Observing the succession of stem families from the second generation to the third generation in Katsunuma Town, we can grasp the new trends in the stem-family life cycle in rural Japan.

As shown in Table 5-1-2, we classified the successors, who are persons of the third generation of stem families, into eight types according to indicators of stem-family succession, which we have mentioned above. Let us think about each type of successor, for a better understanding of the trends in stem-family succession.

2-4-1. Successors in Type VII or Type VIII

In type VIII, a successor is a married person of the third generation who lives with his/her parent(s) and has succeeded his/her parents' property and/or title. He/she has established succession of his/her stem family. In type VII, a successor is a married person of the third generation who lives with his/her parent(s) and has succeeded neither his/her parents' property nor title.

In 1997, there were 44 out of 108 (40.7%) households whose successors belonged to type VII or type VIII. These households had reestablished stem-family households and had been pursuing a typical stem-family life cycle.

2-4-2. Successors in Type III or Type VI

In type VI, a successor is a married person of the third generation who lives separately from his/her parent(s) and has succeeded his/her parents' property and/or title. In 1997, there were eight households whose successors belonged to type VI. In type III, a successor is a married person of the third generation who lives separately from his/her parent(s) and has not succeeded his/her parents' property or title yet. There were 15 households whose successors belonged to type III in 1997.

Stem families whose successors belonged to type III or type VI, were to reestablish stem-family households if they strongly believed in the stem-family ideology. Stem-family ideology declined and rules of residence changed in these families. If the ideology and the rules had kept in these families, in 1997, there would have been 67 out of 108 (62.0%) households that were pursuing a typical stem-family life cycle.

I mentioned above three successors who were persons of the third generation, who lived away from and commuted to their parental homes to work, which was a case that belonged to type VI.

2-4-3. Successors in Type I or Type II
On the whole, successors in type I or type II were younger than those of other types. In 1997, those successors had been single and had not succeeded their parents' property or title yet.

2-4-4. Successors in Type IV or Type V
In type IV or type V, successors had been single and had succeeded their parents' property and/or title. Among them, there were successors such that they were mainly engaged in farming as a manager. They had difficulty in getting married because they were men in their forties. Moreover, there are not enough women who want to marry farmers nowadays. This is a contemporary problem for stem-family succession and also one of the social problems in rural Japan.

3. Conclusion

The aim of this study was to point out evidences of changes in stem-family succession in current Japan by analysis of panel data of around 100 stem-family households in Katsunuma Town.These panels have performed for 31 years from 1966 to 1997. The following results were obtained:

3-1. Trends in Household Composition

During the period of 31 years from 1966 to 1997 many households in family type "Other relatives households" have changed to households in family type "Family nuclei." In 1966, at the first panel, all households belonged to family type "Other relatives households." After 31 years in 1997, there were more households in family type "Family nuclei" (50.5%) than households in family type "Other relatives households" (47.7%).

Married couples of the third generation were found in 1981 in 8 households, 34 households in 1992 and 43 households in 1997. These stem-family households, which contained couples of the third generation, were pursuing a typical stem-family life cycle.

On the other hand, there were households that were slow-paced in circulating the stem-family life cycle or were close to stopping the cycle [Kakizaki, 1977]. In 1997, two households had become households in family type "One-person households." This is a case of "drop outs" of the stem-family life cycle.

Living together with a married son/daughter does not always mean that he/she has succeeded his/her parental home [Kato, 1988]. For Japanese families who hold a traditional stem-family ideology, the successors ought to continue living with their parents even after their marriage. However, there were stem families with married successors whose living with their parents was interrupted. It is one of the new trends in stem families.

3-2. Family Succession

Living conditions between married couples of the second generation and married couples of the third generation were diverse. Some phases of relations between the second generation and the third generation need to be explained, for these phases are incomplete.

We discussed the family succession not only from the fact that family succession had been performed, but also from the requirements as follows: 1) Whether father recognizes a son/daughter as his successor or not, 2) Whether a successor is married or not, 3) Whether a successor lives with his/her parent(s) or not. These are indicators of stem-family succession, as well as the necessary factors of family succession.

According to the indicators, successors were classified into eight types. New trends in stem-family succession were considered under the types of successors. In 1997, there were 44 out of 108 (40.7%) households which had reestablished stem-family households and had been pursuing a typical stem-family life cycle. If stem-family ideology and rules of residence had continued strongly, in 1997, there would have been 67 out of 108 (62.0%) households which were pursuing a typical stem-family life cycle. There was a problem in stem-family succession if successors were mainly engaged in farming as a manager but stayed single. They have difficulty getting married, since there are not many women who want to marry farmers nowadays.

There are other problems on stem-family succession that are left to be discussed. One of them is that more daughters are being recognized as successors by each of their parents recently. We can see this happening in the third generation in Katsunuma Town, but we lack definite information on how much of an increase there was of female successors, because the survey was not done for couples of the first generation with their married daughters.

Moreover, there remains a controversy surrounding the meanings of succession. What are the most important things to be succeeded within a succession is will be our next theme to be discussed[7].

References
Ishihara, Kunio, 1967,"Nouson Chokkei-Kazoku no Sedai-Koutai ni okeru Setainushi-Kengen no

---

7) See Otomo, 1993.

Ikou (Status Transfer of the Household Head in the Stem Family System)," *Japanese Sociological Review*, 17(3): 2-16. (in Japanese)

―――, 1976, "Setainushi-Kengen no Ikou (Status Transfer of the Household Head)," Kiyomi Morioka and Tsuneo Yamane eds., *Ie to Gendai Kazoku* (The Ie and Contemporary Families in Japan), Tokyo: Baifukan, 124-149. (in Japanese)

―――, 1977, "Setai-Shusaiken kara mita Raifusaikuru to Kazoku-Hendou (Life Cycle and Family Change: From the Perspective of Household Directorship)," Kiyomi Morioka ed., *Gendai Kazoku no Raifusaikuru* (The Life Cycle of Contemporary Families), Tokyo: Baifukan, 80-205. (in Japanese)

―――, 1993, "Setai Shusai-Ken no Sedai-teki Ikou to sono Henka (Generational Transition and Change in Household Directorship)," Kiyomi Morioka, Kunio Ishihara, Hiroto Satake, Masae Tsutsumi and Takashi Mochizuki eds., *Kazoku Shakaigaku no Tenkai* (The Development of Family Sociology), Tokyo:Baifukan, 145-162. (in Japanese)

Kakizaki, Kyoichi, 1977, "Setai-Keitai no Shuki-teki Ikou to Itsudatsu (Deviations from the Periodic Transition of Household Structure)," Kiyomi Morioka ed., *Gendai Kazoku no Raifusaikuru* (The Life Cycle of Contemporary Families), Tokyo: Baifukan, 161-179. (in Japanese)

Kato, Kikuko, 1988, "Oyako-Doukyo no Kazoku Hatten-Ron teki Kousatsu (A Family Developmental Approach to the Japanese Three-Generation Family)," *Japanese Sociological Review*, 39(3): 284-298. (in Japanese)

Otomo, Yukiko, 1993, "Chokkei-Sei Kazoku ni okeru Kazoku-Kousei no Henka to Sedai no Koushin (Change in Family Composition and Generational Renewal of Stem-family Households)," Kiyomi Morioka, Kunio Ishihara, Hiroto Satake, Masae Tsutsumi and Takashi Mochizuki eds., *Kazoku Shakaigaku no Tenkai* (The Development of Family Sociology), Tokyo: Baifukan, 99-121. (in Japanese)

―――, 1998, "Chokkei-Sei Kazoku no Hendou ni tsuite no Jisshou-teki Kenkyu: Yamanashi-Ken Katsunuma-Cho ni okeru Paneru Deta wo mochiite (Empirical Study on Change in Stem-family Households Based on the Panel in Katsunuma Town, Yamanashi Prefecture)," *Research Journals on Household Economics*, 37: 70-73. (in Japanese)

―――, 1999, "The New Trends in Household Successions in Rural Japan: A Case of Katsunuma Town," *Asian Rural Sociology*, 1: 115-127.

―――, 2007, "Shukushou-ka suru Setai, Kazoku to Ie no Henka (Shrinking Household Size, Changing Families and the Ie)," The Japanese Association for Rural Studies and Hiroyuki Torigoe eds., *Mura no Shakai wo Kenkyu suru* (Study on Village Society), Tokyo: Rural Culture Association, 76-84. (in Japanese)

Hill, Reuben, 1970, *Family Development in Three Generations*, Cambridge, Mass. : Schenkman.

Tsutsumi, Masae, 1993, "Nouson Chokkei-Sei Kazoku no Yakuwari-Kouzou no Jizoku to Henyou," (Change and Continuity of Role-structure of Stem Families in Rural Areas)," Kiyomi Morioka, Kunio Ishihara, Hiroto Satake, Masae Tsutsumi and Takashi Mochizuki eds., *Kazoku Shakaigaku no Tenkai* (The Development of Family Sociology), Tokyo: Baifukan, 122-144. (in Japanese)

Morioka, Kiyomi, 1973, *Kazoku-Syuki Ron* (The Theory of Family Life Cycle), Tokyo: Baifukan. (in Japanese)
———, 1993, *Gendai Kazoku Hendou Ron* (The Theory of Contemporary Family Change), Kyoto: Mineruva Shobo. (in Japanese)
Morioka, Kiyomi, Tsutomu Shiobara and Kouhei Homma eds., 1993, *Shin Shakaigaku Jiten* (New Encyclopedia of Sociology), Tokyo: Yuhikaku. (in Japanese)

2
Property Inheritance of Farming Families
Masae Tsutsumi

1. Introduction
1-1. Purpose

This article aims to clarify how "mono" (property) is actually inherited in farming families, based on the changes in household compositions over thirty years. How the inheritance "mono" has changed with time or remained unchanged will be investigated[1].

The ways of passing down the homestead and assets including farmlands is a very important matter for a farming family for its continuation. As widely known, Japan's inheritance system has changed from inheritance by a single heir to inheritance by equal distribution as the "Ie" system has given way to the conjugal family system. Through this system the farmland is equally divided, which in turn leads to the discontinuation of farming, farming could not continue. Therefore, it is a general practice that the person who takes over the farming inherits all and other heirs relinquish their rights. In exchange, the successor gives them money on such occasions as marriage and leaving home to set up on their own. The issue of inheritance comes up in a farming family usually when a parent dies. It seldom surfaces as long as no major change occurs to the family members. In order to continue farming, it is important that the heir accedes to the farmland. Recently, however, the heir often has a job other than farming and cannot always take over the family farm. This accelerates the trend of incorporating agriculture. In group farming, private ownership of land holds various challenges. For future farm operations, the continuation of farming needs to be considered from various viewpoints including inheritance.

Japanese rural families usually engage in small farming. Depending mostly on family to work on the farmlands, the heir inherits these lands, which are still privately owned today. Full-time farmers have been farming their farmlands as the means of production. Part-time farmers often do farming in order to maintain their farmlands

---

1) In "Inheritance of farming family assets 'mono' ", in my book *Nihon Nouson Kazoku no Jizoku to Hendou* (Cuntinuance and Changes of the Stem Family Households in Rural Japan) 2009, Gakubunsha, the author analyzed the accessions of farming and property inheritance upon the death of a parent. In addition to "mono", accessions of "hito", or people, and persistence and change in "consciousness" were described. Here, Japanese characteristics of property inheritance will be discussed.

Chapter 5: Family Strategy on Succession and Family Farm Management   225

which are the means of production.

Further development of the industrial structure promoted industry more than agriculture. Land, once the means of production, is now valued as an asset. Fewer children took over their parents' farming, and the farmland somehow lost its significance as the means of production. More people choose agriculture as a profession instead of acceding to it as a family business.

These issues are not limited to farming families. What is important is to discern what to hand down and what to change. Inheritance of "mono" is regulated by a system, but it is also a persistent field of rural families, or Japanese families, as well as a field of reality adaptation.

1-2. Preceding Studies on Farming Families' Property Inheritance and Accession

In Japanese farming families, under the stem family system, farming and farmland have been passed down as a family business and homestead from generation to generation. It was a rational form for a peasant family in the stem family system to maintain and pass down farming and farmland. Inheritance was almost exclusively by a single heir. But as cases in which generation transition did not go smoothly increased, many gave up farming, forcing the conventional methods of maintaining and passing down farming families to change. Behind this phenomenon are changes in family composition. More heirs choose not to take up farming and the family relinquishes farming when the parents retire and a generational transition occurs. In other cases, the heir leaves home and farming is continued by the aging parents until they abandon it. Many of the Japanese farming families are still three-generational. Today, the number of people abandoning farming is on the rise. This trend is accompanied by changes in family composition. Are they within the framework of stem families, or is the stem family system heading toward extinction? Investigation of the changes in farming and ex-farming families, including regional characteristics, living rules, inheritance forms, and family consciousness, is being called for [Tahata, 1993: 58-88].

Earlier studies on inheritance were done in various fields such as sociology[2] [Hosaka, 1990: 156-174], [Sugioka, 1994: 103-128], [Hashimoto, 1996: 82-86], socio-legal study [Toshitani, 1964 & 1974], [Yuzawa, 1964], and anthropology/folklore

---

2) Especially in the field of sociology, Masatoshi Ouchi's "Heir and Generational Transition" in *Nouson-Shakai no Henbou to Nouminnishiki* (Tokyo University Press, 1993) is related to this article. Ouchi analyzes types of generational transition, the successor's life courses, accession and disposal, based on the thirty-year case studies in Akita and Okayama. There are other literatures such as Fuyou to Souzoku by Takatoshi Seki [2006, 43-78], edited by Comparative Family History Society, 1998 (Waseda University Press).

study [Takeda, 1974]. A study on inheritance and accession was also compiled based on reports at academic meetings (under the editorship of the Society of Comparative Family History, 1998).

Here, the whole structure of persistence and change in farming families for the past 30 years will be investigated, and accession and inheritance of "mono" will be analyzed through case examples. As the abandoned land increases and group farming is advanced, it is important to try to foresee in which direction things are going.

2. Characteristics of Challenges and Subjects, and Contents of Inheritance

2-1. Challenges

Let us examine the property ("mono") here. Land, once the means of production, is now valued as an asset. In the past, large-scale farming families were financially affluent, and their social position in the community as well as the position of their "Ie" was high. Recently, however, the management scale and land size are no longer indicative of affluence. As the significance of farmland is changing, how differently is "mono" including land being passed down? Finding this out is important for understanding the persistence and change in rural families [Tsutsumi, 2000].

As for the analysis points: 1) Are land and other assets equally distributed as regulated by law? 2) Is the inheritance method different for different generations? 3) How have the methods of inheritance and accession changed or remained unchanged? Data for clarifying these will be analyzed. Research data taken after an inheritance took place will be studied. There are 107 subject cases, but the inheritances took place on different occasions. Therefore, the total number does not always reach 107.

Inheritances from father to son during the last thirty years will be discussed first. Then case examples of inheritance by the father's year of death will be examined.

2-2. Data Characteristics

The data used here were collected through interviews by questionnaires conducted six times in 1966, 1972, 1979, 1981, 1992, and 1997. Some were also gained during supplemental investigations. The above years were chosen because questions about succeeding farming and inheritance were asked[3] at those times.

Let us analyze what kinds of inheritance existed between 1966 and 1997. Inheritance is an event that takes place when the child's generation takes over from

---

3) The following items were analyzed for respective years: succession of farming for 1966, property succession and succession of farming for 1972, inheritance issues for 1981, inheritance issues for 1992, and inheritance issues for 1997.

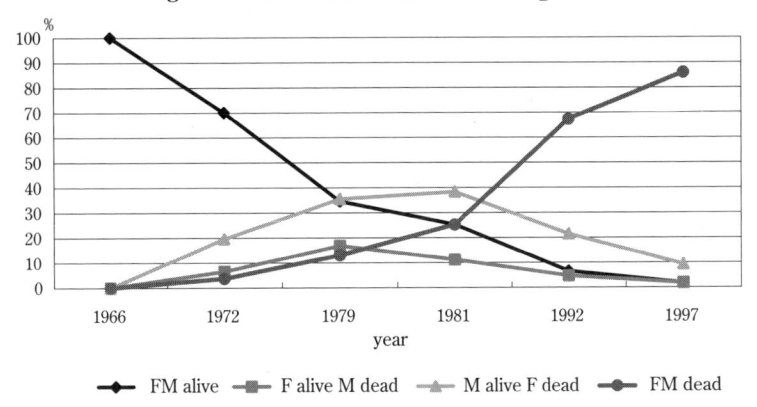

Figure 5-2-1 Parents Alive/Dead Passing Ratio

◆ FM alive ■ F alive M dead ▲ M alive F dead ● FM dead

the parent's generation. Therefore, it is something that is certain to happen. But when it does cannot always be predicted. This is one of the characteristics of this topic. The data collected concern when inheritance actually took place.

There are inheritances after death and inheritance before death. Figure 5-2-1 shows household compositions by whether the parents are alive or dead.

100% of the parents in two-generation families were alive in 1966. By 1997, 86.0% of them had passed away and the generation transition has taken place. 1981 was when the ratios crossed.

21 fathers died between 1966 and 1972 (dead by 1971), 44 between 1972 and 1981, 30 between 1982 and 1992, 8 between 1992 and 1997, making the total 103 cases.

9 mothers died between 1966 and 1972 (dead by 1971), 28 between 1972 and 1981, 40 between 1982 and 1992, 18 between 1992 and 1997, making the total 95 cases.

There is data spread for both fathers and mothers. Half of the fathers died in the 1960s and 1970s. About 30% of the mothers died in the 1960s and 1970s. The number of deaths was the highest in the 1970s for the fathers and in the 1980s for the mothers.

It is presumed that the year of the father's death has a lot to do with how inheritance was carried out. For this, 1970 and 1980 have the highest numbers.

2-3. Contents and Methods of Inheritance

How property is passed down from the parent's generation to the child's generation was investigated. The total number is about 103 fathers' deaths[4]. Inheritance is an event

---

4) Some of the questions were not followed up. The data used here were based on those followed up in 1972, 1981, 1992, and 1997. This creates some limitations, but the data were meticulously collected.

that takes place when the child's generation takes over from the parent's generation, not an everyday occurrence. It comes to pass without fail, but to know exactly when is impossible. This is one of the characteristics of this topic, and the data intrinsically have certain limitations. With this in mind, the data collected over thirty years is examined below.

2-3-1. Methods of Succession of Property
Property includes ①farmland, ②forest land, ③housing site, ④house, ⑤cash, and ⑥others. The following explains what went to who, and how.

① Farmland
Most commonly, the heir inherited the farmland. In 38 cases the heir inherited 50% of the farmland, whereas in 35 cases the heir inherited it all, with only two cases where the heir inherited less than 50%. In all, the heir was the inheritor in a total of 75 cases. There are 7 cases of shared inheritance. Sole inheritance by a sister took place in 2 cases, 50% inheritance by a sister occurred in 2 cases. They all happened in families with no son, and the heiress was the inheritor. In 8 cases, the land was not quite large enough for farming, and the heir inherited less than half of it. Thus, farmland is almost always inherited by the heir.

② Forest Land
Very few families own large forest land. Among those who do, inheritance was mostly shared; partial inheritance of less than 50% took place in 11 cases. In 6 cases, the heir inherited less than 50%. In 5 cases, the heir inherited all. Forest land was usually shared, the priority given to the heir.

③ Housing Site
In 34 cases, the heir was the only inheritor. In another 34 cases, the heir inherited less than 50%. In 11 cases, less than 50% was for shared inheritance. Sole inheritance by a brother was seen in 2 cases, by a sister also in 2 cases. Partial inheritance of less than 50% by a sister was in 2 cases. The housing site was almost always inherited by the heir.

④ House
32 cases were sole inheritance by the heir. 31 cases were partial inheritance of less than 50% by the heir. In any case, the heir mostly inherits the house, even though in 3 cases a brother inherited it. 9 cases were shared partial inheritance of less than 50%.

Chapter 5: Family Strategy on Succession and Family Farm Management   229

⑤ Cash
In 29 cases, the heir took in about 50%. 26 cases were sole inheritance. In other cases, brothers and sisters partially inherited less than 50%. 16 cases were partial inheritance of less than 50%, although the interviewees claimed they had no money. The heir was again most likely to inherit the cash.

2-3-2. Procedure for an Inheritance Waiver
This is a question whether the interviewee went through the procedure for an inheritance waiver at a family court within three months. In the 1981 research, 27 answered yes, and 20 answered no. In 1992, 17 said yes, and 12 said no. In 1997, 2 said yes, and 5 said no. When summed up, the number of those who took the procedure was higher (46) than those who did not (37). The inheritance waiver was more likely to be filed in order to allow sole inheritance by the heir.

2-3-3. Consideration of Gift Before Death
When deciding whether to divide the property and in what proportion, how many took "gift" before death into consideration? In 1972, 7 cases did consider it, while 7 did not. In 1981, 26 out of 45 cases did not, while 17 did (2 unknown). In 1992, 16 out of 29 cases did not consider it, 10 did, and 3 were unknown. In 1997, 6 out of 7 did not consider it, and only 1 did. In total ,35 cases, "gift" before death was given, while in 55, it did not happen. In half of the 103 cases, inheritance was carried out not before but after death.

2-3-4. Troubles with Inheritance Issues
How many people had trouble with inheritance from their parents? The answers to this question in 1981 were "No" in 40 cases, "A little" in 3 cases, and "A lot" in 2 cases. In 1992, 26 said "No", 1 said "A little", and 2 said "A lot". In 1997, 7 said "No". 73 out of 81 said they did not experience any trouble. Only 8, both "A little" and "A lot" combined, said they did. One of these 8 subjects reported that a quarrel escalated to one party demanding the other to pay for signing the paperwork, but this was a rare case. Usually in a farming household, all the immediate and extended family members seem to assume that the heir inherits all. Behind this is a thought that the heir "takes care of the ancestors and the family tomb".

2-3-5. Period of Inheritance
How long did the inheritance process take after the death of the father? The number of total responses was 81. There were 46 cases in 1981, out of which 20 said within three months, 5 said within six months, 8 said one year, 4 said three years, 2 said 5 years, 1

said more than five years, and 1 said "not completed".

1992 had 28 cases, out of which 11 said within three months, 5 said six months, 1 said one year, 2 said three years, 5 said 2 years, 0 said more than five years, and 7 said "not completed".

Out of 7 cases in 1997, within 3 months: 4, within one year: 2, and "not completed": 1. 56 cases out of the total 103 cases were completed within 1 year. Total of 11 cases spent more than three years. The fact that 14 cases remain uncompleted should not be overlooked. As a general trend, it seems that the inheritance process does not require a long period of time. This suggests that there are not many problems about the inheritance. If there are any, they can be quite serious.

3. Characteristics of Inheritance by Investigation Year

3-1. 1972 Investigation

In 21 cases the father died between 1966 and 1971. What characteristics do they have? The property inheritance was done in 10 cases. Sole inheritance of property was in 13 cases, and none was shared inheritance. Has the property been distributed to someone during the last six years excluding the time of death? 13 said no and 2 said yes. The characteristics of this time period were clearly inheritance solely by the eldest son.

3-2. 1981 Investigation

In these cases (44) the father died between 1972 and 1980. Inheritance by the eldest son was still common then. Problems rarely occurred in the process. In 37 cases the deceased did not leave any instructions or will. In 5 cases, the deceased did not draw up a will but left verbal instructions or a note. In 2 cases, testament had been written. Only 1 had problems, while 43 did not. To a question about the difficulty of the process, 27 answered "not as much as expected", 12 said "as expected", and 3 said "more than expected".

Only 8 said that they sought consultation or advice from someone other than siblings. Most of them went to public agencies or professionals such as a judicial scrivener (for procedures and creating documents) and the town office (for paperwork processing). There was also a case in which a priest at the family temple was consulted. Various people and social institutions were consulted depending on the situation. In some cases, cash was distributed to four siblings to help a recently-widowed sister in financial hardship.

3-3. 1992 Investigation

In many of these cases (30) in which the father died between 1981 and 1991, the heir inherited all. In 17 cases other inheritors relinquished the right of inheritance.

Chapter 5: Family Strategy on Succession and Family Farm Management 231

In 12 cases, this was not done. The remaining one case the subject did not respond. 16 said "gift" before death was not considered. No one reported serious problems, and the process was usually completed in a short time. There seemed to be not much difficulty.

3-4. 1997 Investigation

8 cases in which the father died between 1991 and 1997 were examined. The number of cases has dropped significantly. By that time, the majority did not file for inheritance waiver (5 cases). Only 2 did, and 1 did not respond. "Gift"before death was not considered. No trouble was reported. The process was readily completed (within 3 months: 4; within 1 year: 2).

The data shows that even in the 1990s, farming families gave inheritance priority to the heir who often inherited everything. Equal distribution, as regulated by law, was not prevalent. Even as the conjugal family system was spreading, this aspect did not change, retaining the stem family system's rule.

What has been analyzed so far is the inheritance from the father to the child's generation. In 1992, the child's generation was asked how they wanted to pass down to their children (grandchild's generation). Out of 28 responses, 12 were "sole inheritance by the heir". 6 were "basically the heir inherits everything, giving some to the other children". 2 were "the heir gets most, but the other children gets some, distributed as equally as possible". Most gave the heir the priority. 4 said "equal distribution by principle" or "in other forms". The rest were unsure. This indicates that the heir priority probably will not change at the time of the next generation's inheritance.

4. Case Study on Generations of Succession and Inheritance upon the Father's Death

How did succession and inheritance from the father's generation to the child's generation take place? Here, "The Father's Life Course" and "Property and Inheritance Problems of the Heir Generation" will be analyzed.

4-1. Father Dies in the 1960s

4-1-1. The Father's Life Course

The father was born in 1897, as the third son among seven siblings. His two older brothers left home after marriage. He graduated from Ordinary Elementary School and worked at an unknown place for 15 years. He went out on his own in 1923. In 1926, he had an arranged marriage with someone born in 1899. The main family was his eldest brother's family, but he was living in Tokyo and died in 1962. Therefore, the main family did not live in the city of Katsunuma. The father said his was a branch family.

He himself bought wooded area, cut down trees, and sold them to make money to buy farmland.

The father's parents were farmers. The grandfather died in 1930 at the age of 72. The grandmother died in 1924 at 54. The grandfather never retired or discussed having his son take over as head of the family. The father decided to be a farmer after he married. In the 1966 investigation, he was the nominee of "investments in the Agricultural Cooperative" and the account holder of "the family's main savings", but the actual responsibility for the family had already been transferred to the next generation. Farm management and land disposition were done through consultation with the next generation.

He had five sons and four daughters. His eldest son was the heir, and he had an arranged marriage in 1950. The father passed away in April 1967 after two years of suffering from disease. His wife took care of him with the help of his sister. The heir paid for the expenses.

4-1-2. Succession and Inheritance of the Heir

The heir inherited all property. The mother and all his siblings relinquished the right of inheritance. The father did not leave any instructions about inheritance, but the inheritance was completed in about six months without any problems. The siblings understood the position of the eldest son, the heir, very well. During the ten years prior to 1981, all the siblings remodeled or built their houses. To repay for their cooperation at the time of the inheritance, the heir lent them money.

When the father died, the family had about 0.6ha (6,000m^2) of formland. The succeeding generation hoped their child would continue farming at the time of 1972 and live with them, but they did not want to depend on their child. During the 1981 investigation, they said that their eldest son (born in 1954) was going to take over the family. So the son got a job instead of going to college. The plan was to take over the family business after working for three years or so. But because their grape farm operation was not going very well, the son was still working as of 1981. At the time of investigation in 1992 and 1997, the eldest son, the heir, was still working outside the family. Regarding this the father said "I thought it was good for us that he got a job. I was still young and I thought I would take care of the farm. I hoped he would come home after a while. But now, he is making much more than we do. The income from grape farming won't be enough to live on. So I don't think he'll quit his job. Besides, farming is hard. But I think he'll come back eventually."

Chapter 5: Family Strategy on Succession and Family Farm Management   233

4-2. Father Dies in the 1970s

4-2-1. The Father's Life Course

The father was born in 1895 as the youngest of four. He had two sisters and one brother. After his brother, five years his senior, died at the age of 11, he grew up as the heir. After marriage, the eldest sister moved to Saitama and the second sister moved to Tokyo. After graduating from higher elementary school, he became a farmer. In 1918, he married a woman (born in 1896) chosen by his parents. They had nine children, the fifth being the heir. The father's parents were also farmers. The grandfather died in 1935 at the age of 62, and the grandmother died in 1918 at 50. In the 1966 investigation, the father had authority to attend funerals in the community, invest in the Agricultural Cooperation, and dispose of the land. But in reality the responsibility for the family had already been transferred to the next generation. The father was entrusted with the family responsibilities by his parents in 1926. The 1972 investigation data shows that the father had already retired, having given all authority of the household to the next generation.

4-2-2. Succession and Inheritance of the Heir

The father died of heart disease, asthma, and old age in 1974. The heir inherited all the farmland, forest land, housing site, house, and cash. The mother and all the siblings relinquished their right of inheritance. The father did not draw his testament, but left verbal instructions. There were no problems or trouble regarding the inheritance and the process was completed within three months of the father's death. The father had told his children that the heir should inherit everything. The children had received financial support to go to school and were understanding.

During the year in which the father suffered from his ailments, the mother and their daughter-in-law took care of him, and the heir paid for the expenses. At the time of his death, the family owned about 0.8ha (8,000m^2) of farmland. In the 1997 investigation, it was down to 0.55ha (5,500m^2). As for the succession and inheritance from the child's generation to the grandchild's generation, the former is considering giving all of their children some money for school and marriage, and then giving everything to the heir. The eldest son is likely to be the heir, but as of 1997, he was away from home living in Chiba, and therefore it was not definite.

4-3. Father Dies in the 1980s

4-3-1. The Father's Life Course

The father was born in 1904, as the third among nine siblings, and he was the eldest son. His eldest sister moved to an adjoining village after marriage and his second sister to Kamimachi also after marriage. He had three younger brothers and three younger sisters. After graduating from ordinary elementary school, he became a farmer. For two years before marriage, he lived in Tokyo in military service. In 1933, he had an arranged marriage with his wife who was born in 1909. There is a branch family in Kamimachi, but no main family.

The grandfather was born in 1873 and died in 1936 at the age of 63. The grandmother was born in 1877 and was still alive and well at the investigation in 1966. She died in February 1970. The father did not retire nor declared the transfer of responsibility to the son. In 1932, the grandfather told the father to become a community representative in 1932, and around 1935 the father started to manage the farm finances. Around 1936, he started to manage the family's major savings account. At the 1966 investigation, daily farm work was done by the heir, but the father had all authority. At the 1972 investigation, the homestead was in the father's name, but the child's generation had all the authority and responsibilities. The house remodeling and land disposal were discussed between the father and the child's generation. It was during this period that the transfer of the household authority occurred.

There were four children, two sons and two daughters. The eldest son became the heir and had an arranged marriage in 1961. The father died due to old age in March 1987 after a year of illness. The heir and his wife took care of him and paid for the expenses.

4-3-2. Succession and Inheritance of the Heir
The heir inherited all the property. The mother and all the siblings relinquished their right of inheritance. The father did not leave any instructions about inheritance, but the process was completed in six months without any problems.

At the time of the father's death, the family owned 1.2ha (12,100m^2) of farmland. The succeeding generation feels that their son does not have to do farming while young because he currently has a different job. But the succeeding generation hopes that his son will take over farming someday. At the 1992 and 1997 investigations, the eldest son, the heir, was working at the same place. In 1992, the husband of the succeeding generation respected their son's wish when he first got a job.

4-4. Father Dies in the 1990s
4-4-1. The Father's Life Course
The father was born in 1908 as the third among four siblings. He was the eldest son with two older sisters and one younger brother. All of his siblings were living in Katsunuma and were farmers. After graduating from higher elementary school, the father started farming. In 1932, he married someone (born in 1909) his parents chose. They had three sons and three daughters. The eldest son is the heir. The father's parents were

farmers. The grandfather died in 1959 at the age of 84, and the grandmother died in 1937 at 56. At the 1966 investigation, the father had authority over almost everything from community funerals, investment in the Agricultural Cooperative, land disposition, to purchasing of household goods. The child's generation was doing daily farm work, shipping and sales. But the actual authority was still with the father. The father became in charge of the farming around the age 20 because of the fragile health of the grandfather. According to the 1972 investigation data, the father still retained the household authority, and discussed with the child generation planting, shipping and sales, and farming funds.

4-4-2. Succession and Inheritance of the Heir

The father died of pneumonia in 1995. The heir then inherited all the farmland, housing site, house, and cash. All the siblings relinquished their right of inheritance. Two years later in 1997, the mother died of liver disease. The heir's wife took care of both of them before they died. There was no problem or trouble with the inheritance, and the process was completed within three months. At the time of the 1997 investigation, the inheritance from the mother was not processed yet because it was soon after her death.

When the father and mother were sick, the heir's wife cared for them and the heir paid for the expenses. After the father's death, the family had 0.98ha (9,800m^2) of farmland (the 1997 data). As for the succession and inheritance from the child's generation to the grandchild's generation, the former is considering giving all of their children some money for school and marriage, and then giving everything to the heir. The eldest son is likely to be the heir, but as of 1997, he was living in Saitama with his family. The father is planning to pass down the homestead, farmland, family name, ancestral services, and social network. He also said he wanted to pass down the family consciousness to the heir, that only those who engage in farming could have the farmland.

5. Succession and Inheritance Due to Unexpected Family Events

5-1. Child's Generation Dies Before the Parent's Generation

5-1-1. The Father's Life Course

The father was born in 1908 as the eldest of eight siblings. He had six brothers and one sister. All of them graduated from higher elementary school, married around age 24 to 25, and left home. They were living outside the hometown in Tokyo, Minami Koma-gun, Tsukui, and Kofu. The father graduated from higher elementary school, became a farmer, and in 1926 married his wife (born in 1907) for love. They had four sons and one daughter, the eldest son being the heir. The father's parents were farmers. The - grandfather died in 1950 at 68, and his wife died in 1941 at 53. At the 1966 investigation, the father's main authority was over community funerals and investments in the Agricultural Cooperative. He was also the primary holder of the family accounts and discussed land disposition with the heir. All other authority was held by the heir. At the 1972 investigation, the family owned and managed 1.05ha (10,500m^2) of farmland and did supplementary labor. The fourth son lived with the parents. In 1981, their farmland decreased by 0.08ha (800m^2) due to the construction of the Chuo Expressway. The father was the name holder of the resident registration and he owned the homestead but the farmland ownership was shared with the heir. The father declared the transfer of authority to the heir in 1964 and retired. Since then, the heir was the main figure in the family farming business.

5-1-2. The Heir's Life Course

The heir, the eldest son, was the firstborn of five siblings. Born in 1927, he graduated from agriculture school. The school was in Matsudo, Chiba Prefecture, and he was away from home while in school. After that, he engaged in farming. In 1956, he had an arranged marriage with his wife, born in 1930. His father was 48 years old, and his mother 49. His wife was working at a grocery store. At the 1966 investigation, his mother had already left the daily shopping to his wife. His father was given the household responsibilities by his grandfather around 1946. The 1972 investigation data shows that the father still had the household authority and discussed planting, shipping and sales, and farm funds with the child's generation. The eldest son had a boy in 1957 and a girl in 1960. At the 1981 investigation, these children were away from home going to college. Later the boy got a job in Tokyo but came home in 1987 to assume his role as the next heir. But disliking rural life, he left for Tokyo once again in 1988. The girl got a job in Tokyo, married, and moved to Yamagata Prefecture in 1984. Thus, the grandchild's generation left home. The husband of the child generation died of gallbladder cancer in January 1988, leaving the parent generation behind.

5-1-3. Succession and Inheritance to the Heir

At the 1981 investigation, a marriage fund was distributed to the five siblings. The heir's children received money for school and other financial support. The heir was also planning to provide business finance, household goods, wedding expenses, and living expense for the newlyweds. The support would continue until they could fully provide for themselves (1981 investigation).

When the husband passed away, the wife and two children divided the insurance. Because the father died before inheritance, the farmland and homestead were still in his name. The wife was planning to equally divide the inheritance. After the death of the father, the first son of the grandchild's generation promised to take over the farming.

Chapter 5: Family Strategy on Succession and Family Farm Management 237

The authority over farming would belong to the eldest grandson, and his wife would be in charge of "house remodeling," "household goods," and "meal menus" (1992). The resident registration and homestead were still in the late father's name (1997).

5-2. Both Father and Husband Die

5-2-1. The Father's Life Course

The father was born in 1896, the first of four siblings. He had two brothers and one sister. His brothers graduated from ordinary elementary school, and his sister from higher elementary school. Then they left for Kofu, Iwasaki, and the city of Yamamashi. The property distributed to the siblings was a marriage fund only. After graduating from higher elementary school, the father became a farmer. In 1923, he had an arranged marriage (the wife was born in 1902). They had three sons and six daughters. The eldest son, the heir, was the sixth child. The father's parents were farmers. The grandfather died in 1960 at the age 96, and the grandmother died in 1911 at 33. In the 1966 investigation, the father's main authority was over "community gatherings," "community funerals," "planting plans," "land disposition," "house remodeling," and "household goods purchases." The heir had authority over "farm work share" and "judgment of shipping and sales." At the 1972 investigation, they owned and managed 0.75ha (7,500m^2) of farmland. The father was doing supplementary work. The grandfather declared retirement in 1946 and put his son in charge of the household. From then on, the father was the central figure in farming. The father died of a stroke at home in 1975. The heir's wife (daughter-in-law) mostly took care of him, and the heir paid for expenses. There was no support from the heir's siblings who had left home. The mother died of stomach cancer two years later in 1977.

5-2-2. The Heir's Life Course

The eldest son, the heir, was born in 1934. After graduating from junior high school, he engaged in farming. He also went to work at a construction company in Kofu during the agricultural off-season. In 1964 he had an arranged marriage with his wife (born in 1939). His father was 59 years old, his mother 53. His wife was from the city of Enzan and was the ninth child of 11. After junior high school, she engaged in farming. At the 1966 investigation, the mother was in charge of "purchasing daily goods". The wife was in charge of "meal menus" and "rice bin management" with the help of the mother. The father was put in charge of the household by the grandfather around 1946. According to the 1972 data, the father had most of the authority over the household. The child's generation was sharing the farm work, and was the holder of "the investments in the Agricultural Cooperative," "farming fund," and "the major household accounts." The heir had a daughter in 1964 and a son in 1968. At the 1992 investigation, the daughter graduated from junior college and got a job at a hospital. The son graduated from college and was working at a financial institution in the same prefecture.

The heir was managing the farm but had subarachnoid hemorrhage in August 1983. He was in the hospital for six days. His wife cared for him, but he passed away.

5-2-3. Succession and Inheritance to the Heir" (From the Father Generation to the Child Generation)
The heir inherited all the farmland and housing site. The house had already belonged to the heir. There was no relinquishment of the inheritance rights, and the gift before death was taken into consideration. Because the father died testate, there was no trouble and the process was completed within three months.
(From the Child Generation to the Grandchild Generation)
When the husband died in 1983, his wife inherited all the property because the child was under age. The death was so sudden that they had a lot of trouble with inheritance. It took six months. With the husband gone, the wife was the only one to do the farming. The operation size was reduced from 0.75ha (7,500m^2) to 0.58ha (5,800m^2), and she grew grapes for making wine to simplify the labor.

At the 1981 investigation, the grandchild's generation received financial support for their schooling. The wife planned to give support for their living expenses, business funds, wedding expenses, and homestead funds.

The son, the heir, was commuting to work (a financial institution) from home, which his mother was happy about. Her wish was to have him take over the farming. She also wanted him to succeed his father by inheriting the homestead and farm land, and carrying on the family name, maintaining the family tomb, and social network. This idea remained unchanged in 1992 and 1997.

6. Conclusion—Inheritance of property the tendencies that persist
How is "mono" property passed down and inherited when a generational transfer occurs? The following is what became clear from analyzing the subjects for almost thirty years from 1966 and 1997.
1) The method of property inheritance: ①The heir usually inherits all or more than half the farmland. Even if there were only daughters, the heiress often inherits everything. ②Only a few owned forest land. The inheritance priority is usually given to the heir. Shared inheritance is also common. ③The housing site and ④the house are sometimes shared, but the heir is more likely to have the sole inheritance. ⑤Cash is often inherited by the heir alone. But its rate of partial inheritance is higher than that of real estate. The immovables are often inherited by the heir alone, while the movables are shared with siblings.

2) The relinquishment of inheritance rights are more likely to be filed than not in order to allow sole inheritance by the heir. But recently, it is done less frequently. Gift before death is not given in more than half the cases. Property distribution is often conducted after the father dies. Gift before death is, if any, not usually taken into consideration.
3) Few problems occur during the inheritance process, causing little trouble. Some quarrels were reported in a few cases, but there is a shared understanding that a farming family's heir inherits everything. In exchange for that, the heir is expected to maintain the family tomb and care for the parents. The length of the inheritance processing period varies, but half the cases were completed within three months. There are still some unprocessed cases. Problems seldom occur, but when they do, they may become severe.
4) During the 1960s, sole inheritance by the eldest son was in the majority, a trend that continued into the 1970s. There were very few cases of trouble. Most of the subject households lost the father during these periods, and there is almost no case in which the real estate was equally divided. In the 1980s, the heir still inherited everything. The heir was usually the eldest son whose child would take over the farming. By the 1990s most fathers had passed away, the number of new deaths was very small, and generational transfer had already taken place in most households. Sole inheritance by the heir is still the majority, but less people file for the relinquishment of the inheritance rights.

The following is a summary of the succession and inheritance from the father's generation to the child's generation.
1) In one case in which the father died in the 1960s, the heir, born as the third son (1897), had an arranged marriage, and purchased forest land to cultivate it. There were nine children in the family, and the eldest son became the heir. Everything was inherited by the heir. It was hoped that the grandchild generation would take over farming and live at home. A regular job provides better income than grape farming, so the heir kept his job. The inheritance from the father to the son was the sole inheritance, having the mother and all the siblings relinquished their inheritance rights.
2) A father who died in the 1970s was born as the second son of a farming family (1895). After the eldest son died in infancy, the second son practically grew up as the eldest son. After higher elementary school, he engaged in farming, had an arranged marriage, had nine children, and died in 1974. His eldest son, the heir, inherited everything. The other children had received money for school and marriage, so they relinquished their rights of inheritance. The same was the plan for the grandchild's

generation: the eldest son would inherit all, while the other children would get money for school and marriage.

3) A father who died in the 1980s was born as the third child of nine (1904), started farming after ordinary elementary school, went to serve in the military, had an arranged marriage, and had four children. His eldest son took over farming. After the father died in 1987, the eldest son, the heir, inherited everything. The mother and other children all relinquished their rights of inheritance. The grandchild's generation commutes to work rather than farming. It is hoped that he will take over the farming.

4) A father who died in the 1990s were born as the third child and the eldest son in 1908. After higher elementary school, he became a farmer. He married a woman his parents chose and had six children. He died in 1995. His eldest son, the heir, inherited everything. The other children relinquished their rights of inheritance. The same is being planned for the grandchild's generation: the heir would inherit everything, while the other children would receive some money for school and marriage.

5) An heir died in 1988, leaving the father's generation behind, who had already retired. The insurance was divided among the wife and children. The real estate and resident registration were in the father's name. The eldest grandson was to take over the farming. The family lost the father and the heir. The father's property had been passed down to the heir who then died. At that time, his children were under age, so his wife inherited everything. Because the death was unexpected, the family experienced a lot of difficulty during the inheritance process.

The above is an overview of general tendencies and these summaries clarify three points.

1) Even though equally shared inheritance is the legal norm, priority is given to the heir who inherits everything in most cases. Characteristics of the "Ie" system are still retained in the forms of inheritance. The contents of inheritance are different. The system seemed to have changed, but in reality it has not.

2) Inheritance itself has not changed much despite the changing times. In farming family inheritance, the eldest son, the heir, prevails. This is the unchanged aspect of the rural family that is not affected by the changing times and systems. Farm operations can be maintained by not dividing the land or real estate. As the number of people taking over farming decreases, how to maintain the farmland could become a serious issue. Some farm operations are incorporated, to which the farmland would be rented. The family would get money or a part of harvest as a form of rent. This is one of the desperate measures to keep the land, after farmers have become old and could no longer continue working. What to do with the farmland and real estate

Chapter 5: Family Strategy on Succession and Family Farm Management   241

could probably become one of the serious issues surrounding farming, farming villages, and farming families.

3) One of the unchanging aspects of rural families was the method of succession and inheritance. When faced with such reality issues as the survival of rural villages and farming itself, how do people deal with inheritance? The whole community is being asked this question about the land.

There are both merits and demerits of the persistence in farmering inheritance today. How inheritance and land ownership will evolve will affect future farming including group farming, community business, and farming families. Moreover, the inheritance issue presents various challenges that concern the community and society as a whole.

References

Naitou, Kanji, 1973, *Masshi-Souzoku no Kenkyu* (Study on Postremogeniture), Tokyo: Koubundou. (in Japanese)

Hashimoto, Kazuyuki, 1996, "Noto ga Keishou suru 'Ie' no Renzokusei to Kinrinkankei (Continuity of 'IE' and Neighborhood which the Noto Peninsula has Succeeded)," *AERA Mook*, 12: 82-86. (in Japanese)

Hosaka, Emiko, 1990, "Hatasaku-Nouson no Kouzou to Tokushitsu: Nouchi no Bunkatsu to Kazoku-Kouzou no Tokushitsu (Structure and Characteristics of Upland Farming Communities: Characteristics of Farmland Distribution and Family Structure)," *Reseach Bulletin of Kagoshima Women's College*, 11(1): 156-174. (in Japanese)

Japan Association of Private Law ed., 1952, *Nouka-Souzoku no Jittai: Noukabetsu Chousa Shiryo* (Reality of Inheritance in Farming Families). (in Japanese)

Morioka, Kiyomi, 1993, *Gendai Kazoku Hendou Ron* (The Theory of Contemporary Family Change), Kyoto: Mineruva Shobo. (in Japanese)

Morioka, Kiyomi, Tsutomu Shiobara and Kouhei Homma eds., 1993, *Shin Shakaigaku Jiten* (New Encyclopedia of Sociology), Tokyo: Yuhikaku. (in Japanese)

Nourinsho Nouseika eds., 1955, *Noukasouzoku no Jittai* (Reality of Inheritance in Farming Families), 1. (in Japanese)

Otomo, Yukiko, 1993, "Chokkei-Sei Kazoku ni okeru Kazoku-Kousei no Henka to Sedai no Koushin (Change in Family Composition and Generational Renewal of Stem-family Households)," Kiyomi Morioka, Kunio Ishihara, Hiroto Satake, Masae Tsutsumi and Takashi Mochizuki eds., *Kazoku Shakaigaku no Tenkai* (The Development of Family Sociology), Tokyo: Baifukan, 99-121. (in Japanese)

——, 1998, "Chokkei-Sei Kazoku no Hendou ni tsuite no Jisshou-teki Kenkyu: Yamanashi-Ken Katsunuma-Cho ni okeru Paneru Deta wo mochiite (Empirical Study on Change in Stem-family Households Based on the Panel in Katsunuma Town, Yamanashi Prefecture)," *Research Journals on Household Economics*, 37: 70-73. (in Japanese)

——, 1999, "The New Trends in Household Successions in Rural Japan: A Case of Katsunuma

Town," *Asian Rural Sociology*, 1: 115-127.

Ouchi, Masatoshi, 1993, "Nouka Kazoku no Henbou to Nougyo Keiei (Farming Family Crisis and Farm Management)," *Journal of Rural Issues*, 37: 1-10. (in Japanese)

———, 2005, *Sengo Nihon Nouson no Shakaihendou* (Social Changes in Rural Areas of Postwar Japan), Tokyo: Association of Agriculture & Forestry Statistics. (in Japanese)

Seki, Takatoshi, 2006, "Geihoku Chusankanchi ni okeru Nousonkazoku no Sedaikankankei: Keishoukankei to Souzokukankei no Sokumen wo Chushin toshite (Generational Relationships in Farming Families in the Intermediate and Mountainous Area of Geihoku)," *Hakkaido University Literature Study Bulletin*, 119: 43-78. (in Japanese)

Sugioka, Naoto, 1994, "Kazokukeiei no Henkaku to Keishou (Makeover and Succession of Family Management)," *Annual Bulletin of Rural Studies*, 30: 103-128. (in Japanese)

Tabata, Yasushi, 1993, "Nouka no Kazoku-Kousei no Henka to Iji Keishoumondai (Changes and Preservation of Farming Family Structure and Succession Issues)," Toshihiko Isobe ed., *Kiki ni okeru Kazoku Nougyo Keiei* (Family Farm in Socio-Economic Crisis), Tokyo: Nihon Keizai Hyouronsha, 58-88. (in Japanese)

Tachikawa, Masashi, 1989, "Koureikanouson ni okeru Nouka Nouson no Keishou Mondai (Succession Problems of Farming Families and Communities in Aging Villages)," Tadao Hatano ed., *Kourei Kengyo Nouka to Ninaite: Kinki-Chugoku Chiiki ni okeru* (Aging Part-time Farming Families and their Workforce: In Kinki and Chugoku Areas), Chugoku National Agricultural Experiment Station, 51-97. (in Japanese)

Takeda, Akira, 1974 "Sousetsu: Souzoku Keishou no Teigi to sono Bunrui wo megutte (Review: Definition and Categorization of Inheritance and Succession)," Michio Aoyama ed., *Kouza Kazoku 5: Souzoku to Keishou* (Seminar on Family 5: Inheritance and Succession), Tokyo: Koubundou, 303-319. (in Japanese)

Toshitani, Nobuyoshi ed., 1964, *Nihon no Nougyo*, 34. (in Japanese)

———, 1974, "Nougyo no Keishou to Souzoku no Jittai (Actual Condition of Succession and Inheritance of Farming)," Michio Aoyama ed., *Kouza Kazoku 5: Souzoku to Keishou* (Seminar on Family 5: Succession and Inheritance), Tokyo: Koubundou. 364-383. (in Japanese)

Tsutsumi, Masae, 2000, "Noukasouzoku no Jireikenkyu (Case Study on Farming Succession)," *Yamanashi-Kenritsu Joshi-Tankidaigaku Chiiki Kenkyu* (Yamanashi Prefectural Women's Junior College Area Studies), 1: 43-61. (in Japanese)

———, 2001, "Nousonkazoku ni okeru Sedaikeishou no Jisshoubunseki: Hito, Mono, Kokoro (Empirical Analysis of Generational Succession in Farming Families: *Hito, Mono, Kokoro*)," *Reseach Bulletin of Yamanashi Prefectural Women's Junior College*, 34: 63-76. (in Japanese)

———, 2001, "Succession of Stem Families in Rural Japan: Case in Yamanashi Prefecture," *International Journal of Japanese Sociology*, 10: 69-79.

———, 2009, *Nihon Nouson Kazoku no Jizoku to Hendou* (Cuntinuance and Changes of the Stem Family Households in Rural Japan), Tokyo: Gakubunsha. (in Japanese)

Yuzawa, Yasuhiko, 1964, "Nougyo Kazoku no Keieikeishoukatei (Succession Process of

Farming Family Management)," *Nihon no Nougyo,* 34: 62-71. (in Japanese)

244

3

Family Strategy in Farm Succession: A Case of Farming Families Executing the Family Agreement in Takasaki City[1]

Yukiko Otomo

1. Introduction

Each family has autonomy within social changes. In this study we can call the methods to keep their autonomy a family strategy [Maruyama et al. eds., 1998]. In Japan, the traditional family institution Ie has been expected to succeed over the generations, and there is a tendency for family successors to not be able to select their life course by themselves. Their life course selection has to be suitable for continuing their family line. Therefore, we can see elements of a family strategy in the life course pattern of family successors.

Farming families in Japan own their farmlands as a part of their family properties *(Kasan)*. Because of that, farm management is a family business *(Kagyo)*, which should be handed over from generation to generation [Morioka et al. eds., 1993].

However, as it is well known, Japan is a highly industrialized and urbanized country, and the agricultural sector of the national economy has shrunk during the last five decades. There are not that many farm managers who can successfully run their family farm. In spite of that, here we see a case of ambitious farm managers executing a family agreement, which was renewed as a family management agreement today.

2. The Post-war Agricultural Policy in Japan and Family Farming

First of all, we would like to focus on political change in Japanese agriculture during the last century. As mentioned above, the traditional Japanese family institution, the so-called Ie, kept material and spiritual family properties. Family business was based on the material family properties, i.e. land and equipment for its productive activities.

In modern Japan, the Ie institution was modified as a sector that was dependent

---

1) Support for this research was provided by the Japan Society for the Promotion of Science and their 2001 and 2002 Grant-in-Aid for Scientific Research. This study was presented at the 11th World Congress of the International Rural Sociology Association on July 25-30, 2004 in Thronheim, Norwey.

Chapter 5: Family Strategy on Succession and Family Farm Management 245

on the emperor, and was enhanced to a national ideology [Kawashima, 1957]. In 1898, the Meiji Civil Code was created, which stated that material properties must belong to a person and the right to supervise a family has to be transferred from the father to the eldest son. Due to this inheritance system, family succession and family business could continue over the generations.

After World War II in 1948, the current Civil Code was established. The new code abandoned the Ie institution and the right to supervise a family. The inheritance system was changed from a solo-favoring system to an even-favoring one, which meant that not only the eldest son but also all other kin-family lineages were lawful heirs. The institutional background, which guaranteed generational succession of the family business, was abolished.

In spite of that, our case in family farming has been somewhat different, because the post-war Japanese government improved the institution of independent family farming. From 1947, democracy opened farmlands for each farm family from pre-modern large farm owners. This agrarian reform made a lot of the small-scale family farms in current Japan [Sugioka, 2001]. Such small-scale family farms had not possessed basic properties for developing family businesses until the reform.

In 1961, the Basic Law on Agriculture was established, which contributed to the improvement of modernized independent farming families. In order to further its improvement, the Japanese government adopted new strategies for supporting the status of young farm successors on their farm management. One of them was the Family Agreement in farming families [Toshitani, 1990].

Because of industrialization and urbanization, many farming families could not keep their successors in the agricultural field, except for some successful independent farming families. Most of the farm households kept family farming as a side business. Mainly women and senior family members were engaged in farming a trend that was impossible to stop. In those times, the trends were overwhelmingly side-business farming, feminization of the agricultural sector, and aging of the farmers. The amount of uncultivated farmland was growing, and the rate of domestic food supply got reduced. The ecology and safety of food were not secured. Then, in 1999, the Basic Law on Agriculture was changed to the Basic Law on Food, Agriculture and Rural Areas.

The new political enactment gained sustainable agricultural development in Japan. This policy used a concept of Farming Holdings, which replaced the Farm Households, meaning that holdings, which include various forms other than a farm household such as an agricultural corporation and a rural community, are more sustainable than families, because they are not influenced by kin-family lineage. In 2001, agricultural stock company, the strongest type of holding, was constructed because the new law aimed at marketing policy in Japanese agriculture. In these companies, people could choose agriculture as their career.

However, in reality, most of the Farming Holdings are family businesses, i.e. the unit of Farming Holdings is the household. Usually, it is a leading objective in Japanese agriculture to provide good conditions for the family farm. For the Basic Law on Agriculture, the Family Agreement was a measure of improvement of modernized independent farming. It was imported from western countries in the 1960s. At the time, the Family Agreement was operating on a father-son contract for seeking a democratic family relationship and a modernized farm management. However, such a contract among the family did not suit the traditional Japanese farming families and went out of use, except for some rural communities.

After introducing the new law, the contract-system was revived as the Family Management Agreement for partnership within farm families and for empowerment of farming women under the policy toward developing a gender-equal society [Gojyo, 2003][Kawate, 2006]. The Family Management Agreement includes a contract between the husband and the wife, along with the father-son contract.

3. Family Agreement in Takasaki City

3-1. Beginning of Family Agreement in Takasaki City

In Takasaki city, the Family Agreement of farming families has been promoted by the City Chamber of Agriculture since 1966. There are a few communities like Takasaki City that have continued the Family Agreement for more than 40 years. When the most recent investigation was conducted in 2004, 144 farming families had participated in the signing of the Family Agreement in Takasaki City. However, each year the number of farm households executing the contract is around 40. The most recent ceremony for signing the Family Agreement was held on May 12th, 2003. There were 43 farming families, which signed this agreement.

In the 1960's, the Family Agreement was introduced to Japanese farming families in order to keep young farm successors engaging in their family farming. In 1964, the National Chamber of Agriculture published the 'Promotion Charter of Family Agreement Farming.' At that time, as industrialization progressed in Japan, young men left their family farms to engage in non-agricultural occupations. The Family Agreement was to be utilized to improve the working conditions of farming families as well as their family lifestyle. It was helpful in encouraging young farm successors to willingly engage in family farming.

In the 1960's, Takasaki City grew through its combination with the surrounding rural areas, which led to the urbanization of these rural areas. Moreover, in 1967, a new town for wholesale merchants was built in this city, and the city became the center of distribution in the northern metropolitan area. Employment and business opportunities for Takasaki people greatly increased. Young farm successors giving up farming became a severe problem to the agriculture of Takasaki City.

The contract was aimed to keep young farm successors in their family farming. It was a father-son contract. Originally, the age of the son for this contract was restricted to 28 or under, but later this restriction was deleted.

3-2. Types of Family Agreement and Trends in Number of Households Executing the Family Agreement in Takasaki City

There are mainly three types of Family Agreement in Takasaki City as follows:

Type 1: An agreement for reward to farm labor: in this type, for example, a manager of the family farm pays a salary to a family laborer, as to a salaried worker.

Type 2: An agreement for distribution of sales value of products: in this type, a manager and his family laborer make a ratio of distribution in advance.

Type 3: An agreement for inheritance of management: in this type, a farm manager rents his father's farmlands for his farm management.

Type 1 is suitable for young farm successors. Type 3 is mostly taken by a farming family such that it contains the conjugality of two generations: father, mother, son and son's wife. Type 3 is also taken by a farming family such that the father is 60 and over. The father hands over his position as a manager to his son because of his farmer's pension[2]. According to the stages of family life cycle, farming families take different types of agreements.

Table 5-3-1 shows the change in the number of farming families that have participated in the signing of this agreement. There was a turning point between 1976 and 1977. After 1977, farm households that signed the Type 3 agreement increased. This phenomenon shows that many sons had already become managers and new

Table 5-3-1 Number of Households Executing the Family Agreement (Every 5 years)

Unit: households

Year	1966	1970	1975	1980	1985	1990	1995	2000	2001	2002	2003
Number of times	1	5	10	15	20	25	30	35	36	37	38
Total	24	37	32	51	41	45	45	44	44	44	43
Type 1	5	8	6	15	15	13	13	11	11	12	13
Type 2	7	25	15	18	8	4	3	1	1	1	1
Type 3	0	4	11	18	18	28	29	32	32	31	29
Others	7	0	0	0	0	0	0	0	0	0	0

Source: Takasaki City Chamber of Agriculture

---

2) See Chapter 4, Section 4, footnote 4 on p.187.

farmers had decreased. In the 1980's, as urbanization progressed in Takasaki City, the land prices skyrocketed, and the inheritance tax burden for farm successors had become heavier.

3-3. From Father-son Agreement to Partners' Agreement

In 1986, the son's wife began to participate in the Family Agreement. This was put into practice by a proposal from the wives' group. Because of the shortage of farm labor, there was a higher demand for women's labor in family farming. In 1990, mothers also began participating in the Family Agreement.

In the 1990's, the Division of Women and Life in the Ministry of Agriculture, Forestry and Fisheries began to promote the Family Management Agreement[3], so renamed from the Family Agreement. It aimed to empower farming women. In the revision of the Farmer's Pension Act in 1996, women were given the right to take a farmer's pension if they executed the Family Management Agreement[4]. In such movements of the 1990's, the Family Agreement of Takasaki City was noted widely as one of the models of Family Management Agreement.

4. Family Agreement and Rural Communities in Takasaki City

4-1. Areas of Distribution of Farming Families Executing the Family Agreement

Table 5-3-2 shows trends in the development of the number of farming families executing the Family Agreement according to rural community. From this, we can see the geographical distribution of farming families executing the Family Agreement in Takasaki City. There are 13 rural communities in this city. About 40 percent of the farming families executing the Family Agreement are located in the rural community No.9 (the Yawata agricultural area), and about 20 percent are located in the rural community No.13 (the Takigawa agricultural area). This means that somewhat less than 60 percent of farming families executing the Family Agreement of this city is gathered in these two agricultural areas. Another 20 percent is located in the rural communities No.5 and No.6, which belong to the Seibu agricultural area. The remaining 20 percent is spread all over the city. These three agricultural areas are located in the suburbs of Takasaki City and have gathered the full-time farm households.

In the Yawata and the Takigawa agricultural areas, farming families that are executing the Family Agreement are performing cooperative agricultural management within the rural community. From 1977 to 1981 in the Yawata agricultural area, several

---

3) See Chapter 4, Section 4.
4) See Chapter 4, Section 4, footnote 4 on p.187.

Chapter 5: Family Strategy on Succession and Family Farm Management 249

Table 5-3-2 Number of Households Executing the Family Agreement by Rural Communities (Total for 5 years)

Unit: households, %

	Year	1966-1975	1976-1980	1981-1985	1986-1990	1991-1995	1996-2000	2001	2002	2003
	Number of Times	1~10	11~15	16~20	21~25	26~30	31~35	36	37	38
	Total	360	221	159	87	132	227	44	44	43
Community	No.1	36	15	17	8	7	10	2	2	2
	No.2	5	0	0	1	3	5	1	1	1
	No.3	10	0	0	0	2	5	1	1	1
	No.4	5	5	4	1	2	5	1	1	1
	No.5	49	14	9	7	12	26	6	6	6
	No.6	21	17	14	8	15	22	4	4	4
	No.7	9	7	8	4	6	5	1	1	1
	No.8	25	12	4	2	5	10	2	2	2
	No.9	112	79	73	40	54	90	17	17	16
	No.10	6	8	0	0	0	0	0	0	0
	No.11	2	0	0	0	0	0	0	0	0
	No.12	16	8	1	0	0	0	0	0	0
	No.13	64	56	29	16	26	49	9	9	9
	Total	100.0	100.0	100.0	100.0	100.0	100.0	100.0	100.0	100.0
Community	No.1	10.0	6.8	10.7	9.2	5.3	4.4	4.5	4.5	4.7
	No.2	1.4	0.0	0.0	1.1	2.3	2.2	2.3	2.3	2.3
	No.3	2.8	0.0	0.0	0.0	1.5	2.2	2.3	2.3	2.3
	No.4	1.4	2.3	2.5	1.1	1.5	2.2	2.3	2.3	2.3
	No.5	13.6	6.3	5.7	8.0	9.1	11.5	13.6	13.6	14.0
	No.6	5.8	7.7	8.8	9.2	11.4	9.7	9.1	9.1	9.3
	No.7	2.5	3.2	5.0	4.6	4.5	2.2	2.3	2.3	2.3
	No.8	6.9	5.4	2.5	2.3	3.8	4.4	4.5	4.5	4.7
	No.9	31.1	35.7	45.9	46.0	40.9	39.6	38.6	38.6	37.2
	No.10	1.7	3.6	0.0	0.0	0.0	0.0	0.0	0.0	0.0
	No.11	0.6	0.0	0.0	0.0	0.0	0.0	0.0	0.0	0.0
	No.12	4.4	3.6	0.6	0.0	0.0	0.0	0.0	0.0	0.0
	No.13	17.8	25.3	18.2	18.4	19.7	21.6	20.5	20.5	20.9

Note: Data in 1981, 1988, 1989, 1992 and 1993 are unknown.
Source: Takasaki City Chamber of Agriculture

agricultural producers' cooperative corporations for horticulture were formed, which were specialized in producing tomatoes in greenhouses. Between 1974 and 1983 in the Takigawa agricultural area, four farming families formed limited companies (*Yugengaisha*) for hog-raising. These companies together came to receive the management diagnosis from a licensed tax accountant.

In Japan, liberalization of agricultural products began between the 1970s and early 1980s. The competition principle of a market was introduced into agricultural management, and the amount of investment of a farming fund increased. It was the time when the successors in the Yawata and the Takigawa agricultural area had assumed their roles as farm managers, and about ten years have passed after their engagement in their family farming. At the same time, the institution of Family Agreement was introduced in Takasaki City for the farm successor born in 1938 onward.

There were 43 farming families executing the Family Agreement in 2003. Among these farming families, there were 50 males mainly engaged in farming. Twenty-six of them were born between 1945 and 1954, which means that they belong to the generation of the so-called baby boomers and post-baby boomers. In the Yawata and the Takigawa agricultural areas, there were relatively numerous males mainly engaged in farming who attained independent family farming on the basis of the Japanese governmental sanctions in favor of the status of young farm successors.

The next section shows the conditions of farm management styles of these agricultural areas in detail.

4-2. Cooperative Management of Tomato Producing in the Rural Community: the Yawata Agricultural Area

Sixteen out of 43 farming families that executed the Family Agreement in 2003 are in the Yawata agricultural area. Eleven of the 16 farming families are members of one of the three agricultural producers' cooperative corporations, which produce tomatoes in greenhouses. These corporations were organized during 1977 and 1981 by 20 farming families for the purpose of acquiring farming subsidies to construct greenhouses. They own 21 greenhouses altogether and run a workshop for assorting, packing and shipping tomatoes. They employ many part-time workers. It looks like a factory. Eleven out of these 20 farming families are currently executing the Family Agreement.

Most of these 11 farm successors are the so-called baby boomers: 7 were born between 1947 and 1952. When the successors were in school, there were many more classes than for other generations. The students who were not first sons became office workers after graduating from high school. The farm successors were to become farm managers eventually. A community leader of the cooperative corporations suggested they took part in the corporations and engaged in their family farming. They were hopeful for a successful farming career. One of the successors said, "I will earn a lot more than my rival office workers." In those years from 1966 to 1971, they started getting involved with the Family Agreement.

More than 20 years have passed since the establishment of this cooperative management. It is time to pay off the debt for farming subsidies and also time to renew greenhouses. The management is facing a problem of whether to renew these

Chapter 5: Family Strategy on Succession and Family Farm Management   251

equipments or not.

The successors born in this area after the second half of the 1950s had worked in a company as businessmen after graduating from university or high school. But after their early resignation, they started engaging in their family farming. Those who had heirs not currently engaged in farming kept hoping that their inheritor sons would engage in family farming after their early resignation from their companies.

4-3. Agricultural Corporations for Hog Raising : the Takigawa Agricultural Area

Nine out of 43 farming families that executed the Family Agreement in 2003 are in the Takigawa agricultural area. There are four farming families that are each running limited companies for hog-raising. These farm companies were established during 1978 and 1983. Three of them are farming families executing the Family Agreement. These farm successors are also baby boomers.

The biggest company of all is raising more than 160 pigs. It employs many part-time workers. Every company equips themselves with a modernized automatic system to raise hogs; thus, they need not work on holidays and they can enjoy their free time. Together these successors learn management from a licensed tax accountant.

One of the successors' wives said, "I married my husband because of his daring spirit. It is no concern of mine whether he is a farm manager or a factory manager, but I prefer farming to manufacturing. Animals are lovely." She had no experience working on a farm before her marriage.

These farms are anxious about the urbanization of their community. Hog-raising is noisy because pigs oink and they smell awful, and thus, new inhabitants dislike it. As the prices of housing lots rise, inheritance tax becomes a burden to them. For example, when the successor of the biggest farm holding inherits his father's properties, his inheritance tax is estimated at 60,000,000 yen (about US$600,000). However, the successors who are not currently engaged in farming and are working in companies are going to succeed their independent family farming.

5. Farming Holdings and Family-farm Successions

As mentioned above, baby boomers' and post-baby boomers' successors began engaging in their family farming under the Basic Law on Agriculture after the war, cooperating with their neighbors in rural communities and organizing agricultural producers' cooperative corporations. However, how their succeeding generation took the training for becoming under the New Basic Law on Food, Agriculture and Rural Areas? The following two examples are carrying out independent farm companies and are cases in which the family agreement between the parent generation and the child generation was succeeded by the child generation and the grandchild generation.

5-1. A Case of Dairy Producing

5-1-1. Overview

Dairy farming family A established a limited company in 1981, which is located on a hilltop in northwest Takasaki. Their farmland is equal to 10ha, which is quite a large management scale in Japanese standards. When the interview was conducted in July 2000, the ranch kept 300 dairy cows of the Holstein kind, 6 dairy cows of the Jersey kind and 6 young Japanese oxen. Just two months ago, the farming family established another limited company for processing homemade ice cream and yogurt.

Its working force consisted of the manager (b.1943), his wife, the first son and his wife, the second son, the third son, a round year worker, four part-time workers and four temporary workers. The manager's wife took on accounting tasks herself and the third son was in charge of processing dairy products. It takes about 30 minutes by car from their family residence to the ranch. The second and the third son, who were single, lived in the dormitory of the ranch.

In 1966, the manager had signed a contract with his father, the Family Agreement valid until his father's death in 1980. Afterwards in 1990, the first son began to engage in family business and signed a contract with the manager. The first son's wife has also signed the contract of the Family Management Agreement.

5-1-2. Manager's Career

a. Successor- minded Educational Background

The manager was the eldest son in his family. He had 5 younger brothers and sisters. As the eldest son, he helped his parents from a young age. In his junior high school days, he was a member of a baseball team and his wish was to enter a high school that has a well-established and successful amateur baseball team. However, he had to enter another agricultural high school and to learn horticulture in order to succeed his father's peach farm.

He was also expected to engage in his family farm from an early stage, so that he could not enter university, while his younger brothers were given the chance to study at the high level educational institutions by their father.

One of his high school teachers, whose major had been dairy, had significant influence on the manager's occupational selection. During his third year in high school, the manager had already made up his mind to change his family farm from peach farm to a dairy cattle ranch.

b. Initial Engagement in Family Farming

The manager started engaging in family farming just after his graduation from high school in 1961. He started his career as an assistant on his father's peach farm. In 1967, he got married. His marriage was the next important step in developing his farm management abilities. He decided to build a small cowshed for about 15 milking cows in his yard. It was a time for consolidating the manager's business.

c. Becoming a Manager of Farming

In 1968, the manager's mother passed away at the age of 51. In 1970, his grandfather was admitted to the hospital and his father fell ill. All these unfortunate family events urgently required him to manage his family farm by himself when he was only 27 years old, which is a very young age for a farm manager in Japan. Soon after in 1972, the manager legally inherited all of his family properties from his father before his death, and then in 1973, he completely changed his succeeded peach farm to a dairy farm.

d. Establishment of his Company

In 1981, because of a development project of the city, the manager's farmlands were forced to move to another place. Because of the urbanization of rural areas and the large number of children of the baby boom generation, Takasaki city had to construct some new junior high schools in the rural area of the city. A new junior high school was built on family A's farmlands.

The manager and his wife sought for their new farmland to be large enough to run a dairy farm both in and out of Gumma Prefecture. The family bought their current 10ha ranch paying 400 million yen (about US$4 million) and established a limited company. The family raised the capital, which was subsidized by the government, and the wife carried out all accounting tasks by herself instead of hiring a specialist in accounting. She visited a tax information office several times and learned how to pay off their debt in advance. The manager was devoting all his time to selecting the breed of cattle. As a result, he has received several official commendations for selective breeding of cattle, like his award for successful dairy management by the Japanese emperor in 1987. The couple has demonstrated their best capability in carrying out their partnership in their farm management.

e. Fostering the Next Farm Succession

The manager's three sons studied agriculture in schools, and now they all engage in their family business. The eldest son participated in an internship program at a large-scale farm in California, USA. The second son was educated at an agricultural high school in Hokkaido, which is a well-known region for large-scale farm management in Japan. The third son studied milk-processing technology at an Academy for agriculture in Gumma Prefecture. The manager opened two dairies for homemade products in 2000. He will hand over his position as manager of these shops to his third son, as soon as possible after his marriage.

5-2. A Case of Flower Planting

5-2-1. Overview

In 2001, family B had a flower planting farm with a management land scale of 1ha (70a[5] owned, 30a lent), 50a of paddy fields and 30a of greenhouses for cyclamen. Its working force consisted of 6 persons, manager (b.1950), his wife, elder son (b.1978), younger son and two year-round part-timers. The manager planned to expand his farmland and to establish his company in 3 or 5 years, because from 2001 both his sons began to engage in flower-planting.

His family lived together, also including the head of the household, his wife, his two sons and his daughter. The farm family had been executing the Family Agreement for 33 years at that time.

5-2-2. Manager's Career

a. Successor-minded Educational Background

In Japan, the first son usually succeeds the family farm. The manager's father was the fourth son but succeeded the family farm, because his elder brother had passed away in World War II. The father had continued his career as an office worker even after his family-farm succession. As a part-time farm household, the farm family planted rice and barley, and bred silkworm. It was a traditional agricultural pattern in this region at that time, and therefore the manager, his brother and his sister helped their farm operation from a very young age. The manager, as the first son, was expected to be the main work force on his farm. For example, he was obligated to take care of domestic animals, such as pigs and oxen, before going to school. That is why he hates animals nowadays and why he has chosen to start a flower-planting business. Even if he could profit greatly from milking cows, he would never develop such a business.

In his high school days, he was a member of the brass band and he kept a secret longing to be a musician. It was a turning point for him when he first happened to see a planting farm of cyclamen. Now he thinks that planting cyclamen is not just agriculture but also art and a very attractive business. One of his classmates was a successor of a cyclamen planting farm. The manager was given a pot of cyclamen by his friend and he began planting it. After a certain time, he was very happy to see his own cyclamen blooming. During his third high school year he bought 200 pots of seeding cyclamen with his pocket money. He got a secondhand greenhouse from a neighboring vegetable planting farm and placed his cyclamen seedling there. By that time, he had already made up his mind to succeed his family farm.

---

5) 40a=approx. 1ac.

b. Initial Engagement in Family Farming

In March 1967 at his high school graduation, he started engaging in farming by building a small, new greenhouse. Normally, young farmers of his generation had to pass about a two-year internship at large-scale farms. But being fiercely independent by nature, he decided to start his business by himself. At first, he felt envious of his classmates, who already had a regular income as businessmen. Later, however, he realized that he had made the right choice for himself.

c. Becoming a Manager of Farming

In 1975, his father retired. Usually, retirees continued to work on their family farm in rural communities, but his father did not do so, because he was a city community leader with many public duties. Within 5 or 6 years since the manager entered the business, the farmland owner's name was transferred from his father to himself, 10a each year. The postwar Japanese inheritance institution is even between the heirs, spouse and children. In this case, his brother and sister did not need to inherit the farmland, because they graduated from university with by their father's financial support.

In 1976, the manager got married and his wife began to help his business as an accountant. After a short maternity leave, she resumed her family business duties.

d. Fostering the Next Farm Succession and Farm Holding

The manager's first son learned horticulture at university and after that passed a two-year internship at a large-scale farm. From 2001, he is engaging in his family business. In the spring of 2001, he passed a month-long internship in the Netherlands. The second son also learned horticulture at high school and is now engaging in family farming. The daughter graduated from high school in 2001 and is now learning flower gardening at business school. She will be able to engage in her family business as well, if she wants, because of the good management conditions of the family business. They were all willing to help their family farm from a young age, playing games connected to flower planting from early in their childhood. In their high school, they worked part-time on their parents' farm. The first son played an important role as an assistant manager recruiting other seasonal part-time workers among his classmates.

The manager was planning to expand his farmland by renting 0.12ha (1,200m^2) neighboring uncultivated land, and to enlarge his greenhouse with 0.1ha (1,000m^2) more. He hoped that he would be able to establish a limited company in three or five years.

5-3. Common Features of both Cases

The above two farm managers are entrepreneur-managers who were established as a successor of their family farm under the Basic Law on Agriculture after the war. They currently aim to further expand their management scale through bringing up their successors of the next generation, while it is based on family farming.

The common features of these managers' occupations are as follows. (1) Independent personality of the manager. (2) Helping the father's farm as the eldest son in their family from an early age. (3) Attending agricultural high school as a future successor of the family farm. (4) Early engagement in family farming right after their graduation from high school. (5) Formation of family and family succession. (6) Sudden role as a solo manager at an early age because of family complications. (7) Successful partnership with wives in farm management. (8) Giving a special technical education in agriculture to all their children, not only to the eldest son. (9) Letting their children select agriculture as their occupation, which is a rather rare case in Japan. (10) Introducing a large capital and enlarging the scale of their family business because of the fact that several of their children become involved in their family business.

The awareness that the eldest sons would inherit the family farm was formed through the lifestyle of their childhood. Their habits as an inheritor formed their independent personality. Although they succeeded family farming, they reclaimed the management field themselves and have found the management domain in which self-determination is possible.

Early retirement of their fathers, their wives' partnership and their children's expertise gained from a school education made such a thing possible. They also made their children their partners in the family business. These examples make it clear that the management scale expansion of the Farm Holding is based on family-related issues.

6. Conclusion and Discussion

The aim of this study was to focus on the topic of family-farm succession in contemporary Japan. Here, we saw the topic from two different angles: a political macro scoop, and a private micro scoop.

After World War II, the Japanese government promoted family farming, where the essential element is the farm successor. From 1947, farmland was opened for each farm family from large farm owners. The agrarian reform made a lot of small-scale family farms, which had not possessed basic property for developing family business. In 1961, the Basic Law on Agriculture was established and it contributed to the improvement of modernized independent farming families.

However, the number of family farm successors has been decreasing because of industrialization and urbanization. Then in 1999, the Basic Law on Agriculture was changed into the Basic Law on Food, Agriculture and Rural Areas. Under the new law, the policy used a concept of Farming Holdings, which includes various forms other than a farm household, such as an agricultural corporation and a rural community.

Chapter 5: Family Strategy on Succession and Family Farm Management

But in reality, most of the Farming Holdings were family businesses, i.e. the unit of Farming Holdings was a household.

Farming families executing the Family Agreement in Takasaki City were superior independent farming families which were keeping their farm successors. In Takasaki City, the Family Agreement of farming families was introduced in 1966 and continued for more than 40 years. During the period, many farm successors grew up to be managers and brought up the next generation. The life course pattern of these successors changes across generations as follows.

The life course pattern typical to the successors born in 1940: they became engaged in family farming right after graduating from an agricultural high school because they were the eldest son in their farming family. Although they were not allowed to choose a school and an occupation by themselves, they could engage in democratic family farming thanks to the Family Agreement.

On the other hand, the life course pattern typical to the successors, who were born after the second half of the 1950s, was that they were able to choose their education and occupation by themselves. They were initially engaged in a non-agricultural industry and then got engaged in family farming. Their school education usually did not relate to their occupational training.

The life course pattern typical to the successors, who were born after the second half of the 1960s, was different from former generations. They were children of managers who established their modernized farm management by executing the Family Agreement. They studied agriculture in schools and began to engage in family farming soon after their graduation. Not only the eldest son but also other children could be engaged in their family business. They selected agriculture as their occupation by themselves.

As mentioned above, occupational awareness was made based on the family life experienced in one's childhood. It is obvious that the cultural capital of the family farm, which is succeeded in everyday life, was an important inherited property for continuing family business, along with economic capital. Although the concept of Farm Households was replaced by Farming Holdings following the new agricultural policy, sustainable agriculture is greatly based on the family relation of farm households.

References

Gojo, Miyoshi, 2003, *Kazoku Keiei Kyoutei no Tenkai* (Promotion of Family Management Agreement), Tokyo: Tsukuba Shobo. (in Japanese)

Kawashima,Takenori, 1957, *Ideorogii toshiteno Kazoku-Seido* (The Family Institution as an Ideology), Tokyo: Iwanami Shoten. (in Japanese)

Kawate, Tokuya, 2006, *Gendai no Kazoku Keiei Kyoutei* (Contemporary Significances of Family

Management Agreement), Tokyo: Tsukuba Shobo. (in Japanese)

Marceau, Jane, 1989, *A Family Business?*, Cambridge: Cambridge University Press.

Maruyama, Shigeru, Toshitada Kitsukawa and Toru Komma, 1998, *Kazoku no Otonomi* (The Family Autonomy), Tokyo:Waseda University Press. (in Japanese)

―――, 2001, *Kazoku no Regyurashion* (The Régulation of Family), Tokyo: Ochanomizu Shobo. (in Japanese)

Miyazaki, Toshiyuki, 1993, "Nihon no Nouka ni okeru Kazoku Keiei Kyoutei no kihonteki Kadai (Basic Theses of the Family Management Agreement of Farm Family in Japan)," *Nihon Hougaku Kenkyu*, 58(4):3-28. (in Japanese)

Morioka, Kiyomi, Tsutomu Shiobara and Kouhei Homma eds., 1993, *Shin Shakaigaku Jiten* (New Encyclopedia of Sociology), Tokyo: Yuhikaku. (in Japanese)

Otomo, Yukiko, 2000, "Sustainable Family-farming Successions in an Urbanizing Area of Japan: A Case of Farming Families Executing 'Family Agreement' in Takasaki City," *Shakaijouhou Ronsou*, 4:57-70.

―――, 2003, "Kagyo Keiei-Tai no Sonzoku-Senryaku (A Strategy of Family-business Succession)," *Shakaijouhou Ronsou*, 7:89-110. (in Japanese)

Sugioka, Naoto, 2001, *Kazoku Keiei Kyoutei no Kazoku-Moderu no Tenkan ni kansuru Shakaigaku-teki Kenkyu* (A Sociological Study of Shift in Family Farm Agreement), Report of Grant-in Aid for Scientific Research. (in Japanese)

Toshitani, Nobuyoshi, 1990, "Kazoku Kyoutei = Oyako Keiyaku no Tenkai-Katei to Mondai-Ten (The Development Process and Issues of the Family Agreement: The Parent-child Contract), *Nousei Chousa Jihou*, 2-23. (in Japanese)

Yonemura, Chiyo, 1999, *Ie no Sonzoku Senryaku* (Strategies on Continuity of the Ie), Tokyo: Keiso Shobo. (in Japanese)

Chapter 6

Today's Subsistence Production and Agro-food Initiatives in Japan

Chapter 6, the final chapter, is about new trends, potentials, and roles of rural regions. Recently, more consumers in cities are directly connected to farmers in rural areas, and local production for local consumption has been spreading with the government and Agricultural Cooperative's support. This phenomenon draws attention (as it means of increasing consumers') purchasing choices and expanding marketing outlets for local agriculture. In rural life, however, people often grow their own food and share it with friends and families, consuming a substantial amount of local produce. What this indicates is the richness of a rural society where people are in direct contact with nature and have their own social networks, something that cannot be converted into money. Moreover, local production for local consumption has a potential as an alternative movement against globalization of food and farming. This is verified by comparing it with movements in the United States. The local production for local consumption may provide an opportunity for solving various social problems such as environmental, social injustice, and democratic community management. But this cannot be done simply by securing "food safety" or expanding marketing outlets; this is simply a beginning. All the participants in local production for local consumption, farmers in rural regions and consumers in cities, need to expand their awareness for a cleaner environment as local recourses and a better society for community residents.

1
The Present Situation of Local Supply and Consumption of Agricultural Products from the Aspect of Acquisition and Utilization by Local People

Keiko Yoshino
Chie Katayama / Kyoko Morofuji

1. Introduction

These days, various activities related to utilizing local food such as farmers' markets, local food processing, procuring local food for school lunches, are called *"Chisan-chisho"* (local production for local consumption)" nation wide.

In Japan, as income increased from off-farm employment, the share of subsistence production in the food supply continuously decreased. At the national level, food self sufficiency had fallen below 40 percent in 2006 (Ministry of Agriculture, Forestry and Fisheries 2007). The rural population was expected to provide a labor force for urban areas, and agricultural products continued to be exposed to international competition. In 1961, the Agricultural Basic Law was enacted, and policies for "selective production expansion" and the "formation of a base of chief production" were promoted. Changes in food habits (e.g. westernization of diet, increase in eating out, and the use of processed foods) also accelerated the increase of imported foods.

In contemporary Japan, even farm households started to purchase vegetables from supermarkets following the period of the post-war rapid economic growth after the 1950's. Farm women felt this was ridiculous, and the "Self sufficiency movement" started in the 1970's [Hasumi, Negishi and Suzuki, 1986]. It was the very time when the adjustment of rice production, which had been fully supported by the government, began, and farmers felt uncertainty about attaining a steady income. The movement toward subsistence production was regarded as a frugal strategy to reduce household expenses. Also, with rising health concerns on the use of agrichemicals, the call for safe food was increasing among consumers, and chemical free produce from farm households primarily for their family use, appealed to the consumers. The "Self sufficiency movement" developed into the sales of surplus products at small stalls and street markets that were mainly managed by women farmers.

Nowadays, farmers' markets have grown in both number and scale. There are more than 10,000 farmers' markets in Japan [Ministry of Agriculture, Forestry, and Fisheries, 2005], and markets that sell more than 100 million yen annually are not exceptional. *"Chisan-chisho"* (local production for local consumption) is a movement that has been attracting attention recently, and it is expected to support rural communities and economies.

Similar movements like *Chisan-chisho* are developing in other countries, too. "Eat Local", or "Buy Local" is a movement that is spreading in North America and Europe (Sustainable Table 2009). Community Supported Agriculture (CSA), as is described in the next section (Chapter 6-2) of this chapter by Nishiyama is also an activity developed mainly in the United States to encourage local agriculture. These activities not only offer practical value in that consumers can obtain local food, but also have ethical value in how they support local agriculture and enable a sustainable way of rural life.

In Japan, the government took up *Chisan-chisho* as one of the effective measures to improve food self sufficiency in the "Food, Agriculture and Rural Areas Basic Act" which Ministry of Agriculture Forestry, and Fisheies started as a new ten-year plan in March, 2005. In the same year, a *"Chisan-chisho* study group" was organized by the ministry, and annually, plans for enhancing *Chisan-chisho* were made. In these plans, according to the Act, *Chisan-chisho* is promoted "for providing consumers with opportunities to purchase local food through direct interaction with farmers," and it is regarded to be effective "to develop diverse local industries by highlighting local people's originality and ingenuity, and the independence of the locality". Furthermore, by promoting *Chisan-chisho*, promotion of the consumers' understanding about food and agriculture, continuance of local traditional foods, rural development, and a decrease of environmental burdens, by reducing transportation distances, are expected [Ministry of Agriculture, Forestry and Fisheries, 2007]. JA-ZENCHU [Central Union of Agricultural Co-operatives, 2006], is also focusing on the promotion of *"Nihon-gata shokuseikatsu* (Japanese traditional food habits)" by Food and Agriculture Education and promoting *Chisan-chisho* for raising the food sufficiency rate, and is planning to procure local agricultural products for school lunches, and to construct farmers' markets.

In this way, *Chisan-chisho* is being promoted by government and farmers organizations, but the real situation of the local food supply and its utilization is not really understood very well. There have been some attempts to understand the present situation of *Chisan-chisho* from the production and distribution aspect of products using preliminary general statistical data [Ministry of Agriculture, Forestry and Fisheries, 2007: Fujimoto, 2005; Chugoku-Shikoku Regional Agricultural Administration Office, 2003], and also from the supply aspect perceiving related activities such as the number of farmers' markets [Ministry of Agriculture, Forestry and Fisheries, 2005], but the actual situation is not clearly known. Yoshino and Katayama (2004) enumerated the factors that enable *Chisan-chisho* into three categories as follows: i) actual produce, ii) existence of local distribution, and iii) existence of needs by consumers. While studies on factors i) and ii) have preceded factor iii), they are studied little.

The actual supporters of *Chisan-chisho* are the local people who choose to buy this food, and the accumulation of these actions make up *Chisan-chisho*. We think that in order to understand the present situation of *Chisan-chisho*, it is important to look at the distribution and the production of local products from "a local family's dining table", in other words, from the consumers' view point.

Local foods may also move outside the established markets such as direct sales and gifts, which reflects on local social relations. Local food is not just for sustenance, but it also reflects on the local natural environment and food culture, and the use of local food must be deeply connected with the perceptions of local people. We think that the focus should be on local people, on both the aspects of actual consumption behaviors and mentality. From such points of view, the real meaning of *Chisan-chisho* for local people will be understood, and effective measures for promoting *Chisan-chisho* can be sought. From this point of view, producers are consumers too, and both are members of the local community.

In this paper, focusing on the actual acquisition and use of local food (especially on agricultural products) by local people, we analyze the present situation of *Chisan-chisho* from a case study in Iida city, Nagano prefecture.

2. Research Area and Method
2-1. Indicators Selected
As the indicator for grasping the situation of the local food utilization, we selected various "items". We, of course, understand the importance of integrated indicators such as food-self sufficiency rate on energy/weight base, and transport related food environmental load factors, but we wanted to focus on each local product. Local products are the output fostered by nature and local people through many generations, and thus have cultural meaning, also. Among local indigenous products, various wild plants and fungi are often included, but their caloric or net mass value is usually very small, and their meaning will be almost negligible if calculated on energy base. Thus the numbers of items that are utilized as a measure to show the diversity of foods are those typical of the region. Also the net mass value is shown, in order to allocate a position of sample households under consideration.

2-2. Research Area and Method

2-2-1. Research area

We selected Iida city as the research area considering the existence of farm households, existence of urban consumers, and the willingness of local governments to promote *Chisan-chisho*[1].

In Iida city, there are 110,000 inhabitants in 14 districts[2]. The farm household ratio was 13.9 percent in 2000 (national average was 6.6 percent) according to the Agricultural Census [MAFF, 2009]. These 14 districts are quite diversified, from districts with urban characteristics to mountainous remote ones. Iida city functions as the center of "the Hanni region" which contains 14 local governments[3]. There are several farmers' markets managed by various bodies that are managed by the city hall which farmers in Iida city participate in, also those managed by an Agricultural Cooperative which the farmers in the Hanni region participate in, and so forth. The city hall is also trying to procure local food for school lunches at the city level and to public nurseries at the district level. For local people, the concept of own "local area" differed from person to person, and from the questionnaire survey given to the inhabitants (356 respondents, described later), 30 percent thought that the city was the largest area for their own locality, 56 percent thought Iida city and adjacent towns and villages were the largest, while for 80 percent respondents, Hanni region was the largest area.

In this way, everyone's own "local area" was understood as multi strata. Thus in this paper, we defined Hanni region as the largest area for own "local area", and then focused on districts and the city as well.

Regarding sample districts, we selected three districts considering the importance of agriculture, which we thought may affect the situation of *Chisan-chisho*. The sample districts are as follows. Miho district with 66 percent farm households, Kawaji district with 21 percent farm households, and DID (densely inhabited district) with only a few farmers.

Concerning local food utilization, Iida city can be characterized for its main products, vegetables, fruits and fungi, and its low ratio (29 percent in 2002) of local food sufficiency (lower than the national food sufficiency: 40 percent), which is due to the low caloric count of the main products in Iida city.

---

1) According to the questionnaire survey administered to 3,234 local government (1,704 responses, 53 percent) conducted by Rural Life Research Institute in 2002.
2) In October, 2005, Ue village and Minami-Shinano village were reorganized as parts of Iida city, and the district number became 16.
3) The Hanni region is the area covering Iida city and Shimoina region.

2-2-2. Research Method

The study contained three types of research as follows[4].

i) A study of items available at local retailers.

ii) Questionnaire survey given to inhabitants in Iida city.

iii) Questionnaire survey given to households on acquisition and utilization of foodstuffs.

The results of the questionnaire surveys show the relative social position of sample households.

An item survey of retailers and sample survey on foodstuffs were conducted twice, in the winter (December 2002) and in the spring (May 2003) giving consideration to seasonal fluctuation. December is the month of freezing conditions and production is low, and May is an active month, the harvesting season of vegetables including wild edible plants.

i) Item Survey of Local Retailers

Two types of supermarkets, one was local, and the other was nation wide, that were supposed to provide for the general needs of local consumers, and two types of farmers' markets, one was managed by the Agricultural Cooperative and the other by the city hall, both having more than 200 farmers, as the main suppliers of local food, were surveyed.

The survey was conducted on one day in December 2002, and again in May 2003. All of the agricultural products in the markets provided information on the kind and variety of the item, production place, production methods, price and so forth. These items were counted in three ways as follows.

a) Number of kinds (e.g. apples were counted as "one")

b) Number of kinds and varieties (e.g. *Fuji* apples and *Orin* apples are counted as "two")

c) Number of kinds, varieties and seasons. (e.g. *Fuji* apples in December and *Fuji* apples in May were counted as "two")

Supermarkets generally put importance on meeting various needs of its customers, but items in farmers' markets depended on each farmer's concerns. In order to see if the farmers' markets supplied the necessary items for consumers, large scale farmers' markets were selected as samples, but it should be noted that the survey was conducted on only one day, and the items on that day may have been biased.

---

4) Research districts and sample households were selected with the help of the Agriculture department, Iida city hall.

ii) Questionnaire Survey Given to Inhabitants

A questionnaire survey of the people of Iida city was conducted on the acquisition of food (agricultural products and processed foods), and on their interests of using local food and their evaluation of it. One thousand and fifty two respondents in 400 households from three districts were selected randomly, and we received answers from 163 households (41 percent), 390 inhabitants (37 percent).

iii) Sample Survey on Acquisition and Use of Local Foods

To grasp the actual situation of utilization of local foodstuffs in detail, we selected 15 households as samples and asked them to record the acquisition and utilization of foodstuffs.

Sample households were selected considering factors that may influence the use of local foods; whether they were farm households or not, composition of household members, long time residents or residents that have recently moved in. From three districts, seven farm households (three were composed of three generations, two were nuclear families and two elderly couples), eight non-farm households (two were composed of three generations, three newly moved in nuclear families, and two single households).

The survey was conducted over a period of time simultaneous to that of the retailer's survey. The person in charge of obtaining food products and cooking in the household, recorded foodstuff obtained during a week and the recipes and foodstuff used in a day's meals (last day of the recording). For each food product the place produced, acquisition routes (self-produced, purchased or gift/share) and relationships were recorded (Will be called foodstuff survey hereafter). Within those households that produced or gathered foods, name and varieties of produce, harvest season, harvest amount, way of utilization (self consumption, sales or gifts) were recorded (Will be called production survey hereafter). In addition, semi-structured interviews were conducted in sample households on their situation and perception of agriculture, the use of food products, and the use of local food when the surveys were collected.

3. Results and Discussions

3-1. Availability of Local Foodstuffs at Retailers and Acquisition Routes of Inhabitants

Table 6-1-1 shows which locally produced items could be obtained by consumers, compared to those of supermarkets that we presumed met the general needs of the local consumers. Local agricultural products could supply 44 percent of vegetables, 21 percent of fruits, and 58 percent of fungi of those sold in supermarkets[5]. When

---

5) Among the main six vegetables grown in Iida city, five were available at local retailers.

Chapter 6: Today's Subsistence Production and Agro-food Initiatives in Japan 267

Table 6-1-1 Items that were supplied by supermarkets and local products

	(unit)	Vegetables	Fruits	Fungi
Items on supermarkets	kind	107	33	12
	kind+varietes[2]	125	—	—
	kind+seasonality[2]	168	51	21
Items of local products[1] observed in all the sample retailers	kind	57	9	9
	kind+varietes[2]	66	—	—
	kind+seasonality[2]	71	10	14
Items on supermarkets that could also be supplied by local products	kind	47	7	7
		(44%)	(21%)	(58%)
	kind+varietes[2]	52	—	—
		(42%)		
	kind+seasonality[2]	58	8	12
		(35%)	(16%)	(57%)
Items that were unique to local products	kind	12	2	2
	kind+varietes[2]	14	—	—
	kind+seasonality[2]	13	2	2

"seasonality" is considered, the rate decreased because most of the local produce was only seasonally available. On the other hand, minor crops, newly introduced products, and locally unique products such as wild herbs, wild fungi, and vegetables needed to make locally pickled vegetables were found among local agricultural products only.

Figure 6-1-1 shows the actual acquisition of foodstuffs (vegetables and fruits) by sample households from the foodstuffs survey and availability of concerned foodstuffs at local retailers in the retailers' survey in May. Among the 117 items, 41 kinds of products obtained by 13 sample households, local retailers could supply 25 kinds (61 percent)[6].

Regarding 29 kinds of acquired local foodstuffs (underlined ones), 24 kinds (83 percent) were also available at local retailers. Among acquired local food, 32 items of 16 kinds were purchased ("P"s in the figure 6-1-1), 14 items of 12 kinds were produced by the family ("S"s in the figure 6-1-1), and 24 items of 14 kinds were received as gifts ("G"s in the figure 6-1-1), and among 32 purchased items, 13 were bought from farmers' markets followed by local supermarkets (8 items).

As a source of local foodstuffs, purchasing from retailers was mostly chosen, and it can be said that the physical environment for acquiring local foodstuffs is provided by retailers. It is remarkable that considerable amount of foodstuffs were also acquired

---

6) Even though the same kind of products, they are counted as different items if the households, date, source of acquisition or place produced was different.

Figure 6-1-1 Acquisition Routes and Produced Place of Foodstuffs Gained by Sample Households, and Produced Place of Products in Retailers' Survey.

Acquisition Route	Acquired foodstuff (Food stuff survey)	Iida city	Shimoina region	within Prefecture	within Japan	Foreign countries
Purchase only	Enoki mushroom	P2				*Purchase*
	Sweet potato	P1			P3	
	Radish	P3	P2		P3	
	Chicken mushroom	P1				
	Yamabushi mushroom		P1			
	Shitake mushroom		P1			
	Onion	P1			P4	
	Chinese cabbage				P1	
	Beansprout			P4	P1	
	Melon				P1	
	Sweet pepper				P1	
	Garlic				P1	
	Broccoli				P1*	
	Young soybean					P1
	Pumpkin					P1
	Banana					P3
	Pineapple					P1
Self production +Gift +Purchase	Japanese ginger (Myoga)	S1	P1	G2		
	Lettuce	S1	P2	G4	P1	
	Cucumber		P4	G2	P1	P1
	Tomato		P3		P3	G1	P5
	Carrot	S1	P1		P4	
	Butterbur	S1	P1			
	Japanese leek			G1	P1*	P1
	Strawberry	S1			P1	
	Komatsuna leaves	S1	G3	P1	P1	
	Asparagus	S1	G3		P1	
	Cabbage			G1		P3
	Potato			G1		P2
Self production + Gift	Bamboo shoot	S2	G2			
	Young bean	S1				
	Eringi mushroom		G1			
	Spinach		G1			
	Chinese chive		G1			
	Taro		G1			
	Burdock	S2				
	Honewort	S1				
	Wild leek (wild plant)	S1				
	Iyo orange		G1			
	Koshiabura (wild plant)			G1		Local products
	Taranome (wild plant)			G1		

Self production   *Gifts*

Notes: 1) Produced areas with mesh are those areas that were observed on the Retailers' survey.
2) P: purchased, S: Self production, and G: Gained by gifts. Figures on the right of the capital are the number of households that applied concerned acquisition routes.
Source: Retailers' survey and Foodstuff survey

through self production and received as gifts.

3-2. Utilization of Local Foodstuffs and Inhabitants' Interest in It
Among all the respondents of the questionnaire survey, 39 percent were from farm households. Regarding family composition, 28 percent were nuclear families (according to National Census in 2000 [Statistics Bureau and Statistics Center 2009], 52 percent of all the households in Iida city were nuclear families), 28 percent were with more than three generations (21 percent by the Census), 15 percent were single households (20 percent by the Census). Twenty three percent were elderly families (10 percent by the Census), and about half of the single households and three fourths of nuclear families were elderly families. Comparing with the whole population of Iida city, the percentage of farm households, families with more than three generations and elderly families were larger among respondents.

With regards to the utilization of local foodstuffs, 86 households (62 percent of all respondents) produced some agricultural products or processed food, and the food most often produced were vegetables (produced by 78 percent of households), pickled vegetables (66 percent), fruits (63 percent), rice (54 percent) and tuber crops (50 percent). The main advocates of subsistence farming were elderly people (59 percent were more than 65 years old), and regarding food processing 73 percent were women. Ninety two percent of those who produced something at their households, answered that they tasted good. Twenty five percent of households that produce some kind of crop participated in farmers' markets.

Eighty two percent of the households answered that they gave or received products as gifts. Figure 6-1-2 shows the rough ratio of amounts obtained through three routes -self production, purchase and gifts- regarding rice, the staple food of Japan and vegetables consumed by each respondent household using a ternary plot[7]. Concerning the acquisition of rice, single routes such as "all is purchased" or "all is self produced" are in the majority, while most of the respondents obtained vegetables through plural routes and only 16 percent of households purchased all their vegetables. Acquisition routes vary household by household reflecting the production conditions and social relationships of each family.

Figures 6-1-3 and 6-1-4 show in detail the acquisition routes of gifts given and received. Eighty three percent of households for rice, and 97 percent for vegetables have acquisition routes of sharing products as gifts. Regarding vegetables, most of the

---

7) A Ternary plot is popularly used in such fields as petrology, mineralogy, metallurgy, to show the composition of three variables. Any one variable is not independent of the others, and it is possible to graph the intersection of all three variables in only two dimensions.

Figure 6-1-2 Route Wise Acquisition Ratio of Rice and Vegetables in Iida City

Rice (n=150)

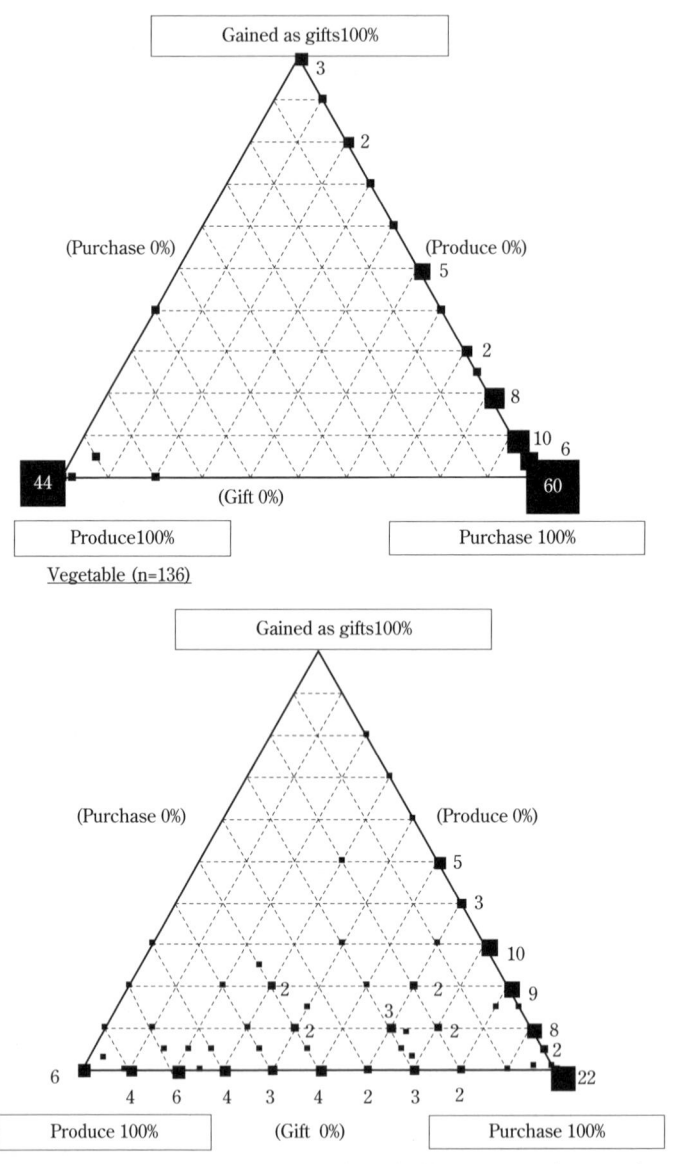

Vegetable (n=136)

Note: Numbers on square means the number of households. Squares with no numbers means the respondent number was one.
Source: Questionnaire survey

Chapter 6: Today's Subsistence Production and Agro-food Initiatives in Japan   271

Figure 6-1-3 Involvement of Iida People in Giving and Gaining the Gifts

	0%	10%	20%	30%	40%	50%	60%	70%	80%	90%	100%
Rice (n=133)			43			10		57		23	
Vegetable (n=140)		29			54			53			4

□ Give only   ▨ Gain only   ■ Give and Gain   □ No give or gain

Source: Questionnaire survey

Figure 6-1-4 The Extent and Relationship between those Who Gave and Gained the Gifts

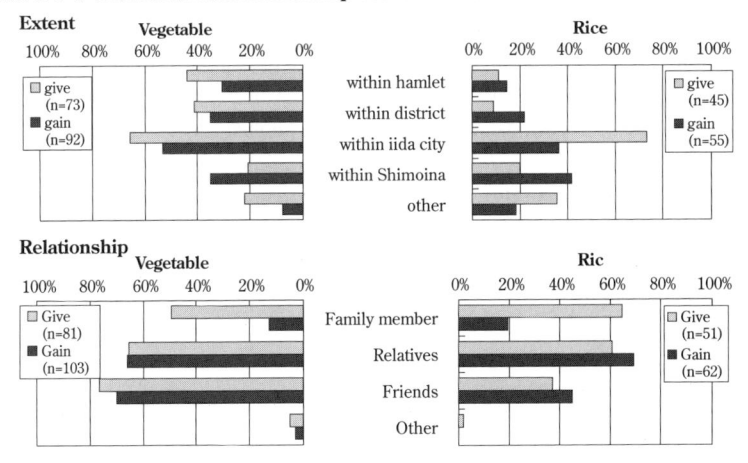

Extent

Vegetable — give (n=73), gain (n=92)
Rice — give (n=45), gain (n=55)

Categories: within hamlet, within district, within iida city, within Shimoina, other

Relationship

Vegetable — Give (n=81), Gain (n=103)
Rice — Give (n=51), Gain (n=62)

Categories: Family member, Relatives, Friends, Other

Source: Questionnaire survey

households had both experiences giving and receiving. Vegetables were distributed in a smaller area than rice and more among friends and neighbors, while rice was shared mainly among family members not living in the house and relatives, which may be due to seasonality and the quick spoilage of vegetables.

Roughly estimating the consumption ratio of the three acquisition routes of all of the responding households in amount consumed[8], for rice 37 percent was from self

---

[8] Calculation of consumption amount of each family was referred to *Nenrei-betus Kome Shohi Jitta Chosa* (Rice consumption survey by age classes) by the Food Agency in 1998, and *Kokumin Eiyo Chosa* (National nutritional survey) [Ministry of Health, Labor and Welfare, 2009] by modifying the age and sex.

Table 6-1-2 Situation of Self Production and Gifts by Districts

	Miho district (n=53)	Kawaji district (n=44)	DID (n=66)	Total (n=163)
Produce something at home**	49 (96%)	23 (62%)	14 (28%)	86 (62%)
Have ever given or gained gifts*	49 (92%)	37 (84%)	47 (72%)	133 (82%)

Note: Significant difference among districts at 5% level (*) and 1% level (* *) by χ^2 analysis.
Source: Questionnaire survey

production, 8 percent was received as gifts, and 55 percent was purchased, and for vegetables 34 percent was produced, 11 percent was received as gifts and 55 percent was purchased.

With regards to the purchasing place of local foodstuffs, 132 households (81 percent) had experienced using farmers' markets. As for personal interests, 258 respondents (68 percent) answered that they were interested in purchasing local food, and the main reasons were "freshness" (88 percent of those who were interested), "seasonality" (57 percent), "safety" (44 percent), "deliciousness" (36 percent), and "traceability" (33 percent).

Table 6-1-2 shows the difference of self productions and gifts by districts. Self production was significantly low among the respondents in DID. The experiences of giving or receiving gifts were also lower than in other districts, but 72 percent had given or received gifts.

Although there were only 30 percent (111 respondents) who had heard of *"Chisan-chisho"*, the existence of local food utilization at the household level in various ways such as by self production, and through giving or receiving gifts was made clear.

3-3. Utilization of Local Foodstuffs by Sample Households

Among the sample households, acquisition route-wise the consumption ratio of rice and vegetables was estimated to be for rice 29 percent self produced, 16 percent received as gifts, 55 percent purchased, and for vegetables it was 24 percent self produced, 31 percent received as gifts, and 45 percent purchased. Comparing the estimation of the results of the questionnaire survey, as shown above the ratio of self production was lower, and the ratio of gifts was higher.

Figure 6-1-5 shows the occupancy ratio of the foodstuffs used for meals during May by the place of production, in two categories such as farm households and non-farm households[9]. Among farm households, 52 percent of the products were produced within their own district including self production, 76 percent were within the Hanni

---

9) Only the number of kinds were counted here. Even if the same kind, they were counted differently if produced in a different place.

Chapter 6: Today's Subsistence Production and Agro-food Initiatives in Japan   273

Figure 6-1-5 Produced Place of Food and Foodstuff (Agricultural Products) used by Sample Households

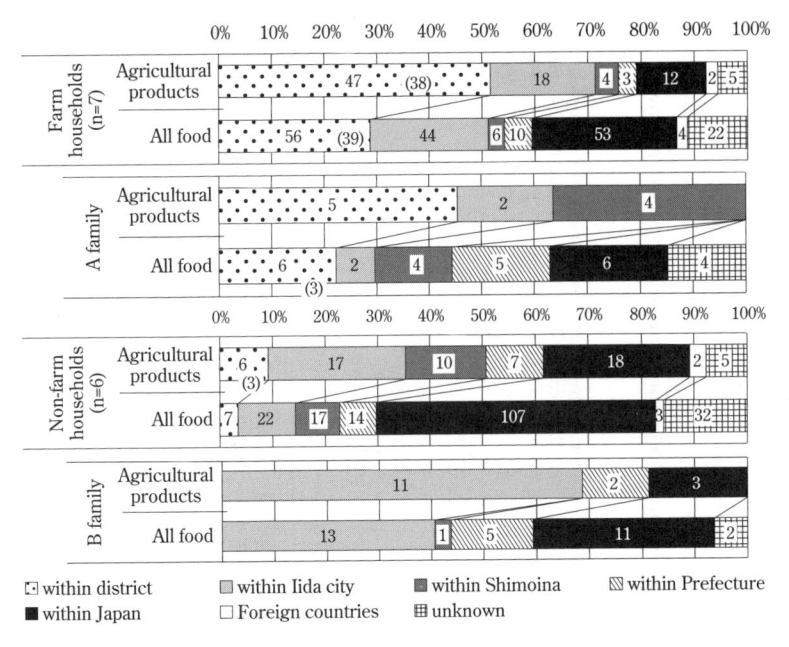

		within district	within Iida city	within Shimoina	within Prefecture
		within Japan	Foreign countries	unknown	

Note: Figures in parenthesis are species number of self products.
Source: Foodstuff Survey in May

region. Among non-farm households, 51 percent were produced within Hanni region. Among 102 items that were produced within the Hanni region, 79 items (77 percent) were vegetables, fruits and fungi, which were the main products in the research area as mentioned above. The reasons why there was some self production among non-farm households was that some of them started gardens of their own by renting land from neighboring farm households.

Next, we will see two cases in detail under different conditions concerning farming, one is a farm household ("A" family), and the other is a non-farm household residing in a DID ("B" family). In a brief look, all the foodstuffs consumed by "A" family were produced within the Hanni region, while no products from the district of residence were consumed by B family (Figure 6-1-5). All the rice was purchased by both of them. With regards to vegetables, 40 percent was produced- 10 percent was received as gifts and 50 percent was purchased by "A" family, and 65percent was received as gifts and the rest was purchased by "B" family.

Figure 6-1-6 Foodstuff Acquired and Used at A Family

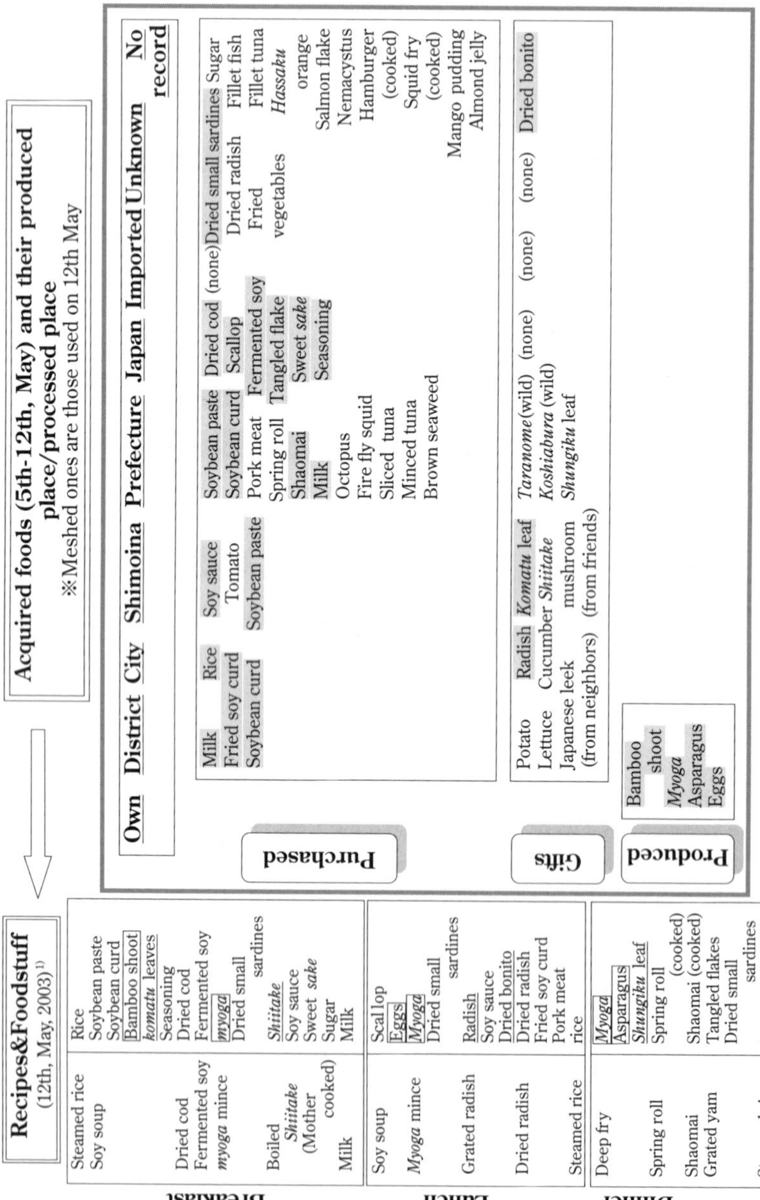

Acquired foods (5th-12th, May) and their produced place/processed place
※Meshed ones are those used on 12th May

	Own	District	City	Shimoina	Prefecture	Japan	Imported	Unknown	No record
Purchased				Milk	Soy sauce	Soybean paste	Dried cod	(none)	Dried small sardines	Sugar
				Rice	Tomato	Soybean curd	Scallop		Dried radish	Fillet fish
				Fried soy curd	Soybean paste	Pork meat	Fermented soy		Fried vegetables	Fillet tuna
				Soybean curd		Spring roll	Tangled flake			*Hassaku* orange
						Shaomai	Sweet *sake*			Salmon flake
						Milk	Seasoning			Nemacystus
						Octopus				Hamburger (cooked)
						Fire fly squid				Squid fry (cooked)
						Sliced tuna				Mango pudding
						Minced tuna				Almond jelly
						Brown seaweed				
Gifts		Potato	Radish	*Komatu* leaf	*Taranome* (wild)	(none)		(none)	Dried bonito
		Lettuce	Cucumber	*Shiitake* mushroom	*Koshiabura* (wild)				
		Japanese leek (from neighbors)	(from friends)		*Shungiku* leaf				
Produced	Bamboo shoot								
	Myoga								
	Asparagus								
	Eggs								

Recipes & Foodstuff (12th, May, 2003)[1]

	Recipe	Foodstuff
Breakfast	Steamed rice	Rice
	Soy soup	Soybean paste
		Soybean curd
		Bamboo shoot
		komatu leaves
	Dried cod	Seasoning
		Dried cod
	Fermented soy	Fermented soy
	myoga mince	*myoga*
		Dried small sardines
	Boiled *Shiitake* (Mother cooked)	*Shiitake*
		Soy sauce
		Sweet *sake*
		Sugar
	Milk	Milk
Lunch	Soy soup	Scallop
		Eggs
	Myoga mince	*Myoga*
		Dried small sardines
	Grated radish	Radish
		Soy sauce
	Dried radish	Dried bonito
		Dried radish
		Fried soy curd
		Pork meat
	Steamed rice	rice
Dinner	Deep fry	*Myoga*
		Asparagus
		Shungiku leaf
	Spring roll	Spring roll (cooked)
	Shaomai	Shaomai (cooked)
	Grated yam	Tangled flakes
		Dried small sardines
	Steamed rice	Rice

Notes: 1) All the foods except for boiled shiitake were cooked by household head's wife.
Among used foodstuff, those in rectangular lines are self products and those with underlines are gained as gifts.

Chapter 6: Today's Subsistence Production and Agro-food Initiatives in Japan 275

"A" family produced and sold fungi, asparagus and flowers through Japan Agricultural Cooperatives. In addition, they operated a self sustaining vegetable garden, and owned a patch of forest. "A" family did not grow rice since they accepted an acreage reduction which was allocated regionally. The family was composed of 5 people spanning three generations. The main person for acquiring and cooking of the foodstuffs was the wife (52 years old at the time the research was held).

Figure 6-1-6 shows the recipes and foodstuffs used on 12 May, 2003, and the foodstuffs acquired the preceding week. This period was the peak season for harvesting fungi and asparagus. As for self production, except for asparagus, wild vegetables, the main products of the family, such as bamboo shoots and *myoga* (Japanese ginger) were also used. There were foodstuffs received as gifts, too, and in every meal, self grown items as well as gifts were used as ingredients.

Among the 56 kinds of foodstuffs acquired during the recording period, 41 (73 percent) were purchased, 11 were distributed (19 percent), and 4 (7 percent) were produced, and among 14 kinds of vegetables, self production and gifts totaled 13. As for the main place for purchasing foodstuffs, in addition to small groceries in the district, and shops ran by Cooperatives, foodstuffs were also obtained from nearby people (rice from the wife's parents' home, and milk from a neighbor) at discounted rates (18,000 yen for 60 kgs of rice, and 70 yen for 360cc of milk).

Regarding harvest seasons and the use of produce, the kinds of produce that were used for their own consumption and for gifts were much more than those that were sold (Figure 6-1-7). They were also used as the ingredients for various processed food. The pickled plums (*umeboshi*) made by the mother of household head was well known for its taste, and many people with the intention of obtaining some, exchanged something of their own. Products that were to mainly be sold were also consumed at home or given as gifts.

"B" family had no farmland, and ran a dry cleaning business. There were 5 family members spanning three generations, and the main person acquiring and cooking of the foodstuffs was the wife (49 years old at the time of research).

Eight kinds of vegetables of the 14 obtained that one week, and 7 kinds of the 13 used in the meals for that day were received as gifts (Figure 6-1-8). The main source of the gifts was the parents of the wife who operated farmland, but some were also received from friends. The things received as gifts were common items such as seasonal vegetables (bamboo shoots, *myoga* (Japanese ginger), asparagus and so forth) and handmade Konnyaku (*a paste made from arum root*), which indicated regular sharing among them.

As for the purchasing place of local agricultural produce, in addition to the Consumers Cooperatives and local supermarkets, a nearby farmers' market was

Figure 6-1-7 Products and their Usage in A Family

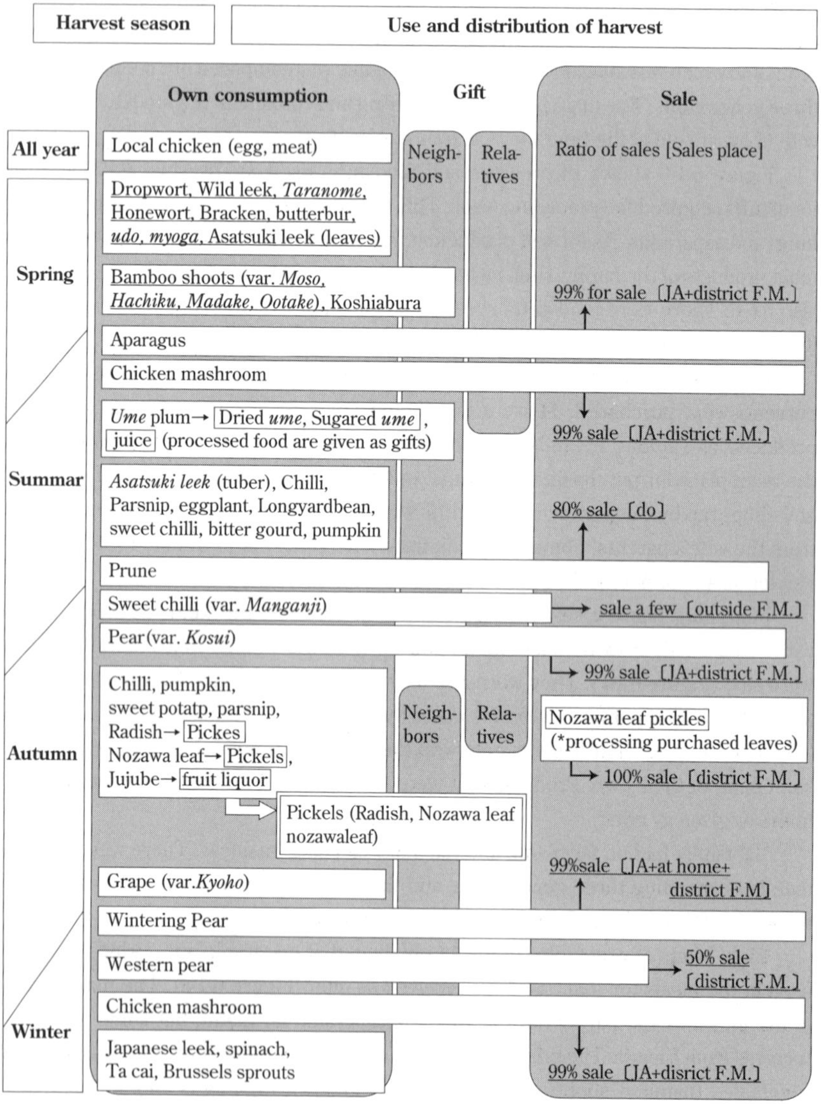

Harvest season	Use and distribution of harvest		
	Own consumption	**Gift**	**Sale**
All year	Local chicken (egg, meat)	Neighbors / Relatives	Ratio of sales [Sales place]
Spring	Dropwort, Wild leek, *Taranome*, Honewort, Bracken, butterbur, udo, myoga, Asatsuki leek (leaves)		
Spring	Bamboo shoots (var. *Moso, Hachiku, Madake, Ootake*), Koshiabura		99% for sale [JA+district F.M.]
Spring	Aparagus		
Spring	Chicken mashroom		
Summar	*Ume* plum → Dried *ume*, Sugared *ume*, juice (processed food are given as gifts)		99% sale [JA+district F.M.]
Summar	*Asatsuki leek* (tuber), Chilli, Parsnip, eggplant, Longyardbean, sweet chilli, bitter gourd, pumpkin		80% sale [do]
Summar	Prune		
Summar	Sweet chilli (var. *Manganji*)		→ sale a few [outside F.M.]
Summar	Pear (var. *Kosui*)		↳ 99% sale [JA+district F.M.]
Autumn	Chilli, pumpkin, sweet potatp, parsnip, Radish → Pickes, Nozawa leaf → Pickels, Jujube → fruit liquor	Neighbors / Relatives	Nozawa leaf pickles (*processing purchased leaves) ↳ 100% sale [district F.M.]
Autumn	Pickels (Radish, Nozawa leaf nozawaleaf)		
Autumn	Grape (var. *Kyoho*)		99%sale [JA+at home+ district F.M]
Winter	Wintering Pear		
Winter	Western pear		50% sale [district F.M.]
Winter	Chicken mashroom		
Winter	Japanese leek, spinach, Ta cai, Brussels sprouts		99% sale [JA+disrict F.M.]

Note: Products with underlines are those gathered wild ones, and with rectangular lines are processed foods.

Chapter 6: Today's Subsistence Production and Agro-food Initiatives in Japan 277

Figure 6-1-8 Foodstuff Acquired and used at B Family

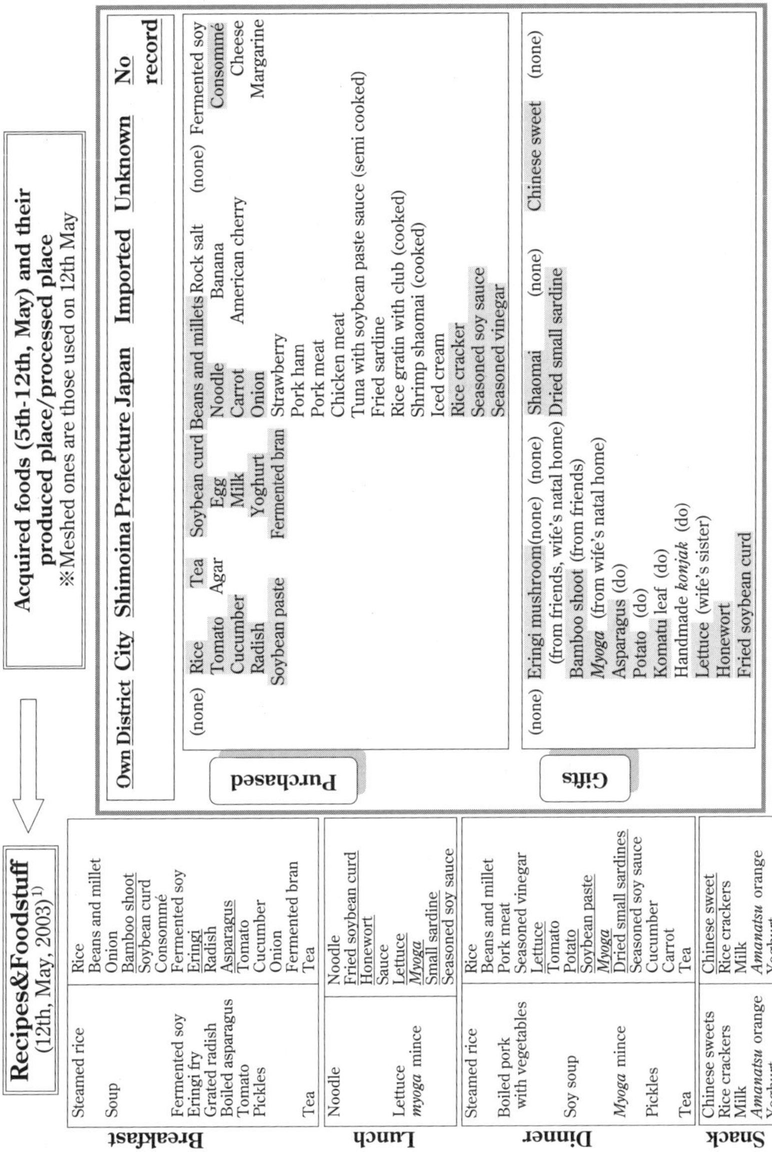

Acquired foods (5th-12th, May) and their produced place/processed place
※Meshed ones are those used on 12th May

Purchased

Own District	City	Shimoina Prefecture	Japan	Imported	Unknown	No record
(none)	Rice	Tea	Soybean curd	Beans and millets	Rock salt	(none) Fermented soy
	Tomato	Agar	Egg	Noodle	Banana	Consommé
	Cucumber		Milk	Carrot	American cherry	Cheese
	Radish		Yoghurt	Onion		Margarine
	Soybean paste		Fermented bran	Strawberry		
				Pork ham		
				Pork meat		
				Chicken meat		
				Tuna with soybean paste sauce (semi cooked)		
				Fried sardine		
				Rice gratin with club (cooked)		
				Shrimp shaomai (cooked)		
				Iced cream		
				Rice cracker		
				Seasoned soy sauce		
				Seasoned vinegar		

Gifts

Own District	City	Shimoina Prefecture	Japan	Imported	Unknown	No record
(none)	Eringi mushroom	(none)	(none)	Shaomai	(none)	Chinese sweet (none)
	(from friends, wife's natal home)			Dried small sardine		
	Bamboo shoot (from friends)					
	Myoga (from wife's natal home)					
	Asparagus (do)					
	Potato (do)					
	Komatu leaf (do)					
	Handmade *konjak* (do)					
	Lettuce (wife's sister)					
	Honewort					
	Fried soybean curd					

Recipes&Foodstuff (12th, May, 2003)[1]

Breakfast
- Steamed rice: Rice, Beans and millet
- Soup: Onion, Bamboo shoot, Soybean curd, Consommé
- Fermented soy: Fermented soy
- Eringi fry: Eringi
- Grated radish: Radish
- Boiled asparagus: Asparagus
- Tomato: Tomato
- Pickles: Cucumber, Onion, Fermented bran
- Tea: Tea

Lunch
- Noodle: Noodle, Fried soybean curd, Honewort, Sauce
- Lettuce *myoga* mince: Lettuce, *Myoga*, Small sardine, Seasoned soy sauce

Dinner
- Steamed rice: Rice, Beans and millet
- Boiled pork with vegetables: Pork meat, Seasoned vinegar, Lettuce, Tomato, Potato
- Soy soup: Soybean paste, *Myoga*, Dried small sardines
- *Myoga* mince: Seasoned soy sauce
- Pickles: Cucumber, Carrot
- Tea: Tea

Snack
- Chinese sweets: Chinese sweet
- Rice crackers: Rice crackers
- Milk: Milk
- *Amanatsu* orange: *Amanatsu* orange
- Yoghurt: Yoghurt

Source: Foodstuff survey
Notes: 1) All the foods were cooked by household head's wife.
Among used foodstuff, those with underlines are gained as gifts.

frequently used, and various local foods were bought there. "B" family also purchased rice directly from a farmer in the same city at a discounted rate.

As shown by the information provided by the two families, various routes for obtaining foodstuffs existed, including sharing, and support by such social networks like their relatives, neighbors, and friends.

4. Conclusion

The study was conducted in order to understand the situation of supply and use of local foods focusing on its actual use in the everyday life of local people.

From the retailer's survey and the foodstuff survey, the characteristics of local agricultural products were understood. They were seasonal and/or locally unique ones, reflecting the diversity and peculiarity of the locality.

From the questionnaire survey, it was understood that local foods were evaluated for their freshness and traceability (which attributes to the physical nearness), and seasonality. From the questionnaire survey and the foodstuffs survey, the diversified acquisition routes of foodstuffs such as self production and gifts that could not be understood by institutional data were observed. Although the local self-food sufficiency was rather low in Iida city, a considerable amount of local foods were utilized through subsistence farming and sharing as gifts. Although the market economy has deeply penetrated into contemporary Japan, self production and sharing as gifts still persists in rural life.

Subsistence farming and processing are the measures to get foodstuffs which requires a long term strategy for getting a good harvest. As "A" family's case shows, various produce is grown or gathered, and processed. It requires direct interaction with the land and/or natural resources in the local areas, which stirs up those feelings of how delicious the produce is, as shown in the questionnaire survey. Main advocates of subsistence farming and processing are elderly people and women, and subsistence farming and processing have the social function of supplying opportunities to contribute to the family even though they have become old. In addition, subsistence farming and processing are activities that non-farm households can take on as Figure 6-1-5 shows.

Sharing gifts is a passive measure of obtaining foodstuffs because the timing and the types cannot be decided by the receivers, but it reflects on the social network that households and individuals have developed through everyday life. Local products moved in various extents as gifts, and particularly, vegetables moved among not just only relatives but also neighbors.

Purchasing is also one of the important ways of obtaining local food, which requires availability at local retailers as a prerequisite. Besides farmers' markets, direct purchasing from farmers at discounted rates observed in the sample households also

Chapter 6: Today's Subsistence Production and Agro-food Initiatives in Japan   279

functioned as an important route for supplying local food. This may be categorized as the intermediate phase of sharing and purchase. While the relationship between producers and consumers are anonymous in farmers' markets, direct purchasing is based on a particular social relationship, realizing a "face-to-face" relationship.

By focusing on the actual utilization of local food by local people, the importance of everyday interaction with nature and of the social networks for the acquisition of local food was understood. *Chisan-chisho* is generally regarded as "supplying local consumers with local food" as shown in the introduction. The standpoint that addresses this *"Chisan-chisho"* is the activities which enable consumers to purchase necessary local food, and also contributes to the development of local industries", where by just separating "producers" and "consumers", and distinguishing them as such in their everyday life in the locality, has adverse effects to the actual utilization and function of local food created by local people in Iida city. The case in Iida city emphasizes how values such as the importance of local food for the local culture, the enjoyment gained from producing and eating such foods, and the establishment of social relationships, all are a sign of the often unseen and uncountable values which rural life has to offer.

Nowadays, farmers' markets are supplying local food to consumers consumption of local food in large volumes such as using it in school lunches are attracting a lot of attention and is promoting *Chisan-chisho*. We agree that such activities are important for expanding the consumption of local food, but when focusing on the "richness" of rural life that is shown in Iida city, other approaches should also be sought such as supplying opportunities to produce or gather local delicacies (and also participate in the management of these resources), and encouraging mutual help or interchange between inhabitants to strengthening social networks. Such activities will not only promote *Chisan-chisho* but also enhance the enjoyment of living in the locality. Effective measures may differ region by region, thus a concrete understanding of the actual situation of local food utilization in everyday life is of primary importance.

Acknowledgement
This revised paper is based on "Jumin-ni Yoru Nousanbutsu no Nyushu to Riyou kara mita Chiikinai Jikyu no Jittai Haaku (Understanding the Present Situation of Local supply and Consumption of Agricultural Aspect of Acquisition and Utilization by Local People), *Journal of Rural Problem,* 172: 45-56.

We would like to thank the administrative personnel of Iida city for cooperating in our research, and the people of Iida city for their cooperation in completing our surveys.

References

Chugoku-Shikoku Regional Agricultural Administration Office, 2003, *Heisei 13 nendo Chugoku-shikoku Shokuryou Nougyo Nouson Jousei Houkoku* (Annual Report on Food, Agriculture and Rural Area, 2001), Japan: 227-234.

Fujimoto, Takashi, 2005, *Chisan-Chisho no Shiten karano Shokuryo Jikyuritsu no Sokutei: Chiiki Sangyo Renkan Bunseki niyoru Apurochi* (Evaluation of Local Food Self-Sufficiency Ratio from the Standpoint of "Produce Locally and Consume Locally" : Using Regional Input-Output Analysis)," *Journal of Rural Economics*, 77(2): 57-66.

Hasumi, Takeyoshi, Toshinori Suzuki and Hisako Negishi, 1986, *Nousanbutsu Jikyu Uundou* (Self Sufficiency Movement), Tokyo: Ochanomizu Shobo.

Central Union of Agricultural Co-operatives, 2006, *Shoku to Noh wo musubu Katsuryoku aru JA zukuri* (24th Resolution of General Meeting).

Ministry of Agriculture, Forestry and Fisheries, 2005, *Heisei 16 nendo Nousanbutsu Chisan-Chisho-toh Jittai Chousa Kekka no Gaiyo* (The report on the Situation of Chisan-chisho in 2004).

―――, 2007, *Heisei 18 nendo Shokuryo Nougyo Nouson Hakusho* (Annual report on Food, Agriculture and Rural Area, 2006).

―――, 2009, *Agriculture Census 2000*. (http://www.maff.go.jp/j/tokei/census/afc/2000/report_archives.html, May 15, 2009)

Ministry of Health, Labor and Welfare, 2009, *Kokumin Eiyou Chousa* (National Nutritional Survey). (http://www-bm.mhlw.go.jp/houdou/2003/12/h1224-4d.html, May 15, 2009)

Rural Life Research Institute, 2003, *Chiikinai Jikyu=Chisan-Chisho no Genjou to Jichitai no Torikumi: Sichouson heno Anketo Chousa kara* (The Present Situation and Local Government Policy on Local Food Marketing and Consumption), Tokyo: Rural Life Research Institute.

―――, 2004, *Rural Life Research Series*, 58.

Statistics Bureau and Statistics Center, 2009, *National Census 2000*. (http://www.stat.go.jp/data/kokusei/2000/index.html, May 15, 2009)

Sustainable Table (http://www.sustainabletable.org/home.php, May 22, 2009)

Yoshino, Keiko and Chie Katayama, 2004, *Zenkoku Sichouson ni okeru Chiikinai Jikyu no Torikumi no Genjou to Kongo no Tenbou* (The Present Situation and Local Government Policy on Local Food Marketing and Consumption), *Journal of the Rural Life Society of Japan*, 47(3/4): 40-50.

2
Alternative Agro-food Movement in Contemporary Japan*

Mima Nishiyama

1. Introduction

Since the 1990's, the context surrounding food in Japan has changed drastically. Multi-national companies have become increasingly dominant over the domestic food system. At the same time, domestic agricultural ability of production has decreased. Consumers' anxieties about food security and safety have grown significantly as well. Integrating the concept of "local" into agricultural policy and practice has emerged as one way to relieve the anxieties about food. The government regards "local food" as a tool to link farmers and consumers. At the same time, local food movements with an emphasis on communication between farmers and consumers have emerged. These increasingly popular movements are termed *"Chisan-chisho"*. *Chisan-chisho* is literally translated as "to produce locally, to consume locally." Since the mid 1990's, numerous *Chisan-chisho* movements have sprouted all over Japan [Taniguchi, 2002].

This paper has three goals. First, we outline the background and emergence of the local food movement in Japan, focusing on the history of the alternative agriculture movement from the perspective of farmer-consumer relationships. Second, we identify the characteristics of the *Chisan-chisho* movement as a new alternative movement in Japan. We analyze and compare government-led *Chisan-chisho* movements with those led by citizens' groups, highlighting in particular their orientation, goals and ways of thinking about the "locality". Finally, we identify the problems and possibilities of the *Chisan-chisho* movement with reference to issues of local food movements in the United States.

2. The Transition of the Relationship between Farmers (Agriculture) and Consumers (food)

Beginning around 2000, local food movements, called *"Chisan-chisho"*, expanded all over Japan. We have some kinds of alternative agricultural movements like *Teikei*[1]

---

* This research is cooperated with Aya Hirata Kimura, was graduated student of University of Wisconsin-Madison. She is now an assistant professor at University of Hawaii at Monoa.
1) *Teikei* is an organic agriculture movement started in the 1970's. In the *Teikei* movement, farmers

after modernization in Japan. But *Chisan-chisho* is a different kind of movement from other alternative movements. The characteristic of *Chisan-chisho* is that they try to encourage food movement within their locality. Farmers and consumers who live in the same locality participate in this kind of movement. In this section, we examine why the concept of locality emerged in the *Chisan-chisho* movement while also discussing the transition of the distance between farmers (agriculture) and consumers (food).

Prior to Japan's economic modernization, agricultural production and food consumption were locally based. Most farmers produced the majority of their own food and sold their remaining products to consumers within their locality. Nakajima says that local production and consumption limited people's food choices and impacted the type of farming in their locality [Nakajima, 2001].

After World War II, the Ministry of Agriculture, Forestry, and Fisheries (MAFF) adopted a policy of modernizing Japanese agriculture to keep pace with industrialization. During this period, many people believed that the localism of the Japanese food system prevented the modernization of agriculture. Additionally, they viewed the ability of consumers to buy food from outside the locality or country, such as strawberries from Tochigi prefecture and wine from France, as symbols of food system modernization and wealth. The new agricultural policies led to a distancing between Japanese farmers and consumers. The policy of agricultural modernization also led to negative health and environmental consequences. For example, chemical fertilizers and pesticides polluted the soil and waterways. The health of farmers was also negatively impacted. Many suffered from an increased incidence of disease related to chemical exposure. In the following paragraphs, we analyze the activities which demonstrate that they were eager not to widen the distance between agriculture (production area) and food (consumption area), because most of them thought that to widen the distance between them would have a negative influence on their food life.

After the 1960, an alternative agriculture movement developed in Japan to counter the negative effects of agricultural modernization. Initially, the movement was comprised of farm women who were concerned about the negative consequences of economic modernization on rural life [Rural Life Research Institute, 2004]. During the modernization period, many farm household members had to seek off-farm jobs to supplement their incomes. As a consequence, many farmers limited their production and stopped growing vegetables for household consumption. Farm women, with support from government extension agents or farmer co-operatives, tried to recover their

---

and consumers who understood the value of organic farming are linked to each other directly. The farmers tried to produce organic food. The consumers supported the producers' life by buying their organic food and to help do some work in farmers' field.

household self-sufficiency and improve the health of their families. They began to grow vegetables on family plots for their own household's consumption [Negishi, 2000]. The movement was limited, however, as the farm women did not attempt to communicate with consumers nor with other farm women outside of their communities.

In the 1970, the *Teikei* movement emerged. The movement, initiated by *Yuukinougyo-Kenkyukai* (the organic farming research group) in 1971, focused on localizing the Japanese food system and promoting organic agriculture. The movement began in response to the negative impacts of agricultural modernization, such as long-distance commodity chains and unsustainable farming practices embodied in overuse of pesticides and chemical products. The policy of *Yuukinougyo-Kenkyukai* focused on the concept of locality, which means it emphasized self-reliance of the food system and economic revitalization, conservation of natural resources and culture in their locality. While most of their efforts centered on developing a sustainable farming system, they also advocated community-wide development that conserved local resources and focused on sustainable practices. The *Teikei* movement was successful at increasing support for organic agriculture, but failed to localize the food system. Urban areas provided ready markets for organic food, while rural areas were not receptive to organic products. Hence, most organic farmers sold their food in the cities, outside of their localities. The *Teikei* movement was successful in connecting organic farmers with consumers, assisting with harvesting and other farm chores.

In the 1980, the *Sanchoku*[2] movement, led by consumers' co-operatives, supermarkets and farmers' co-operatives, emerged. Most *Teikei* movements were conducted by small groups of farmers in rural areas and consumers in the urban area. But in *the Sanchoku* movement, some organic farmer organizations linked up with some consumers' organizations. There were two reasons; one was to respond to the increasing demand for organic food. The other reason was that some farmers' co-operatives therefore are small or periphery production areas away from main policy. They needed to seek their identity and to add other values to their production, for example, organic food or sustainable food. With the expansion of *Sanchoku*, the number of organic farmers and organic consumers increased in Japan. But unlike the *Teikei* movement, the personal connection between farmers and consumers was not emphasized. While *Teikei* continued during this time, the number of *Sanchoku* participants who are farmers and consumers out-numbered *Teikei* participants. The

---

2) *Sanchoku* is direct marketing between farmers' organizations and consumers' organizations. Many *Sanchoku* in the 1980's linked between farmers' co-operatives and consumers' co-operatives. The development of *Sanchoku* then contributed to the expansion of organic marketing and direct marketing.

number of *Teikei* participants decreased because many of its former leaders who were consumers moved on to new jobs after their children started school. *Sanchoku* was thus able to surpass *Teikei*, because *Sanchoku* made it easier for consumers to participate, and *Sanchoku* did not require consumers to work on organic farms like *Teikei*. The role of the consumer was simply to buy organic products. In the 1980's, however, for the first time the government acknowledged the negative impact of industrial agriculture and they introduced the concept of sustainable agriculture. But still the main focus of the government's agriculture policy remained on industrialization.

In the 1990's, many farmers' markets emerged throughout Japan. Farmers' markets influenced family farms in Japan in two major ways. Farm women, prior to the 1990s, did not have many opportunities to earn their own income independently from their family farm. Compared to women in other industries, the ability of farm women to act independently was very limited. Farmers' markets created new and significant opportunities for farm women to earn their own income and take control of economic and social aspects of their lives. For example, a group of farm women started a farm women's market at a nationwide department store. Most members of this group were also members of a "*Seikatsu-Kaizen group*" (the government extension group for the improvement of farm household life). This is the same kind of group that worked in the 1960's to improve farm women's self-sufficiency.

The farm women's markets also influenced production practices on family farms. Prior to the emergence of farmers' markets, most farms produced for the wholesale market, which required large volumes of one or two crops. For those farmers that began selling at the farmers' markets, they increased the diversity of crops they produced to meet consumer's demands [Nishiyama and Yoshida, 2001].

The farmers' markets also influenced consumers. After the emergence of the farmers' market, consumers came to better understand what local food was or what food was in season in their locality. This led them to recognize the freshness and tastiness of local foods, just like the farmers who produced the local foods. We can therefore say that the achievement of the farmers' markets helped the *Chisan-chisho* movement's later expansion. Because of farmers' markets, it is easy for consumers to understand the word "*Chisan-chisho*" (to produce locally and to consume locally). However, farmers' markets served a relatively small portion of Japanese consumers. In the 1990, Japan globalized its food system, importing food from all over the world. The globalization of the food system arguably led to a decrease in food safety. For example, in 1993, underproduction of Japanese rice threatened rice shortages in the country. Additionally, several food imports were found to be contaminated with high levels of chemicals. Many Japanese consumers turned to organic food to avoid the food contamination problems of the conventional food system. After these incidents, organic farmers expanded their markets by participating in wholesale markets. With market expansion, more organic farmers' associations developed [Nakajima, 2001].

In the late 1990s, *Chisan-chisho*, a new alternative agriculture movement, emerged. The movement's primary goal was to change the food system to produce and distribute food locally through cooperation between farmers and consumers in the same locality. Another goal was to educate consumers and promote food safety, agricultural preservation, and environmental stewardship. The movement is primarily concerned with localizing the Japanese food system. This *Chisan-chisho* movement is not related to the *Teikei* or *Sanchoku* movements. Many *Chisan-chisho* movements are led by local governments. The government has significantly contributed to the expansion of this movement. The number of participants is quite large when compared with the *Teikei* and *Sanchoku* movements. And another new characteristic is that the *Chisan-chisho* movement has been realized in localities. Farmers and consumers who live in the same locality are taking part in the *Chisan-chisho* movement. But unlike the *Teikei* movement, participants do not have the philosophy of consciously resolving particular problems. The government-led *Chisan-chisho* is attempting to eliminate consumers' fears about food security and safety. Due to these fears, the *Chisan-chisho* movement's goals became quite limited and narrow. In the following section, we will analyze the *Chisan-chisho* movement in more detail.

3. Emergence of the Localization Movement in the U.S.

Japanese alternative agriculture movements have a history of almost 40 years. But the local food movement, *Chisan-chisho*, has emerged in only about the last 5 years. In contrast, the U.S. local food movement began about 10 years earlier than that in Japan. There are many issues about the local food movement in the U.S. That is to say, in Japan, people understand "local" in terms of geographic area. They don't tend to consider the anti-globalism aspect of "local". But in the U.S., people think that "local" is a tool to realize democracy or social justice in the face of globalization. In this section, we introduce these issues in the U.S. focusing on the potential of local food movements and discuss the importance of these movements.

In the 1980's, activists with in the U.S. alternative agriculture movement began discussing the importance of food localization. However, it was not until the 1990's that many activists within the movement actively began to promote the localization of food systems. Alternative farming movements, for instance, valued the local connection, because they were seen as important in terms of food self-sufficiency [Lockeretz, 1986]. Many argued that food localization could reverse the negative trends associated with global food commodity chains, such as increased pesticide pollution, low produce stand prices and increased food contamination. Family farm preservation groups also emerged and began to conceptualize their activities in terms of reconnecting farmers with local markets. For instance, Hinrichs [2003] considers the roots of Iowa's food localization movement to be Community Supported Agriculture (CSA) and farmers' markets started in the 1980s. Anti-hunger advocates also began talking about re-localizing the food system as a means of addressing food insecurity.

3-1. Why Local?

Why do alternative agriculture and food system activists emphasize the importance of the locality?

We point out five distinct reasons and address them one-by-one.

First, locally-based agro-food initiatives are seen as counter movements to the globalized and corporate-controlled agro-food system [Goodman and Redclift, 1991] [McMichael, 2000] [Raynalds, 2000]. Buttel [2000] suggests that CSAs and farmers' markets are the most common ways in which consumers resist the globalized agro food system. Allen [1999] similarly sees the emphasis on locality as "a form of resistance" to the ever-expanding power of transnational corporations in the production, processing and retailing of food.

Second, strengthening of the local economy is cited by various organizations as the reason to "go local". For instance, the Food Routes Network states that local is good, because "You'll strengthen your local economy-Buying local food keeps your dollars circulating in your community. Getting to know the farmers who grow your food builds relationships based on understanding and trust" [Food Route Network].

Third, advocates of localizing the food system also point out the environmental benefits. The average food product travels thousands of miles, thereby increasing our reliance on polluting fossil fuels. Food localization reverses this trend.

Fourth, locality is seen as being characterized by more social embeddedness, or moral economy. Close social networks, trust, and face-to-face relations bolster locally-based food production and consumption. Improved safety is seen as stemming from the fact that we can now identify the producers' face because of its proximity, rather than any changes in production methods or structural changes in agribusiness marketing. That is, safety and locality is linked through the perceived social embeddedness and face-to-face relations.

Fifth, in contrast to the lack of control and accountability in the globalized agro food system, a locally-based food system is seen as more amenable to improved access of people to shape how food is produced and consumed. In this sense, locality is seen as inherently connected to more self-determination and control [Allen, 1999]. Food localization is also promoted as a means of increasing self-sufficiency. Shortening the distance the food travels from farm to table lessens the vulnerabilities of the food system. As we have seen, the meaning of locality, in the 1990s and in the 2000s, has moved toward emphasizing democratic decision making and social justice in the U.S.

3-2. "Food is the entry point"

Local food movements have a diverse set of goals. But many movements seem to share the fact that they entered their movement focusing on food issues —for example, issues such as food safety or security— and then expanded to more dynamic issues, such as environmental issues or social change movements and so on.

Food is a good entry point for social injustice, as Lappe [1991] argues in her epoch-making book, "Diet for a Small Planet". Kloppenburg et al. [1996] echo this by arguing that food is a good starting point for promoting social change, because of the "centrality of food in our lives and its capacity to connect us materially and spiritually to each other and to the earth." Welsh and MacRae [1998] agree that because "few other systems touch people's daily lives in such an intimate way and thereby provide such a strong motivation and opportunity for citizenship", food insecurity reveals social injustices in a profound way. Food is a "microcosm of wider social realities" [Lang, 1999]. Allen et al. [2003] agrees that food is just an entry point. She sees that food is "a salient issue for everyone", but has the potential to lead to "a politicization that develops into an engagement of other areas of civic life and political issues". Hassanein [2003] argues that food is a "pragmatic" avenue which can transform the dominant agro-food system. "And, within the universe of social and environmental action, food issues, which have come to represent a significant opportunity to construct a new type of environmental and social agenda have also become the place where the local meets the global" [Gottlieb, 2001]. "Food system outcomes - the winners and losers due to the changes in the production and consumption of food - can in turn represent key indicators about the overall state of society and environment" [Gottlieb, 2001].

The Community Food Security Coalition summarizes this larger focus by noting that "small, local, sustainable farms are a building block of any democratic and just food system. This sustainable agriculture perspective has an environmental focus, a rural economic focus, and a labor focus" and "community food security is about sustainable agriculture" [Community Food Security Coalition Newsletter Fall 02- Winter 03]. A similar sentiment is shared by Local Harvest which states that "The Buy Local movement is quickly taking us beyond the promise of environmental responsibility that the organic movement delivered to us, and awakening the U.S. to the importance of community, variety, humane treatment of farm animals, and social and environmental responsibility in regards to our food economy" [Local Harvest Newsletter Fall 02- Winter 03].

From the study of local food movement issues in the U.S, we realize that more emphasis is placed on the aspects of anti-globalism and democracy as food citizens in the U.S. There are some critical issues for local food movements, regardless of class, gender, racial concerns, and so on. Even though these issues are correct, they emphasize a structural perspective, and thus look for social change from the establishment of local food systems or participation of citizens in that process. This is a wider and deeper point of view than most Japanese movements hold. The reason for this difference lies in how the term "local" is defined. U.S. local food movements have developed a more nuanced understanding of "local" in our view. The meaning of locality has come to emphasize democratic decision making and social justice in the U.S. On the other hand, particularly in the many *Chisan-chisho* movements, "local" is interpreted as signifying geographic/ physical scale. Japanese movements tend not to consider the democratic decision making and social justice in their country. In Japan, accordingly, people pay more attention to food safety or food culture than in the U.S. The reason why they have begun to emphasize the concept of locality is that they need to uncover the characteristics of their locality through their local food activities. They tend to overlook the need for social change, even though they really have many problems within the food system. We point out that they should consider what they locally regard as important: not only for food safety but also for sustainable local development.

4. The Alternative Agriculture Movement in Contemporary Japan

In the last few years, the number of *Chisan-chisho* projects has increased considerably. Many of these new projects are led by the local governments or the MAFF. Not all *Chisan-chisho* projects are government sponsored. Since the mid-1990's, citizen groups have organized their own *Chisan-chisho* projects. However, the goals and resources available for citizen-led *Chisan-chisho* projects are different than those for government sponsored projects. In the following section, we discuss the MAFF involvement in the *Chisan-chisho* movement, and we also present two case studies of *Chisan-chisho* movements.

4-1. The Ministry of Agriculture, Forestry, and Fisheries' Involvement in the *Chisan-chisho* Movement

In 1999, for the first time in nearly forty years, the MAFF revamped Japan's agricultural policies. In only three short years, however, they needed to change their policy again in a large part because of the current social conditions of food. During the last three years, BSE (otherwise known as Mad Cow Disease) contaminated meat produced in Japan was found, and many cases of disguised food labeling were publicly disclosed. Other issues such as the chemical contamination of food imported from abroad were also disclosed. Therefore, many people in Japan have serious anxieties about food. In 2002, in response to these food scandals, the MAFF created *"shoku-to-nou-no-saisei-plan"*, a plan to revitalize Japan's agriculture and food system. The term *"Chisan-chisho"* was officially incorporated into Japanese agricultural policy for the first time.

These are two main reasons why the government officially adopted *Chisan-chisho* in 2002. First, the MAFF wanted to increase domestic food consumption. Second, they needed to address consumers' fears about food safety. The role of *Chisan-chisho*, and its emphasis on local food, is to promote consumers' confidence in the food system. One goal is to increase the domestic agriculture market. To realize this goal, the MAFF also advanced strategies for consumer education. This is the most important policy of the new agriculture law instituted in 1999. The other goal is to establish a food system that provides safe food and promotes consumers' confidence. This is the main goal of the *"shoku-to-nou-no-saisei-plan"* (plan for the revitalization of the agriculture and food system). In accordance with this policy, the MAFF focused much of their attention on consumers first. From this, it is clear how important the MAFF thinks this policy, designed to gain consumers' confidence, is. In policy terms, the role of *Chisan-chisho* is to increase consumer confidence while providing fresh local food and a larger domestic market.

To implement this agricultural policy, the MAFF allocated money to local governments for the creation of *Chisan-chisho* projects. Through such projects, the government educated consumers and promoted domestic food markets. However, the government's concept of *Chisan-chisho* was quite narrow. It did not address socio-economic or environmental issues as they relate to agriculture. Originally, *Chisan-chisho* had a very profound meaning. It incorporated *"Shindo-fuji"*, which means that people cannot separate the body from the land. However the *Shindo-fuji* concept was not incorporated into the government's concept of *Chisan-chisho*. The atmosphere of the word *"Chisan-chisho"* gives consumers' confidence in local food, because local food is fresh, and they can see the field in which it is grown and meet the people that produced it.

Local governments promote *Chisan-chisho* as a method to establish a safe, fresh, confident food system in their locality. Their activities include school lunch programs which use local food, events to advertise local food and agriculture, farmers' markets, seminars for consumers, local food systems, and so on. There is no practice of linking up organic farming with movements or certification systems of local food in the *Chisan-chisho* movement. We point out the contradiction surrounding *Chisan-chisho* between the national and local levels. In the following paragraphs, we analyze two case studies; one is government-led *Chisan-chisho*, the other citizen-led. We discuss the differences between them in terms of goals, and then analyze the characteristics of the Japanese local food movement.

4-2. Case study: The Iwate Prefecture's Chisan-Chisaho Project[3]

Iwate Prefecture in northern Japan launched its *Chisan-chisho* program in June 2001. To develop the local food program, the prefecture's government coordinated with several sectors of the prefecture's food industry, including farmers, distributors, processors, traders and consumers. The goals of the *Chisan-chisho* program included increasing the local food market for farmers, thereby changing the local food system so that consumers in Iwate could once again have access to fresh local food. The Iwate prefecture's government was also interested in reconnecting farmers and consumers in order to promote the value of living in the prefecture.

To increase local consumption among the people of Iwate prefecture, the government developed four main programs. Among them was the promotion of "Local Food of Iwate Days." The government designated the fourth Friday, Saturday and Sunday of every month as "local food days" in the prefecture. They encouraged all households to eat local food on those days. To promote this, they asked all supermarkets in the prefecture to set aside space for selling local food on that day. Additionally, the government worked with local restaurants to develop special menus for those days. The second program focused on increasing local food consumption in the schools. The government also promoted local food purchasing in the food manufacturing sector. Finally, the government recommended instituting and disseminating the indicators for a good food system.

The expansion of Iwate's school lunch program was initially the most challenging of the four programs, but in recent years it has proved to be the most successful. Conflicting government bureaucracies delayed implementation of the local food program for the schools. The Department of Agricultural marketing was responsible for increasing local food procurement for school lunches. However, officials within the Department of Education, which has traditionally overseen the school lunch program, did not support the Department of Agricultural marketing program. Finally, after several months of delay, the Department of Education allowed the *Chisan-chisho* program to go forward. A new competitive bidding system was created for school food procurement, which required that food purchased came from local sources as often as possible. By 2002, local food accounted for 47.6 percent of total food procurement for the school district, which represented a 17.6 percent increase from 1999.

The Iwate prefecture held a national forum on *Chisan-chisho* in 2002 with

---

3) This section was analyzed on the basis of the information that I received when I interviewed officer C of the department of agricultural marketing in Iwate Prefecture on April 2004.

financial support from the MAFF. After the success of the forum, people recognized Iwate prefecture as the most advanced *Chisan-chisho* movement led by a prefecture government in Japan. And residents of Iwate became conscious of the importance of this movement. Furthermore, the *Chisan-chisho* movement in Iwate received a lot of attention after BSE and other food scandals were exposed. Soon after, consumers and distributors also started seriously turning to local food as an alternative food source. The school lunch program influenced many people in the prefecture including parents, community members, farmers, and traders. For example, they started growing vegetables in vacant lots for the school lunch program. Additionally, the school lunch program was the impetus for the creation of a new association of food traders and distributors interested in providing local food. Some farmers' co-operatives created a niche of providing local food for school lunches. Now all school lunch programs in Iwate prefecture provide a "local salmon menu" every November 11th. This demonstrates how the *Chisan-chisho* movement has penetrated the entire prefecture. To promote this day, the governor of Iwate ate with students on this day to publicize *Chisan-chisho*. People involved in school lunch programs, parents and community residents - including farmers - paid attention not only to local food but also to the seasonal foods in the area, the way of cooking, local and traditional cuisine, and the nutritional value of local food. They began to educate consumers about these aspects of local food, an initiative now mimicked by the government of Japan.

The prefecture's government began discussions about shifting the management of the *Chisan-chisho* programs from government to local citizen groups in 2003. There are already examples of this happening. Some local NGO's are managing restaurants and farmers' markets to provide local food. The prefecture's government has deemed the *Chisan-chisho* projects nearing success at the end of their first stage. They need to use their funds for other projects. Therefore, they are attempting to transfer the management of the projects to citizens' groups.

On the other hand, the prefecture's government has advanced projects to provide education about food programs for schools in metropolitan areas of Tokyo. They are proud of their food education program, which they have practiced for many years. They want to expand the program to other metropolitan areas which lack agriculture. They seek to create the bonds with urban consumer areas to widen the market for their food. They try to advertise their food by offering not only local food but having farmers disseminate information as part of their food education program.

4-3. Case Study: The Citizen-led *Chisan-chisho* Movement

Citizens began to initiate *Chisan-chisho* movements in the mid- 1990s. But prior to government involvement in its promotion in 2002, the *Chisan-chisho* movement remained small and under-resourced. The original *Chisan-chisho* citizen leaders promoted a different concept of *Chisan-chisho* than that which was later adopted by the government. While the government focused primarily on increasing local markets through *Chisan-chisho*, the earlier citizen efforts had a different agenda. They were concerned with the establishment of a local food system for the economic health of farmers, food quality and environmental conservation in their locality. In this section, we analyze the activity of *"Chisan-chisho wo susumeru kai* (The Club for Eating Locally), the first *Chisan-chisho* movement. In Japan, there are other citizen-led *Chisan-chisho* movements: for example, *"Inaka-kurabu"* (The Rural Area Club), *"Shindo-fuji Iwate"* (Body comes from land), *"Shoku-to-nou-no kakehashi kurabu"* (The association to bridge food and agriculture), and *"Jimoto no shoku to nou wo taisetunisuru kai"* (The association to preserve local food and agriculture). Most of these movements were established at the middle to the end of the 1990's. They all considered the circumstances surrounding local food. For example, to consider the situation of farmers' economics (*Inaka kurabu*), "Why is local food the best for our health?" (*Shindo-fuji Iwate*), "What is the sense of locality?" (*Shindo-fuji Iwate, Jimoto no syoku to nou wo taisetunisuru kai*). We will now analyze the case of *"Chisan-chisho wo susumeru kai"* in detail. Based on our comparison, we realize that these groups have different goals.

4-3-1. *"Chisan-chisho wo susumeru kai"* (The Club for Eating Locally)[4]

The Club for Eating Locally began in 1996 in Akita prefecture, next to Iwate prefecture. The founding members of the club were interested in promoting local food consumption as an alternative to the globalized food system. At first, President T wanted to organize a research group for establishing local distribution and promoting *Chisan-chisho*. His interest was not in food safety like most *Chisan-chisho* movements, but rather in the identity of the locality and the negative influences of economic globalization. Next, he sought a new distribution system to promote rural life that is independent from the negative influences of economic globalization such as destruction of the environment, disintegration of local companies, disadvantages of local value and so on. He identified the lack of networks between farmers and consumers as a problem in his locality. There were many farmers who practiced organic farming and a variety of safe food farming in the area. Most of them sold their produce to consumers outside of their locality, usually in urban areas in Japan. On the other hand, he heard complaints from consumers who were suffering from a lack of safe local food. And there were no consumer co-operatives that practiced *Sanchoku* in the area.

---

4) This section was analyzed on the basis of the information that I interviewed the president T of Akita Chisan-chisho wo susumeru kai on April 2004.

At first, he sent letters to almost thirty people who seemed to be interested in this movement. They were farmers (including organic farmers), owners of breweries, manufacturers, and so on. Almost all people agreed with the goals of the movement and they established the club in June 1996. In fact, after they started considering the local food system, they realized they didn't always know everything about local food or about each other's activities. They recognized the need to conceptualize what exactly local food is. President T defined the characteristics of their activity at the individual, personal level. He suggested that members should start thinking about what they do about *Chisan-chisho* in their own daily lives. So, the membership of this club was open only to individuals, not to members as representatives of any organization. Now, the number of members has grown to about one hundred and fifty people.

They started to learn how to raise local organic crops, how to make tofu, the difference in taste of organic soybeans from conventional soybeans (or fresh vs. packaged tofu), the characteristics of the traditional farm household's life, and so on. The club's other activities include a potluck party using local food and travel to Korea to learn about Korean *Chisan-chisho* movements. The reason why they participate in these activities is to learn about local food for themselves and to try to comprehend the vastness of the subject. But so far, they have no idea how to widen their activities outside of their existing members. But, as President T said, it is necessary for each member to discuss their opinion about *Chisan-chisho* in the club. They complained that they had no other clubs or networks like their club in their community. Since all members in this club have their own opinion about *Chisan-chisho*, they can learn from each other and discover new lessons from their experiences. President T said, "*Chisan-chisho* is the sense of life; it is too hard to realize without practicing it oneself". Seven years after being established, their greatest achievement is that they created a club in which they are confident in each other and learn from each other's opinion.

To approach their next goal, they need to reorganize the structure of their club. They have a plan to become a non-profit organization (NPO) next year, because their present organizational structure limits their activity both in terms of finance and human resources. So far, the club has relied completely on volunteers to publish newsletters and complete administrative work. After restarting as an NPO, their next objective is to create a network which includes all NPOs in their locality. Furthermore, they want to make *Chisan-chisho* not only about food, but also about clothes and residences. And they want to show all people in their locality the principle of the value of sustainable life.

5. Criticism

The major goal for government-led *Chisan-chisho* projects is to widen the distribution markets for domestic food products. Many consumers understand simply that local food is safe and that *Chisan-chisho* is good for the environment. This is a very shallow understanding of the concept of *Chisan-chisho*. The original concept of *Chisan-chisho* is that people can realize a sustainable livelihood by eating and producing many goods needed in our daily lives locally. It is not only the concept of eating well, but also of living well. As President T said, in contemporary Japan, we can recognize the concept of *Chisan-chisho* only in terms of our food life. After modernization, we lost many values associated with traditional or sustainable food life. But, we still have a sensibility for the taste and freshness of food, and we still have a food culture in each locality. So, President T states that we can start considering local food in the *Chisan-chisho* movement. Actually, the main goal of citizen-led *Chisan-chisho* is to encourage local distribution to realize the richness of local life. Most citizen-led *Chisan-chisho* movements tend to value the original meaning of *Chisan-chisho* more preciously. But according to our analysis so far, they have not yet been able to reform or produce new local food systems. After the establishment of the club, their activities have only helped them to understand the concept of *Chisan-chisho* more precisely.

Many participants - especially of government-led *Chisan-chisho* movements - understand that local food is safe and that practicing *Chisan-chisho* is good for the environment. But this assumption may be unwarranted. For example, many *Chisan-chisho* projects didn't prepare any certification system for local food or establish organic farming practices. Most local foods were probably produced by conventional farming. So, they cannot show evidence of food safety and environmental friendliness [Taniguchi, 2002]. We point out the reason why consumers face this complicated situation: In the 1990's, consumers lost confidence in food security due to the experience of the underproduction in domestic rice and imported food contamination. In the 2000's consumers lost confidence in food safety because many food scandals (BSE, disguised food labels and chemical contamination) arose. In response to these problems, *Chisan-chisho* emerged. Most people sought a solution to food problems in terms of both security and safety in the *Chisan-chisho* movement.

So far, these two types of *Chisan-chisho* movements - government-led and citizen-led - have no connection, largely because their initial goals are quite different. But after the accumulation of *Chisan-chisho* movements, many participants may start considering issues on food and then on local food culture, and history and identity of locality. We expect that their areas of interest will expand from food to environment and social change, like movements in the U.S. To create a sustainable society we need to value livelihood, *Chisan-chisho*. So, we point out to all participants the need to discuss structural issues through the practice of *Chisan-chisho* movements. They should discuss the achievements in food localization from the point of view of democracy or the self-reliance of the local area. Therefore, these two types of movements need to be linked to each other or need to establish networks outside of their own movements.

6. Conclusion

This paper analyzes the emergence, transformation, and prospects of local food movements in Japan. From a historical perspective of alternative agriculture movements, *Chisan-chisho* is the first movement to promote the idea of "local food". The most dominant *Chisan-chisho* movement in Japan is a government-led movement, focusing on the MAFF organized consumer education programs concerning local food. But the goal of this project is largely to widen Japan's domestic food market. We argue that this narrow goal has limited the achievements of local movements to issues of local food safety and security. Under this kind of project, it is difficult for participants - farmers and consumers - to have common motives to join the movement. Farmers are eager to widen domestic markets, while consumers are interested in local food safety and security. Therefore, especially in government-led *Chisan-chisho* started activities, participants tend to have a narrower understanding as to the concept of "local food". They don't expect "local food" movements to lead to an ecologically sustainable, socially equitable and economically viable future.

In government-led *Chisan-chisho* movements, we point out two contradictions. The first contradiction is between national and prefectural governments. The national government thought *Chisan-chisho* projects should widen domestic markets and educate consumers. But many prefecture governments saw *Chisan-chisho* as a way to construct a safe and steady local food system. Second, many consumers came to believe that local food is inherently safe and that *Chisan-chisho* is good for the environment. In practice, there is no linkage between *Chisan-chisho* and organic farming, certification systems or environmental conservation. It shows that the government-led *Chisan-chisho* has expanded in a shallow way. The causality between locality and safety is not necessarily evident. Safety and locality are linked through perceived social embeddedness and face-to-face relations. On the other hand, citizen-led *Chisan-chisho* movements have tended to approach their understanding of local food in a more holistic manner. Their area of interest has expanded from food life to sustainable livelihood to the values of local life. They seem to be able to recognize and address more structural problems through the practice of citizen-led *Chisan-chisho*.

We realize that there is an older, more discussed, local food movement in the U.S. than in Japan. U.S. researchers and activists tend to consider the concept of local as resisting trends toward globalization. They argue that the flourishing of multi-national companies threatens democracy and social justice, and therefore, they recognize that certain activities at the local level are important tools for promoting social change. Furthermore, in the U.S. they recognize that local food movements are the entry point for resolving other social problems such as environmental issues, social justice, democracy and so on. The meaning of locality has come to emphasize democratic decision making and social justice in the U.S. In Japan, on the other hand, particularly in the many *Chisan-chisho* movements, "local" is interpreted as signifying geographic/ physical scale. We came to the conclusion that most participants in *Chisan-chisho* movements didn't consider democratic decision making and social justice in terms of local movements. U.S. consumers who participate in local food movements become food citizens, but Japanese consumers who participate in *Chisan-chisho* movements act only as consumers worried about food safety.

We suggest that they need to recognize their food issues as a structural problem in order to reformulate the *Chisan-chisho* movement in Japan. They also need to understand that the concepts of "food" and "local" are tools to gain entry to issues of social justice and democratic decision making. We expect that all *Chisan-chisho* participants' interests will expand from food to environment and social change, just as movements in the U.S. have experienced. But we also recognize that in the U.S., local food movements were started simply by focusing on food issues. Both of them should focus their activities towards the same goals of sustainability, social justice and democratic decision making. So, we believe that people need the values of life found in "*Chisan-chisho*" to establish a sustainable society.

References

Allen, Patricia, 1999, "Reweaving the Food Security Safety Net: Mediating Entitlement and Entrepreneurship," *Agriculture and Human Values*, 16: 117-129.

Allen, Patricia, Margaret Fitz Simmons, Michael Goodman and Keith Warner, 2003, "Shifting plates in the Agrifood Landscape: the Tectonics of Alternative Agrifood Initiatives in California," *Journal of Rural Studies*, 19: 61-75.

Buttel, Frederic H., 2000, "The Recombinant BGH Controversy in the United States: Toward a New Consumption Politics of Food?" *Agriculture and Human Values*, 17: 5-20.

Community Food Security Coalition Newsletter Fall 02-Winter 03 (http://www.foodsecurity.org/, January 15, 2010)

Food Route Network (http://www.foodroutes.org/, January 15, 2010)

Goodman, David and Michael Redclift, 1991, "Introduction," *Refashioning Nature: Food, Ecology, and Culture*, London; New York: Routledge, xi-xviii.

Gottlieb, Robert, 2001, *Environmentalism Unbound*, Cambridge, MA: The MIT Press.

Hassanein, Neva, 2003, "Practicing Food Democracy: A Pragmatic Politics of Transformation," *Journal of Rural Studies*, 19: 77-86.

Hinriches, Clare, 2003, "The Practice and Politics of Food System Localization," *Journal of Rural Studies*, 19: 33-45.
Kloppenburg, Jack Jr., John Hendrickson and G.W.Stevenson, 1996, "Coming in to the Food Shed." *Agriculture and Human Values*, 13:3(summer): 33-42.
Lang, Tim, 1999, "Food Policy for the 21st Century: Can it be both Radical and Reasonable," Koc M., MacRae R., Mougeot L. and Welsh J. eds., *For Hunger-Proof Cities*, Ottawa: International Development Research Center, 216-224.
Lappe, Moore, 1991, *An Entry Point in Diet for a Small Planet—20th Anniversary Edition*, New York: Ballantine.
Local Harvest Newsletter Fall 02-Winter 03 (http://www.localharvest.org/, January 15, 2010)
Lockeretz, William, 1986, "Alternative Agriculture," Kenneth A. Dahlberg ed., *New Directions for Agricultural Research: Neglected Dimensions and Emerging Alternatives*, Totowa, NJ: Rowman and Allanheld, 291-311.
McMichael, Philip, 2000, "The Power of Food," *Agriculture and Human Values*, 17: 21-33.
Nakajima, Kiichi, 2001, "Tabemono no Anzensei wo motomeru San-Sho Teikei no Keisei to Tenkai (The Constitution of the Relationship between Producers and Consumers for Acquiring the System of Food Safety)," Masao Takahashi *et. al.* eds., *Fudoshisutemu no Kouzou-Henka to Nou-Gyo-Gyo* (The Structural Change of Food System, Agriculture and Fishery), Tokyo: Association of Agriculture & Forestry Statistics, 166-190. (in Japanese)
Negishi, Hisako, 2000, "Noukyo no Josei Kigyo Shien-Saku (The Support Initiatives for Farm Women Business by Farmer's Co-operatives)," Masao Okabe ed., *Nouson Josei ni yoru Kigyo to Houjin-ka* (Agribusiness and Corporation by Farm Women), Tokyo: Tsukuba Shobo, 35-50. (in Japanese)
Nishiyama, Mima and Yoshiaki Yoshida, 2001, "Nouson Josei ni yoru Kigyo-Katsudou no Tenkai to Kobetsu-Keiei-Hatten ni kansuru Ichi-Kousatsu: Utsunomiya Agri-Land City Shop (Developing Process of Women's Enterprise and Each Member's Family Farm: The Case of Utsunomiya Agri-Land City Shop)," *Tech. Bull. Fac. Hort, Chiba University*, 55: 59-67. (in Japanese)
Rural Life Research Institute, 2004, *Rural Life Research Series*, 58. (in Japanese)
Raynolds, Laura T., 2000, "Re-Embedding Global Agriculture: the International Organic and Fair Trade Movements," *Agriculture and Human Values*, 17:3: 297-309.
Taniguchi, Yoshimitsu, 2002, "The Chisan-chisho Initiative in Akita Prefecture," *Tohoku Agricultural Economy*, 21: 20-25. (in Japanese)
Welsh, Jennifer and Rod MacRae, 1998, "Food Citizenship and Community Food Security," *Canadian Journal of Development Studies*, 19: 237-255.

Afterword

We have closely looked at the turning point Japanese society now faces through investigating women and families in rural areas, the future of agriculture, and changes in lifestyle. What emerged from each analysis as a common finding is the influence of socio-structural global trends.

We believe that this book clarifies that Japanese society is at a great turning point. This generates various problems. As globalization, aging population combined with dwindling birthrate, and as a decline in population advance, family size is shrinking, farming population is diminishing and aging, successors are lacking, and more farmland is left uncultivated. On the other hand, more women are now starting business, participating in family management, and creating networks. Many of them balance life and work, improving their financial status. New trends such as local revitalization and communication between urban and rural areas through food can be observed, which suggests the future direction.

This book was not written under a systematic positioning. Rather, it presents the research results with solid verification of theoretical studies in specialized areas of each author. In this sense, this is a milestone of current report on farming communities, families, and women in today's Japan with the vision for the future, while demonstrating scholarship.

Because a number of authors touch upon various fields, the editors' contention may not be always clear as intended. But never before have so many researchers united and committed themselves to presenting a study of Japan. We hope that this will lead to significant advance of the study of Japan in the international community.

At first, we express our hearty thanks for Dr. Gyung-Mee-Gim who stays in Republic of Korea that we were able to publish this book. We would like to give our special thanks to Ms. Kazumi Ogasahara, Ms. Kathryn Kobayashi, and all the staff at YES Inc. who graciously met the requests of the editors and authors, and spent an astronomical number of hours checking every English word. We are also greatly indebted to Ms. Chizuko Tanaka of Gakubunsha and her staff for sparing no effort to provide assistance in the difficult circumstances of academic publishing.

The publication of this book was made possible with the 2009 *Grant-in-Aid for Scientific*

Research (*Grant-in-Aid for Publication of Scientific Research Results,* "Academic Book," Masae Tsutsumi, Professor of Yamanashi Prefectural University).

Masae Tsustumi, Chief Editor/Author
November 2009

index

A

accession   225
agrarian (=agricultural) labor   127, 167
Agrarian Reform   163, 184, 245
agricultural business   89
Agricultural Committee   189
Agricultural Cooperative Women's Association (=Group, Club) (*Noukyo Fujinbu*)   36, 63, 73, 75
Agricultural Extension (Service) Center   49, 111, 125, 189
Agricultural Extension Office (Adviser)   64, 70
agricultural globalization   147
Agricultural Improvement Promotion Law   184
Agricultural Producers' Cooperative Corporation   250, 251
agricultural work force   128
agriculture for tourism   26
Agro-food Movement   281
awareness   157

B

baby boomer   250, 251
Basic Law for a Gender-equal Society   188
Basic Law on Agriculture   163, 180, 245
Basic Law on Food, Agriculture and Rural Areas   188, 245
Business Establishment Process (Model)   73, 76
Buy Local   262

C

career pattern   165
child-rearing (=raising, bearing)   77, 97, 99, 100, 102, 103, 106, 124

Chisan-chisho   35, 148, 261, 281
Community Food Security Coalition   287
community funeral   237
community gathering   237
Community Supported Agriculture (CSA)   286
conjugal-family system   8, 9, 109, 211
conventional regional organization   73
co-residence   116
Cultivation Area   132
custom   157

D

daughter-in-law   109
decision-making   52, 59, 115, 125, 157, 296
declining birthrate   124
degree of satisfaction   57
direct selling shop   66
division of labor   115, 142, 179
double income   129

E

Eat Local   262
economic (power) revitalization   283
elderly   76, 124
empowerment   24, 91
entrepreneur   24
Expert Extension Worker   111, 192
Extension Advisor   163, 184

F

"face to face" relationship   279
Family Agreement   244
family business (*Kagyo*)   244
family consciousness   225
family farming (business)   163, 236
family ideology   211
family institution   244
family laborer   247
Family Management Agreement   97, 99, 104-107, 109, 140, 183, 187, 191, 200, 244

Family nuclei   212
family property (*Kasan*)   244
family strategy   244
family structure   133
Farm Life Advisor (*Seikatsu Shido-in*)   163, 175
Farm Management (Agreement)   3, 14, 27, 33
farm management transfer   193
farm manager   105
farmers' life improvement movement   89
Farmer's Pension   113, 218, 248
farmer-consumer relationship   281
farmers' market   149, 284
farming fund   237
farming-related friend   56
Father-sun Agreement   248
food processing   63
food production and consumption   147
food safety   148
Food-self sufficiency rate   263
food system   147
full-time farm household (=farming family)   16, 166
full-time farmer   224

G

gender-equal society   157, 183
gender equality   182, 183
gender issues   184

H

heir   232
High Economic Growth   6
higher elementary school   234
Home Life Improvement Extension Service   36, 61, 163, 179, 184
Home Life Improvement (Practice) Group   73, 75, 184, 173
hornless cow   22
household chore   195

I

Ie   5, 9, 10, 22, 81, 215, 224, 244
independent family farming   163, 245
industrial structure   15, 225
industrialization   10, 245
inheritance form   225
inheritance right   238
International Women's Year   186

J

Japanese Red Cross Society   178
Joining Organizations   52

L

labor force   124
Labor Standards Law   100
large-scale farmer   15
Law of Gender Equality in Labor Opportunities   187
Leaders of Women Farmers   28
life course   73, 110, 114, 163, 244
life cycle   214, 221
(Home) Life Improvement Practice Group   36, 61
life stage   133
lifestyle   4, 22, 155
limited company   251, 252-253
Live-in worker   22
living arrangement   211
local community   159
local farmer   53, 55
local food   151, 278, 281
Local production for local consumption   261
Localism   7
Localization Movement   285
lone income   129

M

major household account   237

maternity leave 99, 100, 103-107
Meiji Civil Code 245
Michi no Eki 36
modernization 8, 32
mother and daughter-in-law dyad 109
Mother-Child Health and Welfare Society 177
multi-generational cohabitation 23
Mura 22, 81, 90, 91

N

national ideology 245
network 47, 55, 142
New Farmer 47, 59
Non-Profit Organization (NPO) 293
Nouson Fujin no Ie 68
Nuclear Family 12
nursing care 142

O

Okamisan Ichi 151
Omodachi 22
One-Village-One-Product 36

P

panel 163, 211
parent-in-law 109
part-time farmer 224
part-time farming family 16
personal network 51
Population mainly engaged in farming 167
public behavior 159

Q

questionnaire survey 127

R

Regional Agricultural Administration Office 192
rural women's entrepreneurial activity
(=entrepreneurship) 27, 35, 38, 61
rural-community food 147

S

sales value of products 247
Sanchoku 283
sandwich-generation 119
self-control demanded 157
self-employed 99, 100, 101, 103
self-sufficiency (movement) 36, 261, 283
sexual division of labor 124, 141
sexual equality norm 82
shadow work 24
Shindo-fuji 289
Shokuno-kyouiku 35
Shoku-to-nou-no-saisei-plan 289
small family farming 14, 163
social activity 157, 171
social justice 296
social network 278
social norm 157
social security 100, 101, 104
sole inheritance 238
stem-family (household) 3, 22, 24, 109, 211, 215
stem-family ideology 215, 216
stem-family system 8, 109, 211
subsistence production 261
successor 109, 216, 217, 244
succession 211, 215, 228
sustainable society 296

T

Teikei movement 283
tense relationship 81
three-generation family (=household) 11, 117
three-generation family arrangement 24
total fertility rate 188
traditional food culture 41
traditional local activity 147

U

uncountable values 279
unit-group 61
urban lifestyle 6
urbanization 10, 23, 245, 251

V

voluntary 85

W

Women's Association (*Fujin-kai*) 63, 171
Women's Department of the Agricultural Cooperative 175
Work Life Balance 99, 124, 134, 188

A Turning Point of Women,
Families and Agriculture in Rural Japan

転換期にある日本農村女性と家族

2010年2月10日　第1版第1刷発行

編著者　　堤　　マサエ

発行者　　田　中　千津子
発行所　株式会社　学　文　社

〒153-0064　東京都目黒区下目黒 3-6-1
電話　03(3715)1501 (代)　振替　00130-9-98842
http://www.gakubunsha.com

乱丁・落丁の場合は本社でお取り替えします。　◎検印省略
定価は売上カード，カバーに表示。

ISBN978-4-7620-2015-5